The Brewster Story

A DEFINITIVE HISTORY OF BREWSTER ACADEMY

The Brewster Story

Read, Remember, Rejoice!
Robert & Shirley Richardson

BY ROBERT AND SHIRLEY RICHARDSON

ISBN 978-1-58973-025-0

Published by Brewster Academy

Printed in the United States of America

The information in this book is true and complete to the best of our knowledge. It is offered without guarantee on the part of the author or the publisher, and we disclaim all liability in connection with the use of the book.

Photographers
Stephen Allen
Alex Green '11
Phil Horton
John McKeith
Marcia Eldredge
Peggy Comeau
Brewster Academy Archives
Wolfeboro Historical Society

Cover Design
Photographer: Ben Larson
Designer: BG Hodges

Contents

Acknowledgments viii

Introduction x

A Tribute to Brewster Academy Teachers, Past and Present xiii
"A teacher affects eternity; he can never tell where his influence stops."
—Henry B. Adams

Recognition of the Support Staff xv
"Only people count. Only people who think and feel and work together make civilization."—Helen Keller

1. The Beginning 17
"The Great Spirit is all things: he is in the air we breathe. The Great Spirit is our Father, but the earth is our Mother. She nourishes us; that which we put into the ground she returns to us."—Big Thunder, Wabanaki Algonquin

2. The Founders 30
"To accomplish great things, we must not only act, but also dream; not only plan, but also believe."—Anatole France

3. Edwin H. Lord, 1887–1907: The First Principal 43
"We all need someone who inspires us to do better than we know how."—Anonymous

4. The Rev. Dr. Charles S. Murkland, 1907–1910: A Man of Service 61
"What you are will show in what you do."—Thomas A. Edison

5. Charles Webster Haley, 1911–1923: Brewster and the Great War 66
"The superior man is modest in his speech, but exceeds in his actions."—Confucius

6. Ralph K. Bearce, 1924–1935: A Man of Conspicuous Ability 83
"The real leader has no need to lead; he is content to point the way."
—Henry Miller

7. Walter G. Greenall, 1935–1942: The Depression Years 98
"When everything seems to be going against you, remember that the airplane takes off against the wind, not with it."—Henry Ford

8. Vincent David Rogers, 1942–1959: Turbulent Times 112
"Do not go where the path may lead; go instead where there is no path and leave a trail."—Ralph Waldo Emerson

9. The Impact of GIs on Campus 124
"Nothing endures but change."—Heraclitus

10. Rogers Gets His Gym 132
"You may give out, but never give up."—Mary Crowley

11. Burtis F. Vaughan Jr., 1959–1965: The Man Who Led the Charge 151
"They may forget what you said but they will never forget how you made them feel."—Anonymous

12. Wilfred E. Paro, 1965–1969: The First "Headmaster" 167
"If you wish to know the mind of a man, listen to his words."—Chinese Proverb

13. Charles Richard Vaughan, 1969–1974: Challenges Brewster to Change 183
"To give real service you must add something which cannot be bought or measured with money, and that is sincerity and integrity."—Donald A. Adams

14. David Minton Smith, 1974–2003: A New Beginning 199
"Be the change you want to see in the world."—Mohandas K. Gandhi

15. The Wish List Comes to Life 218
"Start by doing what's necessary, then what's possible, and suddenly you are doing the impossible."—St. Francis of Assisi

16. Changing Times of 1980s and 1990s 234
"I hear, and I forget. I see, and I remember. I do, and I understand."—Confucius

17. Formulating and Delivering a New Educational Paradigm 255
"If we teach today as we taught yesterday, we rob our children of tomorrow."
—John Dewey
"If a child can't learn the way we teach, maybe we should teach the way they learn."—Ignacio Estrada

18. Doing it All and Doing it Right Across the Campus 275
"If every day you do a little more than is expected of you, everyday a little more will be expected of you."—Mother Teresa

19. September 11, 2001: A Day to be Remembered 295
"There is not grief that does not speak."—Henry Wadsworth Longfellow

20. David Minton Smith: Concluding Years 300
"If your actions inspire others to dream more, learn more, do more and become more, you are a leader."—John Quincy Adams

21. Dr. Michael E. Cooper, 2003–present: The First "Head of School" 311
"Things do not happen. Things are made to happen."—John F. Kennedy

22. Preparing for the 21st Century 327
"What's past is prologue, what's to come is yours and my discharge."
—William Shakespeare

Afterword 340

Board of Trustees, 1887–2010 341

Principals and Headmasters, 1887–2010 343

Bibliography 344

Index 347

Acknowledgments

In any undertaking of this scope, researchers encounter a multitude of sources along the way that contribute to the project. We interviewed more than 70 alums and teachers, tapping their rich memories and conversation for posterity. After our tape recordings had been transcribed and copied, we often returned them to the interviewees for review and comment, all to ensure the greatest accuracy possible. Their first-person voices brought new and refreshing insight into the history of the school. For all their support and encouragement, we express our gratitude to the scores of loyal and enthusiastic alums, teachers, parents and friends who sent us letters, diaries, manuscripts, books, and other documents telling stories of their Brewster connections. Their fortitude, interest, remarkably generous spirits, and resourcefulness have contributed to the unique characteristics of the Academy and this history. We thank them all.

We also would like to acknowledge current Head of School Dr. Michael Cooper who recognized the importance of recording the "Brewster Story." For his patience, understanding, and assistance, we are grateful

Our recognition is extended to Head of School's Secretary Susan Nichols whose tireless efforts and patience exceeded all expectations. During our many searches for the school's records regarding important meetings, events, papers and old primary materials, she was always cheerful and diligent—a true helper. Her efforts made our task easier.

We are indebted to Peggy Comeau for her attention to and interest in our project. Her experience as writer, researcher, photographer, electronic communicator and assistant director of communications, made the job less complicated, not only for the book, but also in developing the text material for our "Writing Brewster's History" columns which were published in *Brewster Connections*. Her electronic skills in sharpening pictures and her suggestions in text revisions added to the completion of an appealing story.

For his help as we sorted through hundreds of photographs and chose the final ones to include in the book, we are much indebted to BG Hodges for his advice and suggestions. Never too busy to pause or to set aside time to work with us to scan and edit both old and new photographs as he brought his considerable graphics talents to the task. The striking cover design for *The Brewster Story* represents BG's special artistic gift. We would have been lost without him during this very important phase of producing the book. For his bright and kind spirit we are thankful.

Barbara L. Zulauf, both an alumna and a former faculty member at Brewster, read an early draft of this book, and we welcomed her careful eye and her encouragement as we completed the history.

Our sincere praise go to our friend Les MacLeod, Vice-President of the Board, for his patient and concise evaluation of "the book." His perceptive comments and suggestions spurred our quest for clarity and adequate explanation, particularly in Chapter 18, which required a complicated rendering of events.

We worked closely with David M. Smith in recording his detailed account of happenings leading to the development of the current school mission statement and the school design model. Headmaster Smith's insightful recollections about his tenure at Brewster bring to life these important chapters in the school's history in which we also shared. His thirty-four-year term at Brewster is a remarkable story in itself.

A most helpful resource was Travis Ball, and we wish to acknowledge the valuable suggestions and advice that he furnished throughout our much longer than expected period of writing this book. Our personal contact with Travis began in 1969 when he was hired to chair the English department and to teach a variety of English classes. Within months he was appointed an assistant to Headmaster C. Richard Vaughan, helping to develop the school publications and publicity. His career since Brewster has taken him to several Indiana and Tennessee universities, colleges, and private schools where he continued to teach writing, but his loyalty to the Academy and its mission remains. Now retired from teaching, he is an active volunteer in his church and the community of his old hometown, Newport, Tennessee.

Each morning, our email beeps with a new thought-of-the-day, along with a superb question about the clarity of one or another of the paragraphs previously sent to him for critique. His energy and spirit are unending. He volunteered to act as a "first editor" of all of our work as we approached the final stages; and he has been a wonderful assistance by providing an independent evaluation of our writings that brought a sense of fairness and balance to our passages for which we will forever be grateful.

At this crucial concluding stage, we are indebted to Doug and Mary Fallon, our long-time colleagues and friends, whom we enlisted to help edit the final manuscript of *The Brewster Story.* Their talents, skills, and 25 years of service to the Academy proved to be, as expected, just the right combination for this important undertaking.

And finally a most significant happening occurred one morning in 2009, when Barb Thomas, an eleventh grade team leader mentioned that the father of her advisee, Sam Joseph, was a publisher in South Carolina. We called Mr. Richard Joseph at Arcadia Publishing in Mt. Pleasant, South Carolina, and he offered to meet with us and discuss our project during the Fall Parents Weekend. With great interest and enthusiasm, Mr. Joseph became totally committed to producing *The Brewster Story*, and he and his staff have advised us throughout the process from manuscript to finished book. Through his generosity and assurance, we were able to complete this project and to publish the history of the Academy from early Native American times to 2010. Mr. Joseph, Brewster Academy salutes you and thanks you most sincerely for your enormous caring for the education of young people and your truly magnanimous gift.

As we conclude our work and look to the future, we recognize that the central challenge and responsibility to prepare students for the future has been a common denominator since Brewster was founded. Whenever the Academy has answered John Brewster's call, finding the courage and vitality to examine what it does and to adapt curriculum and methods to the needs of the students, the school has thrived. When it has become confused or complacent, it has diminished its relevance and perhaps even its reason for existing.

We hope our readers will find interest in Brewster's past, pride in its present, and lessons for its future.

—Robert and Shirley Richardson

Introduction

This story of Brewster Academy was sparked from a chance conversation that took place as Shirley and I approached the end of our active careers at the Academy.

One day as I was rushing to a school meeting, Business Manager Robert Simoneau happened to cross paths with me and said, "Someday Robert, with your love of history and your longevity on campus, you're going to have to write the history of the school."

I paused and then replied, "Sorry Bob, I can't even think of that right now! Maybe later." Our conversation ended abruptly, but it turned my mind to thinking how it could be done. That question would haunt me for months while I wrestled with the daily and long-termed challenges of being partially responsible for the educational welfare of so many students.

It was Herbert Lamb who broke the administrative ground that started Shirley and me upon this long journey. Lamb, an 80-year-old member of the Board of Trustees, arrived at my classroom door one day to tell me that he would like to enroll in the senior course, Modern American History. Because of his long experience with the Sylvania Corporation and his contributions during World War II to the invention of the proximity fuse (a device which exploded an anti-aircraft shell whenever it came near an on-coming enemy aircraft), I was delighted to have him in our class.

During classes, Lamb's wit and thoughtful questions advanced our class discussions, and seniors enjoyed having a man who had lived through much of this history as a member of their computerized learning teams. After classes ended in June, Lamb invited the students to join him at The Wolfeboro Inn for a capstone conversation and a fine luncheon.

Being aware of my passion for history, our imminent retirement and our longevity at the Academy, Herbert Lamb was joined by our longest serving trustee Helen Hamilton in the belief that the Board should take advantage of this opportunity by endorsing and supporting the research and recording of the history of the Academy. Never before had such an in-depth study been undertaken, and it seemed an ideal time for such a venture. In July 2004, the Board formally requested that we consider the task. We agreed, and it has been the central focus of our lives since our formal retirement.

When we first launched our efforts, we recognized immediately that such an undertaking would have to include not only Brewster Academy but also the Wolfeborough and Tuftonborough Academy (WTA) which was founded in 1820 and dissolved in 1888 when John Brewster's Will provided for a new school to be established in his hometown. It is interesting to note, that although Brewster Free Academy (BFA) assumed the role of WTA in educating young people, it wasn't until 1921 that the alumni association of WTA would be merged with the Brewster Academy Alumni Association. Neither Academy was ever a public school, one having been founded by a joint stock venture to serve students who wished an advanced secondary education, the other established by the Will of a philanthropist as an independent school, a free academy, to serve qualified students.

As we researched the founding of the Wolfeborough and Tuftonborough Academy, we began to realize that the reader should also have some knowledge of the land and early history of the town in which they would come to be part of the "Brewster Story." Although we could not share all the results of our research, in the first chapter we opened with the memories of an Abenaki chief who visited with our students in the 70s. From him we learned that our campus is literally fertile ground for more research by students and teachers, an exciting undertaking for "Project-Based Learning."

By the 21st century, Brewster Academy had enjoyed sweeping changes in the size and complexion of the study body, faculty, curriculum development, teaching methods, and buildings and grounds. In our writing, we have attempted, at crucial points, to reflect upon those themes of national importance that influenced young Brewster students. The Brewster students who marched in World War I were in part responsible for the Allied victory in Europe as were the youngsters who fought in a much wider conflict two decades later. Both were supported by the volunteer activities of their fellow students at home. The Great Depression and World War II brought hard times to all, but with sound financial management and hard work by the students, faculty, trustees and administrators, the school survived. When the Nation underwent a transition following two wars, first in Korea and then in Vietnam, economic and social changes affected every Brewster student and parent and brought the school leaders just short of closing the front doors forever. One lesson surfaced—national events do affect the immediate needs of the school and must be carefully considered by the school's leadership. Through these crucial times, the Board remained true to the intent of John Brewster when he wrote his *Will*.

By 1971, bold, vigorous, and far-reaching leadership was needed to sustain an institution beset by uncertainty at every turn yet not willing to capitulate. New school leaders emerged who were energetic and determined to "pull up by the bootstraps" in making a deliberate stride forward in education. The story of Board Chairman Walter DeWitt, '54, is an exciting one. Without his decisive leadership, the school would probably have fallen into financial destitution. His immediate and courageous revitalization of a new board and the selection of a new and yet untested headmaster, set the stage for institutional development few schools have been able to enjoy and led to a comprehensive reexamination of the school program and eventually the Brewster Model. DeWitt and his successors Grant Wilson and Daniel Mudge deserve high praise for their focused leadership and our sincere thanks.

In writing our story, we were fortunate to uncover many sources. We searched into the dark corners of the school, peering into rusted file cabinets, damp dormitory basements, hot attics of old buildings, and the minds of alums, many of whom have since passed. We visited the ancient homes of the Founder and his son William and went to the family plot at the Mount Auburn Cemetery. There we found a granite engraved tribute to William and his wife Clementine offered by Daniel Chester French, the eminent sculptor of statue at the Abraham Lincoln Memorial in Washington, DC, and the Minute Man at Concord, Massachusetts.

We found rich sources of information relating to the formation of the old WTA scattered throughout the town and in previously unexplored corners of Brewster Academy. These included the original secretarial reports of the earliest meetings held at Ichabod Libbey's tavern in 1820 and later at the offices of now defunct local banks where accounts were kept. By far the most interesting and informative accounts of the WTA were told in a lively history booklet written by the Rev. John Hawley, *The History of the Wolfeborough and Tuftonborough Academy.* In the early 1900s, Hawley, a theologian who had served as principal, was asked to write a history of the school. We hope that our successors as Brewster historians may find our efforts to be as helpful as Hawley's were to us.

Hawley's accounts of the daily lives of teachers and students give us a colorful picture of student life and local political conflicts of 19th century Wolfeborough. In addition, the reports of WTA alumni meetings give a snapshot of the last days of this fine old school and their meaningful decision to join officially the Brewster Academy Alumni Association.

With the opening of the *Will* of John Brewster in 1886, Wolfeborough exulted in the reality of being given a new school to use, a town office building, and a new town library and the sources of revenue to perpetuate them.

Today's trustees have been openly helpful to this project by permitting us to have access to trustee records through the decades, and we thank them for this courtesy. These records consisting of both Board and Executive Committee meeting minutes were invaluable. Formal full Board meetings took place usually thrice yearly while the Executive Committee met at the request of the principal or the Board to discuss imminent matters. These documents were of fundamental importance in gaining a clear understanding of institutional development. Fortunately, most often the recording secretaries over the nearly two centuries past were diligent in recording the discussions from those meetings. Their minutes were concise, thorough, and meaningful.

In the garden in front of our Academic Building stands a magnificent granite ball water monument situated in a powerful granite base, suggestive of the hills of New Hampshire. A gift of the Class of 2005, this fountain reflects Brewster Academy today. As the ball spins in the cascading water, it symbolizes a world planet welcoming all students to its doors. From far distant places students come together in Wolfeboro to study, learn, communicate, become friends, and then to go back into the world with a common denominator, "The Brewster Story."

A granite water fountain, gift of the class of 2005, symbolizes world friendship and welcomes all students to Brewster.

A Tribute to Brewster Academy Teachers, Past and Present

A teacher affects eternity; he can never tell where his influence stops.
—Henry B. Adams

As you read this history of Brewster Academy, you will find much information about headmasters, trustees, donors, and buildings, perhaps because the archives of the school—board minutes, legal documents, newspapers and newsletters—all seem to concentrate on these important people and things. Yet whenever one of the authors talked with former students, the conversation turned quickly to the teachers they had encountered at Brewster and the lifelong impact those teachers had on them.

David M. Smith, early in his long tenure as headmaster, recognized this when he said, "Brewster's greatest strength is the quality of its faculty," and headmasters from its founding to the present have reached this same conclusion. Although we have not been able to assemble a master list of all teachers who have served on the Brewster faculty since 1820, we salute each of these educators by remembering some common characteristics they shared.

- Brewster teachers are masters of their subject matter, holding degrees from well-respected colleges and universities.
- Brewster teachers are enthusiastic about their fields of inquiry and enjoy teaching; encouraged by financial support from the school, they continue to learn as members of regional and national professional organizations, as participants at conferences and conventions, and through continuing graduate education.
- Brewster teachers know how to make the complex understandable, how to ask good questions which allow students to "discover" for themselves the points being considered.
- Brewster teachers set high expectations for their students and hold their students to those expectations.
- Brewster teachers know the day doesn't end with the ringing of the last bell, and they are willing to wear many hats—classroom teacher, athletic coach, dormitory master, advisor, and friend—and to move from role to role seemingly without effort.
- Brewster teachers not only talk about the academic life—they model it for their students.
- Brewster teachers remain interested and involved with their students' academic life long after the students have left their classes.

Each alumnus of Brewster Academy, thinking about his or her favorite teachers, can probably add to this list.

Near the end of her long career as an English teacher and department chair at a Midwestern boarding school, Dorothy E. McCullough wrote: "I believe strongly that good education calls for the interplay of growing minds—young minds developing in companionship with older minds that continue to develop. And this condition is achieved best in small classes with teachers who are well schooled, dedicated, and comfortable in their work." Miss McCullough could have been writing about a Brewster Academy education, about the relationship between teacher and student.

But also important to that relationship is what Carl Jung once wrote, "An understanding heart is everything in a teacher, and cannot be esteemed highly enough. One looks back with appreciation to the brilliant teachers, but with gratitude to those who touched our human feeling. The curriculum is so much necessary raw material, but warmth is the vital element for the growing plant and for the soul of the child." This is Brewster.

For their dedicated service, we salute and thank the Brewster faculty since the school's founding. The faculty has been and continues to be the greatest strength of the school.

Recognition of the Support Staff

Only people count. Only people who think and feel and work together make civilization.— Helen Keller

Although we have concentrated on trustees, headmasters, and faculty in telling this history, we recognize that their work would have been impossible without the assistance of Brewster Academy's superb support staff; and we acknowledge their contributions to the Brewster community.

Whether they are called secretaries, administrative assistants, academic assistants, food service staffers, custodians, housekeepers, or maintenance workers, we often don't realize how much school life depends on them. They are at the hub of all that we do—helping enroll students in the necessary programs; keeping good and accurate records of what students have done and are doing; smoothing lines of communication among faculty, students, parents; setting up emergency conference calls; or working miracles to get classes covered when unexpected absences occur. They juggle a dozen balls at the same time and make it look as though they are taking a break.

Good food often assures good morale, and Brewster Academy has been fortunate to have many excellent chefs and food service staffs across the years, including FLIK which has served the school for more than fifteen years. Because the food service staffers see students and teachers throughout the day, greeting them by name and referring to the sports and activities they are involved in, they are both good barometers for school climate and strong influences on school morale.

Sometimes we take school facilities for granted, but a dedicated staff of custodial, housekeeping, and maintenance members keep our buildings and grounds clean and conducive to teaching and learning and perform routine and preventative maintenance so the buildings will serve teachers and students well for years to come.

From our earliest days, faculty spouses have been an integral part of school life. Adept at seeing things which call for attention and "just doing them," they reinforce and complement community spirit and the day-to-day work of students and teachers.

To these varied members of the Brewster community, we say a heartfelt "Thank You" for all you've done without seeking (and often without receiving) recognition. You have enriched our lives and complemented our work.

1. The Beginning

The great spirit is in all things; he is in the air we breathe. The Great Spirit is our Father, but the earth is our Mother. She nourishes us; that which we put into the ground she returns to us.—Big Thunder, Wabanaki Algonquin

The Last Abenaki Indian

In 1978, Director of Studies Robert Richardson had located the last surviving Abenaki Indian Chief whose family had left St Francis, Canada, many years before and returned to their New Hampshire homeland. The chief was at work creating an Abenaki/English dictionary so that his language would never be lost to history. Mr. Richardson invited him to speak to the student body during an All School Meeting on a bright sunny day in October when the leaves were just turning color. The chief shared his memories of the land and the times of the Abenaki Indians. He talked about a time when the land belonged to everyone with no boundaries, when food was plentiful, when Mother Earth gave all that was needed to live, and there was peace in the land. He made us stop and wonder, "Whose land is this?"

This is our heritage. The beauty of this sentiment is what we carry together here in our little school on this great lake. Let us never forget this possibility, this conviction that peace can reign and education can help share and promulgate that sense of peace and the unity of all men.

The Abenakis were distinctive in their dress. Clothing was often embroidered with dyed rawhide mixed with colored porcupine thorns and beads.

The Brewster Story brings that voice to us, and we must reflect on all it means for us as an academic community and a carrier of history.

Much would happen to change that "peace in the land" our chief spoke to us about, much to change the psychological and the physical presence of the land…but the land is still here, we are still here, the story is still here….and we need to remember.

One of the greatest and most jarring explosions that shook this land of "peace," that changed it forever from the "sylvan" paradise of a race of people who venerated it and saw it as the source and giver of life was, of course, the American Revolution. What was to become the site of our school on the pristine shores of Lake Winnipesauke, shores once covered with fir, and hemlock, and oak, and maple, and birch and elm and a system of trails connecting Indian village to Indian village began as a small town before that earth-shattering revolution.

In 1773 Wolfeborough had already emerged as a town of about thirty families who were poor, but successful in clearing land and raising crops. To the Wolfeborough families their arguments as colonists with the Royal ministries over unrepresented taxation seemed never to end, but they were not interested in challenging the power of the royal Governor or the Crown because they respected his rule in the colony, and most people assumed that the success of the Royal governor had a settling effect on the colony. They seemed to prize that stability.

Wolfeborough was a good place to live for a number of reasons. In 1770, the British Crown had made the land safe against the murderous French and Indians raids. With their demise, a colonist could purchase a homestead from a landowner for little money and a promise to remain on the land for 10 years. Second, with the expanding population, lumber would be in great demand and the area around the town was rich with pine, oak and white maple that were highly prized by the Royal Navy and Portsmouth ship builders. While the land itself was not wholly suited for spacious wheat or corn growing, it was productive for cattle, sheep and dairy farming. There were rushing streams to be dammed for grist and saw mills, and there were deposits of clay for brick making along with some

Bridge Village, Main Street looking south.

iron ore deposits. By the time of the American Revolution, there were four staples bred into the New Hampshire economy: beaver pelts, fish, lumber and shipbuilding,

The Rise of Bridge Village

"Bridge Village" included a number of households located on the west and south side of the downtown bridge that spanned the Smith River and connected the inhabitants on North Main from South Main. The North side had a small school located about three miles to the north, while the South Wolfeborough School was located about two miles away.

By 1820, stores began to open around the Bridge Village and commercial interests took over. The Lake Bank opened, and the inevitable demand for clothing, shoes, furniture and groceries took hold as business expanded and gradually moved toward the bridge. Daniel Pickering opened a new hardware and dry goods store and purchased a large plot of land on the northeast side of South Main Street and Center Street. Both sides of South Main Street, adjacent the Bridge, became crowded with new shops and stables, while the heavy industries dominated the Wolfeborough Falls area.

It was into this new part of town that the interest for advanced education soon took hold. Judging from the record of town developments, one can say that by 1820 there was a yearning for intellectual development. A large group of town fathers had gathered at the call of Daniel Pickering to discuss the creation of a town library to be located in Bridge Village. It would contain volumes of books dedicated to the advancement of knowledge. These gatherings resulted in the selling of subscriptions for the purchase of books to be collected in a house probably on Center Street, though the exact location is in question.

The first step toward advanced learning had taken place. The next step would be more elaborate and long lasting with the founding of the Wolfeborough-Tuftonborough Academy and then Brewster Free Academy.

The land that had first been the home of the Abenaki tribe had changed dramatically since those early days. But the splendor of the lakes, hills and mountains remains the same, forever drawing man to its beauty and vista. Somewhere, in all of us, is a lingering connection to this vision of an earthly paradise.

The Changing Land and Population: The Need for Education

The gradual population increase in the Wolfeborough and Tuftonborough area following the American Revolution brought with it the desire for educating youngsters in reading, writing, and elementary math skills. In 1795, the state legislature required all towns to provide a plan for the immediate establishment of schools for children, or suffer fines for the lack thereof.

In Wolfeborough, the townspeople voted to organize single room schools in the most populated areas. Each school had a paid superintendent who was responsible for enlisting help to construct a building, assemble benches and tables, make available a stove with sufficient supply of cord wood, and provide an out-house. Quickly, superintendents were on-duty who complied with the state requirements, and soon there were five standing schoolrooms ready to receive youngsters. Widely dispersed to the north and east of Wolfeborough, most were located on roads twisting through hills and farmland surrounding the present town. In time, there were 19 little schools to accommodate the population increases. Everything seemed settled and in order, but new living patterns were emerging (Parker, p. 330).

By 1810, with the arrival of commercial services, banks, and some heavy lumbering industry, the population of "Bridge Village" quickly saw the need for educating their students beyond the basic skills. The existing schools in the village were too small to accommodate older students for further instruction in language, literature and history of ancient Greece and Rome. Clearly, some had the intention to create an advanced level of education that would resemble the academy concept already established in Massachusetts. Land was needed, and a new building constructed. But a large sum of money had to be raised.

An Academy Takes Form

Education makes good men, and good men act nobly.—Plato

There is very little detailed information regarding the early meetings and conversations of villagers who set into action the planning stages for further education. The first recorded steps were taken on May 4, 1820, when a group of citizens met at the tavern of Ichabod Libby to discuss the question, "Shall we have an academy?" The location of Libby's Inn appears to have been at the present corner of North Main Street (Rt. 109) and its junction with Wambec Road, better known as "Goose Corners" (Bowers, vol. 3).

While this question, shall we have an academy, seems progressive and insightful, it must be understood that the concept of adding more years of schooling to lives of healthy young boys and girls who were needed to tend the harsh tasks of local farm life would not quickly be accepted. As Albert H. Dow, Jr. '41, pointed out, many farmers were reluctant to part with their younger family members, saying,

> "I got through to the sixth grade and it was good enough for me, and it is good enough for you." Young sixth grade boys rose at daybreak, milked five or six cows, fed them, collected chicken eggs, and then made some breakfast before heading out on a mile walk to school, often through winter snow. Returning after school, they repeated the process and added hauling wood, clearing fields, and moving stones. Young girls had similar tasks tending to farm life. Their lives seemed dedicated to spinning wool, cooking meals, sewing clothes, feeding chickens, ducks, and geese, hoeing tomato plants and tending to the sick. Farm duties were exhausting but had to be done (Dow, *Transcribed Interview*, January 7, 2005).

Clearly, then, the task of organizing and planning further education for the young people would fall to those who were deeply concerned about building an academy. Merchants, bankers, tradesmen, and professionals were leaders of the movement—men who could provide the funding necessary for the construction of a school building, provide for teaching materials and hire faculty. Children would either achieve the learning required to enter local trades or qualify for entrance into leading colleges.

Establishing Wolfeborough-Tuftonborough Academy

We do know that during the May 4, 1820, proceedings, this venture for a new school began when a decision was made to establish the Wolfeborough-Tuftonborough Academy Corporation. As that meeting at the Inn progressed, it was voted to raise the sum of "not less than five thousand dollars for the erecting of a school building and collateral purposes." The grantees were Samuel Avery, Jonathan Blake, and Daniel Pickering and their associates. A Board of Trustees was created with Jonathan Blake as president and Daniel Pickering, who had attended Philips Exeter Academy, as secretary. It was agreed that stock shares would be sold, and Daniel Pickering gave an acre of land for the school site. The new school building was to be constructed on a hill near the bridge on Main Street where the present Town Hall is located. An Act of Incorporation was passed by the state legislature on June 20, 1820, and the group was authorized to hold exempt from taxation real estate up to a sum of fifteen thousand dollars.

Daniel Pickering, influential commercial and educational leader of his time.

The Pickering Homestead or Rollins House, one of the oldest houses in Wolfeboro across South Main Street from the Civil War monument.

The progress on the construction of the new school was somewhat slow and at times beset by problems during the summer months of 1820, but it is believed the academy building was raised and somewhat finished through the summer and winter of 1820—1821. In July 1821, benefactors, like Daniel Pickering who had donated the land, and William Guppy, a townsman, who gave $2,000, helped complete the building, and raised an endowment fund. Samuel Avery did the newspaper advertising and acted as the front man in attracting students from other towns who would be boarding with local townspeople. He did this by placing notices in the weekly newspapers of towns around Portsmouth, Rochester and Dover. The freshly painted white building sported a fine feature of a new Paul Revere bell hung high in a new steeple, which would call students to class and townspeople to church (*The Granite Monthly*, p. 380).

Opening of School

The school was formally opened in September 1821. Teachers were hired and a preceptor, John Paine Cleveland, was placed in charge. It is not known how many students were enrolled in the first class; however, by October 1823, the number was 44 gentlemen and 6 ladies. That represented about 1/19th of the town's school population.

Mr. Cleveland came to work almost immediately after his graduation from Bowdoin College in 1821. His preceptorship lasted for three years, and in 1824, he left to enroll at Marietta College in Ohio where he pursued a doctoral degree in divinity. Dr. Cleveland's career led him to serve as the chaplain of the Massachusetts Senate in 1857 and as Chaplain of the 30th Massachusetts Volunteers in 1862 during the Civil War.

Attempt to Draw Boarding Students

In an attempt to inform the outside world of the new school and to draw boarding students from other towns in New Hampshire, *The Portsmouth Journal of Literature and Politics* ran an article in September 1822 describing the location of the school, morals of the students, and the required religious observances. It described tuition as "3 dollars per quarter" and instructed anyone interested "to make application to Joseph Farrar, Esq. or Mr. Samuel

Men with their wagons on the grounds of the Academy as they prepare to raise the Paul Revere Bell to the belfry.

Samuel Avery, a major leader in organizing and maintaining WTA.

Avery, near the Academy" (Haley, pp. 13-14). Mr. Avery lived in a white house on South Main Street across from the present Town Hall and rented rooms to students who wished to board for a period of time during the school year. The original white clapboard house was enlarged over time and is now owned by Brewster Academy and known as Avery House.

School Rules

"School rules are established because some social practices tend to disrupt daily scholastic life." The *By-Laws of 1836* reflect a school community in which behavior was well regulated. The 13-page document identifies the responsibilities of the preceptor and instructors and charges them with a specific disciplinary code. Rules were clear in terms of tuition payment, attendance, and orderly conduct. Students who took it upon themselves not to be governed by the school's rules were asked to leave, but not before having a hearing before the "committee of exigencies," who discussed the issues properly. This committee seemed to have the final decision on action to be taken. Some rules were intriguing. Students were required to provide brooms and brushes at their own expense…and "to take turns sweeping the school floors as directed by teachers." No student was allowed to enter the water for the purpose of bathing more than once a fortnight and then only for ten minutes, nor could a student expose himself to persons passing or repassing on the bridge under penalty of punishment. Students were required to attend church at the Academy on Sundays and to refrain from walking the streets or fields that day. Students had to be in their boarding houses by 9:00 pm and could not leave their residences on Saturday nights (*By Laws, 1836*).

Enrollment

Many of the school enrollment figures during the first decade of operation are left to dust. Some records show that in 1832 the number of students was 33—20 gentlemen and 13 ladies. The principal was Mr. William H. Hoit who did most of the teaching; he had been a pupil in the class of 1823 and had graduated from Dartmouth College in 1831. He served only briefly in 1831 before heading off to a theological seminary (Haley, p.16).

Principals and Teachers

Of the many preceptors and principals of the Wolfeborough-Tuftonborough Academy from 1821 to 1876, ten were graduates of Dartmouth College, six were graduates of Bowdoin College, and the remaining singularly from Brown, Amherst and the University of Vermont. Two were graduates of WTA and two had married ladies from Wolfeborough. Some left to pursue active careers in the ministry, others in law and business. Two of the most noted teachers or preceptors were Thomas L. Ambrose and Joseph B. Clark both Civil War heroes (Haley, pp.21-24).

The Rev. John W. Haley, historian of the Wolfeborough-Tuftonboro Academy in 1915, reflected, "I hold in affectionate remembrance the names of Mr. Clark and Mr. Ambrose. They were my earliest teachers in the Academy, and, as I remember, I owe to Mr. Clark, the Preceptor, the first suggestion that I should look toward college and try for Higher Education" (Haley, p. 24).

Changes in Curriculum

During the years following the American Civil War, the educational direction of schools in America changed, and these changes gradually came to the doors of the Wolfeborough and Tuftonborough Academy. Until then, the curriculum prepared students to enter a classical line of studies at the college or university level. Now less attention was being given to the Roman and Greek classics and more to English literature, poetry, and drama. In addition, more science courses were being introduced. The advent of public education through the high school level was gradually displacing the old academy concept. In 1827, Massachusetts required every town with 500 or more families to establish a public high school, and other New England states soon followed. By 1860, there were slightly more than three hundred high schools in the United States with almost one third of them in Massachusetts and only a sprinkling in New Hampshire (Blum, p.239).

The enrollment figures for the Academy dropped from 229 to 108 during the period between 1863 and 1871 (Haley, p. 25). Perhaps this decrease reflected the fact that young people either left the ranks of common laborers to fill job vacancies in the cities caused by Civil War army recruiting or joined the military.

The Lyceum Programs

An emphasis on self-improvement became the new focus during the first half of the 19th Century, and the Academy proved to be the center for these programs. In 1826, Josiah Holbrook developed a series of lectures in Millbury, Massachusetts, for public entertainment, and it spread through New England. The Lyceum groups were concerned with the dissemination of information on the arts, sciences, history and public affairs, sort of an adult education program (*Columbia Electronic Encyclopedias*). Meetings were held in the evening, and gradually drew many of the most able community leaders to lecture for audiences. The WTA served as a platform for meetings and presentations, which seemed to enrich lives that often had been worn down by the daily chores of farm life. In addition, they offered a social opportunity to exchange conversation and ideas. Ella Thompson Parker, an early WTA student, shared her memories years later.

> The Lyceum was a great factor in the assembly room, when all the townspeople took part in debate, political and otherwise. Nothing seemed so dear, so peaceful as the Academy with its spacious yard... that always looked well" (Bowers, v.2, p.283).

Added to the evening Lyceums was Singing School, held on two nights weekly, which attracted numerous youngsters from the Academy. Jacqueline Rogers Cleary, in her informative book, *Waiting for William*, points out that "Singing School" was held on Monday and Friday nights in a large hall located near the present Wolfeboro Shopping Center. In her story, William Rogers and Martha Orne were both students at the Academy (Cleary, p. 45). William sought to help an irresponsible uncle in Missouri while Martha continued her studies in Troy, New York. Martha's description of Wolfeboro life, cautiously pointing out the most recent marriages and other social happenings in town, illustrates Wolfeboro life during times of change. This story reflects a vivid picture of life and times in Wolfeboro. It also illustrates the point that many youngsters were able to leave the town during the 1830s and early '40s to seek employment elsewhere in a rapidly expanding nation.

The evening Lyceum program was also a favorite of one of WTA's very successful students.

Henry Wilson—Graduate of WTA, Vice President of the United States

Henry Wilson was a graduate of the WTA and a participant of the much respected Lyceum Program who eventually became Vice President of the United States. There is little doubt that the story of Henry Wilson will go down through the ages as remarkable. Although Wilson was challenged by tremendous difficulties that boggle the mind, it illustrates how far determination and high ideals can carry a person. Wilson's strength of character followed him throughout his early years as a common laborer, as an indentured servant, as a merchant in the shoe making business, and through his five elections as the Senator from Massachusetts. He also managed to become vice president of the United States after the American Civil War, serving under President Ulysses S. Grant (Hatfield, pp.233-239).

Henry Wilson, 1812-1875.

In looking back over Henry's past, it is interesting to note how taking a break from the shoe business and traveling to Washington, D.C. by train changed his life. As he passed through Philadelphia, Baltimore, and other towns along the way, Wilson had his first glimpse of hard-core slavery. Entering Washington, he was shocked at the treatment handed out by slave masters with whip, auction block sales, and slave pens. This image, along with black folk working in the Maryland farmland, remained with Wilson. Upon his return trip to Natick and his shoe business, he resolved to do everything he could for the anti-slavery movement, but he also understood the need for a formal education and in 1836, he returned to his native New Hampshire and enrolled at the Wolfeborough and Tuftonborough Academy that later became Brewster Academy. He met with Mr. Samuel Avery and explained to Mr. Avery that he had little money for tuition and board, but would be willing to tutor others and enter into the Lyceum programs. Avery was impressed with the young man and immediately provided him with room and board in his home with Mrs. Avery and their children.

Wilson would be forever grateful to the Avery family for believing in him and offering him an opportunity to better himself and credited them for his success later in life. He had worked hard to illustrate to others that learning required their full attention. His lectures at the Lyceum sessions introduced the audiences to the wonder of scientific advancement by using the orery as an example.

After completing his education at WTA, Wilson returned to Boston and began his political life that would eventually lead him to the United States Senate and to the Office of Vice President where he always stood with the anti-slavery movement and those less fortunate.

Poor health would follow Wilson throughout his years as vice president. In May 1875, he suffered a mild stroke which caused his facial muscles to twitch and his speech to be thick and hard to interpret. Although advised by doctors to rest, Wilson could not. Finally,

The early Avery House where Henry Wilson lived with the Avery family.

on November 10th, 1875, when he was struck by paralysis, he was carried to his bed in the Vice President's Office just off the Senate floor. He remained there until the end came on November 22nd when he rolled over in his bed and died at the age of 63. In 1885, the U. S. Senate placed a marble bust of Wilson by the sculptor Daniel Chester French in the room where the Vice President died along with an inscription written by Wilson's old friend, Senator George F. Hoar:"The son of a farm laborer, never at school more than twelve months, in youth a journeyman shoemaker, he raised himself to the high places of fame, honor and power, and by unwearied study made himself an authority on the history of his country and on the liberty of the individual. As an eloquent speaker, the Senate and people eagerly had listened to him. He dealt with and controlled vast public expenditure during a great Civil War, yet lived and died poor; but he left to his grateful countrymen the memory of honorable public service and a good name, which was far better than riches."

If you travel to Boston and visit Faneuil Hall, as you step up to the second floor and gaze up to your left, you will face an oil portrait of Henry Wilson.

Problems Facing WTA

Years later after Wilson left Wolfeborough, enrollment at the WTA was still declining and tuition fees could hardly pay salaries. By 1866, the school building had suffered through many years of wear, and there had been a lack of careful attention to finances by those responsible for the Academy. It was at this time, that some of the Trustees took a course of action in anticipation of what they felt represented a new opportunity.

The Wolfeborough Christian Institute Established

The Christian Institute located in Andover, New Hampshire, had opened in February 1857, and according to all accounts, it had prospered. The Institute appeared to be financially sturdy, and thus some of the WTA trustees attempted to negotiate for the transfer of the Institute to Wolfeborough. The Institute's founder, The Christian Education Society, had plans on the drawing board to aid in the establishment of the Biblical School in New York. However, at the New England Christian Convention held in Wolfeborough in June of 1886, the Convention voted to change direction and made the decision to transfer the Andover School to Wolfeborough to be housed in the old Academy Building, even though that facility was in need of repair. This angered some townspeople, who were certain the vote had been rigged by some of WTA's stockholders who only wanted their investments returned and were not concerned for the betterment of education. One Christian leader complained that the trustees were just "too stingy" to contribute as they should for the support of a school. A final decision was eventually reached to lease the building and property of the WTA to the Institute (*WCI Exposition,* p. 6).

The Wolfeborough Christian Institute opened in 1871, with an enrollment of 102: 59 boys and 43 girls. But conflict between the townspeople and the Institute continued for several years.

Finally, in 1873, after years of discord, and clashing with town leaders, The Christian Institute shut its Wolfeborough doors and returned to Andover where it reopened under the name of Proctor Academy. Mr. Symonds, the last principal, left for Andover with the Institute and became its first principal (Haley, p.23). The school was to enjoy the endowment of John Proctor and its sports teams were to engage in athletic competition with Brewster for many years to come.

District #19 Public High School

In 1874, the trustees once again reopened the old WTA building for schooling. Then in 1878, with a growing Wolfeborough school population, District #19 sought to obtain the worn WTA structure as its new public high school. As such, the WTA trustees agreed to lease the school for a ten-year period for the admissions of worthy pupils who may apply for academic or high school instruction (*WTA Secretary's Record,* May 6, 1878).

The next several years found the old Academy deeply involved in education as the public school. After 1886, when the Will of John Brewster was made public, the role of the WTA was never to be the same.

Rev. John W. Haley, a former principal who had fond memories of the Wolfeborough-Tuftonborough Academy, offered a final commentary:

"It is clear that the whole life of our beloved Academy, from its opening to its final disappearance, was 66 years, from 1821 to 1887. Certainly, it has had a sufficiently checkered career. It has had its ups and downs, its lights and shadows, its prosperity and its adversity. It has had its periods of success, its periods of dormancy or hibernation, its metamorphosis, its final exit in a blaze of glory.

"With some 40 different preceptors and principals, with about 50 assistants and minored teachers, and with nearly three thousands students, it has proved a fountain of light and knowledge to this community and to the surrounding country.

"From the rising of the sun to the going down thereof, its influence in the promoting of Higher Education has been felt in all the earth. One Vice President, several members of Congress and many other men of distinction have gone forth from its portals. It has sent out ministers, doctors, lawyers, teachers, judges, statesman, missionaries, to enlighten, instruct and bless mankind.

"Noble men and stately women have left their names upon its record. Their example and influence have proven a rich benison to their contemporaries and to prosperity.

"Two generations and more have drunk from the limpid waters of this 'Pierian Spring.'

"God bless the memory, the influence and the surviving students of the old Wolfeborough and Tuftonborough (Haley, p. 27).

The Old Academy Fades

Many modern-day Brewster students have a vague understanding of the relationship between Brewster Academy and the old Wolfeborough and Tuftonborough Academy. Most students view the 1820 date printed on the Academy seal as the founding date of the school, but few understand the relationship between the old Academy and the "new" Academy established by John Brewster in 1886.

Since 1820 the old Wolfeborough and Tuftonborough Academy had been operated as a school, a church meeting center, and a lyceum, and it had also been leased to at least two other entities—the Christian Education Society and finally the District #19 school board. Time had taken its toll on the old building. The records of the WTA Corporation indicate that there was a constant effort to force these groups to use hammer, saw, and paint to repair the damage they had caused. As the darkness of the educational scene in Wolfeborough became evident, local residents began to turn their backs on the old WTA.

At this critical time in 1886, through press and gossip, it became known that John Brewster, former student and businessman, wished to revitalize his old school and other municipal institutions. Unfortunately, Brewster's life passed before he saw his dream in place, but he left that task to others—his son William Brewster, trusted associate Arthur Estabrook, and nephew, John L. Brewster. These men acted quickly.

Moving of the Old Academy

To accommodate a new Town Hall to be constructed under the direction of John Brewster's Will, the old Wolfeborough and Tuftonborough Academy building was moved nearly a hundred yards northeast of its original location where it was later used as the Pickering

Grammar School until Carpenter School was built. By 1925, the structure had been purchased by Greenleaf B. Clark who revitalized it as a hall for community use until it was finally abandoned to the pigeons, then disassembled for lumber—a sad ending to an old helpful friend.

Joined at the Heart

On June 11th, 1887, the new Brewster Academy Trustees petitioned the state legislature to pass an act that would charge them to continue the operation of an academy under the guidelines established in the *Will of John Brewster*. As Brewster's new school took form under the careful eyes of the trustees, the WTA stockholders were compensated for any losses they may have suffered during the long and illustrious career of the WTA. However, the last living trace of that school was its alumni. What was to happen to them?

The first recorded meeting of the WTA Alumni Association (WTAAA) was held on September 2, 1909, at Cobham Hall (now Bearce Hall), the homestead of Mr. and Mrs. George A. Carpenter. It held annual meetings in Wolfeborough and Boston to encourage the camaraderie and spirit of the old Academy. The leadership was in place with Charles A. Hersey as president, Greenleaf B. Clark as secretary and temporary chairman, along with nineteen interested and determined alums. Mrs. Carpenter provided the comfortable surroundings and plenty of ice cream and cakes. The thrust to continue the WTA spirit was the focus of the organization, and a reunion to be held in the Chapel Hall of the new Brewster Academy in 1911 was planned. Accurate accountings of alums were made and letters sent out. The record shows that one hundred joined into an afternoon and evening of gaiety and laughter, accompanied by many speeches recalling the old WTA days (*WTAAA Records*).

Beginning in 1919, with their ranks gradually thinning, the goals of the alumni seemed to change. As the WTAAA continued to meet yearly, there was more discussion directed toward historical preservation. The group explored how they could locate documents, letters and records of the old school. Dr. Henry Forrest Libby volunteered the service of his museum and offered to preserve old artifacts by having them stored at the Tuck Historical Museum in Concord, the Libby Museum, the Town Library and the Court House at Ossipee *(WTAAA Records)*.

With the centennial of the founding coming up in 1920, the alums discussed several alternatives, and one had a special appeal. It was decided that the association would place an appropriate tablet on the site of the old Academy building lot to commemorate the founding of the Wolfeborough and Tuftonborough Academy and Dr. Libby was asked to look into the matter. Following orders, Libby had a $60 bronze plaque cast and placed on the Town Hall, which stated:

> On this acre was the Wolfeborough and Tuftonborough Academy founded in 1820 *(WTAAA Records)*.

Then, at the August 23, 1923 meeting of the WTAAA, a wonderful gesture was offered. Letters from Brewster Free Academy Alumni Association were presented to the group by Mr. Samuel S. Parker and Secretary Cecil M. Pike, '20. The BFA Alumni Association extended its hand to invite the WTAAA into their organization as honorary members. The two groups became now forever joined at the heart. The core of the WTAAA continued their fine work and met yearly until 1927 when Greenleaf B. Clark, Mrs. Emma G. Carpenter, Dr. and Mrs. Henry Forest Libby, Joseph L. Meader, K. E. Parker and Nellie Cate Sawyer formed the Wolfeboro Historical Society. To this day, through lectures and programs, the Society perpetuates the history of the community and enriches the lives of its citizens.

2. The Founders

To accomplish great things, we must not only act, but also dream; not only plan, but also believe.
—Anatole France

John Brewster: A Man Who Valued His Past, 1812-1886.
John Brewster was born into a farm family in a small house located not far from the present site of Kingswood High School. His father, George Brewster, had managed to purchase a 500-acre tract of land covering the top of a small hill that seemed ideal for dairy cattle and hay.

George was descended from John Brewster of Portsmouth, New Hampshire, who had been born in England in 1627, came directly to Portsmouth in 1656, and died there in 1693. George's father and mother, Daniel Brewster and Abiah Flagg Brewster, traveled to Rochester, New Hampshire, in 1775 where they had two sons, Daniel and George. It was this George who later had a son, John, of Brewster Academy fame (Blair Brewster, *Family Tree of Wolfeboro Letter,* May 2, 2005).

John Brewster, founder and benefactor. By the end of his life in 1886, John Brewster had accrued a large fortune, which he generously shared with his family and his hometown. For this he will always be remembered.

On this farmland John Brewster was born on December 14, 1812. We know very little about his youth other than he may have attended the "Bridge Village" public school in Wolfeboro and then spent three terms at the Wolfeborough and Tuftonborough Academy, probably in 1826 and 1827, just before the arrival of Henry Wilson. John's father, George, boarded several students from the WTA each year, so it is likely that John befriended them as they all helped with splitting wood and the usual farm chores (*WTA School Catalogue,* 1823).

Teaching Career and Dry Goods Business

The year 1828 changed John's life forever. Word reached John that there was a teaching job in West Milton, New Hampshire, some miles to the south, where he made immediate application, was accepted and left home, never to return until he had made a success of himself. The teaching job at Milton provided him opportunity to make a major adult decision. He had been paid very little for his teaching and the prospect of financial gain was low. Instead of returning home, Brewster decided to seek employment in a dry goods business with his uncle, Jonathan Tore, in Rochester, NH, who had become ill. Following his uncle's recovery, John served in the dry goods store of William Hale in Dover Landing, NH, where he gained the reputation of being hard working, prompt and careful in his duties. Brewster remained in Dover for five years, and then in 1835, with his savings, and a loan from his previous employers, pledged to enter the dry goods business in Boston.

John Moves to Boston and Enters the Business World

Upon arriving in Boston, John formed the firm of Williams & Brewster, but a short time later, having repaid his loan, he left that business and became involved in helping to organize a new dry goods firm of Brewster, Cushman & Bancroft with their business headquarters located first at 44 and 46 Hanover Street and afterwards at 63 and 65 Water Street (Davis, Vol. 2, p. 628). For sixteen years, John Brewster was a very successful businessman in dry goods. But in 1851, he made another major life decision. Rather than continue in the path he knew so well, he decided to change to the banking profession. He joined with Charles A. Sweet to establish the banking house of Brewster, Sweet & Co. at 76 State Street, and later at 40 State. In 1871, after twenty years, Mr. Sweet retired, and the firm was reorganized as Brewster, Basset & Co, at which time Arthur F. Estabrook joined the group. In 1883, it was again reorganized this time under the name of Brewster, Cobb & Estabrook (Davis, p. 628). Mr. Estabrook had entered the firm as a ten-year-old office boy in 1857, and had become an example of diligence, energy, and determination, which eventually led to becoming a partner in the firm. Arthur never flagged in his admiration of Mr. Brewster.

John's Success in Banking

The key to John Brewster's success as a banker is conspicuously noted. As the Civil War began, Brewster, Sweet & Co., one of the leading banking firms in Boston, was named by the United States government as an agent to sell government bonds. The sales were enormous, sometimes more than a million dollars a week, and probably an average of half a million dollars weekly for the four years of the war. After the war, in addition to the government bonds, Brewster, Sweet and Co. offered the sale of railroad, state, and municipal bonds. During this time, the firm prospered and was very successful (Parker, pp. 438-439). In 1883, John Brewster retired from active business, but Arthur Estabrook continued in the firm under the name of Estabrook & Co.

"As a business man, Mr. Brewster possessed abilities of high order. He inspired confidence in any enterprise in which he enlisted and was a man of genial and generous nature, one whose sympathies were easily aroused and who was never appealed to without a ready response. With no taste for public life or political honors, he devoted his energies to the more genial pursuits of a strictly business career with conspicuously success among the business men of Boston" (Davis, vol.2, p.628).

John Brewster's Private Life

John Brewster married Rebecca Noyes in 1839 and lived in Wakefield, MA. It was in this small town that the Brewster family suffered a tragedy. In September of 1842, just short of two years of age, their first child Elizabeth died, but soon two sons were born to the couple. Three years later John purchased property in Cambridge and moved the family to 149 Brattle Street where the first and second sons of John and Rebecca took to their beds, ill from a contagious disease, probably typhoid fever. The older, John Jr. passed on June 1, 1848, almost five years old. Six days later the younger son, Frank, almost three years old, died, leaving the new house childless and in great sorrow. Upon hearing of the losses, Henry Wadsworth Longfellow, a neighbor living several houses up the street toward town, sent to Rebecca a copy of his famous poem, "The Old House under the Lindens," along with a note of condolence and a book of his poems. Crushed by the losses, Rebecca turned sadly to her house and John to his duties in Boston (E. W. Brewster *Letter*).

On July 5, 1851, their fourth and final child, William, was born during the summertime while the family was visiting their farm in Wakefield. William was destined to bring lasting fame to the family by being recognized as America's most noted ornithologist and the man who brought the plans John had for Brewster Free Academy into reality as the first president of its Board of Trustees. John and Rebecca would also take William on trips to Wolfeboro where they would spend frequent summer vacations on the lake, visiting relatives and friends. As time passed, John encouraged William to enter the banking firm

John Brewster's home, 147 Brattle Street, Cambridge, MA.

in Boston, but after a year of diligent work, William decided that his interests were more directed toward the study of ornithology and he focused his efforts along those lines. Sadly, on November 10, 1874, tragedy struck the Brewster family again when Rebecca suddenly passed away, leaving John and William to fend for themselves on Brattle Street.

Marriages in the Family

It was during this time that two new persons entered the Brewster family. The records indicate that John had taken a second wife, Arabella, age 35. The exact date of the union is not known, but the 1880 federal census of Cambridge had recorded the marriage (*1880 Federal Census Report for Cambridge*, Middlesex City, June 1, 1880).

The second addition to the family was Caroline Kettle of Boston, William's new wife. The couple left the family home in 1878 moving next door to 145 Brattle Street.

John Becomes Ill

In 1885, John became ill, but little is known about the cause of his infirmities. He complained of headaches but no treatment relieved the pain. On January 13, 1886, he died at home, possibly of a stroke or brain cancer. William and Caroline took an active part in the funeral arrangements, and he was buried in the cemetery lot at Mount Auburn, next to Rebecca.

After John passed away, William was faced with completing the family real estate projects and carrying out the wishes in his father's Will, a prodigious task that required William's attendance in Boston and Wolfeboro for many years to come *(Old Cambridge, p.82).*

John Brewster had always been a man who was held in high regard. In business, he had been a man of few words, but those words had been as good as his bond.

Mount Auburn Cemetery, Cambridge, MA, Brewster family's final resting place.

As a young boy in Wolfeboro, John had attended Wolfeborough and Tuftonborough Academy for only three terms before he left his hometown and went off to find his way in the world, ending in Boston to begin a very successful career. It was apparent to John as he progressed in life, the value of an education and how important it was for young people to have the prospect of attending school to gain the skills and knowledge for a vocation. He was reminded of the village in which he grew up and the lack of opportunity for the youth. He was determined to make a difference in their lives and offer them a chance to profit from formal schooling.

John Brewster never forgot his roots and made a remarkable contribution in the field of education. His memory and good deeds live on.

John Brewster's Will

In his Will dated February 23, 1886, John Brewster provided for an Academy in his home village of Wolfeborough for the charitable and educational uses of students with the following conditions: "(1) That the name of said Academy shall be changed to and thereafter continue to be that of the "Brewster Free School" or "Academy"; (2) That no restriction shall be placed upon any person desiring to attend and receive instruction from said school or academy on account of his or her age, sex, or color, provided only he or she is of good moral character; (3) That not more than twenty-five per centum of said annuity shall be spent in erecting buildings or in alterations, improvements or repairs of or upon the same; the remaining income from this provision of my Will to be expended wholly for salaries of teachers for instruction and educational purposes of said School or Academy so, as near as possible, as to make instruction and education therein free....My trustees shall use and appropriate all income from my estate remaining after making all payments and carrying out all provisions hereinbefore made, for the use and benefit of the said Wolfeborough and Tuftonborough Academy."

William Brewster, A Devoted Son, 1851-1919

Two roads diverged in a wood, and I took the one less traveled by, and that has made all the difference.—Robert Frost

William spent his youth on Brattle Street and attended Cambridge public schools, graduating from Cambridge High School in 1869.

The Washington Grammar School on Brattle Street in Cambridge had a unique collection of young students in 1861. Three of these young people were destined to become leaders in the literary, scientific and fine arts world of the United States at the turn of the century. It was here, probably on Brattle Street opposite the grammar school, that the boys, at the age of ten or eleven, played marbles very near Longfellow's "spreading chestnut tree" that "shaded the village smithy." This group was composed of Richard Henry Dana, Daniel Chester French and William Brewster, all neighbors and all, as young boys, very much interested in games, hunting, and fishing. Behind William's family homestead at 149 Brattle Street, his father, John, had built a large barn and behind the barn stood many acres of undeveloped land. Nearby was a small lake surrounded by woods with some clearings that acted as the ideal spot for the neighborhood children to explore. It was here also that William spent hours cataloging birds, developing his skills at taxidermy, and writing about birds (D.C. French in "Introduction" to William Brewster's *October Farm*). By 1900, William Brewster would be called America's finest ornithologist, while his good friend, Daniel Chester French, would be well on his way to becoming America's most noted sculptor for his Minuteman statue at Concord Bridge and marble statue of Abraham Lincoln encased in the Lincoln Memorial in Washington, D.C. Richard Dana

William Brewster, famed ornithologist.

would gain the reputation of being an anti-slavery activist and fiercely interested in the rights of seamen. His book, *Two Years Before the Mast*, a best seller, became a driving force in protecting the rights of seamen.

In 1931, ten years after William's death Daniel Chester French wrote:

> Very early William's particular interest in birds asserted itself, and we made collections of eggs, as was the common habit of boys at that time. I think I can fairly claim that he and Dick Dana and I made a more serious study of the subject than was usual, perhaps because Will's father had a copy of Audubon's Ornithology and my father had Nuttall's, which we studied with a thoroughness that would have put us at the head of our classes, if applied to our school books (William Brewster, pp. ix-x).

Courtesy and kindness were William's guideposts in relationships. He had learned from his father the importance of associations when things had to be accomplished, but he never exploited a friendship for his own welfare. His primary goals were always for the betterment of wildlife and to elevate the existence of man and nature. As a young man, William made ornithology a profession and would bring it to the attention of the American public.

The 149 Brattle Street house was his workshop, laboratory and base of operations from which he would sojourn out into the wilds of New England, venturing to Concord, the White Mountains, the far reaches of Umbagog and Bethel or Dublin.

Caroline, his wife, took to the idea of exploring nature in its habitat as well, and would

William Brewster's home, 145 Brattle Street, Cambridge, MA.

accompany William on his outings and invite friends on these weekend trips. William had purchased an old house in Concord that he named *October Farm.* It was near the Concord River, and became his stage for wildlife operations during spring, summer and fall. It was here that he and Caroline continued their studies and life together.

William and Caroline would spend the next several years making the long journey by car or train to Wolfeboro, staying at the Pavilion Hotel or visiting the home of his friend, Dr. Henry Forest Libby. Libby was a fellow naturalist, preservationist, and dentist who also knew taxidermy. The two understood each other and during breaks in their heavy meeting schedule were content to spend some time tramping in the wilderness or canoeing the lake in search of new wildlife. Libby had the intention of building a museum to house a large collection of bird and animal specimens of the region, and he sought William's advice on the construction. Libby would supply a welcome relief to William's busy schedule.

As the first President of the Board of Trustees of Brewster Free Academy, William's job was to implement the plans of his father in a rapid and detailed fashion. The old Wolfeborough and Tuftonborough Academy building could provide some space, but it was in disrepair and partially used as a town school. Organizing a new school would require a faculty, administration, students, and, most important, the purchase of land on which to construct a new school building. In addition, finding facilities for faculty housing and boarding students was of immediate importance. Plans and directions were needed for a new town hall and library, and scholarship funding must be secured. As required under the Will provisions, personnel had to be enlisted to supervise, develop, and carry out the directives. As each organizational step was completed, Brewster anxiously moved his team forward to the next.

The new Preceptor, Edwin Lord, was hired and moved to Wolfeboro. Upon his arrival in Wolfeboro, he began tending to the thousands of tasks requiring immediate attention: enlisting a faculty, enrolling students, and advertising. A portion of Pickering's old white Academy building would be used for classes, and teachers were boarded at homes in town. Meanwhile, plans for the construction of a new school building were in full swing, and Arthur Estabrook, anxious to lend a helping hand, joined in the task by giving his home, building a new house for Preceptor Edwin Lord, and purchasing property along Main Street for the developing campus.

With the support of Arthur Estabrook and Edwin Lord, William was somewhat freed of the rigorous tasks of attending matters at Brewster Free Academy, and he turned to his journals and sojourns in the wild. He met with Daniel Chester French on their annual outing days along the Concord River, and during one meeting the conversation turned to Father John. As a fitting tribute to the man who helped bring them closer to nature, French volunteered to sculpt a bust of John, today housed in Brewster's Kenison Library.

On the night of July 11, 1919, at the age of sixty-eight, "with Caroline and nurse in attendance, leaving behind the works of his time, his books, his bird museum, his voluminous journals, houses, servants, stocks, rentals as well as his wife and his many male friends," William left this world (Mitchell, pp. 173).

The Brewster cemetery lot on Larch Avenue at Mount Auburn in Cambridge, Massachusetts, displays the graves of each family member in orderly fashion, with the exception of that for William and Caroline. One large polished pink granite stone stands out on the left side of the lot, selected by Daniel Chester French, and engraved with this scripture verse:

> For, lo, the winter is past, The flowers appear on the earth; The time of the singing of birds is come. Solomon 2:11

A bust of John Brewster sculpted by famed Daniel Chester French as a memorial gift to William his boyhood friend.

Immediately upon his passing, the will of William was opened. It was brief and to the point. Caroline was the recipient of his financial estate and house. The bird collection of over 50,000 skins and mountings were left to the Museum of Comparative Zoology at Harvard. His books on natural history were divided between the same museum, the Boston Society of Natural History and Brewster Free Academy.

Upon the death of Caroline on March 4, 1921, $60,000 went to the Museum of Comparative Zoology; $10,000 to found a bed at Cambridge Hospital and $20,000 to the Trustees of Brewster Free Academy to found a museum; $2,000 to the Nuttall Ornithological Club; $2,000 to the Massachusetts Audubon Society; $2,000 to the American Ornithologist Union; $2,000 to the Charleston, S.C., Museum of Natural History; and the remainder to the Boston Society of Natural History.

In another section of his will, William stated "any of such books not taken by said college (Harvard) or Society (Boston Society of Natural History) were to be given to Brewster Free Academy to be kept in the Museum when erected." He stipulated, "$20,000 is to be used in erecting there, at Brewster Free Academy, a one story fire-proof museum."

It would be forty-three years before the Academy would be in a position to erect a museum for William's belongings. In the meantime, Principal Charles Haley would make a space available in Lord House. The room was "cozily arranged, photographs and paintings adorning the walls and heavy rugs covering the floor. Three bookcases are to be found standing in different corners, their crowded shelves supporting the systematically arranged volumes. A desk, a table, several comfortable chairs, three of which are of great antiquity, and a massive leather couch make it an ideal place to read the different books of the collection" (Edward Lehan, 1920).

In a note written in *Commencement Edition of the Brewster Review* of 1962, Herbert D. Tinker, '16, and teacher of mathematics, presented some notes taken by Dr. Nathaniel H. Scott, a trustee of Brewster for many years, which related a story about William. "One night I sat beside him when a class of thirty-six, which he considered an unusually fine one, graduated. He quietly said, "I wish my father could have seen them" and then in a low voice as if to himself, "and perhaps – he –did."

Arthur F. Estabrook, A Trusted Friend, 1847-1919

Do not seek to follow in the footsteps of the men of old; seek what they sought.—Matsuo Basho

After John Brewster, Arthur Estabrook is the single most important figure in the original establishment of Brewster Academy. Even though the men were born thirty-two years apart, it is interesting to note the similarities in their lives, character and personal friendship as previously mentioned.

Growing up, Arthur was a disciplined, curious, dependable and responsible boy as was John. As young men, both were eager to be successful and demonstrated an aptitude for business. Arthur traveled to Boston at an early age to find his future in the city as did John. They were unaware of each other at this time, unaware how their lives would interweave and cross paths until finally they each would become significant players in the other's life.

John recognized the strong moral character and integrity of young Arthur, and perhaps he saw the same entrepreneurial spirit that was at the very core of his own temperament when he hired the young ten-year-old Arthur Estabrook as a messenger boy. Arthur would become the closest associate of John and for the remainder of his life feel a debt of gratitude to this man. Arthur would strive to repay John for the trust he placed in him with his devotion and dedication and would work unfailingly to fulfill the wishes of his mentor. Arthur held a great deal of reverence and admiration for John and in some ways, Arthur may have fulfilled a need in John's life to have someone follow in his footsteps.

Arthur Estabrook, an active trustee who carried forth the dreams of John.

Arthur Builds His Summer Home in Wolfeboro

Through long discussions with John and then finally after visits to Wolfeborough and Lake Winnipesauke, Arthur decided to build a summer home near the shore of this beautiful, tranquil New England lake. Its quiet, peaceful village was a strong draw for Arthur, and in 1886, the same year that the first Academy structure was designed, Arthur began the establishment of his summer home located on the hilltop of land once owned by Daniel Pickering. It was this same Daniel Pickering who ultimately gave the 42 acres of land for the founding of Brewster Free Academy. Thus, Arthur and John are joined once again, this time in fulfilling John's dream for a school for the children of Wolfeborough and Tuftonborough. Arthur Estabrook continued that dream through the acquisition of buildings and property that remain to this day the core of the Brewster campus.

The History of the Estabrook and Main Street Houses

As we researched the history of this fine old building, we discovered that it was one of the first residential structures to take its place as part of the Brewster Academy campus. Arthur F. Estabrook, not only bequeathed a large trust to the Academy, but gave his summer home to the school as well. Likewise, he was instrumental in acquiring several other buildings along Main Street: Lord House, Kimball House and later Main Street Dorm, Haines House, and Richardson House which together greatly expanded the school facilities.

As the Academy began to take form, Arthur positioned himself as not only a long-term trustee, but also as a major player by chairing the Buildings and Grounds Committee which supervised the construction of the original building in 1890 and also the design and construction of the present Main Academy Building in 1905.

Estabrook House, summer home of Arthur Estabrook.

The Estabrook as a Bed and Breakfast

In early years, the Estabrook served as a dormitory for young women and as a formal dining room for boarding students. During that time, it became a place for all students to come together and play games and socialize, and it has remained a center for young people to gather. In addition, the Estabrook served as a summer bed and breakfast from 1913-1921 under the direction and leadership of Lucy Richardson who served as housemother and teacher during the school year. (Some may know Cara and Harrison Moore. Harrison, class of 1946, served as manager of the first student center constructed in 1978 on the stage of Rogers Memorial Gym. He also taught driver's education for many years. Cara Moore, class of 1945, is the daughter of Lucy Richardson). According to the Moores, many alums and summer guests would come and stay at the Estabrook during July and August and enjoy the homey atmosphere, good food, and warm memories of times on campus.

Over the years, the Estabrook has been expanded and redesigned many times to serve the school community, just as Mr. Estabrook had envisioned that it would be many years ago. Despite a major fire in 1897 and several lightning strikes, its special personality remains.

Fire in the Estabrook

The reporting of the fire from the *Brewster Review* of March 1897:

> "FIRE AT THE "ESTABROOK."
>
> SUPPER was hardly finished at the "Estabrook" on Wednesday, the twenty-fourth of February, when it was discovered that fire had broken out on the third floor. In a few moments flames were bursting out in the rooms upon both sides of the hall. Meanwhile an alarm had been telephoned in and those who were the first upon the scene, devoted themselves to saving property.

The various hose and hook and ladder companies of the town responded very promptly and soon they were contesting with the flames that grew fiercer every moment.

The Academy boys assisted by many of the citizens cleared all the rooms of the building with the exception of those of Miss I. Louise Sanborn and Misses Lena O. and Fannie J. Merrill, who were the heaviest losers. After three and a half hours of stubborn fighting, with a scarcity of water, the fire was subdued. The entire third floor was gutted and the remainder of the building was nearly ruined by water. The loss on building and furniture was four thousand dollars, which was covered by insurance.

The destitute " Estabrookers" were sheltered for the rest of the night at the houses of Principal Lord, Mr. Kimball, Mrs.Gilman, and at the "Annex." Temporary quarters have now been provided in the Rollins Block.

Exactly one week after the fire, the contractors began work upon the building. The third floor is to be remodeled and the entire building is to be thoroughly repaired. It is expected that it will be again occupied at the opening of the Spring term.

The Legacy of The Estabrook

Today the Estabrook and the Main Building come together as the heart of the campus, just as John Brewster and Arthur Estabrook came together so many years ago to fulfill their dream of serving students of future generations. The Estabrook stands tall with its welcoming front porch, broad stairs, and expansive entranceway inviting all who open its door to come in and find warmth, sustenance, and friendship within its walls. What more could anyone want as a legacy and testament to his life? For this Arthur F. Estabrook, an active trustee of the Academy until his death, will always be remembered.

The newly re-modeled Estabrook after the fire of 1897.

Arthur Estabrook Passes Away

Forty-five years after his marriage to Ida Fletcher on October 8, 1874, Arthur passed away on July 27, 1919. Although childless, Arthur Estabrook enjoyed the company of young people and took great joy from being in their presence. His enthusiastic spirit made students feel special and valued whenever he interacted with them and in turn, young people responded with admiration, respect, and a desire to please him.

This side of the man was seen when one afternoon he was glimpsed downtown with a group of boys, enjoying ice cream sodas and conversation together. It was during moments like this that Arthur Estabrook was at his best, encouraging young people as John Brewster had encouraged him. The influence of John Brewster had come full circle.

Arthur Estabrook was buried in Mount Auburn Cemetery. When Ida passed away on November 22, 1922, she was buried there alongside her husband. Under the terms of Arthur's will, at the time of Ida's death, $100,000 was to be given to the Academy.

The Pavilion Hotel, where John and William Brewster and Arthur Estabrook would often stay (located where the Civil War monument now stands).

3. Edwin H. Lord, 1887–1907: The First Principal

We all need someone who inspires us to do better than we know how.—Anonymous

The Search for the First School Leader

Charged by the Will of John Brewster to establish a new school in Wolfoborough, the trustees immediately began in 1886 a formal search for its first principal. They had a clear picture of the significant and strategic task placed before them.

The new school administrator was to be the first leader of Brewster Free Academy. He would be responsible for hiring faculty and for enrolling students during the formative years of the school. As the new school moved from infancy to maturity, the new principal would guide it toward fulfilling John Brewster's goal of creating a prime New England preparatory school. This demanded that the new principal not only possess an understanding of what motivates young people, but also a plan as to how to develop a love of learning and a respect for themselves and others. A thorough knowledge of curriculum and business was also essential as were the ability and personality to attract and maintain a superior faculty and student body. He had to have the vision, confidence, and strength of character to be frank and honest while at the same time be masterful and quick to respond to any

Edwin H. Lord, the first principal.

and all demands. Further this person must be optimistic, patient, and able to bridge the gap caused by open uncertainties in the minds of many townspeople. Along with these concerns, binding the wounds suffered by supporters of the old much loved alma mater and somehow bringing them together once again under the banner of the new Brewster Free Academy would be a major challenge for the new leader.

This task fell to Edwin Howard Lord. Born in Springvale, Maine, in 1850, he attended the common school in Springvale and Berwick Academy for a short time before going to New Hampton Academy for three terms and onto Bowdoin for undergraduate study and finally to Harvard for his advanced degrees in 1881. Between 1871 and 1873, Edwin served as a principal of Richmond Maine High School, Brunswick, and later he moved to Lowell, Massachusetts, where he taught science at the public high school until 1880.

Shortly thereafter, he met and married Julia Swift Bennett of Lowell, and they had three children, two of whom were Brewster graduates—Mary Bennett Lord and William Swift Lord. William Swift, class of 1900, became a Brewster teacher and coach.

Edwin Lord's Career Accomplishments

With Lord's innovative skills and pioneering spirit, he was invited to become treasurer and manager of the new Edison Illuminating Company of Lawrence which had been contracted to introduce electrical power throughout the city. Edwin Lord was highly successful and truly peerless in the area of electric power and he was well on his way to enjoying an extraordinary career with the Edison Company when in 1886 major changes took place in his life.

The Offer Made

In 1886, the trustees of Brewster Free Academy, probably through the efforts of John L. Brewster, nephew of John, approached Mr. Lord to become the principal of their unique and nascent independent school in central New Hampshire.

Whatever doubts the trustees may have had in regard to his teaching experience, they were won over by his intelligence, his skills in managing people, and his entrepreneurial ability. They decided to move ahead and offer Lord the opportunity to become the first principal of this new school in Wolfeborough, New Hampshire. His acceptance proved to be an excellent decision both for Brewster Free Academy and Mr. Lord; through his leadership, dedication to excellence, and executive ability, Brewster began its successful journey.

The Task Begins

Time was short, and there was much to be done. Lord's immediate tasks were to develop an admissions plan, hire a small number of faculty members, fashion a curriculum, order materials and develop a housing scheme. Since there were no classrooms yet, arrangements were made with the trustees of the Wolfeborough and Tuftonborough Academy to lease classroom space on the second floor while the first floor was used by the local school district.

Meanwhile, the Brewster trustees were concerned with the development of the newly acquired property on the southwest side of Main Street where construction would soon begin on a new school building. The school had to address many problems associated with the growing pains and the governing of a new foundation that only a clear head and impartial mind could resolve. Trustee Arthur Estabrook was the leader for much of the new building and construction. He immediately turned over his summerhouse to the school and began reviewing property for possible acquisition along South Main Street.

Early South Main Street looking south with the tower of the newly built Town Hall in view.

Main Street Houses

Along South Main Street in the mid 1880s, there was a compact row of ten white buildings backed by barns, gardens, apple trees, and various outbuildings, which interfered with the view of the lake and mountains from Main Street. They also prevented access to the newly developing school grounds. In 1888, under the leadership of Arthur Estabrook, the trustees began to acquire this property. As mentioned earlier, of the ten original houses only Haines House, Main Street Dorm, and Richardson House were not part of this initial transaction, but remained privately owned for a short time before they were added to the Academy grounds by 1890. Two of the houses were moved off the campus but still are in use as private homes, and the others were torn down. The old Pavilion Inn land was acquired in1899, and then in 1911, the old Congregational Church property, located where the Civil War monument now stands, was added. It is estimated that the property acquired by the trustees in this way added about twenty acres to the original grant. More than this, it made possible a beautiful campus and a view of Winnipesaukee from Main Street.

Construction had begun on the new Academy Building in late l887, and in 1891, it was decided that the old Lincoln house where Lord House now stands would be moved and a new house for the principal would be built on that site. Kimball House was built the next year as a faculty residence and dorm.

Opening of School, 1887

In the warm Indian summer days of 1887, Mr. Lord opened the school's first year on September 12th in the old Wolfeborough and Tuftonborough Academy building with two teachers—Miss Lydia F. Remick of Wolfeborough and E. H. Ross of St. Johnsbury, Vermont—and 47 students *(Bowers,* vol. 2, p. 285).

Standard of Behavior

Lord's basic standards of behavior were simple, yet had a lasting effect on each student and faculty member. He required only that, "Ladies must always act like ladies and gentlemen like gentlemen." That statement was further explained in the school catalog: "The formation of character is a leading aim of the school." These ideals he expected from everyone. As Francis Harriman, '94, pointed out, "He was ever ready to advise and then to aid in every

Above, Lord House, 1892, with Kimball House in the background. Below, Herbert Sargent teaching in an early chemistry class in the original Academic Building.

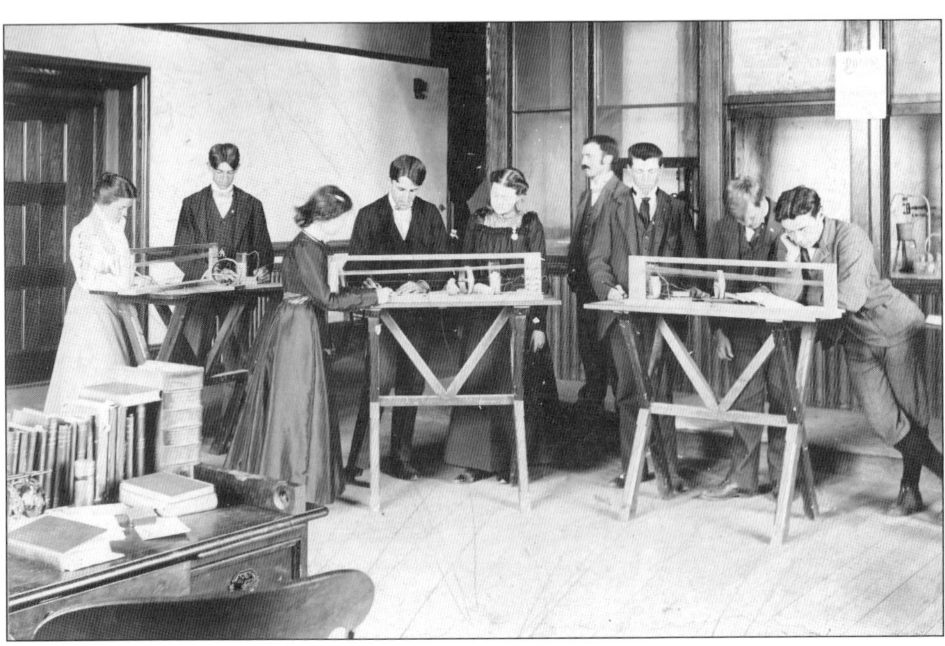

possible way towards the attainment of what seemed best for each individual student. His ideal for every one of us was never low. It was his delight as much as ours if success crowned our efforts....Another ideal which was his aim to impress was earnestness. Idleness was to him not only inexplicable but intolerable. Mr. Lord was, first, democratic in spirit. Equality was to him a right which one surrenders only through some unworthy act of his own" (Clarence E. Langley,'03, *Winnipesaukean*, Mar. 1907, p. 1).

Lord's Curriculum Established

Lord fashioned a curriculum around educating youngsters for college offering two paths of equal intensity. The Classical Studies option set out a four-year program of courses rich in English, Latin, Greek, and French or German, coupled with science and mathematics; and the second, English Studies, while holding to Latin, gave time for more science, mathematics, history and foreign languages (French and/or German). More students enrolled in the English Studies than the Classical Studies (*Brewster Free Academy Catalog*, 1892, pp. 9-14).

First Graduating Class

Of eleven students in the first two graduating classes, 1890 and 1891, three went to Dartmouth College and three to Harvard College. Three men became employed in Boston or Portland, Maine, while the two women graduates remained at home (*Brewster Free Academy Catalog*, 1892, pp. 9-14).

Class Enrollment

There were only a half-dozen rooms provided by the school for boarders at a cost of $4.50 per week. The expense of living in a private boarding house was $3.00 per week and upwards, yet there were no boarders in the first two graduating classes. However, in 1894, Linnie Andrews traveled all the way from Sulphur Springs, Texas, to Wolfeborough as a boarder. Linnie would be one of very few boarding students. But the school's regional day population rapidly increased as railroad transportation was introduced. Enrollment became focused on towns between Rochester to the south, Conway to the north, and Acton, Maine, to the east (Ibid). Before this, transportation to school had been by horse and wagon, stagecoach, or foot.

Class of 1890	7	Class of 1894	46
Class of 1891	4	Class of 1895	57
Class of 1892	9	Class of 1896	45
Class of 1893	18	Class of 1897	49

(*Brewster Free Academy Catalog, 1894*; pp. 12-16).

But these figures can be deceiving since students could enroll by terms—fall, winter and spring. Some students elected to attend school for one, two or three terms, but all prescribed courses in either the classical or English curriculum had to be completed before being considered a graduate.

Lord was a teaching principal throughout his tenure and hired additional teachers depending on enrollment for each year. Between 1890 and 1907, he never hired more than seven instructors, nor did his successor, Dr. Charles Murkland (*Brewster Free Academy Catalogs*, 1890-1911).

The New Building

While classes continued to be held in the old Wolfeborough and Tuftonborough Academy building from 1887 to early 1890, the construction of the new school building progressed rapidly. The structure was located in almost the same plot as the present classroom building but was much different in style. The south wing was constructed first with plans for the addition of two more adjoining sections: a large main entrance hall and a connecting north wing, identical to the south wing structure. These additions would be built when enrollment reached 150 students and the anticipated increase in tuition income permitted.

The four stories included recitation rooms, science laboratories, office spaces, and rest rooms. Windows were tall and large as were the roofs and chimneys. Constructed in a Neo-Gothic style, the outside of the building was rich red brick.

By March of 1890, the new structure was ready for classes, and Lord made careful preparations to move both students and equipment across Main Street to their new home, ending the occupation of the old Wolfeborough and Tuftonborough Academy building. Plans were now to start construction of the new Brewster Memorial Building that would house the Brewster Library and town offices. This meant that the old vacant Wolfeborough/Tuftonborough Academy building had to be moved back and a short bit east to make way for the new structure that John Brewster had provided in his Will.

Recollections of an Old Teacher

The following recollection by Dr. Frederick H. Safford was contributed to *The Brewster* for the March 1926 edition. Dr. Safford taught at the Academy from 1888-1893. At the time of this writing in 1926, he occupied the chair of mathematics at the University of Pennsylvania.

> *The First Years in the Old WTA as Remembered by Dr. Frederick Safford.*
> Brewster Free Academy began its second year in September 1888, with five teachers, of whom Mr. E. H. Lord, Miss Lydia F. Remick and Miss Alice S. Rollins had served the preceding year, while Miss Helen Cobb Clark and myself were newly appointed. A year later Mr. G. C. Kimball was added to the staff and all of the above went to the new building

Original architectural design for Brewster Free Academy.

The Cyclone, *a steamboat on the lake, provided public excursions and transportation as well as a means of travel for Brewster's interscholastic sports.*

in the fall of 1890. The old building occupied in September 2, 1890, had been used previously by the Wolfeborough and Tuftonborough Academy. The erection of the Town Hall in front of it during these years gradually hid it from the Main Street. This building was later moved to the northeast for the use of the town schools and the large columns in front were taken down.

Into these hollow columns students sometimes had climbed from underneath the building and there emitted terrifying noises mistaken for some ghostly speech when a young female student would pass by. There were six classrooms in the old WTA; on the second floor was also a room about 9 x 16 used as a chemical laboratory, its only water supply being a hogshead on a raised framework in one corner. Iron stoves burning wood heated the entire building, and the smoke pipe sometimes dripped creosote. The bell of the Academy was soon removed to the tower of the Town Hall.

In 1899, was held the first Brewster Free Academy steamer excursion on the Cyclone that started at 10:00 AM. On the deck were a cabinet organ and an orchestra composed of students. In the course of the forenoon a rattlesnake was captured swimming off Rattlesnake Island. This was kept in a jar of alcohol on the desk of one of the staff, but it finally "went bad" and had to be disposed of. The excavation for the Town Hall tower was just completed to a depth of twenty feet and the jar was deposited there. Several of the students stood by and sang "Ernan," one of the morning hymns, which was most unpopular. How this jar will puzzle archeologists in coming ages when they explore the foundations of this tower!

The view across the lake was no less beautiful than now. Sounds of distant thunder were credited to the construction work on the Lake Shore Railroad then being built. For several terms the sessions began

Monday noon and ended Saturday noon to allow students to spend their weekends at home.

The house of the principal, first occupied by Mr. Lord in 1891, has been very little changed. Teachers first occupied the Estabrook in the spring of 1891, and in the fall of that year by students also. A fire in the third floor was followed by a slight change in the roof and third floor plans, but the lower part is unaltered. The campus between the main building and Main Street is just the same today as in 1890, although the present Academy does not stand exactly on the site of the original building.

The writer still cherishes a loving cup presented by the students at the time. Almost yearly he visits the campus to renew the associations of that period, recognized by a few of the townspeople but unknown, of course, to present students (The *Brewster*, March 1926).

The Developing School

During the next thirteen years, in addition to being principal, Lord busied himself with teaching classes, hiring new faculty to accommodate increased enrollment of 137 students, developing an alumni organization, staffing the *Brewster Review* with writers, attending to trustees, and preparing students in dramatics and chorus.

Social events were organized and formal dress dinner parties were presented in the Estabrook where each had a dance card and a small lead pencil in order to record their partner's name and dance number for the evening's entertainment.

Sports teams were constantly being organized, and Lord had to plan for space for the teams to play. A baseball diamond was laid out down near the lake, but football was also becoming popular. Brewster boys who had an interest in football had to lug their equipment a mile away to a farmer's hay field where they played and practiced after mowing was done. And no crowds were there at game time to cheer them on. By 1896, Lord had a fine football

The faculty in 1902-1903: Carroll Piper, Reginald Christenson, Edwin H. Lord, Herbert Sargent, Herbert Tirrell, Mary Newton Young, Grace Webster Heartz, Ethel May Garvin.

Above, students enjoyed formal dinner parties in the Estabrook. Below, first campus tennis courts constructed behind The Estatbrook.

field constructed down by the lake near today's baseball diamond, and two tennis courts were built behind The Estabrook. Mr. Lord prided himself as the timer for the football team. Basketball was practiced in the town bowling alley where baskets were erected when there was no bowling.

Indian Joe

A local character, "Indian Joe," lived on the Academy property located down in the woods near Brewster Beach, and he had become a strong daily supporter of Brewster students and particularly of baseball players. Now, with a new team to cheer, "Indian Joe" found himself a hero to the first football boys as well (*Brewster Review*, Vol.2, 1896, p.7).

The 1894 baseball team.

Coach George Kimball and the 1899 football team.

Above, the 1901 boys basketball team. Below, the 1892 girls basketball team in game uniforms.

Pride in the Academy

The period from 1899 to 1903 provided Brewster with a chance to show its stripes and deliver to the town of Wolfeborough an Academy of which to be proud. Brewster had become an important and integral part of the community, and graduates were attending highly competitive colleges while others used their education as a steppingstone to future success. The Academy building and campus had become a significant part of the town's landscape.

Along the north side of the Academy Building, a baseball game is played with spectators enjoying the event.

The student body in 1903 before the catastrophic fire.

Catastrophe Strikes: The Main Building Burns

Then heartbreaking catastrophe hit at 3:15 AM, Monday, November 2, 1903, when neighbors on Green Street were awakened to the sight of flames bursting from the windows on the south side of the new classroom building. William J. Britton, '92, sounded the alarm from the S.W. Clow Company Engine House while Miss Ada Thompson discovered the same scene on the north side of the building. Quickly, the Rollins Hose Co. responded, but by 5:00 AM the fire had done its work throughout the structure. The red brick walls were left standing with only a heap of ashes and rubble at their feet. Evidently, no immediate cause could be assigned. The janitor, Mr. Charles Getchell, stated that there had been no one in the building since Saturday, when he thoroughly swept the building and removed all waste. Sunday morning was spent dusting the floors and rooms and removing the ashes from the furnace. He left the building in proper condition with the doors locked and the windows fastened about 4:30 on Sunday afternoon (*Granite State News,* Nov. 7, 1903, pp. 1-3). Attempts to halt the spread of flames had been futile and all was lost—tables, chairs, shelving, supplies, office equipment and science equipment. For thirteen years, voices of young people and their teachers had been heard chatting and laughing and moving from class to class as they attended to their schedules but now little remained of the pride of students and teachers and the symbol of the school.

The remains of the disastrous fire of 1903.

The original Pavilion icehouse on the shoreline with the Academic Building in the background moved on campus for temporary classroom use.

School Never Misses a Beat

With a hopeful heart, Lord set himself to work immediately, determined not to let the school miss a session. He started out to catch the first morning train to Boston for a trustee meeting but in the process spotted several students lugging their belongings down to the station, thinking there would be no school. He halted them, "Gentlemen, return to your classes immediately. There will be school!"

Lord had already made arrangements for the school to use the new Brewster Memorial Hall for class space. He then contracted for the moving of the old Pavilion or Kingswood Inn's icehouse from its location on the north side of the lower campus near the lake to a position behind Kimball House. It was sometimes affectionately referred to as Lord's 1904 Boathouse. The building was cleverly remodeled and would have new windows and be refitted as the temporary chapel. Then a chemistry lab with steam heat was added. This structure is now located behind The Estabrook and used as the art building. Several rooms in Kimball House were converted to classrooms as well (*The Winnipeasukean,* March 1907).

Lord's trip to Boston was important for the trustees would need to review the events leading to the fire, the insurance policies, plans for the construction of a new school building, and the financial records and approve the ordering of a long list of books, science supplies and materials which Lord carried in his brief case. These were approved for purchase, and arrangements were made to ship them back to Wolfeborough on the next train (*Granite State News,* Nov. 7, 1903, p.3).

Upon return, Lord found everything running smoothly. All classes had met with students in attendance in spite of the confusion. To the students and faculty he reported the progress and stated that the trustees were planning a new building that would soon rise from the ashes of the old.

Mr. Lord set out for the train to visit Boston trustees. Students at the Wolfeborough Station were admonished to return to campus immediately classes were in session.

Constructing a New Academy Building

Construction on the new school building began in the early spring of 1904, with the construction contract awarded to E. P. Cummings & Company of Boston. Ground was broken on August 22, 1904, and the last pieces of the old school walls fell on the 29th. The old bricks were cleaned and set aside to be used wherever possible (*Granite State News,* Sept. 3, 1904 Aug. 29, 1904). As the structure took shape, everyone recognized that the new form was much different than the one before. A new, large hipped roof covered a three-story structure.

The ground floor, open to the lakeside, would house a recreation room, two large locker rooms, a manual training room, separate toilet rooms, a boiler room and coal bunker area. The first floor held an office for the principal, a teachers' room and six large classroom/recitation rooms.

The second floor was noted for the large "assembly hall" which included a platform stage for presentations and which would soon be named the chapel. At each end of the floor were two classrooms with a science laboratory on the south side and an art room on the north end. Two recitation rooms were placed over the front entrance hall. Gone was the red brick of the old building, replaced with a much brighter gray-tan brick. True to the neo-Greco style, four very large concrete pillars supported the roofline and the entrance to the building (The *Winnipesaukean,* Dec. 1906, pp. 6-8).

Teams of horses dragged away the rubble and aided in grading the land around the new structure. The new building was now complete and in exactly the right spot. Since 1905, this structure has always acted as the center of the Brewster campus. All school life seems to swirl around the building, yet it always seems to be in sight. Whether walking from a dorm to the athletic fields or the dining hall, one's eyes seem to settle on the "AC" at some time during the trip.

The new Academic Building 1905 built upon the rubble of the original building.

Dedication

The dedication services at the new school building took place in the chapel on the second floor on November 1, 1905. The platform committee was composed of the trustees—John L. Brewster, William Brewster, Arthur F. Estabrook, President William J. Tucker of Dartmouth College, and Judge Oscar L. Young, representing the alumni. Blaisdell's Band and the school chorus provided music. After speeches by President Tucker and Judge Young, Arthur F. Estabrook, chairman of the Building Committee, gave the keys to the new building to John L. Brewster, President of Trustees. There was no speech by Lord, nor was there a chair for him on the platform. It is believed that Mr. Lord was ill at the time and could not attend the ceremony recognizing what he had worked so hard to achieve (The *Winnipesaukean,* Dec. 1906, pp.6-8).

New School Rule

In order to create an unruffled atmosphere in the building, a new school rule was created. It stated that the use of the front entrance was allowed for only teachers, guests, and parents of students. The students were to enter the building through the two vestibule doors on the lakeside of the building. This would allow easy access to the two locker rooms and keep the floors upstairs somewhat free of dirt and snow. Shortly after the rule was explained, the following poem appeared on the inside front entrance doors.

BALLAD OF THE FRONT DOOR

For writing ballads, one must have
Pathetic themes they say
So on this real pathetic theme
I'll now begin my lay.

Up in our school house nice and new:
As in the one of yore,
Right in the middle of the front
Is placed a broad front door.

Up, up, the student hurries on,
The gong is soon to sound,
He can no more pass through this door,
No, he must go around.

He makes no cry but passes by
O'er rocks and pebbles rough
To reach one of the doors behind,
But thinks it's pretty tough.

"What is the reason?" you may ask,
"Is that door just for show?
Or why is it the bosses make
You by that door to go?"

We have to stumble round behind,
O'er rocks and stones galore,
To enter through the locker room
Where mats are on the floor.

'Tis there that we must wipe our feet
And leave the mud to dry,
And coming up, learn that we're late,
This always makes us sigh.

Our feet are always soiled with mud,
We'll get it on the floor.
And that's the reason we can't use
That handy, wide front door.

Our Principal informs us oft,
When we are in the hall,
The corridors are to pass through,
Don't loaf in here at all.

If that is true of corridors,
Then what about the door?
We thought that was to pass through too,
We think so now, no more.

We've learned it from experience,
(And that's where folks learn best.)
The front doors for the teachers,
The back door for the rest
A STUDENT
(*The Winnipesaukean*, Dec. 1906, p. 17).

It is believed that Albert Dow,'06, editor of *Brewster Review*, wrote this poem.

Athletics
Mr. Lord was in every sense a broad-minded educator, realizing that the training which develops the mind to the exclusion of physical development is unbalanced; he took a keen interest in athletics and encouraged in every way what he believed to be true sport" (*The Winnipesaukean*, Clarence E. Langley,'03, March1907, p.4). It was thus through his direction and dedication that the sports programs during the transition period were successful. Boys managed to have impressive seasons in football, basketball and baseball. Basketball was practiced in the town bowling alley where baskets were erected when there was no bowling. Teams played Tilton, Holderness, New Hampton, Ashland, Plymouth and Fryeburg. *The Winnipesaukean* of 1905 reports a long schedule for all teams and a victorious year in all sports with 25 wins and only 9 losses (The *Winnipesaukean,* June 1905, pp. 5-10).

The football season of 1905 started off with Brewster scoring at-will in most contests until October 14 when it faced two back-to-back games with Tilton, the first at Tilton. Brewster was undefeated to this point, but faced a very heavy line in Tilton and lost the afternoon 6-11. The following game was played at Wolfeborough on Lord's new field, but with several revisions in strategy. With speed and drive, Brewster boys were able to overtake the heavy weighted Tilton defense and resolve the issue 10—0 (The *Winnipesaukean,* June 1905, pp. 19-24).

Athletics Tradition in Song
About this time as Brewster Free Academy was establishing its traditions, a song appeared in the ranks of the student body. As teams returned to campus via steamboat after engaging in athletic competition with schools on the other side of the lake, particularly Tilton School, a red light was hung on the wharf to signify a victory, and as the steamer, loaded with athletes, coaches, equipment, and fans, pulled up to the dock located on the lower field near today's faulty beach, a group of enthusiastic students would stand under the light and greet the team with cheers and song to celebrate the victory. All would join in with the singing of "The Red Light on the Wharf at old BFA."

In later years, the spirit behind "The Red Light on the Wharf" was rekindled in remembrance of Burt Vaughan who helped carry the Academy through the very difficult transition years from 1962- 1965. It was the community's faith in him that kept the Academy's light burning.

Principal Lord's Poor Health
While the good news of the Tilton defeat improved Lord's spirits, his infirmities worsened and gradually took control. On November 5, 1905, just after the dedication of the new building, he traveled to Katahdin Mountain Camps in Maine for a long much-needed rest, returning to school just before Thanksgiving (The *Winnipesaukean,* June 1905, p.16). As time passed, students noticed that Mr. Lord had great difficulty walking from his home to the Academy Building for classes, and supervising the construction of the new classroom building. It gradually became very painful for him to traverse the path from his study in Lord House to the front office of the new main building. Albert Dow, Jr.,'41, remembers his father, Albert Dow,'06, telling him how Mr. Lord would call him to his study and ask that he and another boy help him to his office in the school building. The boys would clasp their hands and arms together forming a 'lion's paw' and with Mr. Lord sitting transport him along the way. Lord's gout was to become much more severe as time passed. Edwin Howard Lord suffered his pain through the remainder of 1905, and as 1906 passed, his pain became intolerable, and he was forced to drop one after another of his responsibilities at school until finally all duties were relinquished. His students would later recall that when he was suffering, he would make an effort to be even more patient than usual in the classroom.

Edwin H. Lord Passes

In December, Lord was taken to the Maine General Hospital at Portland where he passed away on Thursday, January 24, 1907, at the young age of 56. The funeral service was held at his chosen Unitarian Church in Wolfeborough. Shopkeepers closed their doors, and townspeople along with students filled the pews. Each class from 1892 on sent sprays of flowers, and graduates of those classes each presented their eulogies. Lord was then taken to Lowell, Massachusetts, where a family ceremony was conducted the following day. When we review these eulogies, we see the true character of Lord, which was consistently presented by each speaker, "We expect girls to be ladies and boys to be gentlemen," was the common theme.

He had a boundless faith in boys and girls, a faith that was coupled with sympathy so that even the culprit would translate the correction as coming from a friend. Teachers understood Lord as one who would grant freedom in the classroom but would expect results. The entire school community knew that he was always there encouraging and supporting them with his vast experience while letting the students know that he expected the best from them. And, most important, Edwin H. Lord's philosophy set a very high standard for those who would soon follow.

In the twenty years of Principal Edwin Lord's leadership, the Brewster Free Academy, which John Brewster dreamed of, became a reality. It suffered and survived a major catastrophe, but under the leadership of persistent trustees and a dauntless principal, it immediately established its footing as a leading independent college preparatory school.

The Transition

With the news of the death of Edwin Lord, the Board of Trustees immediately fell into step by appointing one of their own to pick-up the reins of leadership, and Dr. Charles Murkland was their man. He had been familiar with Brewster and knew the details of what had transpired since the death of John Brewster. We do not know whether Edwin Lord was aware of the appointment of Charles Murkland as the new principal, but we are certain that he would have been pleased and would have had a smile on his face.

A Final Word on Edwin Lord

Edwin Lord was one of the most remarkable principals to serve the Academy. He came when the demands of the position were most challenging, and he served the Academy well as he established a firm foundation out of which a new school in Wolfeborough continues to be shaped as it carries out the vision of John Brewster. Edwin Lord's spirit and confidence were never blunted by words or catastrophes. He established a curriculum consisting of classical college preparatory subjects, guided the school through two major adversities and initiated both football and baseball by 1894. His high standards would be a benchmark for those who were to follow. It is no wonder that many years later the people were still remembering his kindness and influence.

"But now, in the passing of Principal Lord, we feel that Brewster Free Academy has been called to part with its very choicest possession, and that for us, the alumni, has been severed the one link which bound our acquaintance of the past to that of the present Brewster. The familiar Brewster has passed away, and to the new we of the old shall be strangers. Unknown faces are in our places, strangers are among the faculty, a new building replaces the old; and yet our feelings of sadness over these changed areas compare nothing with our great grief over the irreparable loss of the master mind, our beloved principal (*The Winnipesaukean* 1907, Emma C. Dickens, '98).

4. The Rev. Dr. Charles S. Murkland, 1907–1910: A Man of Service

What you are will show in what you do.—Thomas A. Edison

Dr. Murkland's Early Years and Education

Dr. Charles Sumner Murkland came to Brewster Free Academy as a two-term member of the Board of Trustees and as a superb academician. He was born in Lowell, Massachusetts, on May 20, 1856, and in the early days of his youth, he had become a friend of Edwin H. Lord, who was teaching science at that time in Lowell. After graduating from Lowell High School he went on to Middlebury College, and in 1881, he graduated as valedictorian of his class. A year later he was awarded a master of arts degree with highest honors. In 1883, upon the completion of his course work at the Yale Divinity School and the Harvard Divinity School, he received a bachelor of divinity from Harvard.

On July 30, 1884, he married Helen Tupper of Middlebury. Their only child, Maria, later Mrs. Gilbert Howard, had graduated from Smith College in 1906 and received a master of arts degree from Middlebury College in 1907 (*Granite State News,* July 20,

Dr. Charles S. Murkland, the second principal.

1907). Maria returned to Smith College the next year as a teaching fellow, and received a second master's degree. It is interesting to note that later, after a one year teaching position at Dana Hall School in Wellesley, Massachusetts, she was to join her father and mother at Brewster Free Academy, teaching Latin, Greek and mathematics while her father was principal (Nancy A. Young, Smith College Archivist).

Murkland Enters the Ministry and onto University of New Hampshire

From his very scholarly background, Dr. Murkland entered into the ministry, serving first at the Third Congregational Church in Chicopee, Massachusetts, and then at the Franklin Street Congregational Church in Manchester, New Hampshire. Murkland was elected to the presidency of New Hampshire College (today the University of New Hampshire) by their Board of Trustees on May 18, 1893, and was inaugurated on August 30 of the same year. He was the first to be elected president of the College of Agriculture and the Mechanical Arts following the college's move to Durham from Hanover, New Hampshire. Although as a scholar and executive, he was certainly qualified for the position, his lack of any agricultural experience or background made him a surprising choice for office. During his presidency, he received a doctor of divinity from Middlebury in 1900, and a Ph.D. from Dartmouth in 1903 where he was a member of Phi Beta Kappa and the Society for Biblical Research and Exegesis (Murkland, *University Archives,* Feb.1, 1901).

Murkland's Accomplishments at New Hampshire College (UNH)

Murkland believed in a broad interpretation of the Morrill Act of 1862. That act had been passed by Congress to make higher education more accessible for all young Americans and was primarily directed toward the establishment of colleges in engineering, agriculture, and military science. Murkland, with his very scholarly background in divinity studies, viewed the legislation as a positive attempt by Congress to make educational possibilities more available so that American citizens could receive a college education at a lower tuition rate than that charged by private colleges.

Murkland set his sights for the New Hampshire institution to broaden its curriculum and increase its enrollment, but not without conflict. Some professors felt that the direction of the college must be the expansion of the curricula in sciences and agriculture to the exclusion of the liberal arts and that Murkland's background was overly concentrated in divinity studies (Murkland, *University Archives*). He finally won some of them over and was able, in ten years, to double the college enrollment to double the size of the faculty and staff and to expand greatly the course offerings. By the end of his ten-year tenure at the college, he felt that he had accomplished the goals he had set out to do; therefore, he presented his resignation to the Board in May of 1903. In honor of this fine man and his dedication to the University, Murkland Hall, which is at the center of the university's College of Liberal Arts, is named for Charles Murkland.

Murkland Becomes Principal

With his work at New Hampshire College over and his second three-year term on the Board of Trustees at Brewster Free Academy nearly completed, it was natural for the trustees to turn their eyes to him for leadership as the second principal. His past relationship with Edwin Lord in Lowell, Massachusetts, and also as a Brewster trustee had always been one of great respect and regard, and Mr. Lord would, from time to time, consult him on school issues. It was with this in mind that the Board hoped that Dr. Murkland would be interested in fulfilling the role of principal and carrying on the good work of his dear friend upon Lord's unexpected death.

Realizing that Dr. Murkland was a man who valued scholarship and who had always encouraged young people to seek a higher level of education and reach for their fullest potential, the Board of Trustees elected Dr. Charles Sumner Murkland as the second principal of the Academy. School re-opened on September 11, 1907 with 133 students and eight teachers, including Principal Murkland, who taught mathematics.

The curriculum was revised slightly, making music and elocution a required program through participation in presentations and plays.

"The aim of the instruction in music is to enable every pupil to read music at sight. One period is devoted to individual chorus work. Training for public speaking is required of every pupil. The divisions recite bi-weekly, and in the last two years a standard play is presented" (*Brewster Free Academy Catalogue*, 1908-1909, p.17).

In the same catalogue attention is also given to physical training. "During the last half of the fall, the winter, and the first half of the spring terms the girls have regular drills in proper costume, under an instructor. During the same time, the boys are given daily work in 'Setting up' exercises, in dumb bells and Indian clubs and indoor work on special apparatus. Baseball, football, basketball, handball and indoor gymnastics receive attention during the proper seasons. Special attention is given to securing proper carriage." Dr. Murkland also noted, "A separate building is used for games of basketball and together with rooms in the basement of the Main Building, serves as a rudimentary gymnasium. A well-equipped gymnasium is the most pressing material need of the Academy"(*Brewster Free Academy Catalogue,* 1908-1909, p.9).

Dr. Murkland continued to emphasize the requirement of students to attend chapel exercises each morning and to attend the Sunday morning service at one of the churches in town—either Advent, Christian, Congregational, Free Baptist, Roman Catholic, or Unitarian.

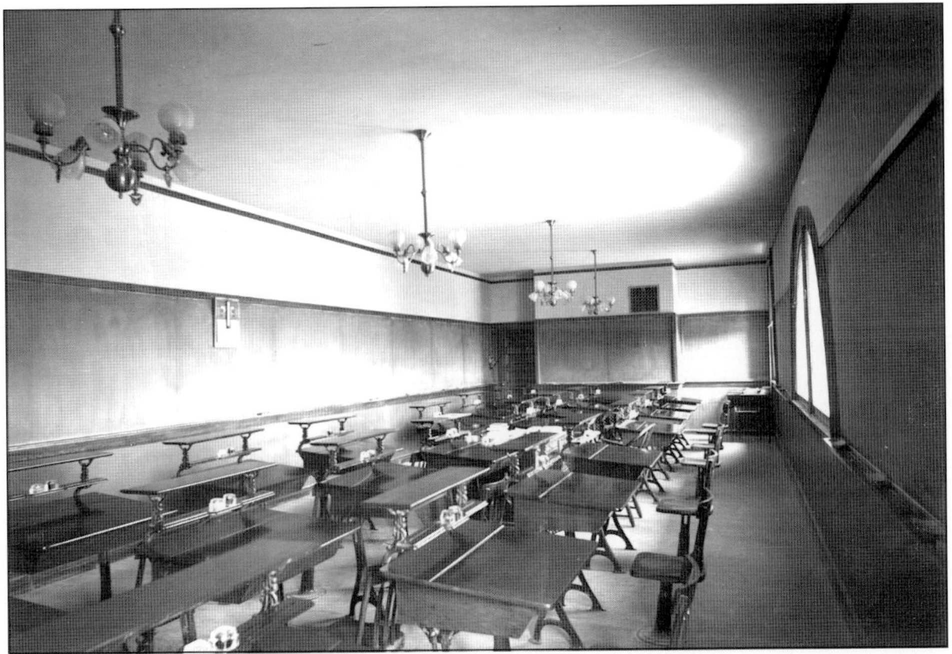

The second floor classroom with the specially designed arched window over the front door of Academic Building.

The Academy Building, 1905, looked down upon the campus before athletics fields.

The Brewster Banner

In 1910, a new student publication, *The Brewster Banner,* was first published, featuring the short stories, poetry, and reports about athletic contests and alumni happenings of the year. The athletic contest notes were especially interesting. A reporter indicated that Brewster's baseball team was superior to both the Rochester and Berwick squads. "The Brewster pitcher, Bill Kolseth, attracted much attention and settled down after the first inning and did not allow another hit, using his spitball to good advantage. Throughout the game, fans cheered and shouted as Berwick players were struck out time after time. A glorious victory was won!"

Bill Kolseth would continue to be an outstanding pitcher for the Brewster team throughout the season. In football Brewster would play against Holderness, New Hampton, Portsmouth High School, and Tilton, but, at that time, baseball was always the most popular sport (*Brewster Banner*, May 1910, p. 22).

Also in *The Brewster Banner* was found an interesting note about the principal and his style of teaching. A student noted that he had seen Dr. Murkland with members of his mathematics class outside on the school grounds surveying the campus, evidently putting trigonometry to work in a practical way.

Murkland Retires From Brewster

Upon completion of his third year as principal, the tall and somewhat balding Dr. Charles S. Murkland decided he needed to move on. He had many options to consider for himself. Certainly, a return to the ministry was possible as was a position in university management. In May of 1910, as his completed resignation letter lay before him on the office desk and as he screwed the top back on his fountain pen, he must have had a feeling of accomplishment. His undertakings at Brewster Free Academy would mirror his work at Durham, opening wide the doors of education. Wolfeboro youngsters reminded him of his humble past, and he was successful at giving these youngsters an education that would provide a firm support for the challenges they would face in the future.

In addition to Dr. Murkland's extensive academic background, his leadership at Brewster had been sterling. He had achieved success in academic life in America when rapid changes were at work throughout the nation. Westward expansion was changing normal life for American youth, and the rapid expansion of American industry placed demands on both schools and their students. As a young man, he had learned the task of hard physical and mental work. As a Congregationalist, he respected God's word and had attempted to combine the talents of those with whom he prayed to the daily chores of life and had sought to bring groups together in service. As the president of a growing college, he had sought to open as many doors as possible to the poor working classes of his state. Now he was leaving Brewster for a life of volunteer service with the church.

Murkland Aids in the War Effort and the YMCA

By 1917, after three years of conflict, World War I brought the United States forces onto European soil. It was the Christian ministry of the YMCA that attracted Charles Murkland's interest. The 'Y' had the responsibility of giving comfort to prisoners of war on all sides, and it organized canteens, religious services, and post exchanges. After seven years of retirement, Dr. Murkland volunteered and was appointed as an educational director in Paris, France, in November of 1917, a post where he remained until after the Armistice, May 1919, when he returned to the United States (*History of the YMCA*, p. 13). It is probable that his daughter had accompanied him during the war years as she was employed in overseas service during that time (Young, email to the authors).

Dr. Murkland Passes Away

Dr. Murkland returned to Waltham and lived there for several years in retirement. On November 12, 1926, following a long illness, Dr. Murkland passed away at Waltham Hospital in Massachusetts (*Granite State News,* 1926). His three younger brothers and his daughter Maria survived him.

AUTHORS' NOTE: Readers may have noticed a change in the spelling of the town name from Wolfeborough to Wolfeboro in this chapter; this change which reflects the spelling used by the town and its businesses, starting about this time.

5. Charles Webster Haley, 1911–1923: Brewster and the Great War

The superior man is modest in his speech, but exceeds in his actions.—Confucius

With the departure of Dr. Charles Murkland in 1910, the Board of Trustees appointed Mr. Carroll Piper and Mr. Herbert Sargent, both senior teachers, to be acting principals until a new principal could be placed in Lord House. Both Mr. Piper and Mr. Sargent were excellent choices since they had been at the school the longest, were fine teachers, and had earned the respect of everyone because of their love of teaching and scholarship. Two terms passed before a new principal was selected. Students commented on how truly first-class the school had been running under the leadership of Mr. Piper and Mr. Sargent and regretted the need for a new leader.

The Board of Trustees selected Charles Webster Haley to be principal in 1911. The Haley family had been original settlers in Tuftonborough. Born in 1857, Haley had attended the old WTA but had transferred to the New Hampton Literary Institute from which he graduated. He taught school for several years in Meredith, New Hampshire, before he entered Boston University Law School. Soon he was offered the principal position at Quincy, Massachusetts, and later the job of organizing the school district superintendency

Charles W. Haley, third principal of the Academy, and his wife Carrie Francis Kelsea.

at Haverhill, Massachusetts. After completing his work there, he was offered the Brewster position, which he accepted.

In 1890, Haley had married Carrie Frances Kelsea whose family lived in Center Harbor. Carrie was a teacher of some experience and would be helpful to the school in the near future. Charles Haley was a stately man—tall, with white hair and beard, and eyes that gave the impression that he was about to comment, "I understand your problem, but I know you can do better."

Academic Changes: 1911-1914

Haley inherited a curriculum that had been founded and tested under the careful eyes of both Lord and Murkland. The school's curriculum was demanding and classical enough to suit the needs of students from Wolfeboro and the adjacent towns, and it was now divided into three courses of study: the classical, the scientific and the commercial. The classical and scientific programs were designed to meet the admission requirements of various colleges and technical schools, while new courses in stenography, bookkeeping, typing, domestic science, commercial law, and correspondence, were added to the commercial program to create a foundation for those entering the business field.

Brewster Free Academy earned a place on the approved list of schools of the New England College Entrance Certificate Board, and the certificates of the Academy were accepted in place of admissions examinations by the member colleges. Certificates were not granted to every graduate of the Academy, but only to those who maintained an average grade of not less than seventy percent throughout their course of study. Mr. Haley's careful review of the curriculum was valuable for the Academy began to further develop over the next three years and secured its positive reputation amongst schools and colleges.

The faculty of 1916: Front Row: Lucy Montgomery, Mary Chesley, Charlotte Hazelwood, Alice Goodwich, and Anna Pitman; Second Row: Harold Melvin, Herbert Sargent, Charles W. Haley, Harry Merritt, and Frank Botonicki.

The Domestic Science Room provided for elective curriculum for graduation requirements.

"Scott's Palace": A Glimpse into Brewster's Past, 1911-1915

As the school advanced academically, Dr. Nathaniel Scott's home just across Main Street from the Academy provided a centerpiece for daily life amongst students, faculty, and parents. Dr. Scott was widely known and respected as a practicing physician and strong supporter of civic activities and became a close friend of both John Brewster and John's son, William.

He was elected to the Board of Trustees of the Academy and was a long lasting influential trustee whose love for Brewster would extend into the 1940s (*Bowers,* vol. 3, p. 433).

Dr. James M. Wallace, class of 1947 and grandson of Dr. Scott, related that he had discovered a remarkable diary of his mother and aunt, who were twin sisters: Ethel Scott Wallace and Edith Scott Tinker, both class of 1915, and daughters of Dr. Scott.

While Edith wrote a daily diary in which she recorded details about her schoolwork, meetings, conversations and social engagements, Ethel carefully not only kept every piece of required written work over her four years of schooling but also instructors' comments. These two collections not only give us a valuable insight into the thriving teenage social life in Wolfeboro, but also the quality of instruction offered by the school and its academic demands. The Scott homestead, referred to as "Scott's Palace," was not only home to the twins and their teenage brother, but also a young male boarding student. This placed the twins in a unique situation to participate in school activities and also carry on their vigorous lives with other students.

With a growing family, living and office space became a problem for the Scotts who had six children: Margaret, Bernice, Louisa,'11, Harlan,'11, and the twins, Ethel and Edith, '15. Dr. Scott expanded the house by building a large addition including a barn where he stored his famous gasoline powered buggy, one of the first in Wolfeboro. Also included in the new addition were several rooms that Dr. Scott rented out to boarding students and served as dorm parent.

Mrs. Scott on an outing with the twins, Ethel and Edith, '15, with a view of South Main Street.

Students could easily scurry to school in the morning, come back for lunch prepared by Mrs. Scott, return for afternoon classes, and later for "hang-out" time with friends to share and discuss ideas, school happenings, and inter-student relationships until the required study hours at night. The term "Scott's Palace" soon entered the school vocabulary, and more than that, it later gave us a vivid insight into student life at Brewster.

Ethel's diary records that Miss Anna Leila Pitman was her English and history teacher. Miss Pitman assigned and corrected in detail nearly two English papers per week while in history she demanded a paper every other week, many more papers than did her colleagues. Papers were assigned on Hawthorne's *Twice Told Tales*, Scott's *Ivanhoe* and *Lady of the Lake,* Irving's *Rip Van Winkle* and *Legend of Sleepy Hollow*, Hans *Brinker and_the Silver Skates*, Havell's *Tales from Herodotus*, chapters from *The Bible,* Whittier's *Snowbound*, and poems by Longfellow and others. Students not only wrote on such topics chosen by Miss Pitman, but occasionally selected topic of their own. Like generations of English teachers, Miss Pitman examined papers for "unity, coherence and emphasis." She read carefully, noting spelling errors, giving suggestions on grammar and structure, writing positive comments and assigning a grade.

As debates were required by each class, one can only imagine the many afternoons at the "Scott Palace" when vibrant and enthusiastic young people practiced their debates and elocution skills. Students were instructed in the formulation of arguments for and against propositions and presented them to judges. By April of 1918, debate had reached a status of such importance that the Brewster Academy boys' debate team defeated the Portsmouth High School debaters and won the championship, gaining possession of the league cup for the 1918-1919 year.

The championship Debate Team of 1917-1918: Francis Sargent, David Thomas, Harold W. Melvin, coach, Nicholaos Steffins, Edward J. Storry.

Ethel reported in her diary that short class trips and outings were planned to supplement the curriculum. Sometimes students ventured on foot to the Libby Museum located at Mirror Lake, a round trip of six miles. (It is interesting to note that some 100 years later, a Brewster graduate and faculty member, Lauren Richardson Hammond, class of 1974, is curator of the Libby Museum.) Some of what students experienced on these and other outings was reinforced through required writing telling about their extra-curricular events.

Ethel's diary briefly describes numerous occasions during which these gatherings promoted social interaction and learning.

January 15, 1912—"Went snow shoeing this afternoon …the snow shoeing really wasn't good but we had a dandy time."

Then, the next day—"A lot of us had to stay after school tonight for whispering….I stayed an hour."

April 5, 1912—"Clayton came to rehearse a violin piece that he is going to play in C.E. Sunday." (This is Ethel's first mention of Clayton Wallace, whom she married nine years later, in 1921. C.E. is Christian Endeavor.)

Later, Ethel writes, "Clinton (possibly Clinton Greenwood, class of 1911, a classmate of Harlan, boarder at the Scott House), had Woodman's phonograph down here after school and we played it all afternoon and evening. It is a Columbia and the records are disks."

And again she writes, "Clinton, again, had Woodman's phonograph down here today. Harlan (Ethel's brother) and I danced up in Clinton's room for over an hour. He taught me the "Boston Two-Step."

On August 28th, she recorded, "Met Mr. Haley, my teacher and principal, and almost started to run because it was nearly seven and it felt as if I was breaking study hours. (During the school year students, even those who lived off campus were expected to keep study hours.)

Another entry, September 3rd, "I have been reading *A Tale of Two Cities*. I have got as far as the knitting women…I don't know as I ever shall dare read farther because I liked Sidney Carton almost better than Evremonde. I had almost rather Evremonde died."

On October 15, 1912, Ethel recorded, "It is lots of fun to study nights with lamps, much cozier." Apparently the house had been electrified, but the family still used oil lamps sometimes (Wallace, p.7).

Both twins graduated from Brewster and the University of Maine, returned to Wolfeboro, married Brewster boys (Clayton Wallace, BFA,'15, and Herbert Tinker, BFA,'16) and continued to be very active community members.

Today, the "Scott's Palace" stands next to the Corner Store gas station and convenience store. The shutters have been removed, the bricks painted grey and an antiques shop occupies the barn.

Only the memories of those familiar with the Scott family and the informative and special collections of Ethel and Edith are left behind to remind us of an era gone by and the wonderful young people who gathered at the "Scott's Palace" as they discovered themselves and their roles in life.

The School Year 1917

But even as life was continuing pleasantly in Wolfeboro, the greater world was in upheaval. While America had been reluctant to take part in the conflict that had enveloped Europe, President Wilson saw no alternative and requested and received a declaration of war from Congress on April 2.

The following September, with war looming, Brewster opened its doors for the 32nd school year with an enrollment of 167, one of the Academy's largest student bodies in its history.

But by 1917, the townspeople of Wolfeboro had little in-depth knowledge of the conditions in Europe that were to bring them into the grip of war. The absence of active radio or reliable international reporting placed the transmission of important events into the hands of the *Granite State News* and the weekly school publication, *The Brewster,* which had been produced and printed since 1912.

For war information, *The Granite State News* and *The Brewster* focused on local events and support groups who worked actively with the American government to enlist troops. In addition, details were published about the war efforts of The Red Cross, YMCA and YWCA. Facts concerning food drives, bond sales as well as announcements about important speakers and letters arriving from graduates serving overseas were also presented in the publications. In addition, during the early war years, Brewster girls gathered in Miss Eaton's room at the Estabrook, busily sewing and knitting for soldiers and refugees *(The Brewster,* Nov. 24, 1914, p. 4).

To Flag and Bugle: Morning and Evening Colors

To encourage patriotism on campus, Judge Oscar Young, a trustee and 1895 graduate, presented a flag to be hung in the chapel on the second floor of the Academy Building until the end of the war. The names of Brewster boys who enlisted in the armed services were to be written on the white strips of the flag. To add to school patriotism, it was decided that the raising and lowering of the flag should be more formal. Students who had been members of the Boy Scouts volunteered to perform this ceremony. A few minutes before classes began at 8:00 AM, a bugler called everyone to the front of the Academy Building where the flag was formally raised. In late afternoon an equally solemn ceremony was held as the flag was lowered. Bert Cropley, '18, the bugler, who raised Morning Colors, soon needed help and the school alumni was canvassed for a $15 donation to buy new trumpets for other students to assist Cropley (*The Brewster,* Mar. 23, 1917).

Supporting the War Effort

In late October of 1917, French teacher Carroll D. Piper, '97, and Harvard, '02, spoke to the student body describing the details about Liberty Bonds. The talk had a marked effect on the students, and it was decided that they ought to purchase one or two bonds to be paid in small installments. The interest earned from them would be used for school purposes *(The Brewster,* Oct. 26, 1917, p.4).

The Wolfeboro chapter of the Red Cross had gathered speed during the summer of 1917 and soon needed more help. An appeal went out to Brewster girls to do their part by helping out on Monday and Thursday afternoons by attending sewing classes. Their help was needed in making surgical bandages and organizing "comfort bags" containing six items suitable for training camp and life in the trenches. "Comfort bags" and surgical bandages came pouring out. Girls also went into "war mode" by soliciting financial help from townspeople to raise money for the Liberty War Fund, and they surpassed their fund-raising goal *(The Brewster*, Oct. 9, 1917, p.4).

Mass public meetings were held in April and May at the Temple Auditorium on Glendon Street pleading with everyone to do their bit, and Brewster students were encouraged to support the requests of the Committee on Public Safety who were responsible for organizing campaigns to help the country. *The Brewster* continued to volunteer space in the newspaper each week to alert townspeople to meetings, campaigns and bond sales. Slogans of "Recruiting Rally," "Save Food," "Do Your Bit," and "Save Water" were advertised weekly. Students on the editorial staff got into the war spirit with the following bid: "Wanted: A Good Patriotic Poem or Essay." A one-year subscription to *The Brewster* was offered to the winner. In addition, a large portion of the land in back of the school building on the northwest side was plowed and readied for planting as part of the food production program, using student volunteer labor to do this less thrilling work. And troop enlistments began to fill a space in *The Brewster* each week.

The response to *The Brewster* editors' offer of a one-year subscription to the student who wrote the best patriotic poem or essay produced interesting perspectives on school life as it related to the war.

In her winning essay, "A Sweater's Soliloquy," Dorothy Brower, '18, recounted a story through the eyes of a mass of newly shorn wool found in a field and picked up by a young girl who tossed the wool into a machine which pulled "her" into a long thread of yarn, before being placed into a vat of hot dye. Soon "she" emerged in the color of khaki, also known as "Red Cross" yarn, when ladies asked for it at the yarn store. "She" was then taken to a home where people wrapped "her" around long needles and shaped "her" into a sweater for a soldier- brother. Packing "her" into a bag, the soldier- brother took her to France and wore "her" into a war zone where other soldiers had similar khaki sweaters. But the soldier- brother was wounded and the sweater lost an arm and "she" found herself in a strange hospital.

War Time Firsts

The first student enlistment was Earl N. Lovering,'19, of Moultonborough who took his examinations and became a member of the First Regiment, U. S. Army. Immediately, a long list of boys signed to join—nine seniors, eight juniors, two sophomores and one freshman, David Thomas. Another twenty-four boys volunteered to support the food production drive and pledged to work on farms where needed. But the enlistments had an effect on sports because many of the boys were key players on the football and baseball teams.

The first to fight were Carroll Scott,'12, and Frank M. Pickering,'11. Scott was a student at Tufts and a past editor of *The Brewster*, who would have graduated from college in 1916, but who instead joined the Signal Corps. When he arrived in England, Scott immediately noticed the absence of men and the fact that women in England did the heavy lifting while their men were away. Pickering, '11, went to France in August with a detachment of railroad engineers (*The Brewster*, Sept. 21, 1917, p.1).

The first to fall in trench warfare was Clarence L. Perkins,'16, who was killed in action on May 10, 1918, and Brewster's first gold star was placed upon the school flag in the chapel after an impressive chapel talk. This spirited the students to war. Clarence's sergeant later wrote of his death. Their company of soldiers had stormed into no-man's land and captured a German trench. In the process, Clarence's eyeglasses had become splashed with mud, and he paused to lean against the trench wall in order to clean the lenses. A German shell exploded near by and he was killed (*The Brewster*, 1918).

The distinction of being the first soldier to return to Brewster from the front fell to Percy Kenney, '17, who visited the campus upon his return. Percy was in the thick of the fighting for six months, was wounded, gassed and shell-shocked. He had many stories to tell, but did not seem to like telling them in crowds, preferring an honorable retreat (*The Brewster*, Feb. 12, 1919).

The 1918 Tilton Baseball Excursion and Game

Not only did the war dampen spirits, but, similarly the rain that poured down on the baseball diamond seemed to create a gloomy attitude on the field as it was often too soggy and muddy for play. On one particular morning with the rain continuing to pour heavily, all hopes for the game at Tilton were in serious question. The story is told that students were out early with their sweaters over their shoulders and lunch boxes in hand asking, "Are we going to have it?" Finally, the news spread that the boat for Tilton would leave at 8:30 AM. After running to the town wharf, everyone boarded. They were soon around Sewall Point and the heavy mist over the mountains and the damp, chilly wind made sightseeing uncomfortable, but the music from the old piano on the upper deck passed the time and the space was cleared for the skillful dancers with their light and springy steps. At noon lunch boxes were opened, and the group soon arrived at Lakeport for the short wait to board the train ride to Tilton and the game with their arch-rivals.

"Singing Brewster fight songs along the way, we found our path up the steep hill to the school where some students were sitting on steps and others peering from the windows to see what this Brewster crowd looked like. At three o'clock the sun was shining and the game began. With loud cheering for support, the Brewster nine fought like never before ending with an overwhelming defeat of our opponents.

"Crowding in a little restaurant in town for supper, the group had been invited back to campus for a Promenade at the large and spacious gymnasium.

"As we arrived, announcement was made as to who was to lead the march and the music filled the air. An elderly amiable teacher introduced us all around and we started on what proved to be a novelty to most of us. This Promenade we had that night was the best ever and well worth the time.

"We left the gymnasium hall at eight o'clock. Twenty minutes later we exchanged cheers with a group of boys who were at the Tilton station to send us off to Lakeport to meet the boat for Wolfeboro.

"It was a silent return trip to campus but as we travelled home we peered through the night mist. Approaching the dock, the traditional red light on the wharf could be seen glowing through the darkness indicating a winning game. Classmates met us singing the familiar, "Red Light on the Wharf for Old BFA."

This was a cherished moment to be remembered during these trying times in history. Brewster won the game 13-7, and continued their winning streak against Proctor 4-3, and then finally their second game with Tilton 2-1, ending the season (The *Brewster*, June 5, 1918, p.1).

This success was the one bright spot in the spring of 1918 until the armistice declaration in November.

The victorious baseball team took great pride and glory in beating Tilton, the arch-rivals of the Academy.

The Influenza Pandemic of 1918-1919

As the war exuberance of 1917 gradually rolled itself into 1918, the country, Brewster and Wolfeboro were to be shocked by conditions that would make the terror of trench warfare pale in contrast. The first epidemic of influenza, an unseen killer, began its devastating and rapid advance throughout the population of most European countries. It probably began in Spain where it killed 8 million, then proceeded to spread throughout Europe, and finally, to the soldiers in the trenches. The most affected were participants in the Great War. With the mass movement of troops and armies, not only on land, but aboard ships as well, where a new name, "La Grippe", emerged. In the U.S., the first phase of the epidemic was felt in training camps in the Midwest where troops were confined in tents or buildings, sleeping in close quarters. The second wave began in Boston in September of 1918 where shipments of large numbers of troops, supplies and machinery took place every day. In October alone, 200,000 died, and the process of dying was fast. As winter took hold, a third epidemic spread, particularly at the end of the war in November. Parades and parties welcoming troops home to towns and cities became a breeding ground for the dreaded disease.

In an effort to control the epidemic, the Red Cross recruits were doubled, and time off was given to workers to assist in hospitals. Gauze masks were to be worn in public, stores could not hold sales, and some towns required a signed certificate before travelers could enter. Bodies piled up at cemeteries awaiting burial when gravediggers had time, and even President Wilson was stricken with flu as he conducted the Peace Conference at Versailles. A story was told of five ladies who played cards one evening. By morning, only two were alive.

On the Brewster campus, action was also taken. Two weeks after the 1918 opening day of school, it was decided by the trustees and Principal Hailey to close the school due to the recent flare-up of influenza in the town (*The Brewster*, Nov. 9, 1918, p1). *The Granite State News* began to record the names of those who were reportedly ill with pneumonia or flu in the "Brief Personals" column near an advertisement for "Mr. Hill's Cascara Quinine Bromide" that admonished the reader, "You Can't Afford to Risk Influenza. Keep Always at Hand a Box" (*Granite State News*, Dec. 14, 1918, p.4). School would not reopen until the later weeks of November.

To this point, the greatest epidemics recorded at Brewster usually were mumps, measles and an occasional outbreak of diphtheria. Mumps outbreaks seemed to be active every spring along with several measles scares. One youngster, Roland Currier,'17, wrote his tale:

I awoke from sleep one morning
And I tumbled out of bed,
And when I looked in the mirror,
Could not find my dear old head
My jaws were like limp sacks of meal,
While my eyes were shut most tight
And on the whole I'm quite sure I'd pass
At a circus for a fright.
They made me haste to bed again,
Though it caused them lots of toil,
And bathed the broad side of my neck
In horrid Camphorated Oil.
I'm on the mend for all of this,
Or at least, I feel that way
And in a week or less no doubt
I'll be back at B.F.A.
(*The Brewster*, Jan. 26, 1917, p.3).

But measles was more difficult to manage than mumps. Measles reached the epidemic stage in the spring of 1918, and it struck with the opening of the spring term. As the days passed, it proved to be the worst on record with twenty-five victims including two teachers, each out of school for two weeks.

The flu epidemic again was the concern of the day, when, in chapel exercises at the opening of the winter term in December 1919, Principal Haley reminded everyone of the delay of the opening of the school in the Fall Term due to the flu epidemic. He stressed how important it was to take great care in helping to prevent its spread. He spoke of how the epidemic had affected the entire world and had caused the death of six times more people than the war loses. He encouraged those who had a cold to stay away from school, but also explained that one who has a cold may not be considered to have the flu himself. He encouraged students to keep out of crowds, not to sneeze near others, and to avoid anyone who is coughing or sneezing (*The Brewster*, Jan. 9, 1919, p.4).

During December and early January 1920, even after the war, the influenza was responsible for the deaths of four Brewster grads: James N. Cook, '98, Cyrus C. Blake, '04, Jason Draper, '13, and Harold Eldridge, Ex. '13. Jason Draper had been fighting in France and increased the number of gold stars on the chapel flag to five.

Still, the demands of war continued to create problems. The drive to preserve both wood and coal had to be met. Everyone was encouraged to sift out their unconsumed embers from the fireplace or cooking stove and save them. Those who used coal-fueled furnaces were encouraged to shut them down each night before retiring and wait until morning to restart. Diagrams for sifters were printed in the papers for the handyman fathers and sons to make out of scrap wood. It was decided that the Academy Building would be closed after school and the coal furnaces banked, then relit early in the morning. This meant that late night office work, club meetings, receptions and dances usually held in the evenings in Chapel Hall would go elsewhere or be postponed.

Somewhere in France

Word would reach school about the fighting at the frontlines. The boys couldn't mention where they were or the names of any towns or villages in which they had been quartered, but they could give a sense of their conditions. The boys in uniform continued to man the trenches in France and write back to school. Lt. Charles Bassett, '14, wrote of his experiences in his manning of a captured German trench. He was in charge of the 101st machine gun detachment and seemed happy to be in the trench rather than back at a rest area. "Most of my company are Yale and Trinity men and they are a fine bunch. One of them plays mandolin and the dugout is a lively place right after mess. We mix right in with the French, and get along fine. The French I had at BFA has helped a lot" (*The Brewster*, April 13, 1918).

Perley Perkins, '17, Leaman Cunningham,'16, Fred Richardson and Linley Moore,'19, alternated in sending back their stories, which were printed under the heading, "Somewhere in France." At times, when the boys had a break in their schedules, they began to write stories of front-line life under the heading "Trench Brewster," and sent them to Mrs. Haley (*The Brewster*, Nov. 16, 1918, p. 1).

In one of his final letters back to Brewster, Perkins wrote, "We began the march southward, out by Verdun, which lasted eleven days and took us far away from the battle scenes.

"To walk again in the halls of Brewster, even though I no longer belong there, will give me a deeper pleasure than I ever knew while I was one of the students, because I have learned a great lesson. I feel even now the handclasps of those who have written me such wonderfully cheering letters of genuine friendship and sympathy and understanding. I think none who have not lived the life over here can understand just what the return will be to us. I only hope I may by my life repay in some measure the nobility of the home people" (*The Brewster*, Feb. 12, 1919, p.3).

Throughout the school year, Mrs. Haley led by example and would sit down with scissors and needles to work with the girls as the boys were encouraged in a louder voice to continue their work planting corn and wheat for feeding of millions of troops and the war ravaged refugees in Europe.

The Armistice

At 11:00 AM, November 11, 1918, "The eleventh hour of the eleventh day of the eleventh month of 1918," an armistice agreement was signed between the Allied powers and the Central Powers to stop the fighting. Troops were to cease-fire and hold to their positions in the trenches until told to do otherwise. In the meantime, the opposing powers were to meet and discuss the details. Germany finally capitulated and a long struggle between the United States, Britain, France and Japan over the final terms of peace would take place in Paris, not ending until 1921.

Post War Activities

In Wolfeboro and Brewster, the war effort seemed to take a turn, shifting from surgical bandages and comfort bags to more food and old clothing. The YWCA put on drives for girls to collect any and all clothing items they could find in reasonable condition. For a while, the knitting still continued turning out long socks, gloves, sweaters and scarves for refugees facing the cold winds of winter.

When the war ended in November, the banks and post offices began to report totals for the purchase of war savings bonds and thrift stamps throughout New Hampshire and the results were interesting. Of the 18 towns in Carroll County, only Conway at $52,603 exceeded Wolfeboro. At $ 31,551 or $14.19 sales per capita, Wolfeboro ranked number two, fine records most likely impacted by the effort of all those Brewster students, the Boy Scouts and the YWCA (*Granite State News*, Dec. 9, 1918, p. 2).

Bronze Plaque Dedicated to Those Who Served

The Board of Trustees immediately ordered that an accurate accounting be made of all Brewster students and graduates who had participated in the Great War and commissioned the casting of a large bronze plate recording their names.

Today Brewster students pass by the lasting reminder of the difficult war years—a large bronze tablet located on the right foyer wall at the entrance hall of the Academic Building. It is dark with age, but it challenges students to gaze and to think of those one hundred and sixteen boys and four girls, as nurses, who stood their duty nearly one hundred years ago

The bronze plaque placed in the entranceway of the Academy honoring all those Brewster students who served in World War I.

and served their country. It is simply dedicated to the students of Brewster Free Academy who served in the war for world freedom, 1914-1918. At the top, it lists the five who died in service - Jason S. Draper, Charles C. Libby, Clarence L. Perkins, Samuel Valley and Lt. George F. Watkins.

The Deaths of William Brewster and Arthur Estabrook

Suddenly, the happy opening of the school year of 1919 turned to sadness with the deaths of the two most prominent and original members of the Board of Trustees who had served Brewster well: Mr. William Brewster and Mr. Arthur Estabrook. They had passed during the summer months, and the boys and girls in the Print Room were grievously affected. It was a tremendous blow for it was these two men who had provided the financing necessary to equip the students with the printing press to keep *The Brewster* in operation. It seemed as though everyone had suffered from untimely deaths of loved ones over the past eight years. Certainly, the loss of life from battle, influenza and causes attributable to a wartime condition of the world had a demoralizing effect, and it did not seem to end.

William Brewster and Arthur Estabrook were viewed by townspeople as pillars of the Wolfeboro community. The two had built the school buildings and dormitories, hired the staffs, brought graduates along to be recognized as college scholars, and fostered great pride in athletic teams. Both men had been guided by the founder who knew of their abilities and developed in them the strength of character to lead the school forth into the Twentieth Century.

Dedication of the First Brewster Academy Yearbook

The first publication of *The SYB* appeared in June of 1921 and recounted in pictures all the events of the class during their four years at Brewster: athletics, plays, sports, and extra-curricular activities. The new book was called *The SYB* for "Senior Yearbook." The class of 1921 honored and dedicated this first edition of *The SYB* to Principal Charles W. Haley.

The class of 1921 had experienced war, food shortages, extra work projects, lethal sickness, and a general shortage of heat over the cold winters. In addition, most athletic team schedules had been cancelled due to transportation difficulties, but their enthusiasm had been channeled into dramatics, debate, skating, pick-up basketball, and hockey when time permitted a breather in a busy wartime work schedule.

But one activity that was not cancelled during the harsh winter was the traditional senior class special event held in January. On a scheduled Saturday night, seniors would outfit themselves with heavy coats, blankets, mittens, and warm woolen hats. They would then board a large maple sugar sled equipped with snow runners and a team of horses. At the crack of the whip, the sled proceeded to the Tuftonboro Grange building where plans were set for a fun night of games, music and a songfest. Supper of hot oyster stew and rolls along with punch and cookies would be served. The long and cold return trip brought them back to school, and the fortunate ones were dropped off at their homes along the way (*The Brewster*, March, 1921). Today, the Grange building still remains as it once did during those cold winter evenings when its halls rang with the joyous voices of Brewster students.

Town of Wolfeboro Requires Refurbishing

The town of Wolfeboro had become well worn and was in need of refurbishing. With speed, the townspeople gathered together and organized the "Wolfeboro Community Association," which took to the task of upgrading the town under the guidance of Clayton Wallace, '12. The old, worn-out 'hand tubs' or firewater tanks were too small and inefficient to act in any fire emergency. They required too many men to operate and couldn't pump fast enough. Wolfeboro's first fire engine was purchased after little discussion. In addition, a new traveler to Wolfeboro could not locate a house or store as street signs had fallen down or were in need of repainting. Quickly, new markers appeared.

Long Term Needs of the Town

But beyond the regular housecleaning needs of the town, new long-term institutions arose from the architectural hand of a Brewster graduate. After finishing Brewster, Albert Dow graduated as an architect from the Wentworth Technical Institute in Boston, moved to Melrose, Massachusetts, and opened his office in Boston. In 1914, Albert Dow was asked to design a dormitory at Brewster for the Josiah Brown Foundation with contractor J. Frank Goodwin. Brown Hall was completed by 1915. Several years later, in 1924, Wolfeboro decided to construct a new public school, and it was Albert H. Dow who offered the proposal of a new Neo-Georgian style red bricked structure designed along the newest concepts of educational needs and known as Carpenter School. But this did not end Dow's offerings to Wolfeboro. The town was in need of upgrading its medical care facilities. The old town hospital was located several streets south of the Academy at the corner of South Main and Clark Road. Plans were developed by Dow to construct a new modern hospital designed along the lines of the Carpenter School and Brown Hall. With the hospital completed, Dow was called once more to perform and was asked to draw up plans for a new Court House in Center Ossipee. When a problem rose with the original architect, Dow completed work on the Tuftonboro School. The St. Paul's School in Concord, NH, wanted a new Chapel, and Dow submitted his plans that were accepted and the building was completed.

Albert Dow, '06, famed editor of The Brewster, *and later a respected architect.*

A major break came in his career when noted architect Sir Henry Vaughan, designer of the National Cathedral in Washington D. C., asked Dow to work with him on the project. Dow designed all the ironwork for the cathedral, and for nine years continued as Sir Henry Vaughan's representative in Washington. Later he designed the church on the campus of Case Western Reserve in Ohio, worked on the Riverside Chapel in NYC, designed Keenan Wynn's home on Nantucket Island, Massachusetts, and an additional 100 Tudor homes in the Newton-Wellesley area in Massachusetts as well as numerous buildings in Maine including Hebron Academy (Albert Dow, Jr., Jan. 7, 2005).

Whatever influences the Brewster experience had on Dow are speculative. Was it his leadership as editor of *The Brewster* during his senior year, his interest in music and writing a school song, or his learning in mathematics and mechanical drawing that he acquired from Professor Herbert Sargent which planted the foundation for his success? Or as a youngster was it watching the new Academic Building blossom to its completion that inspired him? Or was it at the time that his spirit of serving others was illustrated when he helped carry Principal Lord, who had difficulty walking and needed assistance, to his new office each morning? Whatever the influence, Albert Dow was an amazingly talented individual with a deep abiding love for Brewster and New Hampshire.

School in the Early Nineteen Twenties

School spirit was high during this time with continued competition and annual presentation of plays and dances hosted by each of the classes. The attitude that all must live up to the high standards of honor, love, and truth, the principles of our beloved school, was part of the fabric of everyday life. The usual razzing of the freshmen by the sophomores prevailed as a yearly tradition. The young ninth graders would have felt unimportant if tricks and games did not happen and they in turn could not express outrage and hurt dignity. A particular football game with Tilton School, the persistent arch- rival, was well remembered. "On a bright afternoon in October, the cheering crowds were filled in exultation when the football team trounced Tilton in one of the hardest games ever played on the Brewster campus. Bill Hoagland, strong and sturdy, pushed them all around and then some more. The very ground trembled when our stalwart guards crashed to earth with a foe. How we cheered and clapped when Bill stepped forward to receive his well earned and coveted Brewster "B" *(SYB*, 1923, p.6).

For the first time, the girls came forward with a field hockey team. It was the first time that letters had ever been awarded to girls in the history of Brewster. Mary Smart, '29, captain of a later team and a very enthusiastic field hockey player noted," The field hockey uniforms of crimson and blue were very well made and always pressed flat and neat. All of us were proud to wear our uniforms. We played all the Lakes Region schools and Colby Junior College as well as some other small colleges. At times, we would pull up our crimson bloomers to our knees, and the principal would become very upset, and sometimes call the girls over demanding that they pull their bloomers down to ankle length" (Mary Haley Smart,'29, transcribed interview, March 5, 2005).

During that same time, after King Winter arrived, the annual school sleigh ride took place with shots of joy and freezing hands and feet, but no student could help but admit that all had a grand time. It was shortly after this event, on February 22, 1922, that Wolfeboro planned and presented its first Winter Carnival, a tradition, with all of its fun and winter sporting competitions that would be carried forward for many, many years. Snowshoeing, tobogganing, skiing, hockey, ice skating, dog sledding, and ice sculpturing were enjoyed by everyone young and old.

And finally during this era, in October 1922, *The Brewster* reported, "This year the school has returned to the policy of requiring a deposit of one dollar for the use of the textbooks. If the books are all brought back at the end of the year, showing only reasonable wear, the dollar will be returned to the student.

The first girls field hockey team in 1921: First Row-Marian Mills,'23, Marie Breckwoldt,'22. Second Row: Marion Melrose,'23, Charlotte Howe,'23, Ida Averill, '24, Mildred Clow,'25, Dorothy Alexander, '24, Ruby Piper, '24. Third Row: Louise Tobey'23, Elizabeth Hurlin,'24, Helen Smart,'23, Marjorie Rollins, '23, Teresa Hayes, '22, Ethel Clow, '23. Fourth Row: Beatrice Huckins, '23, Esther Lord, '24, Zaida McFadden,'22, Sadie Harriman, '23, Amy Woodmancy, '24.

Two Brewster Bobcats waiting their turn for a toboggan ride located behind Brown Hall, which was often a focus for wintertime fun.

Mr. Haley's Illness

During the November 1922 vacation period, Mr. Haley came down with tonsillitis. The consistent threat of pandemic influenza, the countless meetings with students and the effort to keep school spirits high finally brought him to the point of exhaustion. However, his health became more serious than he or anyone had expected, and he was not to return to school as principal but would resign. The board quietly responded by appointing master teacher Herbert E. Sargent as acting principal, and later Carroll Piper would serve as the Board of Trustees continued the search process for a permanent new principal.

Mr. Haley Bids Farewell

"On Tuesday October 16, 1923, at afternoon chapel the school welcomed as guests and bid farewell to Mr. and Mrs. C. W. Haley who were soon to leave for Florida. Mr. Sargent, acting principal, made a brief address to Mr., and Mrs. Haley expressing the appreciation of the school for his twelve years of tireless service and unfailing interest in all the affairs of the school. The entire school joined in singing "Brewster Days" at the close of which, led by Sheldon Gilman, captain of the football team, they gave three rousing cheers for both Mr. and Mrs. Haley (*The Brewster*, October 1923, p.6-7).

In addition, the class of 1923 also dedicated their yearbook to Charles W. Haley, "To our Friend, In Appreciation of His Unselfish Interest In our Success, We Affectionately Dedicate the1923 SYB."

The Final Years of the Haleys

After leaving Wolfeboro, the Haleys lived in Lakeport, New Hampshire, and spent winters in Florida in an attempt to restore Mr. Haley to good health. In 1937, they returned to Wolfeboro and resided in the village with a cousin, Abel Haley, until Mr. Charles W. Haley's death on September 17, 1943, at the age of 85. His wife, Carrie Frances Kelsea, passed away two years later on October 14, 1945. The final resting place for both Haleys is in the Meredith Village Cemetery, New Hampshire.

6. Ralph K. Bearce, 1894–1935: A Man of Conspicuous Ability

The real leader has no need to lead; he is content to point the way.—Henry Miller

Piper and Sargent Serve as Principal

Following the departure of Mr. and Mrs. Haley, the trustees began a long search for the right man to lead the school during this period of renewal. It would take some time before the actual seating of a new principal, but in the meantime, the Board of Trustees had asked the old standby professors Herbert Sargent and Carroll D. Piper to serve as acting principals, each taking a turn of added duty while awaiting the arrival of a new principal. This delay was a most unusual situation, but the Board felt that the student body had absolute confidence in both Mr. Piper and Mr. Sargent to do the job.

A New Principal Is Elected

During their fall meeting on September 14, 1923, at 15 State Street in Boston, the Brewster Free Academy Board of Trustees heard the report of the search committee who had that day interviewed two leading candidates for the position of Principal. Mr. Ralph King Bearce

Carroll Piper, '97 (left) respected teacher was often called upon to lead the school in the absence of a principal. Herbert Sargent (right), affectionately referred to as "Hoop" Sargent, would sometimes stand as acting principal.)

Ralph K. Bearce, fourth principal of the Academy.

was the second man to be interviewed, and, after a short discussion period, it was decided, by unanimous vote, that Ralph K. Bearce would be the new principal of the Academy (Minutes of the Board of Trustees, Sept. 14, 1923).

However, there was a wrinkle in the agreement that caused some degree of concern. Bearce indicated that there could be nearly a two-year intermission before he could take up the chair of principal at Brewster. He was currently the headmaster at The Powder Point School in Duxbury, Massachusetts, which was closing, and its board had asked Mr. Bearce to remain until all the arrangements for the sale and removal of the school possessions had been made to Tabor Academy at Marion, Massachusetts. The Brewster Board was somewhat taken back by the request, but they considered Bearce's background and talents and felt that arrangements to utilize the experienced teachers at Brewster to cover the principal's responsibilities until Bearce was free would be acceptable.

Early Life of Ralph K. Bearce

Ralph K. Bearce was a native of Turner, Maine, had prepared for Colby College at Hebron Academy, graduated from Colby in 1895, and then received a master of arts degree from Colby in 1902. Mr. Bearce always retained a lively memory of his school days to enhance his understanding of the psychology of youth.

On July 24, 1902, Mr. Bearce married Ellen M. Bradford of Turner, Maine. Ms. Bradford, a ninth generation descendent of Governor William Bradford, and a tenth of Elder William Brewster, taught school at the age of fifteen.

Before his marriage, Bearce taught at Rockland High School in Maine from 1895-1899, and then he went on to the Suffield School in Connecticut as a history and English teacher. Leaving for one year, he taught mathematics at Powder Point School before being recalled to Suffield and appointed dean and then principal, serving the school for twelve years. In 1912, Bearce was prevailed upon to return to Powder Point as headmaster.

The Bearces Arrive on Campus

The Bearces arrived in Wolfeboro July 9, 1924, on the 22nd anniversary of their marriage, and by September, the Bearces were at home along Wolfeboro Bay, living in Lord House. (Bearce Hall never housed the Bearce family.) They came to Wolfeboro during a time when new ideas were urgently needed in all the leading organizations of the town, and their fresh enthusiasm was eagerly accepted. They became members of the First Congregational Church, and Bearce served as moderator of the state Congregational-Christian Conference. He was a director of the Wolfeboro Development Association, president of the Rotary Club, member of the Masons, Morning Star Lodge, and Delta Kappa Epsilon fraternity and soon was respected in a community that needed new leadership in its civic organizations.

Changes on Campus

On campus, through the influence of Bearce, the curriculum of Brewster Academy was modernized and high social standards maintained. Texts were updated and the teaching content in math and science was improved. In addition, the Bearces encouraged dorm parties, and both Estabrook and Brown Hall hosted dinners, serving hot meals to all. Judging activities where students dressed in various types of current fashions and costume were planned; dancing and dramatic presentations were also held several times a year. During the school day, Bearce was always present in the hallways and could be depended upon to mingle and converse with students while never sacrificing his dignity. He was respected for his joviality and sense of humor (*The Brewster*, December 1924).

Both Mr. and Mrs. Bearce were active in directing the religious and recreational activities of the students. Ellen Bradford Bearce, known as Auntie Nell, was a mother to her Brewster boys and girls and fed them cake and milk from her kitchen. Lord House was famous for its hospitality and small imaginative parties where she entertained students, faculty and parents for eleven years.

Restoration Program

With the spirit of renewal extended into Brewster Academy, the trustees saw there was need to upgrade student and faculty housing. The Estabrook wore her colors well after the outside was completely painted and the inside dining area repapered and rooms repainted. Kimball House was completely revised and the inside reorganized to include several new rooms for the increased enrollment of male boarding students. In addition, boys were happy to see the inclusion of a new piano installed in the parlor. Lord House had to be redecorated and new carpentry work completed on the outside.

On the Academic Building, a long copper drainpipe had been dislodged from its fastenings along the roof and melting snow had flooded the roadway to the Estabrook. The bottom step of the Estabrook front entrance was always frozen during the winter months and the students called it the *Prince of Cumberland Step* reflecting their English class study of Shakespeare's *Macbeth*, where Macbeth calls out,

> The Prince of Cumberland! That is a step
> On which I must fall down, or else o'er leap
> For in my way it lies (*The Brewster,* March 1926).

In addition to the repairs on damaged drains, the front entrance columns required more

The restoration of the Estabrook living and dining rooms under the direction of Mrs. Bearce, affectionately referred to as Auntie Nell. These rooms are now part of the campus bookstore and summer program office.

support and painting with a waterproofing compound. Added to this, Chapel Hall received a makeover. All the woodwork and floors were shellacked and waxed. The hanging electric lights and gas fixtures were taken down and new bowl shaped glass domes were put in their places. Two new pianos appeared—a grand piano for chorus work and chapel music, an upright for practice and recreational use.

A new mimeographing machine would replace the printing machines in the commercial department.

School Library and Printing Class

Another change took place that at first caused some concern among students and alums. The trustees decided that a trade-off had to be made between a new library and the printing class activities and workload. Their decision was to reduce the efforts of the students by limiting the production of *The Brewster* to one publication each term with the new edition being increased from four to sixteen pages. In addition, the printing class would take the responsibility of writing and publishing the Senior Year Book (SYB). With the reduction of the printing schedule, the new library would be located in Room 8 and share space with the printing group. Several letters were received which praised the move as now students could use a school-based library instead of trudging across the street to the Brewster Library housed in the Town Hall.

Class Achievements

By 1925, campus accomplishments were visible as class pride led to the printing of class stationary and the adoption of class colors.

Brewster Academy freshman class also set their goal very high. They took a standard achievement test in algebra designed by the Department of Experimental Education at Cornell University and came out at the head of a list of seven hundred schools with a rating of 81.29, and 5% ahead of its nearest rival. Principal Bearce praised all the freshmen in Chapel Hall when the results were announced (*The Brewster,* May 1925).

To celebrate their achievement, the freshmen, class of '28 held a meeting where for the first time a class adopted a class banner. The class chose dark green and white to represent their class. The design was hung on the front wall of Room 1 and each year was moved from room to room as the class moved up through the ranks to Room 4, the traditional "Senior Room," and then eventually to commencement exercises. Its motto, Seneca's "*Non Scholae sed Vitae*" was printed on the front of the banner translated as "*we do not learn for school, but for life*" (*The Brewster*, May 1925).

New Tennis Courts

And there was yet another addition to campus. The athletic program had a new sport. Since the war ended, tennis became popular throughout the country. Carroll Piper laid out two improved tennis courts behind the Estabrook complete with new nets, new tapes and backstop. The Athletic Council approved the organization of interscholastic play with neighboring schools as twenty-two students signed-up to play. Regular matches were scheduled with Kennett High School and Tilton School. Students were awarded the Brewster "B" along with a trophy for the winning team.

Fire in Chemistry Lab

But as changes were being accomplished with much to celebrate, on October 16, 1925, during the noon hour, a fire alarm sounded. Everyone rushed from luncheon to the chemistry lab located on the Brewster grounds in the old Pavilion Ice House that had been brought up to campus years ago from the lake's edge. The fire was the result of a faulty heating stove

Chapel Hall with its rows of ladder-backed wooden benches set for All School Meeting.

and was soon under control; however, there was a silver lining. A new chemistry lab was constructed in the basement of the main building with new equipment and apparatus and was completed by the end of Christmas vacation (*The Brewster*, March 1926).

Enrollment

With the changes on campus came adjustments to enrollment. The 1920s and early 1930s brought an increased student population with an enrollment of 150, but the banner year was 1925 when 225 students were recorded. According to Bearce's records, the upcoming grammar school classes were unusually large due to the numbers of new families moving into the region. Mr. Bearce saw the nature of this enrollment as a two edged sword. While Brewster enjoyed the expansion of its enrollment as a good thing, it brought forth the issue that would haunt the school for the next thirty years, "Should Brewster Free Academy offer to anyone a classical college preparatory experience regardless of their intellectual capacity or their home training experience ?" (*Principal's Report 1930-1931,* p. 1) Each year, in his Principal's Report to the Board, Bearce noted that the drop in ability of day students, whether they were enrolled in either college preparatory or traditional classes, tended to slow down the progress of the class, causing frustration in the teaching staff.

Impact of Train Schedule on School Day

To add difficulty to student progress, the train schedule that brought students to school from nearby towns did not arrive until 9:00 AM, one hour later than the normal beginning time at 8:00 AM, forcing the school to schedule two beginning times, one for 'the train kids,' the other for regular town day students and dorm students. This proved to be cumbersome and inefficient, so the Board of Trustees authorized the principal to require students and parents who had depended on the morning train to use automobile transportation to arrive at school by 8:00 AM and return home on the last train leaving the station *(Principal's Report,* 1930-1931, p.3).

Brewster Publicity

To build the boarding population, Bearce saw the need to publicize the school in a wide national fashion. He had contacted Porter Sargent, a firm dedicated to independent school advertising, and proposed advertising in the well-regarded Porter Sargent Handbook. A broad coverage of up-to-date publicity of school dramatics, musical presentations, athletic activities, and manual training projects would be presented. The Board authorized the expenditure of $600 for the yearly advertising fee (*Principal's Report,* 1930-1931, p. 4). This appears to be the first time Brewster advertised on a wide national basis.

Health of Students

During the Bearce administration, there arose a concern regarding the health of the students. Dr. Nathaniel H. Scott, '11, brought to the attention of Principal Bearce the fact that many youngsters appeared to be under-nourished and pale in complexion. Dr. Fred Clow, the school medical adviser, advocated that periodic health testing of all students be implemented. Information indicating height, weight, condition of eyes, ears, nose, throat and general diet would be kept. The doctor would contact the families of those students who fell behind norms to encourage better health care and diet. Dr. Clow also gave chapel talks to the whole school on good health issues and practices (*The Brewster,* Dec. 1923, p. 6).

Student posture was also evaluated. "The Slouch" became an issue when teachers and Board members noticed that students would slouch against hallway walls and not stand straight. In addition, they would slump on the staircases, and would not sit erect at their desks. As a result, boys were required to attend physical training classes while girls were encouraged to join one of the girl's sports teams. As personal health issues moved into focus, boys and girls were required to take a health class as part of their science curriculum and girls were to participate in "motherhood" instruction taught by members of the Woman's Club of Wolfeboro (*Principal's Report,* 1930-1931, p.3).

Code of Behavior

After many discussions with the Board and faculty, another modification occurred in 1933. Bearce saw a need for the development of a written document regarding acceptable day student behavior. While each dormitory student was assigned to a dorm teacher as an adviser, day students were without behavioral guidance. The document called "The Code for Brewster Students" was published in The *Brewster Bulletin and* the school admissions catalog, and required each student and parent to read and verify by signature. The Code stipulated home study hours, approved school and town organization memberships, required attendance at churches, restricted unsupervised night travel outside the home, curtailed unsupervised automobile usage, and promoted a courteous regard for the wishes of the school and their parents. The supervision of day students was provided by Mr. Bearce and later Mr. Carroll Piper, who work closely with day students and parents in interpreting the philosophy and meaning of "The Code"(*Principal's Report,* 1932-1933, p. 5).

Wolfeboro Enters the Roaring Twenties

As Ralph Bearce came on the scene in the '20s, Wolfeboro was attempting to get in stride with the changes that modernization had forced upon her. The automobile brought easy and faster transportation to American life, and Wolfeboro was undergoing a second transformation as a summer resort. Building contractors went to work with real estate men, and hundreds of new summer cottages appeared on Lake Wentworth and "The Big Lake."

Street signs and direction markers had either rotted away or had been knocked down by winter snows, forcing out-of-town auto drivers to stop numerous times to find the direction to nearby lodgings while old cars with over-taxed mufflers roared up South Main Street. It was reported in January 1923 that there had been a 250% increase in traffic in the last four years, and the town had to post direction signs that seemed to calm the tempers of confused auto drivers. It also marked a time when small gasoline engines powered wooden boats, and hydroplanes delivered mail to the town and islanders (*Bowers,* vol. 1, pp.197-198).

The town quickly added the new entertainment of motion pictures to the summer agenda of things to do, and the second floor of the Brewster Memorial Hall building was converted to a motion picture auditorium where students, town folks and summer residents could find entertainment.

The Impact of the Radio

But a real change was the sale of small and large radio sets. Communication with a modern world became simplified, but it also kept people indoors at night. Plans were made by radio storeowners to have special nights of radio- listening when election returns were being made or important speeches being broadcast. People came prepared with a snack and something to drink while all ears were tuned to the broadcast (*Bowers,* vol. 1, p. 190). Brewster's own musical group "Ray Alexander and His Brewster Academy Orchestra," featured dances given at the Chapel Hall as well as out of town. Mr. Alexander was a teacher who tripled as football and baseball coach as well as orchestra director. The orchestra made itself known by radio broadcasting and newspaper stories. On April 2, 1924, the school orchestra traveled to Boston and broadcast an evening of music on station WEEI, spreading the Brewster message over a wide area (*1925 SYB,* School Activities).

Alexander Band was a popular campus band that entertained at various functions.

School Dress in the Twenties

As the Roaring Twenties progressed to the thirties, this period also marked a time of changes in school dress. School group pictures in 1922 revealed that young girls dressed conservatively during the early days following the Great War. Many wore sailor blouses and ankle length skirts. All had long hair with an occasional headband and string of beads. Boys were dressed in the traditional dark wool suit, white shirt and dark tie, whereas those boys who were varsity letter winners were permitted to wear their dark blue letter sweater with red Brewster "B." Some younger freshman boys wore knickers and sport jackets, probably for the first time.

By 1929 the fashion show had changed. There was no skirt length below the kneecap, legs were stockinged and fitted with black shoes, and dresses were bound at the waist by a low-slung belt. Virtually all wore a sash around the shoulder or black tie. All girls had bobbed hair, and seven senior boys parted their hair in the center. Boys now dressed in different colors. In a group of ten senior boys, only three wore dark blue or black suits, while the other seven had light tan or light grey suits. One had spats over his shoes and three had stripped ties with a light background (*The SYB,* 1929, p. 7).

The Roaring Twenties and Alcohol on the National Scene

The years between 1920 and 1930 brought further turmoil to an already delicate fabric of American life that soon would create an age of revolt against the old norms and traditions. The country was torn when women began to wear short skirts, smoke cigarettes, went mad over jazz and sneered at the conventions of earlier days. The passage of the Prohibition Amendment (18th) brought millions of Americans to the belief that crime would now be terminated. The liquor problem and the sale of intoxicating beverages would be stopped, and

Young people of the Roaring Twenties are dressed in timely attire.

Estabrook Flappers with their housemother are pictured on the front porch of The Estabrook.

that somehow poverty would gradually disappear. Yet millions of others had different ideas. Beer and wine had been served in most American households with or before dinner. They soon learned that physicians and druggists found easy money by issuing over eleven million prescriptions annually to patients under which they might secure alcoholic beverages for "medicinal purposes." Most felt that the questions about how much one drank should be based on personal decisions and not interfere with an individual's freedom or sacred liberty. Some people refused to report offenders to the authorities as required by the Volstead Act or to vote for public officials who supported the act.

When the distribution of a vast supply of barred liquor was discovered and destroyed by government agents, bootleggers quickly found ingenious ways to either manufacture their own or to import it from foreign countries. Inventive citizens quickly found a host of ways to manufacture their own "bathtub gin" and then sold it for whatever they could get. A farmer, pressed for working cash, could hitch-up Old Dobbin to the family cart, trundle over the mountain pass to Canada, and return to his wife who waited patiently in the barn ready to walk to the local wateringhole with a covered laundry basket (Barak and Blake, pp. 373-375).

Radio and Newspapers

While most of Wolfeboro was somewhat removed from this carefree spirit, nevertheless they came into contact with it through newspaper and radio. About this time, new American idols arose in sports—Babe Ruth, Jack Dempsey, Red Grange and Bobby Jones dominated every sports page, and sportscasters hailed their athletic prowess. The labor unions, which were reeling from the Depression following the Great War, suffered from a long series of failing strikes and unrest during the remainder of the decade.

The Evolution Debate

There was another situation that caused rebellion in this time period, and this situation challenged the old standards of religious orthodoxy. Nationwide attention was drawn to a young biology teacher, John Thomas Scopes, in Tennessee, who was arrested for teaching that man was created from a one cell organism which evolved until it got to be a land animal, and kept on evolving until it got to be a man. Scopes was backed by the American Civil Liberties Union. In July 1925, the trial started in Dayton, Tennessee, in a courtroom packed with church officials, prominent lawyers, news reporters and microphones. The Tennessee court convicted Scopes of the charges threw out his fine of one hundred dollars and sent him on his way, but not back to the classroom.

The trial seemed to solidify the feelings of the religious groups into three camps. There were those who saw victory for their beliefs in Scopes' loss. Church officials and loyalists now had the legal conviction to protect the churches from liberals. College students rejected the case findings and immediately began to create dissent on campuses. They campaigned against required chapel attendance; while others felt the church's main cause was thorough spiritual care for the hungry and downtrodden and didn't care much about the divisionary issues (Barak and Blake, pp. 372-374).

Reaction on Campus to National Events

With all of these national issues in the news, the Brewster faculty nervously seated themselves at faculty meetings. They spoke of how obstinate students were becoming and suggested that the school should do something to revive proper social behavior amongst the rebels. The requirement of Sunday church attendance, enforced since the days of Edwin Lord, had gradually eroded, as was the requirement that all students be off the streets and inside studying at seven at night, even in private homes as a signed statement from each parent promised.

The "Toonerville kids," living far from school and traveling to Wolfeboro daily by rail, seemed to be 'carrying on' not only on the train, but also they found it too much trouble to engage in school activities like the town students. However, in fairness, in order to catch the Toonerville train, many students were required to arise at 3:00 AM to catch the train at Sanbornville to be at Brewster by the first period at 8:00 AM. The train schedule was often delayed or simply passed over, leaving groups of students at stations waiting the next train to Wolfeboro and then the long walk up to the Academy. Their spirits were good, but boisterous, when they entered the school door.

The Seniors Take Bible Study

In response to the problems of school behavior and after discussion with the principal, the faculty presented the concept of needed religious instruction. The idea focused on a course for seniors that would require them to schedule one period weekly to the study of the four gospels. Mr. Charles A. Hatch, who became the Bible Study teacher, succeeded in making the life of Jesus a tangible story rather than a vague account with which everyone was slightly acquainted.

Hatch was a Harvard graduate, taught Latin and chemistry, and was in charge of the manual training program where the classes made ironing boards for the dorms, repaired furniture and constructed hurdles for the girls' track team. During the Bible Study, they studied the four books, Matthew, Mark, Luke and John as a whole, and learned from what sources their knowledge was derived. Next they took up a very thorough study of Mark. Discussions were held on passages that were obscured in meaning and quite often they found that the views they held did not continue to satisfy them; the results were apparently very educational. Charles Hatch must have been surprised at the senior dedication of the SYB for the 1928 year—"To Our Teacher and Friend" (*The Brewster SYB*, June 1928; pp. 3-6).

Charles A. Hatch, scholar, teacher, friend, and coach.

What to Do With the Old Wolfeborough and Tuftonborough Academy Building

As education in Wolfeboro began to receive a face-lift with the construction of the Carpenter School, at a trustee meeting on April 2, 1926, the Board read a petition from the Alumni Association requesting their help in adopting a plan to move and restore the old Wolfeborough and Tuftonborough Academy building. Presently, it was situated on the Pickering property near the beautiful new Carpenter School. There hope was to reposition it onto the Brewster campus where it could continue its service as part of the Academy. The old building was in a state of disrepair yet possessed so many old memories that alums wanted to save it for the ages.

After long discussion, the Board notified the Alumni Association that the trustees, "have no means whereby they can aid in the proposition financially and therefore, the most that can be done is to advise that if the old Academy Building can be moved, remodeled as to exterior, and a fund provided for both exterior and interior painting, and a fund of sufficient size so that the income therefore will cover the maintenance and up-keep, the trustees will approve a location on the Academy grounds"(*Trustees Minutes*, April 2, 1926, p. 1-2).

This seemed to be the last effort to save the old building. Nothing ever came of the valiant effort and the building was later disassembled and the wood carted off.

Brewster Gets a New Athletic Field

By September 1928 there was enough alumni interest in town to do something to improve the school's athletic fields for baseball and football. Since Principal Lord had laid out a baseball field for his team in 1890, nothing had been done to level and grade the area. A "Central Committee" had been formed by local alums: Abel Haley, '99, Robert Brewster, '09, Carroll D. Piper, '97, Fred E. Clow, '00, Lottie L. Rust,'16, and Ernest E. Trickey. A sub-committee, established to carry out the work of soliciting alumni in Massachusetts and conduct the fund-raising in the Boston area included three trustees, F. E. Hanson,'03, Albert H. Dow, '06, and Justin M. Tibbetts,'92. Circular letters were sent out, and many personal solicitations were made. Responses proved generous and prompt, but some of the committee members were a little disappointed in the number of alumni who had responded. When the pledges reached well over five thousand dollars, work was started.

With local help Goodwin and Doe contractors of Wolfeboro began the task of removing the many rocks. Ditches were dug and porous tile pipes were laid in rows twenty-five feet apart. These pipes would drain the ground and assured everyone of a dry, smooth field of some four hundred feet square situated parallel to the lakefront. "We look upon this athletic field as a monument, erected by the Alumni and men friends of Brewster. It has been made possible only through many generous donations, and in behalf of the student body, we wish to extend to you our gratitude and sincerest good wishes" (*The Brewster*, December 1928, pp. 1-3).

Christmas Tradition

Principal Bearce seemed ever-present to compliment students and to act as master of ceremony at class parties and banquets. In December 1928, the traditional Christmas Party was held in Chapel Hall. The party was planned for the freshmen and presented by the seniors at 2:00 PM. Instructions had been given for everyone to purchase a small gift of not more than five or ten cents that would be hung on a decorated tree located in the center of Chapel Hall. After presenting several dances and dance games, hot chocolate and cookies were served, and then each freshman stepped forward to pick his or her gifts from the tree. At four o'clock the Toonerville students left to catch their train ride home, while the others continued the dancing and playing of games until five. Principal Bearce, being master of ceremonies, took an active part in the spirit of the day by leading the students in singing popular school songs as the day came to an end (The *Brewster*, May, 1929, p. 6).

The School Population and Finances during the Twenties and Thirties

In 1924 the Board of Trustees had voted to provide the new principal the sum of $37,200, the largest appropriation that he would ever have to run the school. This also included the John Brewster Trust money along with all the school support funding for line items like athletics, maintenance, repairs, coal and power. However, with the Depression influence, the budget gradually diminish until in 1934 the total amount would be only $25,700. Finances were difficult.

Enrollment during the 1920s was reasonably stable around 220 to 226 students, yet in the early 1930s it took a drop to 193. As Mr. Bearce reviewed the situation, he learned that the drop in enrollment pointed to the loss of dormitory students, while the day student enrollment had begun to swell. This expansion of day students was attributed to an increase in population of Wolfeboro as city-dwellers migrated toward the Lakes Region. It was also observed that the quality of the student applicants was suffering and seriousness of purpose was in decline. Fewer students were enrolling in the college preparatory courses and seeking college admissions

Mr. Bearce's concern was that the decrease of boarding students was resulting in loss of tuition dollars. This loss of income had a direct effect on the school operating budget, and the cutbacks, over the years, of $12,000 was discouraging. In an attempt to stabilize the budget, Mr. Bearce recommended the dropping of the commercial course program, the reducing the teacher's salaries by ten percent, and the cutting back of other operating expenses. But costs of keeping the school heated were also rising, and the Board began to search for lower fuel prices. The principal also reorganized the budget to put more funding into the college preparatory courses, particularly the social studies, with the intention of strengthening the background of college bound candidates. Mr. Bearce became aware of the need for further advertising beyond the Porter Sargent Handbook, and anticipated that the future would require that Brewster do more to seek additional money for publicity and made this recommendation at Board of Trustee Meetings (*Principal's Report for 1934-35*, pp.1-2).

At the new year approached, there were many uncertainties in Mr. Bearce's mind that needed answers. He was concerned as to the future amount from the John Brewster estate, and he felt that it would be unwise to attempt any further substantial reduction in the 1935-36 operating expenses of the Academy without an exhaustive study of the school situation. He proposed that the Board study the financial situation and draw conclusions as to attracting more dormitory students to the school. To this point, Brewster had not solicited students through an active admissions plan, nor had it done much to draw public attention to the Academy, yet Brewster was, in reality, competing with neighboring private schools for the same boarding student. He urged the Board to evaluate the admissions situation as soon as possible *(Principal's Report for1934-35*, p. 2).

The Sudden Death of Ralph K. Bearce

With commencement activities ended and summer time approaching, Ralph K. Bearce looked forward to preparing for the 1935-1936 school year. He had been successful in making notable improvements in the property of the school, expanding the teaching staff and was attempting to attract an enrollment of students. At the age of 60, after a two-week illness, on July 4, Ralph King Bearce suddenly passed this life from a heart attack leaving his wife, Bess alone, for their one child, a son, had died at the age of four early in their marriage. This date, July 4, 1935, also marked his 33rd year of marriage. The funeral was conducted at the First Congregational Church, bordering the school on South Main Street and his interment took place at the Lakeview Cemetery in Wolfeboro (*Granite State News*, July 12, 1935).

The Board of Trustee Express Their Respect

> The trustees were overwhelmed by the sudden death of the principal and wished to publicly express their respect and gratitude for this man. At a special meeting of the Trustees of Brewster Free Academy it was unanimously voted to spread upon the records of the Board, to transmit to Mrs. Bearce, and to publish in New Hampshire papers an appreciation of the valued services and the undivided confidence of the Board of Trustees of Ralph K. Bearce, late Principal of Brewster Free Academy.
>
> The unexpected loss of any man from a position of leadership necessarily entails grave problems upon those who are charged with the responsibility of carrying on. But if a man falls out of the ranks the line closes up and the inexorable march of society goes on with measured pace. Assuredly it is a noble fate that strikes a man down in the plenitude of his strength. For him there is no decay, no faltering step, and no pathos of failing days. For the many who will remember Ralph Bearce there remains the picture of one in the full vigor of manhood's best

> years. (For the Board of Trustees, John Abbott, and Justin M. Tibbetts and Geo. H. Evans, Special Committee, Board of Trustees, August 2, 1935).

Mr. and Mrs. Bearce arrived in Wolfeboro at a moment when new blood was urgently needed in all the organizations in town, and their enthusiasm was eagerly accepted by the townspeople as the Bearce family became quickly involved in community activities.

Following the tragic death of Mr. Bearce, Ellen Bradford Bearce remained in Wolfeboro attending to her civic and Brewster interests.

The Dedication of Bearce Hall

Cobham Hall was the name of the estate of George Carpenter, a Wolfeboro benefactor, who lived in the beautiful home at the end of Clark Road. Several years after his death, the Carpenter family decided to sell the estate land and buildings. The Board of Trustees, realizing that the large tract of adjoining property to the Academy was too valuable to be placed on the open market and sold to a new owner, quickly made the decision in 1965 to purchase the estate. The trustees decided that the new possession should be dedicated to the memory of Ralph King Bearce, the fourth principal of Brewster Academy. There were five trustees at the time who had graduated from Brewster during the tenure of Principal Bearce: Mrs. Roland S. Hughes, '26, Judge Frank R. Kennison,'25, Hon. Chester E. Merrow,'25, Charles D. Cilley, '27, and Dr. Harold E. Gregory, '30, and they made the arrangements for the dedication service for Saturday, October 22, 1966 at 4:30 PM, during the regular Parent's Day celebration.

The dedication would take place on the lawn in front of Cobham Hall and then move inside to the new Bearce Hall. Great care had been taken to redecorate the hall with drapes, fine furniture, antique carpeting, and a formal tea setting.

After the football game with Hebron School, parents, trustees, guests and students attended the service led by Headmaster Paro who introduced Mrs. Roland S. Hughes who talked of Principal Bearce, and then presented Mrs. Ralph K. Bearce. Mrs. Bearce spoke lovingly of her husband and their life at Brewster during their eleven-year tenure. The President of the Board of Trustees, Mr. Howard C. Avery, who unveiled a portrait of Mr. Bearce, gave the formal dedication. The group was invited to attend a formal tea ceremony following the benediction led by the Rev. Edward W. Cantwell of the First Christian Church. Mrs. Bearce proceeded to the large reception room of the hall where women graduates of the school formally poured tea. Her heart was full with memories of their life on campus and the honor bestowed upon her husband.

Mr. and Mrs. Ralph King Bearce's final resting place is in the Lakeview Cemetery in Wolfeboro. Ellen Bradford Bearce joined her husband in 1972 at the age of 96.

7. Walter G. Greenall, 1935–1942: The Depression Years

When everything seems to be going against you, remember that the airplane takes off against the wind, not with it.—Henry Ford

Two Brewster principals would guide the school through the difficult times of the Depression years from 1930 to 1942. First was Ralph K. Bearce, who continually faced the bleak reality of expenditures and deficits. Major expenses were deferred, new approaches to admissions tried, but fortunately relationships with the town continued to be satisfactory because townspeople looked to the school as part of their social network. The second man who would assume the leadership position of the school during this bleak period in American history would be Walter G. Greenall.

The New Principal Knew Ralph K. Bearce

Following the sudden death of Mr. Bearce in July of 1936, the Board of Trustees set about to develop a list of possible replacements. From folders that had been sent to them, one candidate seemed interesting. Mr. Walter G. Greenall, Jr., of the Choate School in

Walter G. Greenall, fifth principal of the Academy.

Wallingford, Connecticut, had a broad background of experience in private schools. Added to this, Mr. Greenall had known Ralph K. Bearce and taught with him at the Powder Point School in Duxbury, Massachusetts, for two years in the early 1920s.

Mr. Greenall's Background

In 1891, Greenall was born in Winchendon, Massachusetts, and attended the Murdock School in his hometown before enrolling at Clark University. During the 1920s, after graduating from Clark in 1920, Mr. Greenall accumulated a number of teaching assignments—the Edgartown school on Martha's Vineyard, the Pratt High School in Essex, Connecticut, and the Woodmere School on Long Island, New York, where he taught science and mathematics until 1930. He then served as business manager and a mathematics teacher at Wilbraham Academy in Wilbraham, Massachusetts, until the Christmas of 1934 when he was hired by The Choate School to continue teaching mathematics and serve as their business manager. Mr. Greenall remained at Choate until word reached him of his old friend's death in 1935, and he then applied for the opening at Brewster.

Mr. Greenall had been married to Miss Ella S. Olsen of Brooklyn, New York, for ten years and had one child, Helen Roberta, who was enrolled at the Carpenter School as soon as the Greenalls arrived in Wolfeboro. Helen later attended Brewster and earned several major academic awards and participated on the field hockey and girls ski teams.

New Principal Arrives

When Mr. Greenall arrived on campus, the principal's office was located on the left side of the front corridor. It often appeared gloomy as the morning sun moved away from the window in early afternoon. Tall, and quite thin, with unusually long arms, hands and fingers, Mr. Greenall dressed in dark suits and stood well above teachers and students. When greeting, he presented himself as a person of unquestioned authority.

The Brewster Bulletin of 1936 detailed his rich teaching career and supported the belief that the school was fortunate to have a man who was thoroughly "imbued with his spirit of kindliness and understanding." The article went on to say, "This quality, coupled with his utter lack of patience with shoddy work in the classroom and with his great sympathy for the entire program of the school, will make Mr. Greenall a worthy successor of the fine and able men who have guided Brewster's destinies since her founding." The article went further, explaining that "Our schools no longer cater to those who propose to go to college to enter the professions; they must prepare their young people for the necessary duties of life. Without a firm moral foundation the boy cannot cope with the laxity of our times…" (*The Brewster Bulletin*, Vol.1, No.1, 1936).

Wolfeboro and the Depression

As Mr. Greenall became principal of the Academy, the effects of the Depression were in full blossom. President Roosevelt had instituted a program that assisted states to undertake a series of work projects to improve the condition of public parks, roads and buildings. The projects were slow at first but gathered momentum as the early years of the Depression passed. One of the first projects was to remove the webs of the "brown tail moth" from roadside trees, and in time, progressed to creating storm drains, bridge repairs and finally the construction of federal Post Office buildings. Under this program, the Wolfeboro Post Office was completed in 1936, and the artist's rendition of the building was hung in the lobby.

The town leaders had reopened the Town Garden, unused since World War I, to those in need. Upon application, free seed, fertilizer and planting land were provided. Barter became important for survival until the summer months brought some change with the arrival of vacationers who needed laundresses, cooks and young Brewster girls for governesses. Brewster boys found jobs working on farms or with the Civilian Conservation Corps clearing trails in the White Mountains. Fixing-up old cars, restoring old furniture, and collecting rags and old clothes were ways by which many were able to survive. Moreover, the two excelsior mills at Wolfeboro Falls did not close their doors as the demand for furniture stuffing and packing for auto seats was high. Suddenly the summer months of 1936 brought a marked rise in the construction of new homes and cottages on nearby lakes.

Automobiles in Town

Along with new construction, there were other signs of change in the village. The number of automobiles in 1932 numbered 208 and by 1939 there were 997 vehicles registered. In 1930, there were 400 horses in town, but by 1940 only 53, most used for riding instruction and pleasure.

Other forms of transportation were also being modified. The Boston and Maine Railroad into Wolfeboro stopped running on May 26, 1936, depriving twelve Brewster students from the Sanbornville area of the age-old way of getting to and from school. After trying an electric locomotive, the rail company developed a bus system from Sanbornville to Wolfeboro to help both students and business folks, but that was soon terminated. As a result, parents found themselves making the long drive to Wolfeboro over snow or mud covered roads.

By the late 1930s, a noted increase in trucks and automobiles is visible in this downtown Wolfeboro winter scene.

Some Bright Spots during the Depression

By Christmas of 1938, conditions improved and the town bustled. Shops were open, purchases were high and stores reported a brisk and active sales period. The Town Hall became the center for movie nights throughout the week. On Saturday and Wednesday nights, there was "Bank Night" that brought "standing room only" crowds when prizes of $25 to $100 were awarded the winning ticket. The town rescinded its old rule of no movies on Sunday in March 1937, and showings immediately began. Radio, for those lucky enough to own one and for their neighbors lucky enough to be invited to listen in, was a major recreational tool. Young boys found that they could build a small "cat's whisker" crystal radio set from a diagram found in a Sunday newspaper (*Bowers,* Vol. 1, pp. 219-265).

Brewster Academy's 50th anniversary celebration also offered an opportunity for people to celebrate during these trying times. Leading members of the local community had offered their pocketbooks and talents in service to the Academy for many years and now they again came to campus for the special festivities. Other out of town alums, who had become quite successful in their own right and had remained loyal to the Academy, arrived in Wolfeboro for the anniversary merriment of this significant landmark.

Depression Enrollment

During the Depression years of Bearce and Greenall, Brewster enrollment figures hovered between 144 (1938) and a high of 160 (1936) and seldom more than three PGs. After 1938, girl enrollments began to exceed boys by one, two or three students each year. Generally, there were enrolled from 24 to 28 boarding students, and the freshman classes were always the largest. Brown Hall remained closed, drained and unheated, and boarding students were

Trustees and leaders of the Brewster Community gathered in 1937 for the 50th Anniversary of the Academy: Robert Irish, William Britton, Oscar Young. George Evans, Herbert Mills, Justin Tibbetts, Arthur Gale.

boarded in The Estabrook or Kimball House throughout these years (*Executive Committee Reports*, 1935-1941).

1939—First Time Tuition Is Charged

After reviewing the financial climate of Brewster Free Academy, the Board of Trustees for the first time imposed a tuition charge for all day students in order to maintain financial stability.

> The public considered Brewster a "rich school" when in fact the Academy had few additional funds to put toward growth, new facilities, and improvements. Once the basic educational costs had been met, the income had been depleted. The public was largely unaware of the situation until 1939 when alumni, parents, and general public responded to the appeal, helping to ease the crisis. In that year, it was necessary to charge tuition for the first time. This amounted to $50 per local non-boarding student, which was assumed by the town, resulting in a small increase in the tax rate (*Brewster Academy Catalogue*, August 23, 1946).

Heating System Problems

Mr. Greenall and the Executive Committee of the Board were concerned about the inefficiency of the coal-fired heating systems in all campus housing. The main school building was always cold on the second floor as was the Estabrook and all other faculty homes. The furnaces were stoked in the late afternoon and left until morning, and it was not unusual for pipes to freeze during the night hours. The Board was also alarmed by the rapidly rising cost of coal, and plans were made to evaluate a new automatic stoking system which would reduce the amount of coal burned and evenly heat the building. The new Huggins Hospital had experimented with an "Iron Fireman" automatic stoking system and found it excellent. Plans were made to try an "Iron Fireman" in the Estabrook on an experimental basis. The results after one winter were superb, and subsequently a pair of them was installed in the boiler room of the main Academic Building. They gathered high praise, especially from students and teachers who had choral or drama practice at night on the second floor of the Academic Building.

The Executive Committee Supports Principal

Fred Ellsworth Clow, MD, '00, and Judge William J. Britton, '92, were of great assistance to Mr. Greenall as members of the Executive Committee. Dr. Clow had long been a friend of the school and was well respected for his determination to improve the physical development of students. An interesting story concerning the doctor was related by Albert H. Dow, Jr., '41, who upon returning to his room in the Estabrook late one afternoon after football practice found a man asleep in his bed. The man awoke and said, "I am due at the hospital at 4 o'clock – wake me up then. It's too noisy at home! I'm Dr. Clow" (Dow Interview, 2005).

Judge Britton, also a support to the principal, was well known in Brewster history too. It was William Britton who had discovered the flames bursting from the second floor of the school building and had given the fire alarm on that dark night in November 1903. While a student at the Academy, Britton had been a key running back on the football team of 1892, and was now a prominent lawyer in town.

Both of these men fielded questions of procedure and advice from the new principal. Together, they planned a new physical education program for boys and girls that emphasized health and physical development and encouraged the expansion of the sports program,

Dr. Fred Clow tended to the medical needs of both the village and school.

bringing into play field hockey, midget six-man football and ice hockey on a new rink located on the northwest side of the Academy Building.

Also with their encouragement, competitive skiing was organized in 1937 by Coach Robert Page with regular meets at the new Abenaki ski slope. In addition, three new tennis courts were constructed behind the Estabrook to replace the old ones. However, the demand for hiring young Brewster boys to perform tasks for neighbors and local storeowners apparently kept some youngsters away from athletics in the afternoons. Ned Bullock stated that he had to serve many local farms during the afternoon hours: There was always a need for a work boy (Bullock Interview, 2004).

As the effects of the Depression began to recede Brewster students found themselves becoming more interested, not only in athletics, but in extracurricular activities as well. The attraction for dramatic arts, although never fully faltered through trying times, was in full blossom with the traditional yearly junior and senior plays sparking the pleasure of young people; the 1938 senior play, *After Wimpole Street*, was presented and enjoyed by an enthusiastic audience.

Clow and Britton continued to support Principal Greenall as they organized a plan to bring noted speakers to graduation and special events. The 150th anniversary of the U.S. Constitution was noted on campus as Senator H. Styles Bridges gave an address and planted the "constitutional elm." Dr. Fred Englehardt, President of UNH, was commencement speaker in 1938, and Senator Bridges gave the commencement address in 1939. During that commencement week, twenty-five Brewster boys helped extinguish a massive fire that broke out on Cotton Mountain.

In 1939, another event that was promoted by Clow, Britton, and Greenall was the granting of permission for Dr. Perley Perkins, BFA,'17, of World War 1 fame and now the Director of Debate at Middlebury College, to hold the annual debate with the University

Above, both players and spectators enjoyed a campus1939 hockey event. Below, Coach Ralph Estey with the 1939 ski team.

The 1932 baseball team gathered on the north steps of the Academy Building.

of New Hampshire in Brewster's Chapel Hall. This event gathered crowds from town and dorms (*Principal's Reports,* 1938, 1939).

Curriculum Improvements

Under Principal Greenall, the academic standing of the school saw change. As time passed, 1939 became a good time to evaluate the academic improvement of the student body. That year, it was reported that there were only 39 failures out of a possible 542 courses. The curriculum was extended in 1940 to include instruction in music, dramatics, debate, Bible study and world affairs study groups. In early April, the New England College Certification Board extended the Academy's privilege for another four years *(Principal's_Report,* June 9, 1941, p. 4).

Given the new additions to the school curriculum and the increasing demands of the physical development of its youth, it was felt that plans should be made to provide adequate space for their instruction. A place for basketball and physical training was needed. Board members had considered moving and reconstructing the old Wolfeborough and Tuftonborough Academy Building located behind the Brewster Memorial Hall, but the facility had deteriorated to a point where it had no value.

Home economics and manual arts instruction at the Carpenter School was a possibility, but it was found to be impractical and financially difficult for the school. An in-school library was needed so that students could quickly withdraw needed books and teachers could have access to research materials or place such materials on reserve. With no ready solutions, space concerns would loom overhead for many years as patchwork alternatives were attempted to address the issues. It became obvious to the school community that the Board of Trustees would very soon have to confront the need for additional facilities as the enrollment of the Academy increased.

Seniors of '41 and the SYB

The *SYB* Staff for the class of 1941 produced the finest yearbook of that era. It reflected

The 1938 Senior Play, After Wimpole Street *cast, l–r: Mary Witham, Barbara Lewando, Francis Colman, Leon Dunbar, Joseph Stevenson, Richard Goodhue, Gladys Cox, Robert Thurrell, Jr., Iris Lord, Jeannie Mulvey.*

attention to detail, humor, and a seriousness of purpose that extended throughout the class' four years at Brewster, and it was the first hardback *SYB*. All photographs were well presented and fashioned to show students at their best. Whether the picture was a formal or a casual one, they were characteristic of young men and women ready to enter a new life.

Faculty and senior photographs were large and well posed and clear. Boys were dressed in dark suits with white shirts and dark ties while girls all wore sweaters and skirts or dresses with stockings, high-heeled shoes and appropriate jewelry. Athletic uniforms were clean and neat and showed no frays or tears, while helmets, skis and field hockey sticks were evidently cleaned and polished. Snapshots of outdoor activities reflected school spirit and energy. A careful examination of senior photos brings a happy spirit to the viewer when so many Wolfeboro town leaders of today are immediately recognized: Howard Bean, Ned Bullock, Doug Bowles, Sandy Dow, Forrest Durkee, Curtis Pike, Bob Hanson, Barbara Lewando—they are all there.

But it was a sad *SYB* in one respect. The dedication was given to Fred Ellsworth Clow, MD, class of 1900, who had passed this life on January 4, 1941, having suffered a heart attack while tending his medical rounds in a freezing snowstorm.

Problems from the Depression on the Academy

By 1940, financial deterioration had wormed its way through both town and school. Bearce and Greenall had witnessed its insidious effects perpetuated on everyone, whether parent, teacher, student or school administrator. The school saw that changes had to be made in hopes that even meager investments in the school program would begin to bring more students to their doors, but their efforts were in vain. Advertising in Porter-Sargent's book proved too little, too late and had only modest effect in drawing new boarding students to the school. School admission records reflected a large freshman class each year, but comparatively few of them remained for four years; fewer went on to college. Tuition from boarding students was small and vacancies in Brown, Estabrook, Kimball and any other potential dorm went unfilled by new boarders. Brown Hall had been closed for years, and fewer boarding students applied for admission.

Dr. Fred Clow's efforts to expand the athletic program were pioneering in developing physical fitness, but parents with limited funds were left to personally provide transportation and equipment needs. Alumni heard annual appeals from their class agents for increased giving, but these donations were small. Often records of donors were lost or improperly recorded. Long delays in the scheduled maintenance of the school facilities had resulted in conditions approaching dilapidation and danger. Leaking roofs, rusted water pipes, broken hinges and cracked windows went unattended for years. The two new Iron Fireman automatic stokers continued to do their job in keeping the Estabrook and the Academic Hall reasonably warm, but their cost detracted from other much needed repair work. Most perplexing, the trustees of the school seemed at a loss to establish a process by which these conditions could be set right. The Depression period had begun to wear away at the school's financial foundation to a point where the Board of Trustees needed to rethink their strategies. Since the general educational objectives bestowed upon it by the school's founder from the earlier days had long supported the concept of free education for young boys and girls to pursue a better preparation for advanced training, the demands upon the Board to continue that goal soon became financially difficult to realize.

Board Faces Financial Reality

By 1940, the Board of Trustees began to face the stark reality of the limitations placed upon them by the Depression and the passage of time. Several Board members began to feel the need to capture a broader view of the assets of the school and to take action to use the potential of the school as a stepping-stone to attract individuals of wealth or foundations that were known to have funds earmarked for distribution to institutions of learning (Hanson letter to Justin M. Tibbetts, July 10, 1940, pp 2-3).

Preparing for the1939 Commencement when Senator Styles Bridges addressed the graduates.

The Greenall Faculty of 1939; Robert F. Meader, Carroll D. Piper, Fred K. Higgins, Robert Page, Jessamine Shirley, Principal Walter G. Greenall, Herbert E. Sargent, Marie Frosberg.

F. E. Hanson Joins the Board and A New Direction Emerges

The first recorded hope that could engender enthusiasm was the election of F. E. Hanson to the Board of Trustees. Mr. Hanson, '03, a respected Boston attorney and a close friend of Justin Tibbetts,'92, had a sharp mind for business. In addition, Hanson seemed to have an optimistic outlook. He wanted to change strategy by developing a broad and highly publicized plan to bring about financial stability. To accomplish this, he would enlist the best and brightest from the Alumni Association, complete a feasibility survey on the potential fund raising capacity of the school, revise the accounting procedures being used to offer more fiscal clarity, and formulate a plan to attract potential givers to the school.

Hanson saw Brewster Academy's potential by examining its long history. He examined each word of the Will executed by John Brewster in an effort to bring clarity to what the intentions of the founder were. In the Will, he saw nothing that compelled the school to be exclusively for Wolfeboro and surrounding towns. As a graduate of the class of 1903, Hanson could reflect on the educational system instituted by Principal Lord that cultivated so many graduates who enrolled in Ivy League colleges and moved into careers bringing them financial success.

As he read the Will, Hanson saw the entrepreneurial skills of John Brewster at work in almost every word. Why would John Brewster place the school on the most beautiful piece of real estate he could find when he could have purchased land elsewhere at much cheaper rates? Why would he build only one-third of the school building, leaving the other two thirds to others of similar entrepreneurial skills as himself? Why did John Brewster stipulate that the majority of the Board of Trustees was to be of non-residents of the surrounding towns?

The conclusion is that John Brewster, in all his wisdom, left for those who were to follow the challenge of his Will.

Hanson saw the rapidly declining Boarding population with the closing of Brown Hall and declining occupancy of other dorm rooms as a dangerous sign. He saw the necessity of reaching far beyond the borders of New Hampshire for residential students. Another concerning factor was the high attrition rate of incoming freshmen who left school before graduating. Using these points, Hanson carefully constructed an overall view of how the Board could approach the coming years with a firm plan of action.

Up to this point, the Brewster Academy Alumni Association had done its part to augment the financial underpinnings of the school, but now much more help was needed. The alumni had long tailored their support of the school through the annual Boston Brewster Club meetings, by individual contributions, and by festivities held during commencement week. These were helpful to the school's annual budget, but because of the Depression, they had little impact when measured against the total growing needs of the Academy. Hanson believed that alumni giving efforts could be improved through better record keeping, consistent contacts, and improved financial management.

Hanson Takes Action

Hanson let his ideas be known to other Board members, and they too became convinced of the need to change the direction of financial management of the school.

Hanson wrote, "It is within the power of management to change this situation and place the Academy in a position to attract increased income and funds in the future; while at the same time restoring it to the same relative position in regard to the average free school system that it formerly held. Unless that is done, it is not difficult to foresee for it the same destiny that befell its predecessor (Wolfeborough and Tuftonborough Academy) which continued for 58 years as a privately operated institution, and then became a local high school in all but corporate existence…." (Hanson letter to Tibbetts, 1943).

At its annual meeting in 1943, the Board of Trustees designated F. Ernest Hanson to act as a committee of one to consider the possibilities of increasing the income and funds of the Academy, particularly through increased dormitory occupancy and donations and bequests. The undated eight-page Hanson report was probably given at a subsequent Board meeting or possibly distributed by mail to all Board members. The report is thoughtful, precise and well framed. It quite clearly defines Hanson's perception of the intent of John Brewster. It was now for the full Board to follow Hanson's lead and move the Academy forward (Hanson, *Brewster Free Academy: Income and Funds*, 1943).

Ominous Awareness of War

But for the class of 1941, the clouds of war and uncertainty were gathering. All students and teachers understood the conflict that had begun in 1939 in Europe and the gradual rise of a very aggressive Japan in Asia. Students gave news reports during chapel service, and these were a point of discussion and debate during World Affairs presentations. Most boys understood that their role would be as servicemen, but they did not know where or when. After that Sunday afternoon, on the seventh of December 1941, life in Wolfeboro and Brewster would never be the same and would be dominated by an uncertain future.

Pearl Harbor Attack

It had become the custom after church services on Sunday afternoons for dorm students to gather at 5:00 PM in the Estabrook dining hall and listen to "The Shadow," a mystery radio program. If there were snow on the ground, the group would first divide into teams and play "Fox and Hounds," a game in which a boy and a girl would be foxes, and with a fifteen minute head start, blaze a trail through the snow with deception in mind. The trail would usually lead across the campus and down through town lots, over to Sewall Road and beyond. The Hounds would then follow the tracks until the confusing footprints revealed the Foxes. Capture was inevitable. The gang would then return to the Estabrook for hot chocolate and the opening words from the radio, "Who knows what evil lurks in the hearts of men?....The Shadow knows!" (Dow Interview, 2005).

But this Sunday afternoon was different. Instead of the mystery program, the announcer broke in: "We interrupt this program for a special announcement: the Japanese have attacked the United States fleet at Pearl Harbor in the Hawaiian Islands. Keep tuned to this station for further details." That afternoon Wolfeboro church bells chimed, and their doors opened for those who wished to come. At noon the next morning, Monday, President Roosevelt went to Congress to deliver his famous "Day of Infamy" speech requesting that a state of war be declared against the empire of Japan. The speech was short, but at least now everyone knew what had to be done. School was called off that day, but Headmaster Greenall had the dorm students report to Chapel Hall where he had set-up a radio so that everyone could hear the famous broadcast. Emily Sargent,'25, the daughter of Professor Herbert Sargent, was at Honolulu when the Japanese attacked. She had joined the Civil Service and had been sent to Shanghai, China, then transferred to Hawaii. After the attack she wrote a letter to the citizens of Wolfeboro describing the attack tactics, the spirit of the soldiers and sailors ('fighting mad') and the battle damage (*Bowers,* vol. 1, p. 271).

Brewster Responds to the War

It seemed that the forces of uncertainty took a slow turn for the worst. Those male students who had hoped for peace were suddenly faced with signing-up now or waiting to be drafted. It seemed a good choice to sign now since most enlistees were given the option of service branch and to then wait until after graduation to report for duty. To be drafted meant that one had to report immediately to the army when called by the local draft board, and there was also the thought that to be drafted would not look good on your record either when serving or in the future. Throughout the war many male students each year conversed actively as to what to do, and the enrollment figures show that many from all classes, freshmen through seniors, enlisted knowing that their turn would come. As Ned Bullock, '41, stated, "Everyone in school knew the war would soon come. We were kind of preparing ourselves ahead of time. Many of the boys would bring their hunting rifles to school and adjust the sights for accuracy by practice shooting at targets down by the lake during lunch period under the supervision of one or two teachers" (Bullock Interview, 2007). Girls took on the task of collecting clean old bed sheets from around town. Their task was to tear them into long sections several inches wide, and fold them into neat squares for delivery to the Red Cross.

Brown Hall and the War Effort

But there were larger plans unfolding in town. Since Brown Hall was not being used as a dormitory, the town won an appeal to the Brown Trust and was utilizing it as headquarters for various wartime groups. It became the headquarters for the Wolfeboro Civilian Defense Committee and the Civil Air Patrol, and was equipped with telephones and other apparatus. Brown also became the headquarters from which citizens could receive ration stamps for food and gasoline.

Air Raid Drills

Just two weeks preceding the Pearl Harbor attack, Wolfeboro citizens and students attended a demonstration on the Academy field of how to douse incendiary bombs that might be used by German bombers in an attack on the East Coast. Air raid drills were held in town with wardens on duty. Each dorm had a designated air raid room that was equipped with drawn "black out shades." All other lights were turned off in rooms and hallways. Wardens patrolled the streets reporting those windows bright with lights (*Bowers,* vol. 1, p. 269).

Saving Stamps, Saving Bonds and Victory Gardens

The school initiated a program of savings stamps and bonds and students had their purchases registered during homeroom period. A "Victory Garden" was again created on the now Memorial Field and another behind the Clark House on Green Street. Students would gather scrap metal from homes and bring it to the school flagpole where the pile grew almost to the front steps of the school building, then awaited trucks to haul it away for separation and melt down.

The First to Fall

As the years passed, students soon were aware of graduates who had died or were wounded. Hallway talk seemed anxious and efforts were made to write letters to those grads who were serving. Helpfully, the *Granite State News* published the names each week along with the location of hospitals where boys were recovering (Moore Interview, Feb.15, 2005).

The "First to Fall" was Clayton E. Hale, '37, of South Wolfeboro, who died September 10, 1942. Clayton attended Boston University and graduated in 1941, after majoring in business administration. He joined the United States Air Force and became a pilot (Anita Hale Interview, 2007).

Greenall Resigns

After the class of 1942 graduated in June, a major change took place in the school's administration. During the summer, Mr. Greenall made a decision to resign as principal of the Academy. During his tenure, he had accomplished the goals set by his predecessor, Mr. Bearce, by his strict enforcement of the Code of Behavior required of each student. He had placed great energy into requiring each student to do his or her best. In doing so, he had "saved" many students. Robert Hanson, class of 1941, remarked that, "Mr. Greenall saved me because I had not spent my study time wisely and he knew that I was capable of much more. We had a talk that changed my whole attitude about the future" (Hanson Interview, March 10, 2004).

And Hanson was not alone. Howard Bean, class of 1941, remarked that Mr. Greenall heard that Howard and others were constructing a hockey rink during the evenings when they should have been studying. Bean and others were called to the principal's office and berated for the way they had been wasting their evening study time. Greenall was a strict disciplinarian in every sense and seemed to be everywhere, verifying that everyone was doing his or her job (Bean Interview, 2007).

Leading the Academy through the Depression era was difficult at best. With declining enrollment, school facilities in disrepair, little funds for athletics, the realities of world war looming, and worry about fiscal responsibilities when the everyday task of living was an uncertainty—all took their toll. With these overwhelming issues and perhaps personal problems, Walter Greenall presented his resignation to the Board of Trustees in late summer, and it was immediately accepted. There is no record of the reason for his decision, but the Board without delay began a search for a new school leader.

The record indicates that Mr. Greenall served in the armed forces during the reminder of the war, returned to school administration and served out the remaining days of his career at Phillips Academy Andover. He retired in 1963 and passed away on December 4, 1964.

8. Vincent David Rogers, 1942–1959: Turbulent Times

Do not go where the path may lead, go instead where there is no path and leave a trail.
—Ralph Waldo Emerson

Pre War Fears and Concerns

The resignation of Principal Walter G. Greenall in late summer of 1942, just months following the attack at Pearl Harbor, brought an added concern to the Board of Trustees who had been struggling to balance finances throughout the Depression years. There were justified fears that war would bring reduced enrollment to the school and wartime inflation with rising costs in food, coal, gasoline, and labor would cripple any school budget plan.

With the opening of school scheduled for the first week of September 1942, the Board had only a few weeks to choose a new principal. By August applications were received from many candidates, all of whom were well qualified. After thorough review, the Board voted unanimously to hire Vincent David Rogers.

Principal Vincent David Rogers and Mrs. Rogers with their children David, Richard, Davena, and Dianne in Lord House.

Rogers was a descendant of an old Rogers family who had played a large part in the civic affairs of Wolfeboro during the life of John Brewster, and his father had attended the Wolfeborough and Tuftonborough Academy. The oldest Rogers child, Richard, attended Dartmouth for one year before enlisting in the Navy and the three younger children, Devena, David and Dianne would attend Carpenter School and Brewster.

Rogers was a former student at Brewster Academy who had transferred to Philips Andover Academy for his junior and senior years. He then attended the University of New Hampshire for two years, earning letters in a variety of sports, before transferring to Dartmouth College where he continued his lifelong interest in athletics, including lettering in track. After graduation, he taught at Barre, Vermont, for two years; in 1926, he was hired as a teacher at Manchester Central High School where he remained until 1942. Rogers earned high praise from the principal of Manchester Central High School not only for his dependability, but also his ability to analyze youngsters and handle difficult cases in a very diplomatic way. "He knew when to put pressure on, and when to give a boy a pat on the back…I hate to lose him, but I like to see a good man get ahead" *(Granite State News,* September 25, 1942).

Judge William Britton noted Rogers' love of farming would help the school during wartime. Rogers had taken several courses in poultry and animal husbandry at UNH, study which would help him when raising livestock on the family farm in Sanbornville or later raising poultry in the Haines Barn for use by the chef. (*Principal's Report,* Fall 1942).

Rogers built a large chicken coop in Haines House barn (now the Climbing Barn), using wood from an old toboggan slide which had run from Brown Hall to the lake. (*Granite State News,* Sept. 25, 1942).

It became obvious that this tall, trim man loved athletics. Any coach could have pictured him as a tight end or as a rugged catcher on a baseball team. He had coached a wide variety of sports during his career and had the ability to spot good coaching. He entertained strong opinions regarding the role of physical education in the development of youth, and these ideas would be guidelines in future curriculum planning for the school. During the fall of 1942 he converted the tennis courts, in back of the Estabrook, to a basketball court and got together a group to play. Rogers clearly saw the need for a gymnasium and made his thoughts known to the Board in an early report to them *(Principal's Report,* October 1942).

Rogers Takes Charge as the War Affects Enrollment

The Academy enrollment figures for the first two years of the war were bleak and telling. In 1942, from a total enrollment of 160, 19 students left during the year. While only four boys decided to enlist in the service, eight lost interest in school work and seven changed residency, probably following families to better wartime employment.

When school opened in the fall, many boys did not arrive on time because they were needed to help bring in the fall harvest; and the school delayed the formal opening a full week. The six boarding boys were placed in Estabrook and the five girls in Kimball House. From 1942 to 1945, female day students were in the majority, and freshman classes were always the largest at 55—almost double the size of senior classes.

This trend seemed to verify Mr. F. E. Hanson's letter of 1940 to the Board in which he questioned whether John Brewster intended to create a school for day students alone, or whether the Board should increase the scope of applicants from a broader geographic field, concerns the Board later addressed. Learning problems also seemed to be a concern. Rogers wanted freshmen placed in classes that would remediate their educational problems.

The Brewster Board was not alone in confronting the problems of the day. Headmasters throughout the New England area unanimously expressed their opinions that the "1943-

The often snow-covered basketball court with Coach Principal Rogers.

1944 academic year had been the most difficult year for every principal and headmaster." Rogers remarked to the Executive Board that all schools were faced with similar problems: enrollment, food, fuel, teacher recruitment, and wartime anxiety.

He also commented on the sad death of Judge Britton who had been a constant, faithful advisor to him. His kindness, generosity, and good friendship would be greatly missed, especially during these trying times.

Retaining Faculty and the War

During the war maintaining a teaching staff was always a worry to the Board and principal. Male teachers were continually leaving for the armed services. Women teachers often felt that their employment was more needed in wartime production, and they withdrew. Rogers had to depend on older men and women to serve as teachers, but this proved difficult when they were asked to perform multiple tasks such as coaching, taking charge of plays, and planning weekend activities.

Not only was the retention of teachers a problem, but also inefficiency was an issue. The husband of one of the teachers was hired to teach art and other courses; his personal style was difficult, and he managed to offend both students and teachers. Although Rogers made every attempt to accommodate him, his unwillingness to comply and cooperate forced Rogers to ask him to resign.

Food and Fuel Rationing and the War

Along with enrollment, faculty retention and learning issues, the war brought the rationing of both food and fuel. Since teachers who lived on campus were permitted to take all of their meals in the dining hall with the boarding students, a top priority was keeping the dining hall kitchen well supplied. The coop in Haines barn was big enough to nest a great number of chickens and to provide the cook with eggs and poultry. A large freezer stored meat and perishables. Rogers purchased two fat cows, had them killed, and the meat delivered to the freezer. He tapped the large maple trees on campus and prepared maple syrup in the spring. Daughter Dianne reports boiling it down in the Lord House kitchen with the resulting loosening of the hall wallpaper. The school victory garden located on what is now called Memorial Field needed constant tending, often by Rogers, especially during the summer evenings throughout the war. The problem of supplying fuel for school buildings was difficult as well, and Rogers had the janitor report the status to him daily. Coal was shipped from Concord to Wolfeboro on a schedule, but there were times when supplies were low, and he was apprehensive that the furnaces would burn out causing pipes to freeze. Alums remark to this day about the heat pipes in Chapel Hall in the Academic Building that made it the best place to keep warm.

World War II and Athletics

Because of the rationing of gasoline and the lack of tires, the athletic program did not do well during the war years. The school depended upon the good will and spirit of parents to assist in transporting teams. The *S.S. Mount Washington* was also used for transportation from Wolfeboro to Lakeport, New Hampshire, where a short train ride would bring teams to Tilton. When the lake was frozen, or the steamer could not run, games would often be called off. When parents either could not purchase gasoline or find replacement tires, games were also cancelled. Weather also was a major deterrent.

Student Anxiety and World War II

Messages about the war were received everywhere—radio, newsprint, hallway chatter, morning chapel, letters from an older brother, movies and comic books. The anxiety aroused by these messages sometimes produced in a student an attitude of carelessness and neglect; in some cases, academics took a back seat, resulting in a poor or failing grade and continual lateness or absence which led to a talk in the principal's office where Rogers was

The SS. Mt Washington *used for athletic transportation from Wolfeboro to Lakeport.*

at his finest. But this issue was one of commonality with other boarding schools, perhaps and more intense at schools located near defense or military centers (*Principal's Report,* October 25, 1943).

Student anxiety and boy/girl relationships during war-time evidently reached a high point at many other schools as well. During the annual gathering of New Hampshire headmasters, held in October 1944, at St. Paul's School, the eighteen headmasters focused their discussion on the future of co-education in the private school. Rogers came away from the meeting believing that a trial period limiting dormitory life to boys should be considered. Although he presented this suggestion to the Board, the policies regarding coeducation were not changed then (Rogers, *Executive Board Report,* October 10, 1944).

World War II, But "The Show Must Go On"

In some way, the war had an impact on the lives of all students and their families. With that in mind, the principal felt it important that there continue to be a source of joy and spirit on campus.

Barbara Lewando, '38, had returned to Brewster as a teacher following her graduation from the University of New Hampshire in 1943. Her assignment was to teach sociology, economics and history and also to direct student dramatic productions. Over the next several years, Ms. Lewando (later Mrs. Edward Zulauf) would direct five plays—*The Man Who Came to Dinner, Our Town, You Can't Take It With You, When We Were Young and Gay,* and *Dear Ruth.*

The Music Flows On During the War

The boys' and girls' Glee Clubs presented evenings of music to towns and surrounding villages. The clubs, directed by Burt Vaughan, had 60 voices combined, each with a different repertoire. Vaughan also began to develop the school orchestra with 11 students. Following his return from the Navy, the 1945-46-concert season was superb. Both glee clubs and the orchestra which had grown to include forty-four girls and twenty-four boys, all presented concerts at the Carpenter School, Brewster, the Cate Fund, and the Boston Brewster Club.

World War II: Clubs

In addition to the Civil Air Patrol, two more groups were organized during the last years of the war that were directly related to the war effort. Seven Air Corps boys passed the Reserve's mental and physical tests and were sworn in. They were allowed to complete their schooling before being called up after graduation in June.

Junior and senior girls were inducted into the Red Cross Home Nursing Course, which taught them basic nursing procedures. Certificates were awarded to all girls.

Civil Air Patrol

Carpenter School was also used as a workshop for students to make recognition models of German and Japanese aircraft to be used for helping new Air Force pilots to recognize enemy planes quickly. Brewster girls were enlisted into classes to learn Morse code and study the designs of German and Japanese aircraft so that they would be able to alert headquarters. Once the girls had passed their tests, they were allowed to wear a CD uniform and stood watchtower duty, spotting and reporting all airplanes in the vicinity to headquarters. Curtis Pike, '46, remembers joining the Civil Air Patrol and, after being trained under Fred Tuttle, the chief warden, serving as a spotter in a special tower built on the property now occupied by the Palmers' house on Clark Road.

Organized early in the war years, the Civil Air Patrol continued operating throughout

The Boys and Girls Glee Clubs, conducted by Burtis Vaughan, were a major part of school life.

Young boys often enlisted in the Air Corp while they were students. Young girls joined Red Cross classes.

The Civil Air Patrol was part of the town's civil defense program.

the war. Curtis Pike related an interesting story. His sister Emma, who had completed her Morse Code training, was assigned to act as spotter and stationed in the aircraft watchtower located on Clark Road. Her job was to search for airplanes and report any unidentified aircraft. While on duty one afternoon, she spotted a plane resembling a Japanese Zero fighter plane. Her fellow watchers laughed and chided her, but she persisted and reported her find to headquarters in Concord. The Civil Air Patrol headquarters had reconditioned a captured Japanese Zero and were using it as a decoy to test the watchers. Emma had been the first not only to spot it but to report it as well. She was awarded a certificate in honor of her attention to detail and her watchful reporting (Pike Interview, February 17, 2006).

The 1944-1945 School Year and the End of the War

School opened in September 1944 with 178 students—26 seniors, 44 juniors, 51 sophomores, and 55 freshmen, along with two postgraduates. There were seven boarding boys in Kimball and seven boarding girls in Estabrook.

Along with the administrative responsibilities of the principal's office came the task of recruiting new students. Unfortunately, up to this point, the principal had neither the time or funds to fulfill this significant role, and there was no admission office. Alone, the principal simply reviewed and evaluated all students who applied, and his decision was final.

Rogers explained to the Executive Board that he wanted to place a school advertisement seeking new students in the *New York Times'* Sunday edition to help increase boarding enrollment. Ads appeared in 13 alternating issues with the first ad appearing January 14, 1945. "We have had two new girls at the Estabrook as a result of the advertising" (*Executive Committee Report*, January 1945, p. 1). This was the first attempt to seek boarding applicants from out of state by advertising in a prominent national newspaper.

The Aircraft Watch Tower located at the top of Clark Road.

The 1945 Brewster yearbook records that 231 local boys had enlisted or were drafted into the armed services and were heavily involved in the war effort. This included five brothers from the Tutt family and five sons of the William Massey family.

Along with the commitment of its sons to the war effort, the school year brought persistent and worsening problems and the list seemed to be endless. Boarding enrollment was down. Because the school was not using Brown Hall, the town continued to rent it from the Josiah Brown Fund for use by the Red Cross, the Rationing Board, and the Civil Air Patrol. Finding teachers was very difficult. Principal Rogers was faced with food and maintenance problems at every turn. Obtaining food was a priority. He continued to buy beef and chicken wherever he could find it and to tap the campus maple trees for syrup making. Brewster Beach road had to be closed because it had become a "hangout" for young people who abused the facilities, and the costs of repairs were too much for the school. The water lines into Haines House and the Academic Building froze during the winter of 1945 and had to be restored. The old iron stove and refrigerators in the Estabrook failed and had to be replaced at a cost of $900.

The winter of 1944-45 brought very deep snows and most roads were closed. Campus paths had to be hand-shoveled by students. There was no skiing at Abenaki because the rope tow engine could not be supplied with gasoline, so students had to carry their equipment to Hart's Hill off North Main Street to ski.

Though the list was long with problems to solve, there were a few positive notes. Fortunately, Mrs. Marjorie Hatch was able to take over the glee clubs and orchestra when Burt Vaughan was sent off to the Navy. Florence Paige, dedicated and respected English teacher who lived in the Estabrook and was affectionately known as "Ma Paige" and whose daughter would later become Mrs. Burtis Vaughan, was a strong and positive influence not only during the war years, but later while the GIs were re-adjusting to school life. Joseph Melanson,'10, (Bucky'53) a local banker, volunteered to coach the hockey team, and it appeared that he could arrange transportation for out-of-town games. The team had a good season.

For the class of 1945, the end of the year was in sight as the war news was encouraging. The costs were enormous, yet there was relief to know that the tide seemed to be changing each week. Finally, with the surrender of Germany in May of 1945 and the surrender of Japan in September as the result of the explosion of atomic bombs, the war finally ended.

Roosevelt Agrees to be the Graduation Speaker for the Class of 1945

Sometime in February of 1945, thinking how wonderful it would be to do something very special for her class, senior Hope Whittum MacDonald, '45, came up with several creative possibilities. Finally, she decided that the best and most incredible gift would be to enlist the President of the United States as the graduation speaker for commencement services in June. Hope related an exciting story to us, part of which we share below.

One night we were sitting around the Estabrook, talking, and we thought, [in] what other country than the United States can you call the President when you want to speak with him?

"Go ahead, Hope, call him!" one of the girls said. I picked up the phone and rang the White House.

"How may I help you?" came the answer.

"I want to speak with the President," I said.

"Just a minute, please," came the response.

Hope was connected to Secretary Perkins who inquired where she was calling from and why she wanted to speak with the President. After hearing her request, Secretary Perkins told her, "Well, I don't know why he wouldn't. It sounds very nice. No one else has called."

After giving Secretary Perkins her phone number and other information, the group considered what to do next, finally deciding it would be good to tell Mr. Rogers what they had done. He was less than enthusiastic when they told him they had invited the President to be their Commencement Speaker.

An attempt was made to verify the call with Lillian Osgood Brookes, '38, the town telephone operator, but she was not allowed to give out such information.

Hope continued her reminiscence: "Principal Rogers was distressed and agitated by the news, and during a special called school meeting the next morning, he told the students, "I have never seen anything like it in my life. A group of the seniors have taken it upon themselves to call the President of the United States and invite him to be our commencement speaker without asking my permission. What is the school ever going to do? We don't have the accommodations for his support staff, or the ability to tend to the requirements of such a visit" (MacDonald Interview, January 2006).

Unfortunately, in early April, President Roosevelt died, and the nation was cast into a long period of mourning. The class of 1945 could still say that the President probably would have been their speaker.

The 1945 SYB (Senior Year Book)

In 1945, the yearbook staff expressed the love for their country when they wrote an editorial about the soldiers who were far away from home fighting for freedom.

> The Yanks today are fighting for Main Street and what it means to them – for their ideals of freedom and happiness in a land to which they hope to return. We can never pay the debt to these men and women –

In Chapel Hall, Principal Rogers conducts morning meeting.

> for those who are our brothers and sisters, friends and sweethearts, and those whom we do not know. May every one of us be worthy of their sacrifices. May we prove to the world in the years to follow that our boys have not fought and given their lives in vain, and may freedom, equality, and lasting peace be the rewards of their labors (*SYB, 1945*, Editorial).

Preceding this editorial was a "Roll of Honor" listing of 231 Brewster students and graduates who were serving or had served in the war.

Wolfeboro and the Victory Celebration: World War II

The Japanese government formally accepted the terms of surrender on August 14, 1945. Before the White House could formally accept the surrender, news broadcasts released the long awaited word at 7:00 PM that evening. Wolfeboro church bells first announced the surrender to the town while local people listened carefully by their radios. But it was not long before crowds began to rush to the center of town where every kind of noise making device was improvised and forced into service. The town fire truck with its ringing bell, shot guns, old fire crackers, cooking implements, even old water heaters dragged behind a car, all played their part in making victory noise and celebration. Boats appeared in the harbor with horns blaring and a massive bonfire was started on the campus. Crowds demanded music and before long a loud speaker system was set-up in front of a downtown store. This immediately reenergized boys and girls who wanted to snake dance up and around the street lamps. Finally, the music turned to "Country," and the square dancing started and seemed to never end. It was a joyous time for everyone, and no harm was done *(Bowers*, vol. 1, pp. 276-277).

The Death of Herbert E. Sargent

Despite the joy of war ending, there was also sad news. Early Sunday morning, October 27, 1946, the Brewster community and the Alumni Association were shocked by the news of the sudden death of Mr. Herbert Eugene Sargent. It was his 54th teaching year at Brewster.

Mr. Sargent had gained the nickname "Hoop" in an unusual way. He had never really understood the reason for cheering at football games before he first arrived at Brewster in the late 1890s. *The Brewster* reported a funny incident when Mr. Sargent attended his first Brewster football game. As Brewster scored a touchdown, Sargent stood with the students and joined in shouting, "Hoop, Hoop, Hoop, Hurray!" Later when the opposing team scored, he stood and bellowed "Hoop, Hoop, Hoop, Hurray!" As he turned to the crowd, he realized with astonishment that he was standing alone. It was explained to him that, "We cheer only when our team scores." But, he retained the nickname, "Hoop" to this day.

He was Acting Principal of Brewster between 1910 and 1911, and then again in 1923 and 1924. By 1946, it seemed that everyone in town knew Sargent. If you were a town student, your father, uncle, aunt, brother or sister had had a Sargent in a math, science or mechanical drawing class at one time or another. His son, Edward "Ned" Sargent, also a Harvard graduate taught science and coached at Brewster as well.

When the school was preparing to move from the old Pickering building to the new school across the street in 1894, Principal Edwin Lord had hired Sargent to teach science and mathematics. His botany classes at Brewster were "ground breakers," and they so thoroughly explored the woods and fields of the area that they found many specimens never before found hereabouts. Sargent prepared a great many specimens that were placed on exhibition in the Libby Museum (*Granite State News,* November 1, 1946, p.1).

Mr. and Mrs. Sargent lived all their Brewster days in the white house directly opposite Lord House, but facing South Main Street. The barn behind is long gone, but the apple trees in back of the kitchen remain. "Hoop" Sargent had a deep respect for Abraham Lincoln and in his study a statue of Lincoln gazed down on Sargent's desk along with a wide variety of books on Lincoln. After his passing, there lay open on his night table a copy of A *Teacher in America (Granite State News,* November 1, 1946, p. 3).

Campus Mall in 1906 with Sargent House (formerly Health Center and currently Main Street dorm) where Herb Sargent and his family lived.

9. The Impact of GIs on Campus

Nothing endures but change.—Heraclitus

After the War

After the final collapse of Nazi Germany in May1945, the Allied Forces shifted their attention to the Empire of Japan in the Pacific. The defeat of Japan in September 1945 marked not only a major turning point in world affairs, but also in the life and culture of Brewster Academy. The U.S. Congress passed legislation that would offer a temporary solution to their threatening financial solvency. The Servicemen's Readjustment Act, often called "GI Bill of Rights," provided funding for those servicemen who wished to refresh or continue their education after they completed their military obligation. Designed to prevent the disastrous aftermath of World War I when returning GIs could not find work, the bill allowed GIs to enroll in certified schools to take refresher courses, complete their high school diplomas, and then get jobs or go on to college.

With this prospect in mind, the Board focused on the future use of Brown Hall which the town no longer needed to house wartime emergency service. To keep the water and heat working properly, a husband and wife team was offered the living quarters in the building in return for janitorial services. The school appealed to the town to turn over Brown Hall (still under its 99-year lease from the Josiah Brown Trustees) to the school for the expected rush of ex-servicemen.

In 1946 sixty veterans returned home and attended Brewster to complete their high school education.

The federal government reimbursed Brewster the cost of room and board for each GI who was accepted and enrolled. As predicted, Brown Hall filled quickly with the new students. Some GIs were allowed to live in town, but all GIs dined in the Estabrook. This pattern of increased GI enrollment continued throughout the Korean War (1950-54) and beyond as Congress extended the GI Bill to all those veterans.

1945 Summer Plans

Rogers had put in a plea for a "good station wagon" for the transportation of athletic teams, helping make possible football team wins over Proctor Academy 20-0 and Fryeburg 36-6 but a loss to Berlin 6-0.

The power lawn mower finally wore out; a new one was ordered for delivery in May with payment due in June since there was no allowance in the 1945 budget (*Executive Committee Board Reports*, October1945 and November 1945). Rogers delegated the job of keeping the lawns mowed to students hired during the summer for roughly $94 a month. In 1945, Steve Hatch, '48, was hired as a summer groundskeeper to mow the campus. The summer days were long and hot, and Steve wore short pants while mowing the grass. When Mr. Rogers saw Steve wearing shorts while hand mowing by the lake, he immediately called him to his office. "Short pants are not manly, and you will wear long pants regardless of the heat. You will not enter the lake to swim unless the temperature is 104 degrees. Now, don't let this happen again!" (Hatch Telephone Interview, February 2007).

Although the old problems of paying regular operating expenses continued, there seemed to be a more relaxed feeling on campus. Rogers had spent much of his summer time making curriculum changes, painting Kimball House with pre-war paint, restructuring the Main Building basement to include more room for a new athletic storeroom, raising a considerable amount of garden produce, and caring for the two hundred and fifty chickens in the Haines House barn.

School Opening 1945

Soon the new school year began. Enrollment for 1945-46 jumped to 198 with 12 boarding boys in Kimball and 9 boarding girls in Estabrook. The senior group was small at 28, but

Veterans who lived on campus took their meals in the Estabrook dining room.

there were 51 juniors, 47 sophomores, and 45 freshmen. Seven postgraduates enrolled. Rogers reported to the executive committee that the enrollment was the largest since 1942, due in part to the attendance of GIs who came to review science, math and English. In 1944 enrollment had been 160 but fewer than 150 students in both 1943 and 1942.

Hilary Masters, '44, a tenth grader, a young boy away from home for the first time, was made to feel accepted and comfortable by the Rogers. Later he became a successful writer and a professor of English at Carnegie Mellon University.

In a letter to the authors, Masters recounted his mother sending him to Wolfeboro before school actually opened. Mr. Rogers met his bus, set him up in a room, and invited him to take meals with the Rogers family. "How generous and caring they were. Once school started, we were often invited to the Rogers house for parties and light suppers. I remember winter nights when we would pull up the rugs in their living room and supply records for their player for dances."

Assembling Faculty

Because many young men and women were still in the armed forces or working in war industries, recruiting faculty became a major challenge. A new teacher, Mr. Monroe, Latin and English, and Miss Amanita, commercial teacher, were impressive hires. In the spring of 1945, Rogers contracted Robert Meader to teach English but soon ran into difficulty when parents argued that Meader, a conscientious objector who had not served in the war, should not be allowed to teach. Mr. Rogers limited Meader's teaching schedule, but when unrest among some parents continued, Rogers let him go. That left the baseball team without a coach, and Rogers coached while he continued to search for a replacement *(Executive Committee Board Report,* March 30, 1945, p. 2*)*.

The Impact of GIs on Campus

When the leaves turned in the autumn of 1946, the school year was well underway. For the first time the student body included many GIs who were older and more mature students—battle tested, wiser, and anxious to get on with life. Most entered school with the idea of seeking refresher courses or regular diplomas and moving as quickly as possible to college. As soon as they completed the necessary requirements for college admission, they were gone.

Enrollment Increases

The total enrollment for 1946 was 279 students of whom 86 were veterans; 32 left the school during the year to attend colleges or take jobs. As there was limited dorm space for the vets, many were permitted to live off campus.

Overcrowding

Classrooms and study halls were crowded. Combat-hardened GIs were restless and bored with the underclassmen; Headmaster Rogers and Dean Piper concluded there had to be a change. Rogers decided that GIs would not have to attend study halls provided their grades were good; this relieved the pressure on them and the teachers (*Executive Board Committee Report,* September-November 1946, p. 1).

Because many young men who enrolled did so on recommendation from a college admissions director, they took refresher courses in math, English and science, leaving Brewster after they had completed a semester with solid grades and teacher recommendations, and enrolling in college, often for second semester.

Study Halls (above) were scheduled in the large second floor classroom on the north side of the Academic Building. Below, students are doing an assigned task at the blackboard in the 1940s classroom.

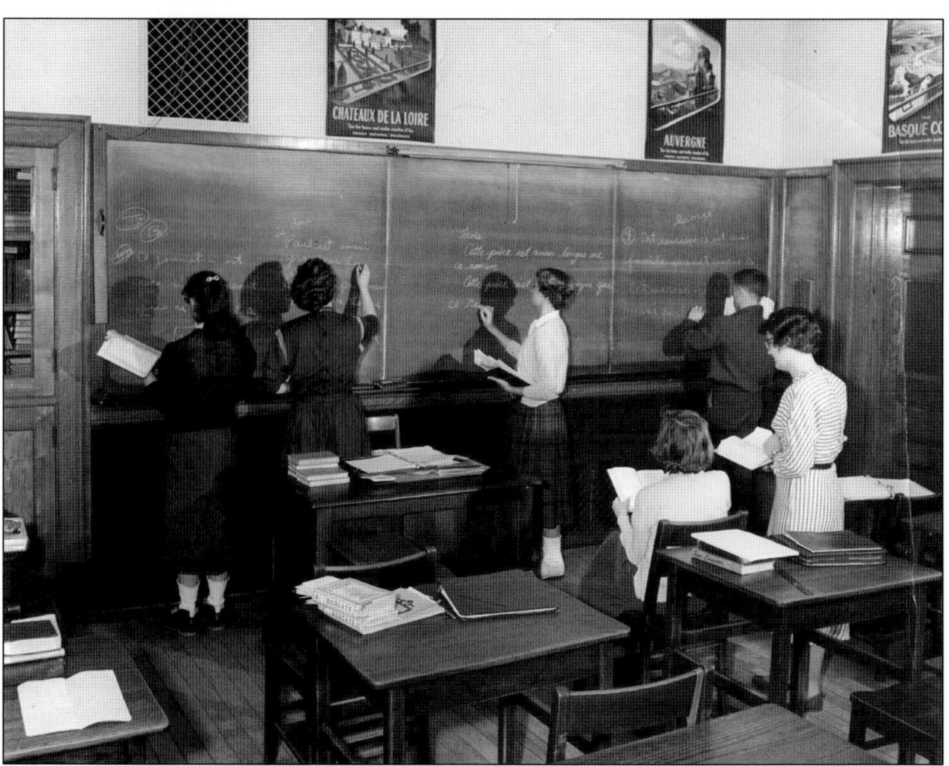

Conflicts of Seniors and GIs

A split feeling developed between the members of the senior class and the GIs who were not familiar with the school traditions to which seniors were accustomed. Class parties, field trips, dances, oratorical presentations, class debates, and all the preparations for graduation and formal procedures had long been ceremonies in which seniors took great pride, but the GIs were uninterested. The following year Mr. Rogers reported to the Board, "Certainly there seems to be a better association between veterans and the regular students than usual. This is probably due to the fact that the veterans new to us this year seem younger, and most of them have had less combat experience" (*Executive Board Committee Report,* October 1947, p.1).

GIs and Sports

During the next few years all athletic teams prospered across the seasons with the contributions of the GIs. Their successes led to a special celebration in Brewster Memorial Hall with noted speakers Sherman Adams, Paul Swaffield, Bump Hadley, Bill Stearns, sports writer for UNH, and coaches from Dartmouth, Brown University, Boston College, Boston University, and UNH. In 1949, certificates and warm-up jackets were awarded, signifying membership on the Prep School Championship Team.

Budget Problems Arise

When the federal government was very slow in releasing funds to GIs to pay for their educational and living expenses, the school budget was strained; and further budget issues confronted the Academy. Unsettled feelings about the relationship with the Academy accumulated in the town. During the summer, the executive committee initiated talks with the local school board regarding their understanding that the salaries of the two Brewster teachers who taught the commercial courses would be paid in part by the town. Later the local school board denied payment, requiring the executive committee to underwrite the teacher payment from its operating budget (*Executive Board Committee Report,* September-November 1946, p.3).

Later that year, the relationship with the town again soured when state legislation was introduced to permit the towns of Wolfeboro and Tuftonboro to use tax-raised money to pay their pupils' tuition to Brewster. Rogers remarked, "Passage was doubtful. I believe it is obvious that there is considerable opposition to its passage by Wolfeboro residents and members of the local school board as well. With this expressed opposition combined with no definitely organized local group working for its passage, it would seem doubtful if the bill will pass" (*Executive Committee Report*, April-May, 1947, p.1). And it did not pass.

Change in Dormitory Assignments

By the 1948-1949 school year, a change had to be made in the dormitory assignments because there were now far more boys than girls (54-8). Estabrook housed 22 boys, Kimball, 13, and Brown had their traditional 19. Four girls each were assigned to Haines and Sargent Houses.

Lobbying for Physical Education

With most of the concerns over GIs resolved, Rogers lobbied the Board for further required daily physical education classes. With no physical education facilities other than two rooms in the basement of the main building and a make-shift outdoor basketball/tennis court area, usable only in fall and spring, it would prove difficult to arrange. He knew, however, that this would put more pressure on the board to move on the plans for a Brewster Recreational Center and Museum.

Winter Carnival events were held each season on the campus ice rink including broom hockey and skating races.

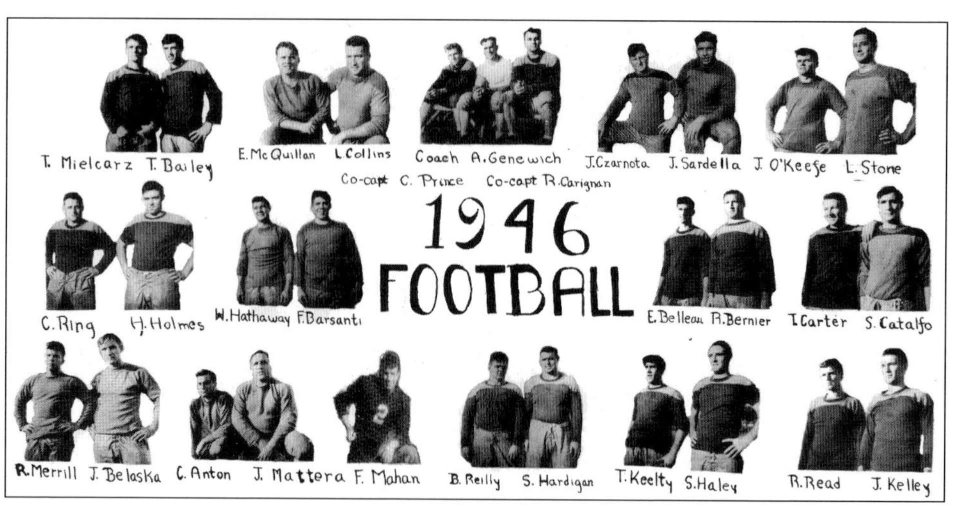

Mr. Genewich coached the 1946 victorious football team (above). The 1946 hockey team (below) coached by Mr. Sikorsky, fortified by a number of veterans, was the League "C" Champions.

Beginning Fund Raising Efforts for a Recreation Center

An initial appeal for raising $30,000 had been issued to alumni and friends of the school, and by June 1947, $2,500 had been received. When word of the appeal reached Bernie Landman, he deposited a further $1,700 to the Brewster Free Academy Gymnasium Account. This would make a start on the long awaited gymnasium.

In addition, committee organizations began to fall in line. John H. Clow, President of the Board Arthur Gale, Albert Dow Jr., Vincent Rogers, Edwin Edgerly, Fred Stackpole, Esther Britton, Beryl M. Kramer, Marjorie Hatch and Chair Charles Severance composed the Finance Committee. The Building Committee, chaired by Vincent Rogers, included Edwin Edgerly, Fred Stackpole, Albert Dow Jr. and John Kimball. About this time, Judge Frank R. Kenison and Chester E. Merrow joined the Board of Trustees. Merrow, a New Hampshire state congressman, was a man with immense poise who was respected by all, and he would become an important player in raising funds for the gymnasium.

The Passing of Dean Carroll Piper

In June, Carroll Piper, after serving for 28 years at the Academy, took leave from his position as teacher and dean. During the summer months of 1948, increasing pressure in his chest troubled the dean, and the only relief seemed to come with continued rest at home. As the months passed, it became obvious that he needed closer care and was moved to Huggins Hospital. Rogers kept in touch with Piper's progress each week and made frequent visits.

During the fall of 1948, Dean Piper expired at the age of 68. He had served the Academy long and selflessly as teacher, dean, acting principal, counselor, and friend. His magnanimous spirit is remembered in the hearts all of the youth he served so well. Always a level-headed problem solver, he is remembered for his quiet, unemotional approach in dealing with school predicaments as he established stability in the life of the school. Students respected his judgment and academic professionalism. He never faltered when encouraging students to do all that they were capable of doing, and they felt comfortable in seeking his advice because of his long experience in placing Brewster seniors into the best colleges.

Dean Piper had graduated from Brewster in 1897 and from Harvard in 1902 *magna cum laude*. After several years in business, he joined the Brewster faculty in 1920, becoming dean in 1935. In addition, he had served Wolfeboro as Town Clerk and Chairman of the Board of Fire Precinct Commissioners. He also founded the Wolfeboro Chapter of DeMolay. Dean Piper and his wife, Clara, had three boys, Charles, Elmer and Clinton, all Brewster graduates. Son Clinton served for two terms on the Brewster Academy Board of Trustees. During the dedication of Piper House in 1983, Burtis Vaughan noted, "Dean Piper is remembered for his commitment to developing the ideals and objectives that make the Academy what it is today."

10. Rogers Gets His Gym

You may give out, but never give up.—Mary Crowley

The Appeal for a Gym

With the war at an end, Rogers renewed his appeal for a gymnasium. He had spoken to the executive committee about the need several times since 1942, and his appeal during the January 1946 meeting of the Executive Committee is clear:

> There is a very keen interest shown by the alumni and townspeople, and certainly the need for one is urgent if we are to keep Brewster in a favorable position with other schools. Couldn't we get the $40,000 from the Brewster fund (William Brewster) cleared by the Massachusetts courts by providing a museum or trophy room in the proposed building and thus make a beginning? I really believe the alumni and friends of the Academy would respond generously to an appeal for funds if we showed them that we had $40,000 available to match a similar sum to be raised. I would welcome the opportunity to work with a committee with some such plan *(Executive Committee Report,* January 1946, p. 1).

Accounting Concerns

At that point, however, other money matters concerned the Board. Rogers stated that Fred. E. Hanson, a financial committee trustee, had reported that the school expenses were exceeding the income and that a trustee meeting should be called to discuss the problem and to find a resolution (*Executive Committee Report,* September 1946, p. 2).

As accounting procedures and business practices were updated, it became obvious to the Board that the school had to bring expenses into line with income. In reality, the investment yield had not and would not present a yearly income that would be pleasing to the eye. After a long discussion, the Board came to the decision that a student charge of $50 would be required in the next school year. They realized that this could not happen without "strained personal relationships" between Brewster and the town (*Principal's Annual_Report,* June 1947, p.2). At the same time, Rogers was concerned about another financial problem—painfully slow GI payments for their tuition. Rogers worried that once graduation took place, the payments would not be made; thus to clear GI accounts before graduation became his priority.

The Start of Fund Raising

Following a solicitation of local alumni, parents and business owners, plans for the center slowly began to evolve. In Rogers' January 1949 report to the Board, he indicated that the campaign had now collected $74,427, noting this sum included an estimated evaluation of $48,000 from the William Brewster Fund, but no appeal had yet been made to enlist out-of-state alums. He cautioned that to reach the final $250,000 objective, much more had to be done to encourage out of state alums to contribute. He hoped that if everyone participated and cooperated in the drive, the school might be able to begin the construction of the building before September 1949 *(Executive Committee Report,* January 10, 1949, p. 2).

It was shortly after Roger's report to the Board that the school was informed of the Cowan estate's $90,000 gift. What a timely boost to the building fund.

Professional Fund-Raising Help Sought

Realizing that professional help was required, in 1949, the Board of Trustees asked the John Price Jones Company, Inc., of New York City, to study the fund raising potential of the school and to submit a campaign proposal. Their thoroughly detailed proposal arrived at Brewster in February 1950.

Their greatest concern was the solvency of the school. The school budget needed to be balanced; it had been operating at a deficit for more than 10 years. Their plan recommended increasing the number of boarding students to eliminate this problem.

The proposal then presented a detailed roadmap for a campaign; used guidelines to evaluate leadership strengths, sources of gifts and giving potential; and showed how to develop workers to join with the leadership.

Rogers must have felt both elated and doubtful by the report. He had run an excellent administration for almost 10 years with very limited resources, and had done so at his personal financial expense, having taken either a salary cut, or at least no salary increase, over several years. At times he had sold family property in Sanbornville to make ends meet. Yet this report must have given him the personal validation that his work and effort were justified. If the master plan were to be successful, it would depend on how well he could get everyone to work together.

Never before had the school ventured into a large financial campaign, and the trustees had questions. Would it be possible to raise $250,000 for a new gym when alumni giving had been traditionally low and focused on an annual Boston banquet? Could an accurate listing of current alums be generated quickly for such an undertaking? Could the local townspeople realistically provide enough funding to augment the needs of the school? Should the school focus the giving campaign in one area, when it was obvious there were many other needs that required attention—a school library, manual arts area, more classroom space, modernized and properly equipped science laboratories? Should all of these needs be put before that for one gymnasium?

There were more questions. Would alums feel that they had had no gym and did very well in athletics? "If it was good enough for me, then it is for you." Others would feel that a new library should be first, then the gym. Some would feel that if the will of John Brewster had kept the school all these years, then there must be enough money for a new gym. Others might demand that plans should be made to accommodate a museum room, a place for art and dramatics, and a manual arts area. Others wanted town needs considered: a place for town meetings, concerts and public celebrations, even music and choral instruction. And beyond this, the school needed a place where general school maintenance and repairs could be performed.

The Jones Report

The Jones report clarified the case for a new gymnasium—recreation hall. But the report offered a chilling footnote. It reminded them that "with the growth of public high schools, many academies died during the first quarter of the 20th Century because they lost the spark of their founders, had ceased to generate new ideas, or had failed to keep abreast of the changing needs of the changing times. Those academies, which remained alive and vital, had done so because they had continuously adapted themselves to the constantly evolving task of preparing youth for life, and had been leaders rather than followers. Those who do not grow with the times will write their own obituaries." The report reviewed Brewster Academy's history to date, classifying it as a product of the New England Academy concept. "The Academy has long been described as a good and accredited school under the most exacting standards of the New Hampshire State Board of Education, the New England Association of Colleges and Secondary Schools and the College Entrance Examination Board" (*Jones Report*, p. 1- 5).

The general public living in the Lakes Region saw the school as a good institution for students from families of moderate means; they viewed it as an opportunity for a free education that they had taken for granted. There had been no serious effort to cultivate students from families of means outside the state; thus there was almost no wealthy alumni support. The school seldom made appeals for funds and apparently existed handsomely on a large endowment fund. As a result, many regarded it as a fabulously rich institution. But the true significance of Brewster was not adequately appreciated. Many were not aware of all that the school had contributed to the area. The public was only recently aware of the financial problems the school was facing and when it became known, the reaction was one of shock and skepticism. The local public, as a whole, did not realize that if the town built a public high school, the cost would sky rocket and the upkeep would considerably exceed $200 a year per student (*Jones*, pp. 10-13).

The report reminded the trustees that Wolfeboro and the neighboring towns were confronted with a state educational mandate that, if it were to be met, required the community to start planning immediately. The Brewster Trustees must decide what kind of school Brewster ought to be and could be. Three possible courses lie ahead:

1. Brewster could become another strictly 'private' school, which lived within its income and prepared a select few superior students for college. Wolfeboro and surrounding towns would then be compelled to build a new high school.
2. The Academy could then abandon its boarding department and become to all outward appearances a public high school, or
3. It could strengthen itself and adjust itself to the new needs of the new times, continuing to serve the traditional dual function of the New England Academy.

The Jones group hoped Brewster would take the third course. "Our reading of John Brewster's will leads us to the belief that the founder would have chosen that course. We hope that in making their decision the trustees will have the counsel of the citizens of the community and the alumni" (*Jones*, pp. 17-20).

Dream to Reality

Funding the much-needed building would require tapping three sources—increased tuition fees; gifts or bequests from private benefactors; and state, federal or town funding. The final section of the Jones document presented a "Plan of Campaign Organization," which detailed steps in reaching all groups that were good prospects in raising funds for the school.

The trustees carried the full burden for a decision to hold a campaign, the type of campaign, and pre-campaign planning. The Campaign Executive Committee would actually run the campaign, make policy decisions and meet frequently and regularly. A time schedule divided the campaign into seven phases based on Autumn, Winter, Spring and Summer terms, starting in1950 and concluding during the Summer of 1951 (Jones,

Board of Trustees, 1950: Fred A. Stackpole, Joseph Melanson, Chester E. Merrow, Vincent D. Rogers, Frank R. Kenison, Justin M Tibbetts.

pp. 58-84). However, there were greater forces at work that would interrupt the plans of the Brewster Trustees.

Invasion of South Korea

At 4 AM, Korean time, on June 25, 1950, an all out invasion of South Korea by North Korean Communist troops took place. Americans in Wolfeboro watched in distress during the first two months of the war as Americans went on a buying spree that caused aggressive price increases and scarcities. But more important, it awakened them to a new peril of possible expanding Soviet aggressions in Western Europe, the Middle East and Asia. The Cold War was now beginning, and draft boards in every village and city in America hurriedly composed lists of potential draftees who were to report for induction. Congress moved swiftly to pass legislation that would set mobilization allocations, crank up defense production, build industrial plants, and double our armed forces from 1.5 million to 3 million servicemen. By early June 1951, the war in Korea and the stabilization of Western Europe began to wear on the American people who were encumbered with taxes, high prices, and scarcity of materials, and who were frustrated with petty political party annoyances.

Korean Conflict Uneasiness

Both faculty and students also were uneasy over the war situation, and the school suffered from several problems brought on by these forces that were beyond its ability to solve. While there were no GIs enrolled in 1951, as the year progressed, 12 boys either were drafted or enlisted, some of whom were boarding students; and one teacher was called to active duty in the Naval Reserve. Of the 212 total enrollments on opening day for the 1950-51 school year, only 188 students remained at closing.

This uneasiness continued as the faculty complained of a lack of coordination and unusually high work demands, and some felt that the administrative duties of the principal were keeping him from attending to the needs of the faculty. Several threatened to leave and did. But, as the springtime weather improved, some who wished to return were denied. New faculty recruits for the fall term were very good. Dartmouth graduate Joseph Sardella had attended Brewster as a student and wanted to teach history and coach football. Coach Sardella was a great success, earning the respect and admiration of students and athletes alike. Other teachers applied for open positions in art, science, English and music, and were hired.

Trustees View the War and Fund Raising
The Brewster Trustees recognized that The Korean War cast a shadow over the fund-raising campaign, and they sought further advice from Jones Company. H. W. Peters was skeptical about initiating such an important measure given world economic circumstances—high inflation, low wages, building restrictions under war emergency conditions, and, more important, the manpower reserves that would be called into action. Peters urged that the Board not target the gymnasium as a fund -raising goal, but rather as a secondary product in a long-termed and well-defined program (Peters, pp.1-2).

Merrow's Trip to New York
Trustee Chester Merrow's visit to Jones' New York offices was productive and a meeting was planned for July 21, 1951 when H. W. Peters would come to Wolfeboro and meet for the first time with the full Board of Trustees. At that meeting, the Board finally decided that necessary money to employ Mr. Peters to organize and run a fund raising campaign for Brewster Academy under the direction of the executive committee of the campaign committee, could be "hired" from the "Recreational Hall Fund"*(Minutes of the Board of Trustees,* July 21, 1951, p. 1).

Planning the Location of the Memorial Building
In 1949, Mr. Rogers had written to Bremer Whidden Pond, a landscape architect from Boylston Street, Boston, to visit the school and make recommendations about location of the new building. Following his visit, he emphasized the need to preserve the natural setting of the school and the open lands and lake to the west. The new building should be secondary to the main building, the dormitories and dining hall and should have easy access to parking spaces within reasonable walking distance to the doors. Pond indicated the necessity of keeping the building low to the ground and further to the east where the natural grade would not detract from the beautiful setting (Pond, pp. 1-7).

1951: Life at School Continues
While plans were underway for the new building, the winter of 1951 was an active one in Rogers' office. The curriculum was remodeled and refashioned with Domestic Science being added to serve the needs of women. The Kimball House first floor "kitchen" was expanded to include new stoves, refrigerators, a broad selection of utensils and cutlery, and appropriate tables. Kimball then became the girls' dorm, rather than the Estabrook. Until the new Gymnasium/Recreational Center was completed, make shift plans were developed to have the new art program take over one or two rooms in Haines House and a new athletic equipment space be provided in the basement of the Academic Building while the winter outdoor sports program continued.

New Catalog
By June 1951, the board had approved the publication of a new school catalog. They carefully studied and reviewed each page, revised and approved new text, compared the

Home Economics and Sewing Classroom in Kimball House redesigned and refurbished.

The 1951-52 ski team with their coach, Dean Rupert Brown.

new with the old, and approved thoughtful suggestions. Specific emphasis was placed on "coeducation." Mr. Rogers consulted with Wayne Davis of Boston, a professional publisher who would begin the layout for a new edition; $1,000 was approved for its immediate publication (*Trustee Minutes,* April 21, 1951, pp. 2-3).

Town People's Uncertainties about Brewster

With the looming national issues and the current school fund raising plans consuming the leadership of the Academy, a deepening uncertainty developed in town about Brewster's future: Should Brewster become the public school of Wolfeboro? How could the State of New Hampshire take over its operation? Some citizens complained that the trustees and Mr. Rogers were not administering the school properly and contended there was no need to charge a tuition fee. Rogers became the target of unrealistic criticism, and, as Ned Bullock, '41, pointed out, "Mr. Rogers was blamed for everything"(Bullock, 2007). As Mr. Rogers stated in his report to the Board in June 1951, "the year has brought out more conflicting criticism than is good for the school. However, in the final decisions and conclusions, it is pleasing to note that the faculty, trustees and townspeople, as a whole, seem to be loyal to the principal and in sympathy with his problems" (*Principal's Report,* June, 1951, p. 2).

Organization Phrase of Building Project

During the spring and summer months of 1951, Rogers and the trustees, along with the Campaign Committee and the chairman, the Honorable Chester Merrow, had completed a gigantic task. Working closely with H. W. Peters, the planning committee under the direction of John J. Ballentine, '46, executive director of the school's Building and Development Fund Office, completed the organizational phase by enlisting volunteers—

both alums and non-graduates—to serve as office staff and door-to-door canvassers. Instruction booklets for alumni canvassers were written to detail the approach to be used in soliciting contributions. John published announcements of the Academy plans for the major development program. Other staffers researched the names, addresses and phone numbers of over 3,600 known alums. Card catalogs were established by Barbara J. Lyman Currier, '50, Mr. Rogers' secretary, and carefully watched over by John Ballentine in his new office in Mr. Sargent's old house.

Ballentine made notations on 'special donors' who were either capable of or offered larger donations. He then turned to developing plans for Brewster's first Homecoming to be held in October, and published a booklet, *For a Better Brewster,* which outlined Brewster's goal in building a new gymnasium. He also produced *A Sound Mind in a Sound Body,* a publication clarifying the case for a new gym and showing how it would serve the needs of both students and the town.

The Academy decided to reinitiate the old *Brewster Review* newsletter used during the 1920s to communicate with alums and townspeople. It was a four-page monthly paper covering meetings, school elections, sports events and alumni news. The initial edition bannered plans for the school's first Homecoming Day scheduled for October 13, 1951, that would include guided tours of the campus, a football game with New Hampton, and, as the capstone, a special dinner at which Congressman Chester Merrow would speak. After dinner an alumni dance was planned in the Academy Chapel with music furnished by Al Columbus and his band. Alumni news would be included and up-dated in each edition by Mrs. Lillian Osgood Brookes, '30, President of the Alumni Association.

The first homecoming celebration in October 1951.

Students Support Fund Raising

Congressman Merrow met with students, faculty and administrators in a school meeting to enlist their support to raise funds by sponsoring projects.

In May of 1952, the school erupted in a flurry of activity. All of the classes seemed to consider the fund drive a measure of class competition. Freshmen took on the project of selling trays that were decorated with a painted and colored picture of the main school building. In addition, they held an auction which earned the fund $200. Sophomores earned $200 by canvassing the town in search of scrap metal that was dragged to the back of the Estabrook where it awaited the scrap dealer to arrive and pay his rate. The junior class placed containers in all the local shops and stores to gather pennies to make a "Thousand Miles of Pennies" for the fund, and seniors presented a "Senior Carnival," selling tickets and earning $250. These student activities created great enthusiasm on the school campus that spilled over into the town as well.

Enrollment Concerns

As fund raising was underway, the challenge of increasing enrollment was uppermost on the mind of the trustees and principal as they tried to balance the budget. Dormitory enrollment in 1952 was still low with only nine boys and nine girls, but boarding inquiries for 1953 were up. If the Academy were to improve its financial position the boarding enrollment must be increased.

By June of 1952, matters had changed. Rogers reported a total enrollment of 220, an increase of eight more students, but for a variety of reasons there were withdrawals during the school year. Testing scores of all classes that year were among the highest in school record—all well above average and some students with exceptionally high ratings.

Major Trustee Decisions

During the Board of Trustees meeting of June 7, 1952, the trustees made two major decisions to bring finances into line and to get the building program off to a good start.

From two finalists the firm that seemed a little stronger and more experienced was hired. Henry C. Newell and Howard A. Goodspeed of Concord would develop detailed plans for the general contract work, excavation, masonry, structural steel, plastering, carpentry, glassing, electrical work, heating and plumbing, and all other work to be completed on the new structure (*Specifications: Memorial Building for Brewster Free Academy, Inc., Wolfeboro, NH*, Newall–Goodspeed, Architects and Engineers, 20 Pleasant Street, Concord, NH).

Second, Trustee Kenison reported that the income from certain funds could be used "towards Vocational Education" because of a recent decision handed down by the Superior Court of the State of New Hampshire in the October Term of 1951, on Equity 2834. The Court reviewed the trust funds managed by Brewster Academy and concluded that the proposed allocation of the income from those funds could be used by the Academy to carry its plans forward.

The excitement over the campaign was briefly interrupted by a tradition that seems to infect most seniors at that time of year. As the warm spring breezes began to blow across campus during the school day in 1952, seniors suffered the usual case of Spring Fever. "Spring is that certain time of year when everything is blooming – everything, that is except the student's mind. That cranium which contains that so-called scholastic brain just seems to fill with everything but the initiative to study. This, of course, presents a problem for both the student and his teachers. His mind keeps telling him that he needs a rest, or at least shorter working hours, while on the other hand his teachers demand that he work even harder in order to keep his work at top grade" (*The Brewster Review,* April 1952, p. 2).

Senior carnival events to raise funds for the new Memorial Building were celebrated on the Brewster campus and were well received.

And spring exploded in another way. Students, teachers, administrators, trustees, coaches, athletes, alumni and even important businessmen at the local and national level were enlisted to get behind the drive to support the Academy's building and development program.

Massachusetts and all states other than New Hampshire were grouped under the leadership of Mrs. Adelaide Robinson Hughes,'26, of Braintree, MA. Twenty Massachusetts town chairpersons organized themselves into brigades of leaders who solicited alumni living there with a booklet titled, "The Minds of Our Children," which told the story of Brewster's needs and the development program planned to meet the needs. The target goal for everyone, Maine to California, was to raise $208,000 for urgently needed facilities. The target goal for Massachusetts was $10,000, but the entire "Brewster family" was urged to solidly get behind the effort.

Commencement and Alumni weekend was scheduled for June 6-8, 1952, only a short time away. Mrs. Lillian Osgood Brookes, president of the Alumni Association, had made arrangements to house visiting alums in the homes of local alums and in dormitory spaces.

The alumni banquet was held at the Masonic Hall and was open to everyone whether or not they had ever attended Brewster Academy, an obvious open invitation to anyone who was curious about the school plans or wanted a free meal! Among the speakers was Dean Charles C. Noble, the Dean of Hendricks Chapel, Syracuse University, who was well known to the Wolfeboro area. He announced that the intensified fund drive would begin that night, June 7th, and run through the month of July, though no solicitations would be made during the turkey dinner banquet. Mrs. Brookes called for help from alumni volunteers who could give a few hours to help in the Development Office during the next several weeks (*Brewster Review*, May 1952, pp. 2-4).

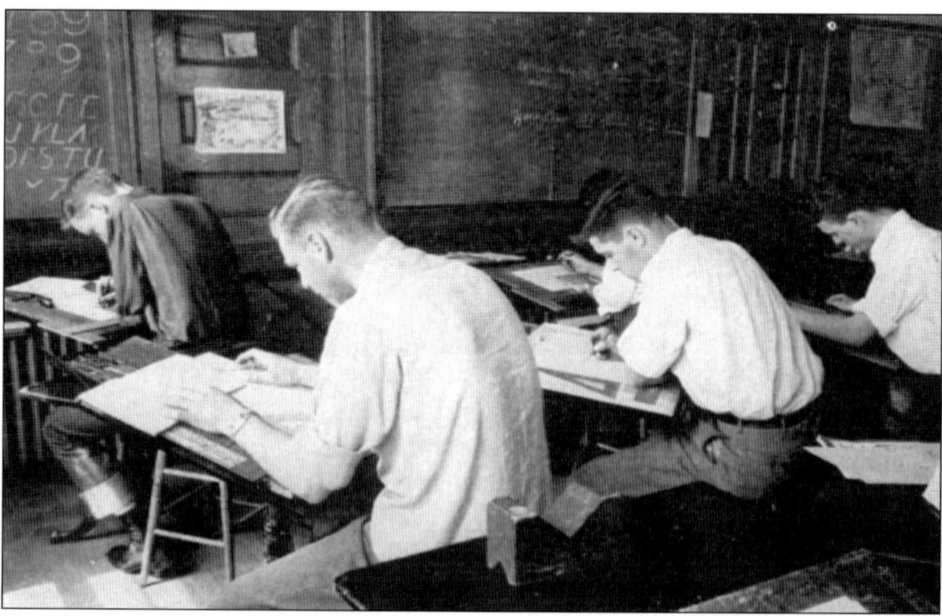

Students in class attempting to focus their attention on school work and avoid the spring fever epidemic.

Principal and Mrs. Rogers always had time to visit with students in Lord House.

Competition for the Fund Drive Continues Through the Winter

By December, two Brewster alumni classes were fighting for the lead in the race for the highest percentage of class members contributing to the fund: 1903 with an impressive 62% participation and 1907 with 60%. The December *Brewster Review* reported gifts and pledges totaled just over the $65,000, and Howard C. Avery, chairman of the drive, declared that the drive would continue until the total of $208,000 is reached" (*Brewster Review*, December 1952, p. 4).

The Boston Brewster Club, in February 1953, planned to celebrate their 60th anniversary (really their 57th) by inviting all former students to the club's annual spring reunion at the Commander Hotel in Cambridge for a record turnout on April 26th. The feature presentation would be the combined boys and girls glee clubs under the direction of Dean Burtis F. Vaughan, also the director of music at Brewster. In addition, an orchestra would provide music for dancing throughout the evening.

The freshmen, class of 1957, continued selling their 12" x 18" trays featuring a full-color view of the academic building and lakefront against a maroon background (*Brewster Review*, January-February 1953, p. 4).

Ground Breaking

On February 21, the Board of Trustees accepted the bid of the Weare Construction Company of Weare, NH, to construct the building for $255,873. On the wind-swept campus in early April in 1953, the groundbreaking ceremony for the Memorial Building (later renamed Rogers Gymnasium) took place on the hillside at the south side of the school. A photo taken at the event includes almost all of the trustees who had planned, organized and helped fund the first structure to be erected by the school since 1905.

The 1953 ground breaking for New Memorial Building with President of the Board, Arthur P. Gale, turning over the first shovel of dirt.

Arthur P. Gale, President of the Board of Trustees, pictured with shovel blade pressed into the solid soil by his left foot, carefully lifted off what was to be the first of many loads of dirt to be removed for an immense cellar hole. To his right was Vincent D. Rogers, the principal, who had made this new building not just a personal dream, but a matter of ultimate concern to the student body, alumni, faculty, town officials and other trustees. Construction would begin immediately and would take a predicted 200 working days to complete, but there would be delays caused by bad weather, late deliveries of building materials and the inconveniences of mechanical and electrical breakdowns that are sometimes not anticipated in such a large building project (*Brewster Review*, March-April 1953, pp. 1-4).

Construction Continues Through the Year 1953-54

The construction crews worked through the rain storms of early June when the clay-like consistency of the soil made it difficult at first for much digging, but the cellar hole gradually took form until suddenly the crews found the remains of the old Academy building which had burned in 1903. In the midst of the debris were found two of the original entrance pillars later to be incorporated in a campus landscaping project. As the old timbers, bricks and crumbled cement were gradually removed, the new walls were secure, and the construction continued with the erection of steel beams and roofing over the gym floor and stage. By the end of the 1954 school year—in time for graduation—the crews had completed their work.

The new Memorial Building was completed in 1954.

The construction of the new gymnasium offered the principal and trustees a clearer view of the future of the school. With its completion, athletics and physical education became immediate priorities. School spirit soared and within two years the school won the New England championship in basketball. Women's basketball was started, and soon they were on the road to many great victories.

Rink DeWitt, '54, Remembers These Years

Walter "Rink" DeWitt, '54, shared many memories of his years as a Brewster student during this time period. Rink was a student leader, member of the Glee Club, football letterman and a champion skier who had great respect for Mr. Rogers and his school. Completion of the gym led to a conflict between students and administration. Traditionally Commencement had been held outdoors, and the Class of 1954 embraced that tradition. The Academy wanted to hold the ceremonies indoors in their new gymnasium. DeWitt recalls:

> Rogers held high standards and expected you to live up to your own high standards. He was a no-nonsense guy, but had a sense of humor and enjoyed the funny side of life. He had a spring in his step, wore a camel hair topcoat with a fedora pork pie hat and drove a slightly used Lincoln convertible. When classes would change, he would stand in the doorway of his office, and say hello to those who acknowledged him first. Many walked by with heads down and eyes elsewhere. He was an authoritarian figure.
>
> As time came for graduation, "the administration", and Vincent D. Rogers, decided the class of 1954 would graduate from the new gymnasium. Oh, my, the Class of 1954 wasn't pleased with that news… we had no connection with that building…it wasn't ours… we wanted to graduate out front, like everybody else had done for so many years. Somehow, Ramona Stevens and I were chosen to 'plead our case in chains' before Mr. Rogers…in his office. We prepared well, and would have impressed the United States Supreme Court, but we didn't impress Mr. Rogers: we graduated from that gym. And now we can proudly say, we were the first class to graduate from Rogers Gymnasium." Ramona Stevens and I were voted 'Mr. and Miss Most Popular by our class… not the Brightest…not the Most Convincing…not the Most Likely to Succeed… Just Popular.'

Impact of New Building on Athletics, School Spirit, and Campus Life in the Late 1950's

Despite enrollment issues, the new building had tremendous impact on all areas of school life. The lessons learned in physical education classes, directed by new instructor Paul Whalen, engendered more self-pride and brought students into better physical condition.

The growth of music, dramatics and choral work seemed to explode. With a practice area, a new stage and space to support programs, BurtisVaughan and his assistant, George Hall, whose specialty was band and orchestra, were able to present musical productions that were of advanced quality. Large numbers of townspeople could comfortably attend their concerts.

Students in the vocational training program designed by John Nay, the director, worked with excellent equipment and presented their results at national conferences, winning many prizes. Boys learned how to use tools in an effective manner and to express their ideas. Art

"Rink" DeWitt and Monie Stevens, leaders of their class. "Rink" DeWitt would later serve for many years on the Board of Trustees.

students, under the direction of Rupert Brown, took their instruction with thought and diligence, participating in state competition and winning many awards.

The 1954 School Year and Expansion

With the increased enrollment of boarders from 18 to 51, the school was forced to rent space in nearby homes to accommodate new enrollees. In his *Principal's Report to the Board,* Rogers indicated that the expansion in day enrollment would continue. "With every living space occupied by boarding students, the graduation rates from Carpenter School increasing, the Board must be prepared for an increase in day enrollments, but we should also consider the further expansion in residential students."

The boarding enrollment increase had prompted the school to build a beautiful new addition to the south end of the Estabrook, a dining hall where all boarding students could be seated at one serving. It forced improvement in the science facilities, located in the basement of the school building; better equipment was installed to accommodate the new students.

A new roadway entrance to the Academy was designed east of Kimball House that helped to control the traffic around the entrance to the campus center, and the roadways in front of Lord House and the Estabrook were reserved for foot traffic.

But the increase enrollment although a positive measure, also placed a burden on faculty. Teachers were now required to teach a full academic program as well as to coach, supervise students who had free time during the day, and plan activities during the weekends.

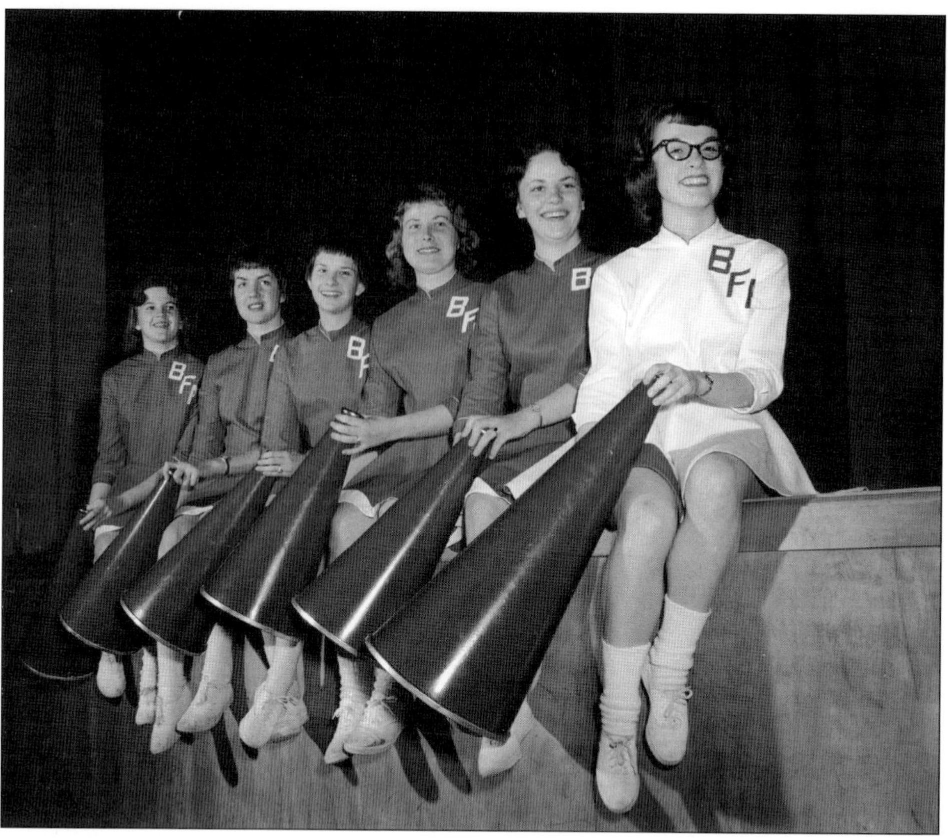

Cheerleaders played an important role in creating enthusiasm and spirit within the school community. M. Leavitt, C. Johnson, B. Fernald, M. Glidden, H. Jutras, and M. Reissfelder.

Problems of Increased Enrollment and Signal Flag of Things to Come

Although expanding the residential population was the goal of the trustees in order to balance the budget, the growth far exceeded dormitory space, and a waiting list was begun. In addition, the numbers of grammar school students at the Carpenter School preparing for their graduation to Brewster were alarming. By 1957, the housing situation for both faculty and residential students had reached a point where the Board needed to find additional space and focus on this growing issue.

In addition, although it was first time that a major construction project had been accomplished without the dependency on the earnings of John Brewster, the addition of the new building seemed to send a signal flag that there were other needs to come.

As the school was feeling comfortable with its academic programs, a shift in national events from the Korean War to the Cold War would not only have lasting national economic and social ramifications, but would force the administration to again review its curriculum in order to better serve its students.

With the launching of the first satellite by the Soviet Union, the United States reacted with the need for improved instruction in mathematics, chemistry, physics and basic sciences. Students were urged to take four years of high school science and mathematics and to seek at least a four-year college degree. Those not entering college were advised to enroll in a two-year technical school program. Advanced training beyond high school was becoming a "must," and schools everywhere urged students not to end their education before graduating from high school.

Brewster Academy must consider carefully how it was to prepare its students for this new challenge.

What Did John Brewster Intend?

With future enrollment increases expected and national educational forces at work, these concerns would demand every trustee, school administrator, faculty member, graduate, student and townsperson to look very closely into the very meaning of the Will of Founder John Brewster. Was Brewster Free Academy meant to be a school for the education of students, not only of Wolfeboro and Tuftonboro, but for all the neighboring towns: Wakefield, Osspiee, Brookfield, Alton, and Moultonboro? Should the school dissolve its boarding department entirely and focus on educating a full day school enrollment? Should the school dissolve its obligation to Founder John and continue to serve the needs of the towns under the supervision of the State of New Hampshire? These were difficult questions to be pondered by the Board of Trustees over the next few years; and as population increased, determining the answers would become crucial.

The Rogers Retirement

By June of 1958, having given careful consideration to his retirement, Rogers wrote to the Board of Trustees indicating that the school year of 1958-59 would be his final year of service to the Academy. He had accomplished his final goal, and the new Memorial Building was serving the school well. Understanding his decision and accepting his wishes, the Board began planning for a recognition celebration in his honor.

In 1959 after sixteen years as principal, Mr. and Mrs. Rogers retired to their Sanborn farm.

The Celebration

On the evening of May 23, 1959, the Memorial Gymnasium was the scene of much activity as over two hundred friends and supporters met to pay tribute to Vincent D. Rogers. Following a roast turkey dinner, many people addressed the gathered guests: Howard C. Avery, president of the Board of Trustees, Burtis F. Vaughan Jr., Principal-elect, James A. Wales, Jr., representing the Brewster parents and friends, and Kilburn Culley, '59, representing the Brewster student body. Congressman Chester E. Merrow was present and spoke in praise of Mr. Rogers, as did a telegram from Senator Styles Bridges.

Featured speaker was Hubert V. McDonough, principal of Manchester Central High School and longtime friend and associate of Mr. Rogers. Rogers had coached and taught for 16 years at Manchester High with "Hubie" McDonough.

The Master of Ceremonies, John Ballentine,'46, editor of the *Somersworth Free Press,* kept the evening moving at a good pace and climaxed the affair with the presentation to the Principal and Mrs. Rogers of a mantle clock with an inscribed plate, and a monetary gift. A lighter moment came with the presentation of "Pat," a frisky white goat, in reference to Principal Rogers' intention of retiring from the field of education to that of farming, but at least "Pat" would help with the lawn mowing.

An era had come to its conclusion; and after serving the Academy so well for sixteen years. Vincent Rogers was ready to resume his life as a gentleman farmer. As his daughter Dianne recalls in her reminiscences, "He once told me, when we were looking out at the Sanborn Hill fields, that 'There's a need in every man to stand on land that is his.' He was to fulfill this long-awaited wish for the next twenty years" (Dianne Rogers Quayle, May 12, 2008).

11. Burtis F. Vaughan Jr., 1959–1965: The Man Who Led the Charge

They may forget what you said but they will never forget how you made them feel.
—Anonymous

Burtis Vaughan Files for the Principalship

Following Vincent Rogers' decision to retire at the conclusion of the 1958-59 school year, the search committee, chaired by Mrs. Adelaide Hughes, began the process of reviewing applications and interviewing candidates for the position of principal. During the summer Burtis Fleming Vaughan Jr. filed his formal application with Mrs. Hughes, asking to be considered for the position.

The search committee reviewed the applications of over twenty candidates; four of the best qualified, including Mr. Vaughan, were personally interviewed by a majority of the Board of Trustees. The process was finally completed on March 7, 1959, with the selection of Mr. Vaughan as the seventh principal of the Academy, beginning July 1. Early that summer, Mr. Vaughan and his family, Virginia, Janna, JoAnne, and David left Sanborn House and moved across campus to Lord House, the official residence of the school's leader (*Minutes of the Brewster* Academy *Board of Trustees,* July 1958).

Principal Burtis Vaughan, the seventh principal of the Academy with his wife Virginia, and children Janna, JoAnne, and David in Lord House.

Mr. Vaughan's Arrival on Campus in 1939

Upon completing his bachelor's and master's degrees from Columbia University, Burtis Vaughan came to Brewster in 1939, traveling by railroad from New York to The Weirs in Laconia, and then by steamboat to Wolfeboro, arriving at the town docks. He had interviewed with Principal Greenall for a position in Latin, English or French and was accepted as a teacher, living in Kimball House. With the exception of two years' service with the U.S. Navy as Lieutenant (jg) in the Joint Intelligence Center, Pacific Ocean Area, Vaughan served as teacher for nineteen years and was dean of the Academy for the last ten of those years. He had coached junior varsity and varsity teams in football, baseball and soccer, where he carried off two New Hampshire State Prep School Championships. He directed the Academy glee clubs and bands that were a significant addition to the extra-curricular program on campus for many years (*Brewster Review,* March 1959, pp.1, 3).

Through a mutual devotion and an appreciation of music, a partnership bloomed between Mr. Vaughan and English teacher Virginia Paige Whiting. In December 1952, Virginia, a gracious and gentle woman of Yankee frugality and dry wit who also fulfilled the roles of teacher, concert pianist, library devotee, mother, and congenial hostess, married Burt Vaughan. The Vaughans, with daughters Janna, '62, and JoAnne,'65, and son David, lived in Sanborn House, now Richardson House, bringing meaning and accomplishment to the Brewster community for many years before Burt became principal in 1959 *(Brewster Review*, June 1988, p.6).

Students Remember Burt Vaughan as Teacher and Coach

Stories abound about Burt Vaughan as a teacher and coach. His Latin and English classes were attentive and demanding and his approach was objective. If a student were having difficulty in perceiving a major concept, Vaughan would never chastise, but would bring clarification—"What you say is good, but you need to elaborate a little more; what is the author's main point?" And as a coach, he would never criticize a player for what he had done, but always pointed out exactly what the player should have done and why. In this way, he was able to get the most from each student/player, and it seemed that he was ever present for extra help for students.

Dan Ford, '50, remembers, "Due to Mr. Vaughan's amazing ability to get his students engrossed in the subject, I recall becoming completely immersed in first year Latin as we studied Caesar's Gallic Wars. ("Having done this, Caesar…") This was true of his English class as well when we studied Homer's *Odyssey* ("When Dawn the rosy-fingered…"). Teachers at Brewster seemed less interested in the process and more interested in the students and the subject matter" (Dan Ford Mongraph, 2005).

But Vaughan had an incredible influence on those who had difficulty in classes. Allan Bailey, '60, spoke openly of his respect for Mr. Vaughan and how his academic career changed with having him as his teacher. "Alan, you are starting off the same as you have for the last two years, and I am not going to let that happen. You are going to study hall every night and get your work done! Mr. Vaughan was a gentle giant, and his strength was Latin and coaching soccer. I just didn't fit in until my junior year, and Bert was the one who brought me into reality. He was the greatest thing since sliced bread" (Bailey Interview 2008).

Donald "Chip" Brookes, '65, declared, "Burtis Vaughan was the best teacher I ever had anywhere, anytime, anyplace. He loved his subject and his heart and soul was teaching. He would ask questions, rapid fire, pointing to you, but if you asked a question, he stayed with you until you got it, ignoring his lesson plans for the day. He had a passion for his subject and his students, and you can't teach that, it's just in you. He walked in the door and the car was in gear. You were ready to go!" (Brookes Tape, 2008).

Burt Vaughan's Durability

The daily chores of schooling challenge any teacher, but Vaughan had a durability that was heat-treated, and his overwhelming teaching load would have humbled most aspirants. He was always present where students were, and always offered extra help. His class preparation and paper–grading, coupled with long hours coaching and dorm supervision, then the limitless practice sessions with glee clubs, church choirs and organ practice at the church never seemed to deteriorate his enthusiasm. He had the endurance that he expected everyone to have when it came to schoolwork. It was natural that Rogers would look to Burtis Vaughan to be Dean of the Academy in 1949 and be in charge of the guidance program. Vaughan was used to hard work and had followed Rogers' leadership, but he was much the academician. With a keen eye toward the future and foreseeing a growth in student attendance at boarding schools, Vaughan saw a need to improve academic standards, make courses more demanding, strengthen student outcomes, and expand the curriculum to better prepare students for college. His immediate goal was to "make Brewster an effective instrument in the education of our young people for the complex world of today" *(Principal's Report,* October 7, 1959, p.1).

Vaughan's First Year as Principal

On opening day in 1959, 276 students arrived, 76 of whom were residential students. There were six new teachers—one to replace the chalk throwing, Mr. Herbert Tinker, who had retired after twenty five years teaching math at Brewster, and one to replace a commercial teacher who had moved to Massachusetts. The other four new instructors would assist in English, Latin, and math courses, but also take classes during the new activities period. This new core of teachers would soon become part of an eight period daily class schedule instituted by Mr. Vaughan, a schedule that had never been tried before at Brewster. Even as

June Tilton, a talented, well-regarded English teacher.

new faculty members were getting settled into their teaching assignments, during a special ceremony in the chapel, Mr. Vaughan honored Herbert Tinker for his years of service to the school. The student body and faculty presented him with a set of golf clubs. Later that day, at a formal reception at Lord House, the Director of Athletics, Paul "Pop" Whalen, gave Mr. Tinker a new golf bag and putter to round out the collection *(Annual Report to the Trustees,* June 6, 1960, p.1).

Vaughan's new plan for the school day was organized with eight periods; seven periods of classes and one for lunch. However, he designated that one of the seven would be an "enlightenment" period, and would include everyone. The "activities" period, as he later called it, would cover a broad selection of courses and would attract excellent enrollment—Band (23 students), Glee Club (101students), Typing (51 students), and a number of students in music appreciation, debate, public speaking, a shop club, a radio club, a coin club, journalism and a driver training class, (two sessions yearly).

Mr. George Hall assumed the leadership of the music program after Burt Vaughan became principal and successfully continued the well-established music tradition at Brewster. Two new upper-level math courses were introduced—Analytical Geometry and Calculus—taught by V. David Rogers '51, the son of Principal Rogers. In addition, national testing of all students took a priority. All 9th and 10th graders were required to take the National Educational Development Test, while 11th graders took the Merit Scholarship Test. All seniors took the College Board Scholastic Aptitude Test and achievement tests as required by their college selections. And these were all given at Brewster, scheduled throughout the school year. But Vaughan did more. He petitioned the National Honor Society to institute a chapter at Brewster, and the school was granted the right to recommend students each year for membership.

Not only did Mr. Vaughan overhaul the academic day, but also when residential students returned to school in the fall, they were happy to see many changes in Brown Hall and the Estabrook. Vaughan had Brown Hall completely refurbished. Every nook and cranny had been cleaned, painted and decorated. The Estabrook would not be recognized at first glance. A new four-bed infirmary was built on the second floor and Mrs. Audra Piper, RN, was engaged to be the school nurse with regular hours. Dr. Harold Gregory was the school doctor and would be called when serious cases arrived. The Estabrook kitchen was enlarged and the two lounge areas on either side of the entrance door were redecorated with new wallpaper and paint and sported new magazine racks with four popular periodical

George Hall, a talented musician, directed the many very successful music programs after Burt Vaughan became headmaster. The Brewster band, part of the orchestra, brought music and spirit to the Friday night pep rallies.

David Rogers, '51, teacher, coach and dean of students.

selections on display. In one lounge, Vaughan had a new television set installed.

To encourage better communication between the faculty and administration, Vaughan held planning sessions for the faculty before opening day and frequent meetings throughout the year at Lord House.

A new tradition of inviting boarding students to special dinners with Mr. and Mrs. Vaughan at Lord House was begun, and in an attempt to continue his efforts to establish a more home-like atmosphere for these students, he asked dormitory faculty to invite residential students into their home for a Christmas party before vacation time. During the winter of 1960, Vaughan initiated a snow sculpture competition between dorms and the results of student ingenuity and creativity were amazing. The sculptures, which were larger than life, caught the attention of out-of-state tourists driving through town who would stop on Main Street, jump out and take snap shots. The sculpting competition was so competitive that Vaughan decided to award the winning dorm or group with a snow sculpture trophy that went on display in a new cabinet located in the main hallway opposite the front door of the school building (*Midyear Report to the Trustees*, March 1, 1960, p. 3).

Success in sports competition throughout the year was good. Varsity football, under the able direction of Coach Ed Murphy, played a schedule that included mostly college freshmen teams, and, although they had a 1-7 season, spirit and enthusiasm were high. Varsity soccer, hockey and baseball all won Lakes Region Championships, while the varsity and JV basketball had winning seasons of 10-6, and 6-5.

Principal and Mrs. Vaughan would often entertain students in Lord House for dinner.

Annual Report to Trustees

In his *Annual Report to the Trustees* for 1960, Vaughan posed a warning: "The large expected eighth grade enrollments pose a problem for next year, for after careful count I have estimated that between 315 and 325 students will be enrolled on opening day next fall. We are being taxed to our capacity and our pride and talking point of having small classes for individual attention may make it mandatory to engage one or two more teachers on part-time to help keep the small classes" (*Annual Report,* June 6, 1960, p. 1).

That statement by Burtis Vaughan was the beginning of a long five-year series of events that would lead to the organization and cooperative partnership of several nearby towns to provide adequate programs and facilities for their children. It would also bring the Trustees of Brewster Academy to define their school with more institutional clarity. A second request in his annual message to the Board of Trustee was to bring attention to the school's admissions system:

> I should like the trustees to consider the establishment of a new office at the Academy, namely a Director of Admissions. This person would be a teacher at the Academy, would work with the principal, but who would have charge of the details and procedures of the admissions process. If the school were to succeed in drawing students from lands afar from Wolfeboro, it would be immediately important to have someone assist the principal in the daunting tasks ahead (*Annual Report to the Trustees,* June 1960, p. 3).

Although the Board did not take action on this request for a formal director of admissions, Paul Whalen was successful in attracting athletes from the Boston area to supplement the boarding enrollment numbers.

While the majority of faculty spent the summer months gaining new ideas in teaching methodology at graduate schools like Middlebury, Boston University, Plymouth and UNH, Burt was busy revising the room structure of the Estabrook in order to provide more space for additional dorm students. At the same time, expansion took place in the dining hall kitchen in order to serve over 100 people at both lunch and dinner.

The Enrollment Explosion Begins

The enrollment picture for 1960 was bright. On opening day, a whopping 332 students, including 88 dorm students, arrived. This included 92 freshmen, 65 sophomores, 70 juniors and 102 seniors, plus 3 post graduate students from Wolfeboro. This impressive picture was 55 over 1959, and brought the average class size from fifteen, to 25 and 30. This caused Vaughan to wonder if the school should plan for a cutback in the large number of students enrolled from towns other than Wolfeboro and Tuftonboro. His master plan was to keep class sizes in the college preparatory subjects to fifteen so that teachers could give more individual attention to students, and at the same time keep up with the curricular demands expected at the college level. Vaughan commented to the Board:

> It will be remembered that Brewster ranked first in the State in 1959 in sending the greatest number of graduates on to college. From the Class of 1960, it will be seen that perhaps we shall be on top again, for 76% of the class has gone on to post secondary study. We have been indeed fortunate to place three junior students in the upper 3% of the country in the National Merit Scholarship tests. Of these, one is a semi-finalist, ranking 7th in the State (*Principal's Report to the Board,* November 1, 1960, p. 2).

Even with crowded conditions, student achievement was impressive.

The athletic teams still continued to be an important part of the life of the school and were urged on by a new Friday night activity—the pep-rallies, held in front of the Academy Building. A line of eight peppy cheerleaders, accompanied by Mr. George Hall's Brewster Band, led the student body in school cheers to energize the football and soccer teams. These teams won the Lakes Region Prep School titles and were awarded their championship jackets along with a testimonial dinner by the Rotary Club.

Both basketball and hockey teams lost their bid for the Lakes Region championships to Tilton, but basketball went on to the New England Prep School tournament in March.

A Christmas Dance, decorated in the holiday theme held in Chapel Hall.

The ski team, composed mostly of freshmen and sophomores, was one of the best in recent years. Five of the boys were able to enter the New England Prep School races at Middlebury (*Brewster Review*, Fall 1960, pp.1-3). Along with the sporting events, music, plays, and dances were very much a part of the social life on campus, and the traditional Christmas dance was always well attended.

Brewster football was superb because many of the boys were postgraduates and talented enough to play against college freshmen teams as well as the regular Lakes Region teams. Unfortunately, because of the number of postgraduate players on the team, Tilton dropped Brewster in football and Holderness refused to play Brewster in all sports. Vaughan did his best to address the problem at the annual Headmaster's meeting that did soften the hard feelings, and soon reconciliation took place.

As the regular winter sports season closed, and the season changed from snow to mud, the school concentrated on a new intramural basketball program for boys. The major focus was to keep athletic interest high and to keep students active as everyone waited for the snow to melt and the fields to drain and dry out (*Midyear Report to the Trustees,* February 23, 1961, p.1).

Deepening Enrollment Issues

At this point, Vaughan saw a deepening problem with future enrollment prospects. His mission had been to develop a school along the lines of a traditional New England Academy, where an educational program was directed toward preparing students for college admissions. Class sizes were usually held to about fifteen which permitted close attention between teacher and student.

In the spring of 1961, Vaughan completed a survey on enrollment of both residential and day students for the years 1961 to 1965. He noticed there was a sudden change taking place. Vaughan had been approached by the superintendents of Ossipee, Moultonboro, Wakefield and Sanbornville, inquiring if Brewster could take their day students beginning in 1961, and Alton requested that Brewster take 80 students if the very small Alton High school were to close. (It would not close.) There was no public high school in Wolfeboro at the time, so students graduating from the Carpenter School had to go to Brewster, Rochester, or Kennett in Conway. From the numbers, he calculated that to keep class sizes to the "15" he wanted, the school would have to drop its entire boarding component and become entirely a day school, and he did not like that idea.

He wrote, "If Brewster Academy increases its enrollment to the point that it serves as a regional high school for this area, we may as well drop our dormitory plans, as our admissions talking point is small classes and individual attention. The problems connected with the regional school are many. Discipline, increase of facilities for a more expansive program to take care of a comprehensive curriculum are, I feel, too much to hope to do… Brewster Academy has been and is unique in its campus, its facilities and its standing. The principal feels that it should be kept this way" (*Report of the Principal on the Future Enrollments at Brewster Academy,* May 8, 1961, pp. 1-2).

A short time later, a meeting of the local trustees and Principal Vaughan was called to consider the expanding enrollment patterns. It was decided that "effective in September 1961 to accept no more freshmen from the towns of Moultonboro, Wakefield, and Sanbornville. Only those students from Wolfeboro and Tuftonboro will become members of the freshman class" *(Report of the Principal,* May 12, 1961, p. 2). But it is evident that there were problems with this and, as cooler heads prevailed, a change took place. Mr. Vaughan proposed to the full Board that keeping with the wishes of John Brewster, "in the years to come we hold entrance examinations for day students outside the Wolfeboro-Tuftonboro area so that all towns may have an equal opportunity to send students to the Academy" (*Annual Report of the Principal.* 1960-1961, p.1).

The Transition Begins

But there was a greater problem threatening the core of Brewster Academy that immediately brought concern to trustee Chairman Howard C. Avery. Principal Vaughan and some trustees met with the Superintendent of Schools and the Wolfeboro School Board to discuss the issue of over-crowding at both Brewster and the Carpenter School and the expansion of classrooms and related facilities.

Mr. Avery pointed out apprehensions in a letter to John Carr, Brewster Estate Trustee: "The consensus of the meeting seems to be that an added building or buildings will be needed to take care of junior high students, or the full four year high school grades, either with a local building providing for Wolfeboro students possibly with day students from surrounding towns, or a school built on a cooperative basis with towns in the area. The second alternative, which, I believe, the Board of Trustees and administrator of the school do not want, is for Brewster to expand and become another large central high school and lose the "private school" benefits of small classes and high standards necessary to prepare students for entrance into colleges and other institutions of higher learning."

The issues that Chairman Avery and the Board felt they needed to address with the Brewster Estate Trustees, were complex. First, if Wolfeboro built its own high school and the Academy reverted to its original status as a "private" school without state regulation or state accreditation, would any income from the Brewster Estate be affected and if so, in what way and for what reason? Next, if the Academy enrolled only boarding students and day students, whether or not Wolfeboro or any other town paid tuition, what would be the impact? And finally, if the Academy limited its curriculum to strictly college preparatory,

The Board of Trustee Executive Committee: Principal Vaughan, Mr. Howard Avery, Mrs. Adelaide Hughes, Colonel Hugh Wilkin, Dr. Harold Gregory.

what would occur in regard to funds from the Trust and just what obligation did Brewster have to provide secondary education to students from Tuftonboro, beyond that which is stated in the Will *(Avery, pp. 1-2).*

The Carr Report

John P. Carr focused his response directly on the two articles of the Will of John Brewster that were of concern. First, there was the question of annuity payments to the school from the estate:

> An annuity payment of $10,000 which was not subject to the discretion of the Estate Trustees in any way as to time and amount, nor the right of the school to receive from the "divisible income" such monies would not be affected. It might have some bearing, or effect on the exercise by the Trustees (estate) of their discretion as to how much of this money might be paid to Brewster Academy in any one particular year. It has been the practice of the Trustees ...to pay the entire share of the "divisible income" to the Academy...after the amount of the money has been determined, usually at such time as request has been made by the Academy.
>
> It is my opinion that Brewster Academy has no obligation to provide secondary education to students from Wolfeboro and Tuftonboro by reason of the fact that such students come from Wolfeboro and Tuftonboro. I presume that the language in your question, "beyond that which is stated in the Will and applies to any student," you refer to the language of the Will which is one of the conditions of the gift which is stated in the Will, "so as near as possible to make instruction and education therein (in the Academy) free."
>
> No restriction has been placed upon any person desiring to attend the school by reason of his or her age, sex or color"; and the program mentioned in your letter contemplates the imposition of no such restrictions. The rest of the condition is that the money, "be expended wholly for the salaries of teachers, for instruction and educational purposes of said school or Academy, so nearly as possible to make instruction and education therein free"...."The very language of the Will indicates clearly that it is contemplated and understood by the Trustees (estate) that the education furnished cannot be totally and entirely free of cost to the student.... Or, in other words, the bounty of the trust is not intended to relieve the taxpayer's burdens but rather to enhance and enrich the benefits to the students.

In response to the curriculum question, Mr. Carr stated, "Nowhere in the Will is there anything at all which says how the school shall be run; what its curriculum shall be; and what its objective from an educational standpoint shall be" (Carr, pp.1-4).

The letter must have been a relief to both school trustees and Vaughan for it added some strength to their plan to retain the ideals of the Academy in the face of becoming a "central high school." The issue was discussed at the next Board of Trustees meeting on April 7› and the text of Carr's letter was thoroughly reviewed. It was the consensus that the Trustees "should draft a resolution to help clarify the Academy viewpoint in order to give the public school committee a direction to follow in their future meetings."

The resolution stated: "From information available at this time it is the consensus of the Trustees that Brewster Academy revert to its former status as a private Academy not later than the fall of 1965. However, the Trustees invite the towns, school boards or any other interested groups to present any other plan as an alternative solution to the problem" *(Board of Trustees Minutes,* April 7, 1962, p. 1).

Brewster Caught in the Crossfire

At the next Board meeting on June 15th, Vaughan realized that considerable preparation must be undertaken in the area of admissions should the town school board plan to build a new public high school. He knew that far more effort would have to be given to increasing the boarding student population.

"It would be my hope that the trustees would appoint committees to study the costs and design of a new dormitory to house between 30 and 40 newly enrolled boys. We would certainly need to have 125 boys on campus by the fall of 1965 at $2000 each to start with a budget of $250,000." Vaughan went on to describe his summer plans to visit educational consultants in Boston and New York to attract more four-year students"(*Annual Report to the Trustees*, June 5, 1962, p. 5).

The State of New Hampshire required that the new state standards would go in to effect in the fall of 1963. Thus several neighboring towns had enlisted study committees to present plans that would provide their students with adequate programs and facilities that would fulfill the state standard**s,** but none were acceptable to the state. The immediate problem was the overcrowding at Brewster Academy and the Carpenter School, and it would not be easy to solve the problem in such a short time. Brewster was attempting to provide an educational program to 350 students in a plant designed to accommodate fewer than 250 students. The Carpenter School was excessively overcrowded and wanted to combine with Brewster to create a new comprehensive high school, a partnership that now seemed impossible since the Academy Trustees voted "to revert to its former status as a private Academy not later than the fall of 1965, with emphasis to be placed on the training of students for college entrance." It did welcome any other plan as an alternative solution to the problem.

The town of Wolfeboro would have to make arrangements for the secondary education of its youngsters by other means. A comprehensive high school would be needed that would provide, first, a general education for all; second, provide good elective courses for those who wished to use their acquired skills immediately on graduation; and third, provide a satisfactory program for those whose vocations would depend on their subsequent education in a college or university. According to authorities, that school should be of sufficient size to provide for a minimum of 100 in a graduating class.

It was financially impossible for Wolfeboro, Tuftonboro, New Durham, Brookfield, Ossipee, and Sandwich to join the venture, each for different reasons. Sandwich declined when it faced the problem of distance, and Brookfield declined for financial reasons, but was willing to send students on a tuition basis. Alton decided to build a new high school and Wakefield a new elementary school. But the study team clearly saw the need for founding a cooperative district, which would include a public school system for grades one through twelve. As such, Kingswood Regional High School was the result of the very long deliberations (McDermott, p. 1)

The Brewster Transition

Along with the Board of Trustees, Vaughan took charge of the situation at Brewster by organizing a new Transition Committee composed of: the principal, Dean Rupert Brown, Trustees Mrs. Hughes, Mr. Avery, and Dr. Harold Gregory, and Mr. George Goodwin, representing the dormitory faculty. It was determined that an administrative assistant be hired to work with the principal on facilities, foundation bequests, and all other matters pertaining to the problem of maintaining Brewster in its private status.

It was also voted to engage an architect or campus planner to examine the campus to make recommendations for a long-range building and layout situation, as surely a new dormitory would soon be necessary. Vaughan was deeply concerned that the dorm postgraduate enrollment had to be replaced with younger students, the majority of whom should be 9th and 10th graders. It had been previously decided that no student who had a diploma from another school could engage in interscholastic sports other than being a manager of a team, or helper in the athletic department. The dropping of the PG program as such would permit Brewster to return to the Lakes Region Preparatory School League. But the committee recommended that Principal Vaughan should also be the director of admissions, and should, with the assistance of the dean, have charge of talking with educational consultants and headmasters of the Lakes Region League who might be helpful in resolving problems connected with enrolling younger students. It was agreed that the enrollment of younger students should begin with the fall of 1963, a task with which Vaughan was to struggle for the next several years (*Transition Committee Minutes*, July 26, 1962, p.1).

Vaughan traveled extensively during 1963 to recruit private students. Many of the interviews were discouraging for various reasons. First, Brewster had no recent record as an exclusive private facility. Second, library facilities were inadequate in comparison to most New England preparatory schools. Third, the transition itself was reason for the lack of interest in the school as few outside students wanted to be part of what was perceived by many as an experiment *(Bowers,* Vol. 2, p. 297).

But there were some redeeming factors: the Academy building was beautifully constructed, the campus buildings were well cared for and orderly, the magnificent views of the lake and mountains were certainly attractive, and the proximity to a bustling downtown gave students a chance to join in Wolfeboro life. The headmasters of other independent schools in New England were supportive in believing that Brewster had great potential to move forward, after experiencing a few lean years, and be successful.

A "New"Recreational Hall

In the meantime, there was a movement underway by students, teachers, and parents to seek a place for a recreational room, a place where students could congregate after school and on weekends. The old boathouse building, situated behind Kimball House, was used only for storage. (Principal Lord brought this icehouse (boathouse) from the lake onto the upper campus, when the school building burned in 1903, and it was used for a chemistry lab. It has been since moved to the east side of Academy Drive and converted for art classes). It was quickly decided that it would be a perfect location for a recreation hall, and everyone helped to clean out the old junk. New linoleum was installed on the floor, and Mr. John Nay and his woodcraft boys replaced the windows and pine paneled the entire room. Parents, trustees and students contributed to the purchase of a ping-pong table, a pool table, TV set and a radio. The principal then made arrangements to have soft drink and candy-cracker machines installed. A faculty-student committee set up rules and regulations for administering the facility. It was a wonderful solution to give students a place to go during off hours (*Midyear Report to the Trustees*, February 23, 1961, p. 1).

To add to school spirit, the winter snow sculpture contest for the Winter Carnival was in full force and won by Furber House dormitory students for their work on a large statue that included the original four Mt. Rushmore Presidents, and added the face of John F. Kennedy as a fifth. Estabrook won second prize and Haines third (*Brewster Review*, Spring 1961, p. 1).

Furber House's unique first prize snow sculpture, Mt Rushmore, with the addition of President Kennedy.

Proceeding through the Transition

The trustees were eager for professional assistance in gathering advice on how to proceed through the transition period. Dr. Gordon O. Thayer, the headmaster of Thayer Academy in Braintree, MA, a friend of Mrs. Adelaide Hughes, and one who had spent some summers in nearby Brookfield, reviewed the plan of the school's academic, athletic and administrative structure from top to bottom. He emphasized the importance of an education committee that would work closely with the principal and report directly to the trustees. The committee would study the curriculum and be in charge of hiring and firing. The principal would work through and with the education committee, who would take matters directly to the Board. Thayer's presentation was detailed and thorough.

The Herbert E. Sargent Hall

But there were immediate matters to be attended before the transition could be completed. Vaughan was very concerned about the construction of a new dormitory to house the additional residential students for the 1964-65 school year. The Board had been receptive to the idea, but time was passing and Vaughan's enrollment figures called for an additional 50 boarding students. On March 7, 1964, the trustees voted "to take all necessary steps to build a dormitory in the general vicinity of $207, 000 plus $10, 500 for furniture, to arrange for financing of it, and to have it be available and ready for occupancy by September 1, 1965." As the early summer drew on, it became obvious that the cost of the new structure was too great to achieve in such a short time. At the next meeting on June

The ground breaking ceremony for Sargent Hall: Board President Howard Avery, Dr. Lawrence Tee, Mr. Edward Zulauf, Mr. Roland Hughes, Mrs. Adelaide Hughes, and Dr. Harold Gregory under the watchful attendance of the student body.

15, it was voted to accommodate only 40 boys by reducing the size of the structure and the total cost to $175,000.

Immediately, Trustee Hughes passed out pledge cards to the trustees and turned in her own pledge of $5,000 for the new building. The new dorm would be located east and south of Brown Hall. The roof was to be flat in case another floor should be needed later. A fund raising project was organized to develop a new library as well as the dormitory. The project would follow the lines used in raising money for Roger's Memorial Hall, but with an alumni secretary who would set up a class agent system to contact alumni. All of this would be under the direction of Mrs. Hughes. It was also voted that a Special Gifts Committee be organized under the direction of Trustee Gregory. The class of 1964 had voted to leave the school $75.00 to start a Class of 1964 Alumni Fund and donated $500 to the school for a new library and dormitory. Trustee Justin Tibbetts contributed $10,000 toward the new dormitory.

Finally, Sargent Hall was completed and ready to serve the campus as a boys dormitory and faculty housing. Over the years there would be changes and additions to the building, but on October 2, 1965, it was dedicated in honor of the longest standing mathematics and science teacher, Herbert E. Sargent.

Letter of Resignation

In the late hours of June 13, 1964, as the meeting was drawing to a close, Burtis Vaughan read a letter to the Board of Trustees, resigning as principal of the Academy effective on July 1, 1965. Several trustees asked him to reconsider and change his mind, but he could not. Trustee Hughes made a motion that we accept Mr. Vaughan's resignation with deep regret as of July 1, 1965. Trustee Kenison moved that the president appoint a selection committee of three trustees to recommend to the Board a successor to the principal. Trustee Merrow made a motion, "that accompanying the letter, which was going to the press, should be included a statement from the trustees that elaborated their appreciation of the devotion and untiring service that Mr. Vaughan had given for a quarter of a century during his years at the Academy." The motion passed unanimously (*Minutes of the Annual Meeting Board of*

Sargent Hall completed and dedicated in 1965.

Trustees of the Brewster Academy, June 13, 1964, p. 2).

But this was not the closing stage of his career at Brewster. Burt saw that he had one more year to bring the school into a position of stabilization. He wanted to increase the enrollment of the lower grades, complete the new dormitory, fashion a college preparatory curriculum, which was more intense, and limit the number of post-graduate students. Concurrently, Vaughan was faced with tuition increases at the same time when Brewster was competing with other independent schools whose tuitions were also rising. The tuition ratio between boarding and day students was about five to one. The boarding tuition for '65 was $2200, and day was $420, both well below the national average for independent schools. Soon, he realized that he could not realistically drop the post-graduate program, but would still broaden the search for younger students. The increased enrollment of boarding students would be absolutely necessary for 1965-1966.

Vaughan's Last Year at Brewster

The enrollment for 1963-1964 was the highest ever at 366. There were 99 juniors, 78 sophomores, and 80 freshmen, and the largest senior class ever at 108, but this would be the high mark for many years. While keeping a sharp eye on the daily admission inquiries during the winter and spring of 1965, Vaughan, as he anticipated, saw that the enrollment picture was being impacted by the transition. The total enrollment for 1964-1965 was 132 total, with 96 dorm students and only 36 day students. There were 9 freshmen, 25 sophomores, 29 juniors, and 54 seniors, but 25 students were lost, and ten new students took their places during the year (*Annual Report to the Trustees,* May 19, 1965, p.1). While Mr. Vaughan had little enthusiasm for the post-graduate student, he did understand that they did, in fact, need an extra school year to prepare for college. He had stated that it might be necessary for the school to carefully screen them before admission, but he saw that as a decision the new principal would have to make.

When Burtis Vaughan announced his decision to retire as of July 1, 1965, the Board of Trustees appointed a candidate search committee and began accepting applications. By the end of the summer, the committee developed a list to of candidates and made contacts for interviews. On September 12, 1964, the committee arranged for Mr. and Mrs. Wilfred E. Paro of Berwick Academy to join the Board meeting to answer questions and for Mr. Paro to discuss his ideas about how to proceed at this point in Brewster's future.

After a long question and answer session, the Board announced, "Mr. Paro was to be the next 'headmaster' of the newly designed Brewster Academy" (*Minutes of the Brewster Trustees Meeting,* September 12, 1964, p. 3).

Vaughan Leaves

In July 1965, the Vaughans moved to Hampton, New Hampshire, where Burt was Chairman of the Foreign Language Department at Winnacunnet High School and, not surprisingly, head soccer coach, and Virginia was head librarian of the Hampton School System. Their service to the Congregational Church in Wolfeboro—Burt as organist and choir director and Virginia as choir member—carried over to the Congregational Church in Hampton. Both became involved volunteers at the local hospital.

Vaughan Honored with Excellence in Teaching Award

Much more can be said about Burt and Virginia Vaughan, but one thing that seems to say it all is that in a poll of three thousand Brewster alumni Mr. Vaughan was the overwhelming choice as their most popular teacher. Burtis Vaughan was the first teacher to be honored with the newly established "Excellence in Teaching" award in 1985.

It was in his honor and in honor and memory of his wife, Virginia, who had passed away in 1985, that Brewster Academy dedicated Vaughan House. It was done with admiration and appreciation shared by all those whose lives and hearts were touched by the Vaughans.

The Vaughan Legacy

Burtis Vaughan was truly an exceptional man who led the Academy through the tumultuous times of transition. The old adage of "do the times make the man or does the man make the times" was so apparent in the life of Brewster under the leadership of Principal Vaughan during the early 60s. Burt Vaughan understood better than anyone that change was necessary for the ultimate survival of the school and the future education of its young people no matter how difficult that change was for the students and townsfolk to acknowledge and recognize.

As he accepted the mantle of daily leadership of school life, he realized very quickly that revolution was required in order to fulfill the very different needs of its students. The school in its present format was unable to serve all of its constituents. Appropriate and acceptable education could not be delivered to the student body due to overcrowded conditions and educational needs. Space requirements and facilities were inadequate and the conflict of offering a curriculum that would prepare college-bound students as well as students whose education would terminate with a high school diploma could no longer co-exist. Additional funds, curriculum, and facilities had to be acquired and this he believed could not have happened under the present conditions. A new regional high school was the answer, he believed.

With a heavy heart but also with the understanding that the very survival of Brewster Academy was at stake, Burtis Vaughan determined that to continue John Brewster's vision and commitment the school would have to assume a new direction. This Burtis Vaughan delivered. He led the charge up the mountain to a new beginning. It was one of the most difficult challenges of his career, and it was met with great obstacles along the way. But the only way he was able to achieve this new direction, which he knew to be absolutely necessary, was by keeping his eye on the ultimate goal, and for this Brewster will be forever indebted to him (*Brewster Review,* 1985).

Burt passed away on September 3, 1998.

12. Wilfred E. Paro, 1965–1969: The First "Headmaster"

If you wish to know the mind of a man, listen to his words.—Chinese Proverb

Wilfred Paro the Man

Wilfred Paro had been selected by the Board of Trustees to be the next principal of Brewster during the fall of 1964 and would take the office as of July 1, 1965. He would assume the title of headmaster, which seemed to befit the position because the school was again recognized as a private institution. Wil would be the first leader of the Academy under the new designation and re-organization. Where Burtis Vaughan had brought the school through the initial stages of developing and instituting a college preparatory curriculum, organizing the construction of dorm facilities, enlarging dining areas, hiring a teaching staff that was of higher grade than before, and bringing the school through its transition period, it would fall upon Wilfred Paro to bring the spirit and traditions of the independent school to Brewster. During his tenure, Wil was not only headmaster but was also for all practical purposes the chief admissions officer, the dean of students, and the staunchest supporter of the Academy's athletic teams.

Headmaster Wilfred Paro, and Mrs. Betty Paro.

Wilfred Paro was born in Adams, Massachusetts, and attended Deerfield Academy where he was a student under the supervision of Dr. Frank Boyden, the legendary headmaster, whose guiding hand directed Wil toward Arnold College in New Haven, Connecticut, from which he received his bachelor's degree and later he earned a master's degree from Boston University. His career spanned a professional life dedicated to young people at both the high school and college level. His desire to return to independent school life took him to Lakemont Academy, Lakemont, New York, where he served as assistant headmaster. In the early 1960 he returned to New England in the same post at Berwick Academy, South Berwick, Maine, to assist the school in developing its new expansion before coming to Brewster in 1965.

Wil arrived on campus at a time when the Academy was in the process of transition from what had been considered Wolfeboro's local high school to an independent school whose student population, in the low 100s, was to be primarily boarding and all boys. It was a school that would see a number of its faculty travel down the street to the then-new regional high school in Wolfeboro.

First Faculty to be Hired

In the spring of 1965, Wil was not only trying to close out his academic year at Berwick, but was also hiring his Brewster faculty and enrolling its student body for the coming year. Even before arriving in Wolfeboro, he put out the call to Bob Richardson, a former colleague at Lakemont Academy, asking him to accept a position at Brewster.

Realizing that a functioning library was key to the academic program, he also contacted Libby Sanders, a librarian who was living in Water Village, and hired her to become the school's first full-time librarian. But more additions to the faculty would be forthcoming as Headmaster Paro arrived on campus.

New Faculty for the School Year 1965-1966

The opening of school in September 1965 brought excitement as an almost all-new, but mostly experienced, teaching staff arrived at Brewster.

Robert Richardson, who would serve the Academy for the next 45 years, was among the first to be hired. Bob had earned his B.A. in History and Government from Otterbein College, had finished a master's from Syracuse and had taught with Wil at Lakemont Academy. At Brewster, Bob was head of the History Department, then administrative assistant to the headmaster, and finally director of studies where he would bring major changes to the curriculum and also initiate many new programs, such as Senior Project, Senior Seminar, and the Honors and Leadership Programs. The Daughters of Colonial Wars of the State of New Hampshire named him American History Teacher of the Year. He would be head coach of tennis, winning several league championships and assistant football coach. Bob was called upon to serve in many capacities and was a man who willingly wore many hats whether it was in admissions during the early years or helping in student life advising the Student Council and the yearbook. In short, he was a talented, dedicated Renaissance man who believed in and lived the private school life. Students often remarked, "We never had a history teacher before who didn't need the book to teach the course. Knowledgeable, creative, compassionate, and challenging—that was Mr. Richardson."

Three other new hires in that first year were James Wright, who chaired the English Department and was head football coach, Eugene M. Dea, in the English and drama area, and Thomas Pierce, who would teach French and Spanish and serve as assistant basketball coach.

Returning Faculty 1965

The returning faculty members, who rounded out the teaching staff that first year, were impressive and experienced. Rupert Brown was dean of students, having served Burtis Vaughan well; V. David Rogers would continue in math and as ski coach with Mr. Brown. Bill Bradford would remain in the History Department, David Pollini in the Science Department, and head of foreign languages would be Luis Gomez (*Brewster Review*: Fall 1965, pp. 2-4). All teachers were males and would work with each other with zeal and camaraderie not only in the dorms, but in the classrooms and on the athletic fields as well. Two female teachers who were on staff would find it difficult supervising boys in the dormitories or assisting the coaching staff in athletics and would find jobs in the public schools.

Independent School Traditions Established

As the school year began, Wil's style as a traditional New Englander was evident. He was a strict disciplinarian in the custom of his old headmaster at Deerfield, Frank Boyden. Among the "old school" traditions that are associated with Wil's tenure and which were the practice among the New England independent schools of the time were the "teas" after sports contests, presided over by faculty wives, where cocoa, punch, or cider and cookies or doughnuts were served to both school squads. The Friday night pep talks at the headmaster's home before Saturday games emphasized sportsmanship first and foremost.

Wil also initiated Sunday afternoon gatherings at the headmaster's house with faculty and seniors. Student dress code in those days mandated jacket and tie. Although Brewster was a non-denominational school, Sunday church attendance was required for students and many teachers. Each student had to sign out to attend services at local houses of

Headmaster and Mrs. Paro regularly entertained seniors for a Sunday afternoon gathering at Lord House.

worship where a faculty member invariably took attendance and removed any buttons found deposited in the church offering plate.

During Wil's first year, as was the tradition of the times, every meal was a sit down meal, and the dress code of jacket and tie was in effect. Each meal was served after the headmaster, or his designee, offered "grace," and each student table waiter served the table-head with the evening meal. The faculty table-head then served each student "family style." When everyone finished, the waiter collected plates and utensils, and when each table had been cleared, the headmaster gave announcements. After evening meal had been completed, at 7:00 PM, extra-help sessions were held in the Academy Building—English on Monday, history on Tuesday, math on Wednesday, science on Thursday, and foreign language on Friday—Glee Club and Drama Club held practices on Friday nights.

Continuing with past traditions, each school day began with an all-school meeting in the "chapel" at 8:00 AM which Wil led, opening with the Lord's Prayer, the Pledge of Allegiance, and two readings from the Bible, and each Thursday evening there was a vesper service. He expected more from students in terms of their social behavior than from their academic performance. It was a tradition in which he had been educated, and he was a strong proponent of its value through that tumultuous period of the 60s.

As admissions officer, Wil ran "a one-man shop." There were few admissions trips or visits to educational counselors. Students seeking admission to Brewster came to the office door and met with the headmaster. It was simple, direct, and traditional.

Disciplinarian that he was, he was also an extremely understanding man with a gentle nature and a soft sense of humor, but his masterly voice was known to carry a note of displeasure on certain occasions when the situation warranted. Second chances and more

Teacher Don Smith with a group of young men looking their best in required coat and tie at a club meeting.

Robert Black, president of the student body, as monitor and greeter in the front hall.

were not uncommon to offenders, but he did not suffer fools lightly. Wil loved golf, a sport that he continued to play until his death, enjoyed basketball, and took pleasure in faculty get-togethers. Wil was a conscientious worker and would put in long hours. He also had a quick sense of honor and as an individual required very little personal gain. The pleasure he derived was from the job itself, not from material acquisitions. Giving of himself as he did, he held high standards for those around him and derived strong satisfaction from personal relationships.

Mrs. Paro

Mrs. Betty Paro was a lady of the highest order but was also down to earth. She was positive and saw the good in every boy and was truly interested in being of help to everyone, student or faculty member. She kept in contact with parents, offered suggestions and was supportive of her husband. They were the team that ran the school.

Activities on Campus 1965-1966

One hundred and thirty seven students appeared on opening day in 1965; one hundred and twenty were boarders and seventeen were day students, three of whom were girls. Forty-two boys reported for early football practice four days before opening day, and the team kept its spirit up through a difficult season, winning two games—Exeter JV's and Proctor. But basketball did well, winning ten games and losing six. The local Lion's Club encouraged Brewster to participate in their Winter Carnival celebration, and when the trophies were awarded, Brown Hall was awarded first place in snow sculpturing with their team of huskies pulling a dog sled. The school play, *Stalag 17* was ideal for an all-male cast. After the play, the Alumni Association honored Douglas Bowles, '41, with a silver Wentworth Bowl; Bowles had been a pilot and prisoner of war confined in a Stalag during World War II.

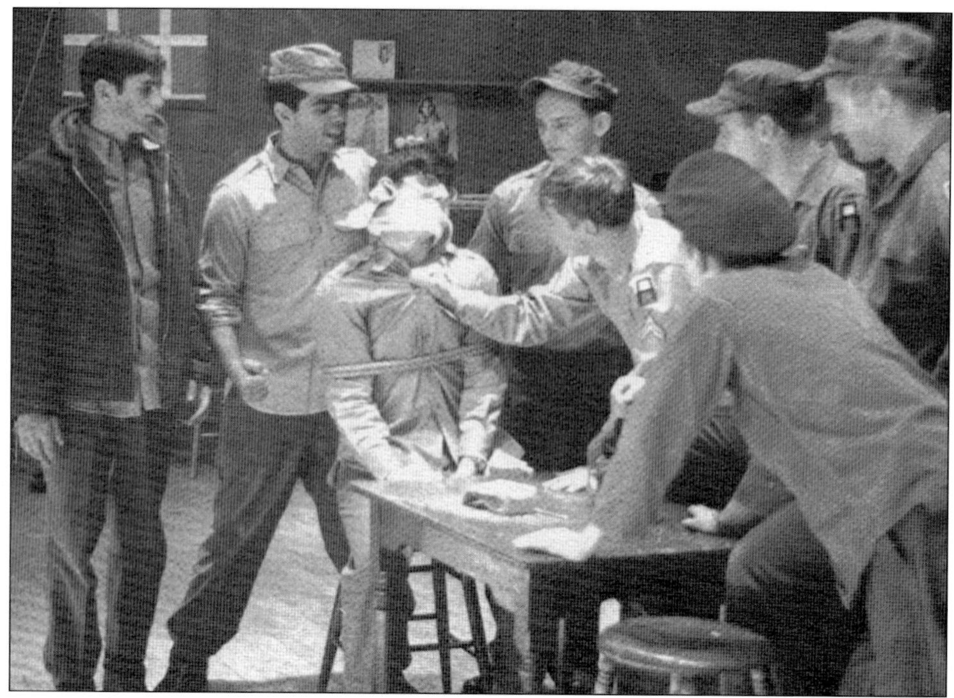

The famed play, Stalag17*, directed by Gene Dea.*

School Life Changes 1965-1966

By all accounts, the school year 1965-66 produced lots of positive results in a school that had made a dynamic transition to a "boarding" school. Students had a selection of elective courses in the curriculum and a solid selection of extra-curricular activities. The school year had also been divided into three trimesters instead of two semesters. While the dress code was very formal, few complained, and there was a noticeable improvement in the way dormitory rooms were cared for. The school finally had a more than adequate infirmary with a highly efficient nurse, Mrs. Hazel Stubblebine, in charge, and a doctor was always on stand-by.

Headmaster Paro ran a very strict school, and during the summer months of 1966, he completed a new edition of the student handbook, a twenty-one page document that detailed all the rules, schedules, and important information students and their parents needed. The handbook also encouraged every student to "become all that he is capable of being."

Campus Changes, 1965-1966

Along with instituting modifications in curriculum and student life, the 1965-1966 school year brought immense changes to the Brewster campus beginning on October 2nd with the dedication of Sargent Hall. This largest dorm housed forty-two students and two faculty members and provided a new recreation room in the basement. Mrs. Herbert E. Sargent was the guest of honor who charmed the audience with a speech about her husband and his many long teaching years at Brewster.

The second change was the purchase of the Ralph Carpenter II property, also known as "Cobham Hall," a twenty- five-acre estate that joined the school campus on the south

The home of Ralph Carpenter, Cobham Hall set on a 25 acre estate.

side bordering the athletic fields. The large home could easily accommodate ten boarding students and a resident teacher as well as being the headmaster's home for the Paro family.

The third major change was the expansion of the Estabrook dining facilities. A large extension was added to the hall to accommodate new dining facilities for two hundred and to provide more space for food preparation. Day students were to join boarders for lunch each day.

A fourth change was that the campus was lighted for the first time using underground wiring, and soon the old telephone poles with their maze of wires were removed. The summer was spent developing a walk and roadway lighting system to light the campus. The school building was equipped with fluorescent lighting in all classrooms and study areas.

A fifth significant change to campus was the loss of the elm trees. The Board of Trustees became concerned about the gradual deterioration of many of the beautiful elm trees bordering every roadway on the campus. The American elm trees were gradually dying of disease and had to be cut down and stumps removed at very high cost. Trustee Mrs. Adelaide Hughes, '28, came to the front and took on the project of their gradual replacement with maple trees. The project was long and, while she provided most of the funding, she enlisted support from interested alums to help defray the cost. The project was well worth the expense and ended with a campus that was beautiful and finally cleared of dead trees and stumps.

In the World, "The Times, They Are a Changin' "

As changes were occurring on campus, there was a darker shadow in international affairs that was gradually creating deep concern among teenagers and dividing the country.

In Southeast Asia, the communist forces of North Vietnam, having had success during the 1950s in defeating the old imperialist forces of France in Indonesia, challenged the free country of South Vietnam. By 1963, under the presidency of Lyndon B. Johnson, the United States along with other allied forces began to increase the arms commitment of the West for military action in defending the little country. In doing so, Johnson increased the drafting of young men into service to a point where troop commitments to Vietnam rose

The tragic loss of the magnificent elm trees that lined the paths and roadway on campus.

to 550,000. The country quickly became polarized by peace demonstrations, draft card burnings and marches on the White House. Sons and fathers soon found themselves facing each other, square jawed and white knuckled.

To compound the unrest, Martin Luther King, Jr. began his peaceful demonstrations against racial discrimination and black poverty with his famous speeches in Washington at the Lincoln Memorial and then continuing the unrest throughout the southland. In many cases, young men refused to be inducted into the armed forces by leaving the country and fleeing to Canada. Angry impoverished blacks in the North began the "long, hot summers" of looting and burning in major cities, and, in the South, demanded their civil rights to voting and equal treatment in transportation and education. The nation was split in its loyalties, and by 1968, Richard Nixon, who sought to bring the country together, was elected president as a Republican, and the nation waited for times to change. "The Times, They Are A Changin' "sang Peter, Paul and Mary and Bob Dylan, as Brewster students reacted each in his own way and not as one spirit.

In addition, the assassinations of Martin Luther King Jr. and Robert F. Kennedy, both leading political figures of the Democratic Party and prominent national figures of the times, had a devastating impact on the country.

The Pill

Changes and unrest seemed to infiltrate every corner of American life. The introduction of "The Pill," approved by the U. S. Food and Drug Administration in 1960, and on the broad American market by 1965, made young American women open to changes in life-style never before experienced. Unmarried women were having sex prior to the pill, but they were using different, dangerous and less effective means of contraception. In the midst of the civil rights and anti-war movements, women of a younger generation questioned authority, rejected parents' values, and intensified the collision between the traditional values of an older generation and the emerging demands of a newer one. Helen

Gurley Brown's book *Sex and the Single Girl* championed career women and open sexuality, effectively destroying the notion of the "old maid." These changes did not stop with the pill but expanded female demands for equal pay with males, unfettered access to advancement on the job and an open door to safer medical treatment for abortions.

Including these national issues into a history of the school is necessary to frame the administrations of two headmasters, Wilfred Paro and C. Richard Vaughan, both of whom struggled with the changing times, and, of course, the challenges facing the youth whom they sought to lead. The impact of the war would affect student life for many years to come with demonstrations, draft- dodging, candlelight vigils, moratorium study sessions, and general unrest. Mixed emotions would run high, and the leadership of the school would be tested.

The Carpenter Estate Becomes Bearce Hall 1966

Nevertheless, as national events continued to rage, the summer months of 1966 proved to be constructive and encouraging on campus. Paro reported that the Carpenter estate was being renovated and brought up to date with papering, painting and pointing up of plaster by the buildings and grounds crew. Plans were set to use the furnishings on hand, but additional furniture for the public rooms needed to be purchased. The public rooms would be used for faculty meetings, student meetings, and weekend guests; the headmaster and family would reside on the second floor. Three boys would also be housed in Bearce Hall. This would permit tax abatement from the town. For furnishing the first floor, $5,000 was set aside for the painting, papering and renovation. Mrs. Hughes, Mrs. Gregory, Mrs. Paro and Mrs. Avery were to select furnishings and to approve all purchases. They did their job well because the first and second floors were decorated with antiques, oriental carpets and comfortable furnishings suited to bring any group together. The trustees felt that it would be appropriate to have the opening and naming of the building, Bearce Hall, at a service on Parents Day, October 22nd, 1966, and to notify Mrs. Bearce of the board decision (*Minutes of the Board of Trustees*, May 7, 1966, pp.1-3).

Long Range Planning

At the same meeting, the board discussed the question of the adequacy of the library allotment in light of the trend in education toward encouraging the study and use of more outside materials. The headmaster brought up the problem of balancing library acquisitions with the available space and felt a survey should be made not only to determine the acquisitions of future materials in relationship to required space, but also to consider the future needs of the school in general. In August 1966, the Long Range Planning Committee consisting of Dr. Harold Gregory, Charlesworth Neilson, and Wilfred Paro reported their findings to the Board. With a proposed enrollment of 250 boarders and twenty-five to thirty-five day students, their responsibility was to determine and prioritize the future needs of the school. Their prioritized list of essential buildings and renovations were:

a. A library. This would free the present chapel for library expansion. There was a possibility of acquiring an existing church nearby, placing it on a foundation and expanding it to meet the needs of the school. Cost: less than $20,000.
b. Dining and kitchen facilities to feed three hundred and fifty persons and include lounges for students and faculty. Estabrook would then be free for classrooms and a faculty lounge. Cost: $300.000.
c. Science and mathematics complex of four lab-classroom units, four general classrooms, a small auditorium for forty, offices, science library space and museum. Cost: $500,000.

d. Two dormitories housing forty students each with suitable faculty quarters. Cost: $500,000.
e. Auditorium seating 500, including equipment. Cost: $300,000.
f. Gymnasium addition to include exercise rooms, wrestling, handball and squash courts, training room, swimming pool, lounges, and locker rooms. Cost: $300,000.
g. Additional athletic fields and tennis courts: Cost: $40,000.
h. Buildings and Grounds workshop. (Not included in priority list, but immediately needed.) Cost: $10,000.

Bishop Lord's house on the northwest side of the school property near the lakeshore was offered to the school, and the figure of $35,000 was mentioned. It could house six to eight students and provide a faculty facility.

In addition, it was discussed that a covered artificial ice rink for hockey and recreational skating, although expensive, could provide year around income from the summer population. Cost: $500,000 (*Long-Range Planning Committee Report, Buildings and Grounds Meeting*, August 28, 1966, pp.1-2).

The Buildings and Grounds Committee reviewed the factors presented by the Long-Range Planning Committee and developed a plan which focused their attention on a fund-raising program that would be tied to the 150th birthday (1970) of the school and would accommodate the first phase of the expansion program—the raising of $5,000,000 (*Meeting of the Sub-Committee on Academic Standards of the LRP Committee Report*, August 21, 1966, p.1). This revelation set the stage for an ambitious undertaking. It embraced all the major building blocks necessary to place the school in a position to compete actively with other college preparatory schools around the country and to bring the best modern educational facilities into play. But, more, it would act as a guide for the future success of the school by bringing into focus the two goals: the improvement of admissions and regeneration of alumni interest in the school.

The alumni had gradually become split: those forever loyal to the school and those who felt the school had "thrown out the town students." Much repair work was necessary. John Ballentine, representing the alumni, spoke of "building a bridge" to the alumni who, in many cases, represented the "town reaction." As a start, the association would plan a special get-together on November 2nd. Ballentine wanted to uncover a "great deal of richness" that could be cultivated and recapture a sense of the good Brewster had done for its graduates. He hoped to enlist their services as class agents and agents of referral for prospective students. The results of this meeting would test waters for future group leaders and volunteers *(Minutes of Meeting of the Board of Trustees, October 20, 1968*, pp.2-3).

School Year 1966-67

Even with Long Range Planning underway, as the school year 1966-67 began, it was a good one for students but not for enrollment. Although the school had projected an enrollment of 125 boarding students, only 105 actually enrolled. This shortfall made it obvious that the school must reduce spending on things that should have been done and place someone in charge of recruitment and fundraising as soon as possible. The school needed to undertake action to identify and correct the factors that had caused the reduction in admissions applications and to develop a plan to increase alumni contributions.

Almost all independent schools in the New England area had noticed a definite slowdown in the number of inquiries and admissions. It seemed as though the Vietnam War was causing economic chaos throughout the nation. On top of the political unrest, rising prices for food, fuel and building materials were absorbing income that might be saved for the future. The federal government had invested millions to upgrade a sagging public school curriculum, but the war and its demands for more recruits had introduced a feeling of resentment and rebellion in the youngsters it needed to refill the ranks of soldiers at training bases. As the cost of independent school tuition rose, fewer and fewer candidates appeared for admission interviews. The Brewster Board of Trustees and the headmaster appeared helpless to promote themselves as effectively as they might, but during the coming school year, even with the concerns of rising costs and admissions, new programs and a new home for the library were introduced to campus life.

The Library under Headmaster Paro

With admissions always a concern for the Academy, Mr. Paro still continued his concentration in developing the school library. The first real formal library on the Brewster campus was established under his leadership for he understood that at the heart of every school is the library.

It is interesting to follow, however, the growth and changes in the library not only in numbers of books, but also as it changed location and grew to fit the needs of the school. When John Brewster developed his school plan in the 1880s, he provided a space for a town library to be located in a room of the new Town Hall, but by the 1950s, patrons found themselves pressed for reading space as students from across the street flooded the reading room. The only alternative seemed to be to set aside space in the Academy Building for an easier access to reference books and novels. In reality, the classrooms served as sources of information, and teachers gradually collected books specifically for class usage. Room 8 took on the title of "Library," but it was far too small to house a meaningful collection. Barbara Zulauf, with the financial support of $1,000 from Adelaide Hughes, made the first attempt at establishing a school library. Barbara remembers that 800 books were donated from the home library of boarding student Charles (Chuck) Barnard of Manchester. Barbara and her husband picked up the books, cabinets, and shelves from the Barnard home and set them up in the second floor classroom at the top of the stairs "Mr. Dewey would not be pleased with our cataloging system," Barbara related.

The First Formal Brewster Library

Mrs. Elizabeth (Libby) Sanders, the school's first full-time librarian, came to Brewster in 1965 along with Wil Paro. Before school opened in fall of 1965, the library that Barbara Zulauf had created had been formally established during the summer, using the two classrooms located on the second floor of the Academic Building. An unusual half moon window just above the front entrance doors to the Academy building uniquely marked the new library. The library housed a collection of some 1,500 volumes, and Libby Sanders remembers that that early library was dark and small, but active. "We had some furniture and adjustable shelves. Additional books had been donated in response to an appeal made the previous year. Many had bookplates in memory of John F. Kennedy. Although the library was not large, there was no real cataloging system, only title and author cards.

Libby Sanders helped students check out books along with Elizabeth Crawford, her co-librarian. Libby soon learned that "you can't run a library in an academic day." Filling in for one another, their day stretched from 8 AM to 6 PM as they worked to build and strengthen the library facilities. In Libby's words, they "begged and borrowed" books to build the collection.

As the library collection grew and needs changed, it soon became apparent that more space was needed, and the school began to look around for an appropriate setting. It soon settled on the space that had been divided into two classrooms and had also served as a study hall area on the second floor and on the north side of school building. The new

The new library established on the north end of second floor of Academic Building.

quarters would provide double the area and would offer a vital service to the academic program.

The new library grew its collection to about 3,000 volumes during those years as a bequest of the late Miss Elizabeth Brewster provided for the purchase of many books along with the regularly scheduled acquisitions.

The next goal was to have 5,000 volumes in the stacks, and friends of the Academy were most generous in assisting toward that end. Libby and Elizabeth, jealously guarded every square foot of shelving for the book collections given by parents and friends of the library and also meticulously created space for research and reading, but more changes were to come in 1979.

The Outing Club, Trail Crew and the Rowing Club

Along with the changes and additions in the library, the fall, winter and spring of 1967-68 brought Mr. James N. Ramsey to Brewster as a French teacher, but much more. Young Jim had recently graduated from Dartmouth College, and his great desire was to start a program of outdoor education in which young boys could learn and physically develop using the outdoors as a learning center. Jim was young, tall and open to new ideas. During the fall months, six Sunday excursions led the group to the mountains, while during the week daily work trips were spent clearing trails in the Wolfeboro area.

In September of 1967, Mr. Howard Avery offered to Brewster the use of nine hundred acres of timberland near Rust Pond, known school-wide as the Avery property. As time passed, academic and recreational uses for the land blossomed forth under Ramsey's leadership. The Science Club conducted field trips; the Cross Country team trained along the four miles of pine-carpeted lumber roads, and the Outing Club took daily two hour hikes around the property and planned for the construction of an Adirondack-style shelter in the valley which would be used for spring and winter camping. The area brought not

Under Coach James Ramsey the first group of oarsmen: C. Foss, P. Kimball, A. Shiro, D. Rolph, R. Schiavoni, B. Hirsch, W. Bradford, C. Noble.

only cross country skiing but a chance to construct wooden duck boxes to inhabit the area. Mr. Walter Carlson, Jr. '53, a local forester, made practical suggestions for reclaiming an old beaver pond by reconstructing a small dam and restocking the pond with fish they were advised would thrive (*Brewster Review, Holiday Issue*, 1966, p. 3).

The work continued, but Jim Ramsey's interests extended to rowing. As a member of the Dartmouth Rowing Club, Jim searched out the possibilities of attaining one of the newly discarded rowing shells from the Dartmouth Club. Jim was successful in his request when Dartmouth handed over a rowing shell named The John Dickey after a renowned Dartmouth president. The 62-foot, 8 man racing shell arrived at Brewster during the early winter of 1967 and was ready for open water practice in the spring of 1968. The first team was Charles A. Foss, '68, Peter Kimball, '68, Alan B. Shiro, '67, David Rolph, Richard Schiavoni, '70, Bennett Hirsch, '68, Bill Bradford, '69, and Carlos Noble, '70 (Bradford, Interview, 2007).

Football and Hockey on Campus

Athletics, in general, were superb. In 1965 Jimmy Wright, dean of students and chairman of the English Department, served as the head football coach with Bob Richardson, chairman of the history department and director of studies, as the line and defensive coach. Although Bob characterized that first year as "not successful," the varsity football team of 1966-67 set the standard for the year. He credits much of the success of the team to two elements: the will of the individual players and the "winning spirit" created by coaches who invented

Coaches Jim Wright, Bob Richardson, John Staples, and Neil Abeles and the 1966-67 winning football team.

individual nicknames for each player. The squad was led by All-New England quarterback Frank "Red" Harris of Malden, MA, and gleaned six wins, one tie and no loss. Red Harris would go on to play quarterback at Boston College and the Detroit Lions.

Coaches Jim Wright and Bob Richardson praised the roles played by all members of the squad with many of the boys intensively recruited by college coaches. Coach Bob Richardson recalls one of the highlights of that season was the game against Proctor Academy that ended in a 14 to 14 tie. "In the last seconds of the game, Proctor attempted to break the tie with a field goal, and the ball was kicked from the 40 yard line. It sailed through the air, hit the crossbar and bounded out. It was a thrilling moment and cheers went up from the crowd. That moment will always be remembered!"

Pop Whalen's varsity hockey team won eight games again with Frank Harris as leading scorer. It should be noted that Harris, after the hockey match was over, would run to the gym, suit-up in basketball uniform, and finish the final quarter. The team was hampered by the abundance of snow most of the season that seemed to appear during the early morning hours. But this did not prevent their defeating Tilton (twice), New Hampton (twice), Proctor, Berwick, and North Yarmouth. Their only losses were UNH freshmen and Holderness (4-3).

The Woe of 1968 Summer Admissions

The summer of 1968 brought discouraging figures to Wil Paro and the school. The Executive Committee faced a bleak prospect; the admission report showed a sharp drop in applications and final acceptances, resulting in a projected loss of $13,300. By August 24, the school had enrolled 94 boarders and seven-day students. Mr. Paro had placed advertisements in the *New York Times* and *Christian Science Monitor* as well as 17 local newspapers in the area, and he had contacted summer schools and camps (*Minutes of the Executive Committee Meeting*, August 28, 1968, pp.1-2).

However, as August turned to September, just after opening day, Mr. Paro reported an increase to 108 boarders, 8 day students and 3 PGs; the slight up-turn was credited to the contacts made with local football camps and regular camps, plus helpful advice given by the Advisory Service for Private Schools in New York City. The Board reported that Mr.

The outstanding 1966-67 hockey team with Red Harris, coached by Paul "Pop" Whalen.

L. Thurston Pendleton, one with experience working in fundraising and development, had been hired to be assistant to the headmaster. "Penny" would offer assistance in the Business Office and work with the headmaster on searching out avenues leading to improved admission numbers (*Minutes of Board of Trustees*, October 20, 1968, p. 2). But the national political and social unrest coupled with rising costs would not abate, and most all independent schools were reporting stressful times forcing them to seek relief from mortgage payments and increasing the number of gift requests made to their alumni.

School Year 1968-1969

As the life of the school year continued, a student newspaper, *The Subterranean*, emphasized student concerns over the smoking issue, the question of hypocrisy in the present morning chapel format, mixed messages in the handling of discipline with overly restrictive policies, and the emphasis on athletics over academics impacted school spirit. However, the publication did present a step forward in attempting to open student/faculty dialogue. It would be important for the students to present their concerns in a manner that would contribute to the progress of the school in a constructive, objective, and responsible manner where judgment could be made on the ideas presented rather than a defense of one's self (*Monograph*, Peter Greer, 1968). As the faculty and the headmaster began to listen to the voice of the students, they began to work together in a respectful way to resolve concerns.

The impending loss of some of the school's best faculty members, the fragile alumni relations with the Academy, and the school's ever nagging enrollment issues as well as the dim financial picture, raised the trustees' concerns for the welfare of the school.

Paro's Resignation

At the Board of Trustee meeting in May 1969, Wilfred Paro formally announced his resignation as headmaster of Brewster Academy, effective on September 1, 1969. His

The senior class of 1968-69 was comprised of only male boarding students—one of the few years when this occurred.

decision had been reached after close consultation with Mr. Neilson, Board chairman, on April 1st, and after long and careful consideration of many factors. Paro stated, "He found it difficult to make the decision, but felt it was the right one to make for all concerned." He expressed his appreciation for all the help the Board had given him and said that he would continue to identify himself with the Academy and its growth. He felt that there would be sufficient continuity of personnel at the Academy and that everything would be ready for normal operation when school opened in September. The Board went on record with their expression of appreciation for what Mr. Paro had done for Brewster. During his tenure, Mr. Paro had brought the structure and spirit of a traditional New England prep school to the Brewster campus and established the groundwork for future headmasters to build upon. To carry on the good work that had been done, a selection committee was appointed to proceed with interviewing and recommending to the Board such candidates as they felt qualified for the headmastership (*Minutes of the Annual Meeting of Board of Trustees*, May 31, 1969, p. 3).

Mr. and Mrs. Paro would find a new home in Peterborough, New Hampshire, where Wil would become assistant to the president at Franklin Pierce College. In April 1987, Wil Paro passed away peacefully in his sleep after a day of golf. Betty, in 2009, at the age of 95, is living in Concord, New Hampshire.

13. Charles Richard Vaughan, 1969–1974: Challenges Brewster to Change

To give real service you must add something which cannot be bought or measured with money, and that is sincerity and integrity.—Donald A. Adams

Following the resignation of Wilfred Paro, a Selection Committee—John Ballentine, Arthur Mason, Dana Cotton, L. T. Pendleton , Peter Tyler and Charlesworth Neilson—went to work gathering resumes from candidates throughout the United States. After thoughtful discussions and with the full approval of Brewster Academy Board of Trustees, they announced that C. Richard Vaughan had been appointed headmaster of the Academy succeeding Wilfred E. Paro who had resigned effective September 1 (*Minutes of the Board of Trustees,* September 1, 1969, p. 1).

Mr. Vaughan, age 41, had been principal of Telstar Regional High School, Bethel, Maine, since 1966 where Mr. Vaughan was known as an innovative and imaginative educator not only in this country, but in Europe as well.

Mr. Neilson commented on Vaughan's wide experience and modern educational techniques. "He is ideally suited to carrying on and broadening the progressive instructional

C. Richard Vaughan, the ninth headmaster of the Academy.

approach, which will be initiated at Brewster in keeping with the tradition of the fine education of our young people. This is urgently needed in these unsettled times, and we are indeed fortunate in obtaining Mr. Vaughan's leadership in this important work."

Mr. Vaughan was a graduate of Kimball Union Academy, attended the University of Vermont, and received his B. S. degree at the Northeast Missouri State College in Kirksville. He held a "masters degree in education" from the University of Maine.

Vaughan and his wife, Margaret, and three children, David, 15, Ellen 11, and Susan, 9, expected to find Wolfeboro an ideal place to carry on their recreational interests in fishing, camping, and other outdoor activities (*Granite State News,* July 24, 1969).

Opening of the School Year 1969-1970

As school opened in the fall, a competent administrative team and faculty were in place to support the new headmaster and his innovative approach to education: veterans Robert Richardson, Albert Powers, Paul Whalen, David Rogers, Lee Gridley, Mal Murray, David Pollini, Carlos Noble, Bill Slack, Bruce Hermann, Chris Harlow, Libby Sanders, and, recently hired Travis Ball, John Clayborne, Bill Morrison, Paul Perry, and David Smith were all prepared for this new beginning. Along with educational innovations, the main focus had to be to increase enrollment. If the school were to survive, this had to be the top priority for the new headmaster.

Wolfeboro's Tax Bill Confronts New Headmaster and Board of Trustees

As Mr. Vaughan began his first year as headmaster and was confronting the problem of dwindling boarding enrollment, another obstacle that had been in the background was brought to the attention of the Board of Trustees, a matter that had to be handled with extreme care, as it appeared it could darken the already chaotic financial footing of the school.

In the fall of 1967, the Town of Wolfeboro gave notice to the Academy that some form of taxation would be levied on the school. A meeting with selectmen would be scheduled to review the proposed Academy tax bill of $3,967.50 due for 1968. The selectmen submitted a report that described the basis for their evaluation, but left it to the school to review the report for the legality of their calculations.

With the purchase of Bearce in 1966 and the construction of Sargent in 1965, the value of these two additional buildings plus Kimball, Haines, Estabrook, and Brown where students were housed, and the Estabrook kitchen and dining room where students were fed, finally exceeded the exemption, and thus the first taxation was levied on the Academy in 1967. It was, however, in the province of the town to set the tax rate.

The Board decided to accept the taxation levied by the town, and it was agreed that the school should pay some tax in light of the services maintained by the town—police protection and fire fighting—and to comply with the New Hampshire statute.

The Board pointed out that there were many services offered to the town by Brewster and they too should not go unnoticed as the town set the tax rate (*Minutes of the Board of Trustees,* January 3, 1969, pp.1-2).

First Impressions—Travis Ball

Travis Ball, a young English teacher, was hired by Wilfred Paro as an English teacher during the days of transition in July 1969 but was told that Mr. Vaughan would be his headmaster when he started work. Ball had been assigned to be a master in Sargent Hall, serve as English department chairman, and tend other duties in the area of publications and publicity.

Travis tells the story that the "faculty in 1969 was diverse and all had enthusiasm for their subjects and focused on student achievement. Teachers were used to a large degree of autonomy, which later proved to be both a strength and weakness. I was particularly impressed with their communication skills, often thinking that if I had had a Malcolm Murray for high school math, I would have understood the subject; a David Smith, Chris Harlow, or Bob Richardson for history, I would have a greater enthusiasm for the story of civilization; if I had studied biology with George Mikulis, I would have seen how all life forms fit together; and so on. Despite all the uncertainties about Brewster and its future, faculty members went into their classrooms and taught.

"During my first months at Brewster, the days were long, and most activities were mandatory. I still remember the early mornings, making sure the students were up and dressed in school uniform for breakfast at 6:00 or 6:30 AM, and I concluded early on that a student could fulfill the letter of the dress code and yet defy the spirit of it. The handbook had an incredibly large number of things to be accomplished even before breakfast, and the day was packed from breakfast through evening study hours. At meals we all had assigned tables and assigned seats.

"During orientation about school rules and codes of conduct, students asked about situations not covered by a specific rule. Dick Vaughan replied, 'When in doubt, don't!' I borrowed that line many times when writing faculty and student handbooks for other schools. Slowly there was a shift of responsibility to students to make decisions for themselves and to accept consequences from those decisions. This is, I think, the heart of true discipline. Each individual becomes responsible for himself and the adults in the community guide students toward becoming self-disciplined" (Ball, pp. 3-4).

The School Year 1969-1970

During the fall and winter of 1969-70, Bill Slack, Travis Ball, and Mr. Vaughan went to work on redesigning and publishing the school catalog. Also during that year, in addition to the overhaul of the viewbook, the entire curriculum and scheduling process needed revision, and departments had to begin the hard work of restructuring courses and time allocations so that 12th graders and some advanced 11th graders would enter into trimester courses which allowed more concentration and in-depth study, rather than the broad survey type of study. Typical courses were "The Roaring Twenties," "Authors of the Twenties," "Science of the Twenties," "Blacks in America" and "Native Americans." The campus was ideal for the last trimester of "Native Americans" as an archeological dig was started down by the lake in search of artifacts. A sense of discovery and wonderment seemed to erupt with every shovel (*Brewster Review,* Summer 1969, p.1).

School Year 1970-1971

By the fall term of 1970, the new school scheduling scheme called Flexible Modular Scheduling, which had been in the works for some months, was ready to be instituted. The new schedule would eliminate the repetition of each class meeting at the same time each day. It would permit a staggering of classes so that a teacher could adjust each class and have at least three choices of duration time based on need for instruction. Flexible Modular Scheduling resulted in students being exposed to more elective course choices, a more college-like atmosphere, and less monotony and routine. Advanced Placement courses in English, American History, calculus, biology and foreign languages were offered.

But the schedule had a down side. It was very labor intensive, requiring at least three weeks to prepare the initial paperwork and then more time to convert it to a conflict-free master schedule, and then additional time to prepare three final copies for student, adviser and school files. This process was then repeated two more times for the winter and spring terms.

Still there were even more changes in the planning stages waiting to be implemented.

Developing School Management Team, 1970-1971

Travis Ball's experience as a teacher and then as administrative assistant for operations reflects the changes that were to come within the administrative team.

"When I came to Brewster, the headmaster and the business manager were the only full-time administrators. A dean of students, V. David Rogers, whose father had earlier served as headmaster, and a dean of studies, Robert R. Richardson, assisted the headmaster. Both men carried a fulltime class schedule, coached, and served in various ways in the residential life program.

"In March 1970, Dick Vaughan appointed Paul W. Whalen as an administrative assistant to the headmaster. 'Pop,' as he was known to generations of students, had been at Brewster since 1954, serving as athletic director and at times taking on other responsibilities in the classroom and as interim business director. Paul also assumed much of the day-to-day responsibility for discipline and coordinating dormitory activities.

"At the same time Dick asked David Pollini to serve as alumni and development director and me to help with school publications. The annual fund was a relatively new venture, and David brought his long association with the school and his friendship with many alumni to the job. Alumnus John Ballentine, a very successful and creative printer and publisher, provided invaluable assistance as we revamped the publications and developed an in-print identity for the school" (Ball, p.14).

Brewster Student Anxiety Over National Issues

The newly formed administrative team was eager to be a part of educational change at Brewster, but at the same time, beginning at the college level, a national unrest in higher education was sweeping down into the secondary schools. Issues of dress codes, hair length, traditional curriculum, required church and chapel attendance, formal dining room meals and required study halls had gradually ignited dissent among Brewster Board members, faculty, and students. Students caught the TV film clips of riotous college students at Kent State, Berkeley, and the Chicago Democratic Convention and questioned what their future role would be, whether in army green or college sweatshirts, especially in light of a draft law which required every male from 18 to 25 years to report to his local Selective Service Board for registration and a possible call to active duty. President of the Board of Trustees, C.K. Neilson, appointed a Trustee-Faculty Development Committee to meet from time to time to discuss student unrest issues and make detailed reports to the Board of Trustees (*Minutes of the Board of Trustees*, March 15, 1969, p. 2).

The changing times seemed to hit home with Brewster boys both young and old when Mr. John Staples, a respected history teacher and coach, responded to his sense of duty by rejoining the U.S. Marine Corps and left campus with his wife and young son.

In 1967, Daniel F. Ford, class of 1950, wrote a remarkable novel entitled *Incident at Muc Wa*. The story centers on an American Special Forces unit accompanied by a detachment of regular South Vietnamese soldiers who were ordered to secure a small village called Muc Wa. When they arrive at the village, they find the physical remains of a French army battalion, which had perished under the fire of the Viet Cong years before. Ford uses the image evoked by ancient Greek writer Simonides' epitaph for the three hundred soldiers who died fighting Persian invaders at Thermopylae, Greece in 480 B.C.: "Go, stranger, and tell the Spartans that we lie here in obedience to their laws." In 1978 Ford's tale, *Incident at Muc Wa,* was developed as the film *Go Tell the Spartans*, and actor Burt Lancaster immediately agreed to star, even paying for the last $150,000 to complete it (www.danfordbooks.com). The book and film played a significant role in reflecting student and adult anguish over this tragic war, and by 1978, America had seemed to accept the fact that the loss of over 53,000 American military personnel was far too great a price.

Boarding schools often appear to be insulated from the outside or "real" world, but that is an illusion. One of the greatest challenges to the Academy came when the national movement at colleges and high schools called for a moratorium on usual academic activities one day each month, using this class time to learn more about Southeast Asia's lands and people. In addition, there were times when students held candle-light vigils and protest discussions regarding an unpopular and apparently ineffective war in Vietnam.

A number of students wanted to participate in this national movement. Some faculty supported their desire, while others desired to hold to the letter of every school regulation. The conflict between students and faculty escalated: some students threatened to leave if they didn't have freedom of speech, and some faculty members tossed letters of resignation on Mr. Vaughan's desk when they felt he didn't hold firm to school regulations.

Again the underground newspaper, *The Subterranean*, sprang up, and senior Bobby Arnold emerged as the leader of the Brewster moratorium protests. Later Bob would become an accomplished poet and publisher in Vermont, a writer-in-residence for a time at a prominent independent school, and a master stonemason. Eventually the fine art of compromise prevailed, balancing protests and academic obligations. Faculty still remember the students with protest signs and anti-war buttons demonstrating along the main street in front of the campus.

Environmental Humanizing

In order to address and alleviate some of the unrest demonstrated on campus, Headmaster Vaughan targeted the 1971-72 school year to begin part two of his master plan for the

Students demonstrating on campus against the Vietnam War.

school, which he referred to as the "environmental-humanizing" phase. This plan would bring broad revisions to the current, so-called regular or traditional academic, athletic and disciplinary tone of the school. The revision of many yearlong courses in social studies, English and some science courses into elective trimester courses were carefully planned, while most all mathematics and foreign language courses would remain yearlong studies. Students would still compete for Honor Roll status. In order to reduce the ever-creeping spring disease of "senior slump," two new projects were proposed: Student Assistant Volunteers in Education (SAVE) and Senior Project.

Student Assistant Volunteers in Education

SAVE was designed for those seniors who wished to remain on campus during the final term, still enrolling in four major courses, but taking SAVE as their fifth. SAVE students were enlisted to act as teacher helpers at the Carpenter School or at Kingswood Regional. Each SAVE senior would report to his or her Brewster adviser weekly and at the end of the term present to the Brewster faculty an oral recounting of his or her teaching experience. They would live in their dorms and abide by school rules. They could participate in sports, which pleased the coaches. Usually there were ten SAVE seniors each year.

Senior Project

Senior Project was much different. Seniors, during the winter months, made arrangements to complete a four-week study on some specific area which interested them. In most cases, seniors made arrangements to work as employees in a corporation or business where they would learn the operations of the organization. Several seniors used this time to complete the Outward Bound programs in Maine or Colorado, while others developed projects at Woods Hole Oceanographic Institution with Dr. Robert D. Ballard, whose son attended Brewster. Their final examination consisted of an oral presentation to the Brewster faculty, an evaluation by their program director and a graded written report on their experiences. This project was very popular because it was unusual and almost fully self-directed.

Athletic Program

The Athletic Department was also to see revision, and Headmaster Vaughan's modification in 1970 was broad. With a school enrollment of about one hundred students and a football team that was very small but played against teams who were highly competitive, changes had to be made. In the opening games of 1971 with Hyde School and then Dracut High School, the team suffered several serious injuries, which forced the coaching staff to recommend that the remainder of the scheduled games be dropped. Mr. Vaughan agreed, and the opponents were notified that their schedule would have an open date as Brewster was closing its football season. As English teacher and soccer coach, Trevor Peard recalls, "It was the happiest day of my Brewster life as all the remaining football players ran over to my practice field and wanted to be on my team! We finished with a great season with many victories and became Lakes Region Champions for 1971" (Peard *Interview*, 2008).

Vaughan saw interscholastic sports as a part of athletic fitness but also felt that interscholastic sports were only one area of physical development. Traditionally, Brewster had placed interscholastic football, basketball, soccer, hockey, and baseball as a top priority in its sports program with very little choice provided for students who had other talents and interest. Vaughan felt that the requirement of three terms of interscholastic sports was too confining and that the requirement should be changed to two seasons of interscholastic sports and one term of a recreational activity. Outing Club, sailing, crew, golf, tennis, biking, fishing, fencing and recreational skiing were offered. The Father's Club had just purchased three new sailboats and had given three new tennis courts, originally located on

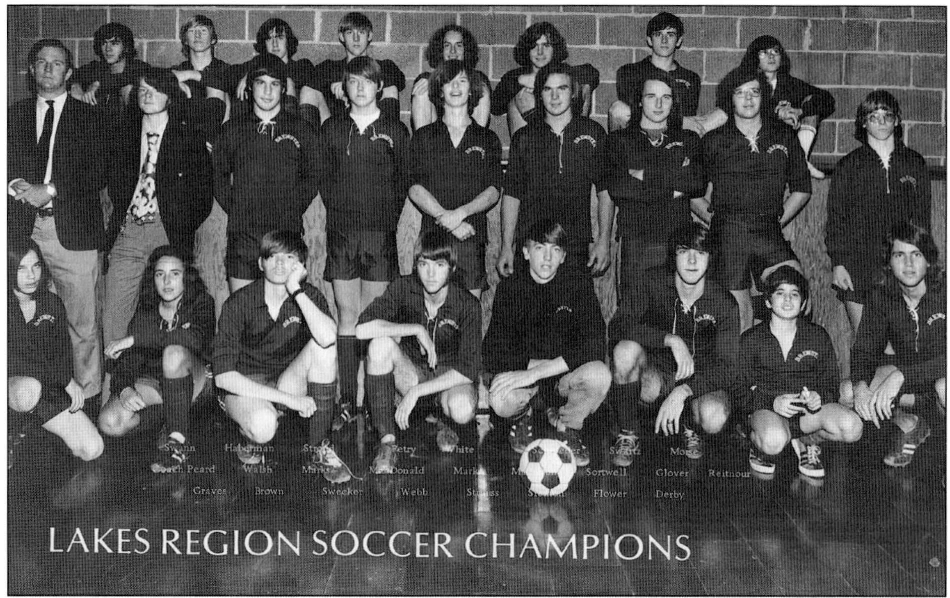

Coach Trevor Peard with the winning soccer team of 1971.

the present Brown Field. Teachers would supervise instruction for each one of the activities, and Bill Morison, a science teacher, became the first sailing coach.

Revision in Student Handbook and Haircut Issue

With the changing times, Vaughan felt the rules written in the student handbook were in need of modification, and he instituted further revision of citizenship rules. The old student handbook, written during the headmastership of Wilfred Paro, had rapidly become far too rigid for students of the 70s. Vaughan revised dining hall usage so that breakfast attendance became optional. Students protested the haircut rule, many refusing to cut their hair or emphatically refusing to return to Brewster. Tempers flared and threats were exchanged whenever teachers and students discussed personal grooming. Vaughan proposed a new haircut standard that allowed longer hair and sideburns but still prohibited moustaches and beards. Again, some faculty members objected, stating that "the school gave in" and fearing that Brewster students would become longhaired hippies, but others felt the issue was reasonably settled.

Informality had also become very important in public traditions and in 1973 graduation attire no longer included caps, gowns, and gold cords, but now the accepted dress was coat and tie and fancy dresses.

Thunder Clouds over Wolfeboro Bay

Change did not come easily to a school over one hundred and fifty years old or to its alumni and veteran teachers. Most independent schools exist primarily to give better and more individualized attention to aid young boys and girls to realize their full intellectual potential, to prepare them for the relatively unsupervised college life, and to motivate them to do so under their own drive and desire. Each student must be tested thoroughly in reading, mathematics and intelligence, and to accomplish this, the school had to revise

Three new asphalt tennis courts (above), with backstops and shades, given by the Father's Club. Golf practice (below) held out on campus under the magnificent elms trees soon to be all removed due to Dutch Elm Blight.

its program to accommodate the needs of each student as it planned for classes, advisers, teaching methods and practices, and benchmarks of individual progress. A special needs reading program for those who had fallen behind had to be established, and Vaughan found Bruce Finkle, class of 1967, who had graduated from the U. of Massachusetts with a master's degree in education, to head this program.

Several teachers and even more alumni felt that the reduction from three seasons of athletics to two terms represented a de-emphasis on sports that would result in losing students and prevent the school from having "winning teams." Others felt that the school should move in the direction of becoming a two-year junior college. This divided opinion created an atmosphere of stress and confusion.

Paul Whalen, Administrative Assistant to the Headmaster

Richard Vaughan's tenure as headmaster took place in very difficult and contentious times for the entire country. Obviously, many of the issues that were causing conflict throughout the nation spilled over into the school.

This stress also extended to the relationship between Pop Whalan as administrative assistant to the headmaster and Headmaster Vaughan. Since there was deep disagreement between them on some basic policy issues and Mr. Vaughan felt the need to cut back the budget for administrative positions, the position of assistant to the headmaster was eliminated. The headmaster then assumed all responsibilities of the discipline task.

This change came as a shock to the community because Whalen had for years developed athletics at Brewster and was recognized as an outstanding coach in all sports. He was widely respected in Wolfeboro and at many of the larger high schools in the Boston area for helping those students who had completed their high school education but needed one year to develop their academic preparations to meet college standards. For a number of years, Whalen, as director of athletics, had been instrumental in recruiting a large number of post-graduates each year to supplement the school enrollment and bolster the athletic line up. Under his leadership, the school had gained a reputation for having a strong athletic program.

Ultimately, the Board supported the headmaster's decision. However, out of respect for Whalen and all he had done for the school, Pop was asked to continue his supervision of the two football camps held at Brewster during the summer and remain living on campus. Mrs. Whalen was commended and thanked for her assistance in the library, and Whalen was recognized for his contributions to the Academy.

Brewster in the Crossfire

Another crisis in the school had to do with admission figures which, for the next several years, nearly brought the school to its knees. The admissions for 1971-72 indicated a drop in all grade levels to a total of 60 boarders when 110 were needed, along with 13-day students, and a faculty of 13 including one new full-time instructor. The now unoccupied Furber House on Main Street was sold for $30,000, and Bearce Hall would be closed to students but be occupied by Mr. and Mrs. Peter Cole and their two daughters. Mr. and Mrs. Vaughan and family would move to Lord House where the headmaster could more closely supervise campus activities. Needed income from the rental of the new tennis courts, plans to operate an adult parent summer camping-sports program, and the football camps seemed the only prospects for the school to earn summer income.

The substantial damage done to the annual alumni giving programs was discouraging and was mostly focused on two issues. Many alums felt the school's emphasis on admitting students who were classified as "underachievers" did not bode well, even though the school would provide a reading and study skills program to remediate the deficiency. The prospect

Mathew Gregory, '72 (left), in traditional cap and gown, receives his diploma from Headmaster Vaughan and Academic Dean Robert Richardson. Below, Student Council President Robert Baylis, without the traditional cap and gown, receives his diploma and special award during commencement ceremony.

of losing David Rogers, Malcolm Murray, Lee Gridley, Albert Powers and Paul Whalen seemed unthinkable. Even some endowed funds from alums and friends of the Academy were recalled from the school's annual budget, further crippling the school operations.

On the positive side, to help with enrollment, the Board of Trustees again, gave serious thought to the admission of young women as boarding students and agreed that it certainly was congruent with the Will of John Brewster. At this time, many boarding schools for girls were making plans to combine with boarding schools for boys. Others were closing their doors, and some male boarding schools such as Deerfield, Choate, Andover and Exeter all lined up to admit young ladies. Even the Ivy League colleges like Harvard and Brown were joining forces with their female counterparts, Radcliffe and Pembroke. Within the year, Brewster made the decision to admit boarding women, and Bearce Hall, somewhat separated from the campus center, would become an ideal dormitory for at least ten new boarding girls.

The hair issue was also settled, at least for as long as it could be—it would be a compromise, melding the anxieties regarding the transition from the World War II standards with those of the "Me" generation, Woodstock and the Rock and Roll era. But it did indicate to students that the school was emerging and trying to adapt to a more modern standard. Yet the pictures in the 1972 *Winnipesaukean* clearly display the images of smiling students, all boys dressed in coat and tie, complete with long hair and looking sharp, intelligent and actively enjoying campus life. Day student girls, well dressed and groomed, seemed to take the leadership in leading class discussions, writing papers and playing active roles in a production of *The Rainmaker,* the school play.

Friends forever, classmates of 1971: "JJ" Jimmy Jameson, Danila Berenbach, Bob Gibson, Ralph Botticeari, Hunter "Bucky" Craig, Anne Vodola, and Steve Chorney.

The 1972 production of the The Rainmaker *supported by leading actors Joan Bozuwa and Peter Sortwell.*

By 1972-73 the Board of Trustees, and its president, Mr. C. K. Neilson, had a full plate of tasks. Aside from resolving the issue with the town on taxation of Brewster lands and buildings, they were faced with the continuing problem of admissions. To accomplish this formidable task, Vaughan would need to enlist the help of Peter Cole, David Smith and Bob Richardson to do the roadwork from Illinois and Ohio through the New England states. Then there was the job of hiring several new and qualified teachers to replace those who had decided to leave Brewster; since he would be on-campus, Mr. Vaughan would tackle this responsibility.

The Alumni Association would require damage control work. The Alumni Office needed to regain its enthusiasm and that of alums and together roll-up their sleeves and plan for the continuation of the *Brewster Review*, the Boston Brewster Club and the annual alumni fund drive. And the Board added another major sales job: private foundations and trust funds. They decided to research all of private trust funds available to secondary education, determine which ones would be open to schools like Brewster, and then make applications.

Problems Continue

The summer months of 1972 brought more problems to Richard Vaughan and Brewster Academy. These problems compounded to the point that the question of the continued existence of the school was perhaps as serious as was the case in the summer of 1872 when the Christian Institute folded its school and the Wolfeborough-Tuftonborough Academy resumed a failing operation.

The headmaster's traditional office in the corridor of the Academic Building was now used for admissions while a smaller room down the hall was temporarily used as the head's office while plans were in progress to convert Room 1 into a more spacious headmaster's office. There were, however, no funds for the construction, nor was there Building and Grounds Committee approval for the expenditure, a situation that later antagonized the Board. With this new office arrangement, Mr. Vaughan spent most of his time in the Lord House study, choosing to interview prospective students and their parents in that location.

Despite the continued support of a significant portion of his administrators and faculty, Mr. Vaughan's efforts to reform various aspects of the school presented him with unanticipated difficulties.

With the departure of Paul Whalen in the early days of 1971, many school alumni became disenchanted, and a half dozen experienced and respected teachers lost confidence in the direction of the school and would soon depart.

The priority attention to admissions, which remained critically important to survival of the school, needed to be addressed. In 1972, admissions inquiries dropped and the ratio of applications to paid enrollments was about 16-1. This harsh reality placed unwanted pressure on the school resulting in the admission of a score or more students who, sadly, were inappropriate in relation to the academic, athletic and behavioral expectations of the school.

Further pressures to retain currently enrolled students led, at times, to inappropriately acceding to their wishes. One such example was the revision in the evening study rules, in reality not study hours but instead "quiet hours permitted 'til midnight." The late hour forced significant burdens on overworked faculty/dormitory masters, and the students also felt the resulting strain of sleep deprivation. Few appeared to be accomplishing much.

Female Students Admitted

In order to increase enrollment, Mr. Vaughan supported the discussion held in 1971-72 that the time had come to admit girls as boarding students, using Bearce Hall and Kimball House if needed for female students. The menacing issue of admissions for the 1973-1974 school year thus had one new positive dimension—it was the first year since the early 60s that female students were admitted as boarders

Kim Barney, Lauren Richardson, and Marion Hubbard, first boarding "lifers "to graduate.

Those first boarding girls were also instrumental in supplementing the sports program by establishing teams in field hockey, soccer, softball, and a new riding program coached and advanced by Mr. Richard Fahy, a much appreciated history teacher, and his wife, Anita.

Of the ten girls who entered the academy in 1973, three became the first modern female "lifers." Kim Barney, Lauren Richardson, and Marion Hubbard entered as freshman and graduated as seniors in 1977. Many more would follow in the years to come as the percentage of girls within the student body grew steadily.

The 1973-74 Energy Crisis

The energy crisis of '73-'74, which accompanied a deep recession and high inflation, was now added to both the challenges Vaughan inherited and those that came into being during his tenure.

Whether it was a fear the oil shortages might lead to an inconsistent supply of heating oil or the rising fuel prices might not be able to be met or some combination of the two along with other factors, Mr. Vaughan announced that the Thanksgiving and Christmas breaks would be merged. The result was the students would be leaving campus in the third week of November and not returning until the first week in January. Meanwhile, back on campus, thermostats were turned down, teachers were put to work taping window sash cracks, placing aluminum foil behind radiators, installing storm windows, and building storm doors around entryways to keep out the cold blasts. Teacher work squads were sent out to cut firewood in Moultonboro, truck it to Wolfeboro, and then stack it behind the Academy Building, where it could be used in the school building's boiler, if necessary.

In addition, the faculty set about laying-out the school hockey rink on the upper athletic field complete with lights and began to spray the first critical layers of ice each night (*Brewster Review,* January 1974, p. 1).

But as January's thaw began to set in and classes once more returned to a normal daily routine, grumbling reignited. The break had been so lengthy it proved difficult to recapture a sense of commitment from a significant portion of the student body, a factor that had a draining effect on faculty. The winter sports programs went badly. The business manager required that coaches check the van gas tanks with a yardstick and keep a record of the purpose and number of miles on any trip. The faculty was further frustrated and angered when the business manager ordered the thermostats in buildings, including faculty apartments, to be equipped with locking devices, which prevented the settings from being changed; and with winter winds penetrating some of the older buildings, pipes were freezing all over campus.

When the faculty was surveyed as to their teaching plans for next year, Vaughan was disappointed to find that many newly hired teachers let it be known that they were looking elsewhere. They wanted more security as daily life on campus seemed to be so uncertain and it appeared to be a good time to move on.

As dissatisfaction spread around the campus, Mr. Vaughan became increasingly inaccessible to faculty and students. Amidst these developments, one could feel a tone of resentment or frustration in his speech when he engaged a group of students during a meeting, and his sense of humor seemed to have vanished.

Vaughan Leaves Brewster Academy

When the Board of Trustees met in March of 1974, they recognized that there were many areas of concern resulting in a negative culture and low morale. If the school were to survive, they saw the Academy needing an immediate rebirth with measures that would stop the financial bleeding. In addition, the campus wide situation was critical and required urgent action.

The Board of Trustees 1973: Back Row: Herbert P. VanBlarcom, Carlton W. Spencer Arthur J. Mason, Dorothy Bovaird, Charles D. Cilley '27, Elvira Avery, John J. Ballentine '46, Lloyd B. Waring, Warren P. Tyler, Walter N. DeWitt '54; Front Row: Charlesworth K. Neilson, Adelaide R. Hughes '26, Colonel Hugh Wilkin, Fred C. Brokaw.

During that meeting, led by President Rink DeWitt, the Board determined that the school must have new direction and new leadership and that they must immediately begin the search for new management and guidance.

They had no choice but to try a new course for the preservation of the school and the hope that the vision of its founder could and would be realized in the near future.

Although Richard Vaughan had faced some nearly overwhelming challenges in his service to Brewster Academy, he offered the school some new insights and innovative approaches. However, the school needed a more hands-on directorship, and the Board made the decision to hand over leadership to someone who could integrate himself more fully into the community and set a rhythm for innovation and change that the faculty could accommodate.

Charlesworth K. Nielson, president of the Brewster Board of Trustees, had given C. Richard Vaughan good advice when he assumed the position of headmaster in 1970 when he stated, "You are ahead of your time in education management and must be careful because there are those who are not as willing to take the risks as you are." Unfortunately, this forecast became a reality.

David Smith Prepares for the Opening of School as Acting Headmaster

David Minton Smith, was an energetic and well-regarded history teacher who, as dean of students, had done his best to keep the morale high and students on task during this difficult period. With the departure of Richard Vaughn, he was appointed the acting headmaster.

The faculty rallied with him, and they set out on the daunting challenge of moving the school toward the fulfillment of its mission to students and achieving financial stability

As summer moved forward, activity on campus was intense as David Smith, the acting headmaster, established an *esprit de corps* fueled with optimism. With a shared sense of duty and a bountiful supply of energy, they set out to capitalize on what they began to believe was an unleashed opportunity to create a special environment for young people and the professional community that would serve them.

In addition to an all-out admissions effort that included contact with returning families, telephoning potential new families who had shown interest in the school, and interviewing students and parents, the summer months were devoted to cleaning and painting, hiring some new and very good faculty members, and producing publicity. All of this had to be done without spending money. Every member of this summer team was well aware of a budgetary caution from the Chairman of the Board.

A New Headmaster is Appointed

The Search Committee made up of trustees, faculty, staff, alumni and students, interviewed candidates from a variety of independent schools as well as selected Brewster faculty members, and by August of 1974, the Search Committee had completed its work and made its recommendation to the Board of Trustees. David Minton Smith was offered the position of headmaster, which he accepted. Now under the leadership of a new headmaster, faculty and students were able to put the past behind them and move forward as he chartered a new course.

C. Richard Vaughan's Life After Brewster

Dick Vaughan had a major heart attack just after he left Brewster and recovered in Maine where he was on the Board of Directors of a preparatory school. Later the Vaughans settled in Winter Haven, Florida, where Dick joined an educational consulting firm, placing students in prep schools. After a time, they moved to Dyke, Virginia, where Dick became director of the Blue Ridge Summer School, the most rewarding job he ever had as he did lots of traveling and hiking in the Blue Ridge Mountains. Upon his retirement, he and Peg went back to Randolf, Maine, where he died in 2000 at the age of seventy-one.

While living in Georgia near daughter Ellen, Peg Vaughan passed away in 2009.

14. David Minton Smith, 1974–2003: A New Beginning

Be the change you want to see in the world.—Mohandas K. Gandhi

By the time David Smith arrived on the Brewster campus in August 1969, he had developed many of the insights and formulated many of the ideas that would serve as the underpinnings of a student-centered approach to education, an approach which would become the hallmark of the Brewster experience. For the next thirty-four years, David Smith served Brewster in various capacities, bringing growth and a spirit to the school that would be far reaching, transforming the very fabric of the Academy as it moved into the twenty-first century. His early life at home, at school, at part-time jobs, at church, and at college had taught him some important principles that would guide him throughout his life, i.e. to fully commit to the task at hand, to search for meaning in his daily routine, and to apply the lessons he had learned about respect and concern for each individual to the situations he would encounter in his impressive and singular tenure at Brewster Academy.

David Minton Smith, the youngest and longest serving headmaster, with his family: Timothy, James, wife Sheila, and Daniel.

David's First Year at Brewster and His Teaching Philosophy

It all began in the summer of 1969 when Headmaster Will Paro, Director of Studies Bob Richardson, and Department Chair Chris Harlow hired David as a history and political science teacher, dorm master, and coach. David was ready to put his principles to work, and the test began immediately.

Despite his many talents and abilities and his deep respect for and understanding of the student, David affirms that his first year at Brewster was definitely a learning experience based on a set of new and unexpected challenges that arose from the many different hats teachers in a boarding school must wear. Luckily, he was able to work with and learn from more experienced members of the faculty.

However, as David affirms, it was Bob Richardson who became his primary mentor. In fact, they shared a similar philosophy of education. Bob was able to make specific suggestions to help David hone his approaches in the classroom. For example, Bob emphasized that there must be continuity in the curriculum and that each day's lesson plan should begin with stated outcomes. Further, Bob was able to show David that students at Brewster were expected to be active learners setting their own ambitious goals rather than playing a passive role by memorizing and regurgitating the teacher's ideas. Finally, to his great delight, David discovered that Bob Richardson was also a proponent of the idea that study skills development had to go hand in hand with the advancing demand of the content curriculum. This would become a guiding principle throughout David's years at Brewster Academy and a fundamental driver as the school adopted and advanced the "Model" program in the 1990s.

Pop Whalen proved to be another important mentor for David in the area of athletics and coaching. Pop emphasized teamwork and sportsmanship. David states that he also generated principles that inspired young people to step up to the challenge of their potentials

Robert Richardson, academic mentor to David Smith.

while the teacher/coach took responsibility to provide them with the knowledge, skills and confidence to go out onto the field and to fully commit themselves to excellence.

Dave Rogers, the dean of students, also influenced David that first year by teaching David to accept total responsibility as a dorm parent. When David asked for help with a difficult dorm situation, he was asked "What are you going to do about it?" David was grateful for this lesson. "It was a lesson and model I was able to practice as a headmaster, that is, to allow the teacher or student to grow and build confidence by working out his/her own solutions to problems. Thus, they each could take pride in having the ability to handle difficult situations."

Smith's Teaching Assignments

After signing on with Brewster, David Smith first taught US History and World History. However, when mini-courses came into vogue, students were asked to choose what they would like to see offered in the History Department. Not surprisingly, they selected Russian/Soviet history. Bob Richardson then informed David he would teach that subject. David attempted to beg off, saying he had never had a course in Russian/Soviet history; but Bob told him that was no problem because he had all summer to develop his course. David would go on to teach Russian and Soviet History for the next twenty years and to teach it with passion and expertise.

Smith Appointed Dean

Halfway through his second year at Brewster, at the age of 26, David was offered the position of assistant to the headmaster for student affairs or dean of students. Headmaster C. R. Vaughan explained that he recognized David's extraordinary capacity to relate to students and their resulting faith and trust in him.

David Smith and athletic mentor, Paul Whalen.

Challenging Times

This faith and trust in David was illustrated by an incident David still remembers with warmth and good humor. He writes, "As an example of how I felt about them and how they chose on one occasion to demonstrate their special relationship with me, one early evening Peter Tinkham, Rick Olfene, Bob Scanlon, Frank Cole, Dominic Valarioti of the class of '72, with group ingenuity and the strength of teenage young men, planted my Volkswagen in the Estabrook dining room and then gathered around it for a picture much like big game hunters. I displayed that picture in my office throughout most of my headmastership. As dean, I knew that if I wanted something done or someone to look after what I needed done, the student leadership would take hold of the morale of the community during difficult times. I only had to ask, and it would happen. In fact, right from the beginning of my tenure as dean, I did not have to go far to find some of those key students."

David Smith Appointed Acting Headmaster

Following the resignation of C. Richard Vaughan, the President of the Board of Trustees Rink DeWitt, called a meeting of the Board to affirm asking David Smith to be acting headmaster until a search committee could conduct a full and thorough exploration for a new headmaster. He received the Board's approval, and soon after David accepted the position, Rink asked for an All-School meeting in Chapel Hall where he announced David's appointment. There was much applause, and as David and Rink were leaving the meeting, Rink turned to the new acting headmaster and said, "They really like you."

Smith took on the responsibilities of the position because he was asked to fill an immediate need. Again it was in his nature to realize that the compliment was not only

A prank: The Dean of Student's car discovered in the Estabrook dining room.

a show of faith in him, but also brought with it an obligation to fulfill the expectations and needs of those gathered in Chapel Hall. The needs were many and included a dire economic situation—so dire that it threatened the very survival of the school.

While Smith was fully aware of the challenges, his focus, his faith, and his enthusiasm rested in what he saw as the school's potential. He recognized that it was only by truly serving the needs of each individual student and their parents that the school would survive and prosper (Smith, *Monograph*, pp. 14-15).

The Board gave him no specific direction other than the implicit idea of holding the institution together until a search could provide a leader who somehow, in some way, could lead the school back from the brink. For the remainder of the spring term, the faculty and student body came together under the leadership of the acting headmaster. The school year ended with dignity and spirit.

The Selection of a Headmaster

During the following summer, a headmaster search/selection committee reviewed over 100 applicants from all parts of the country and formally interviewed 30 individuals from which they selected a group of ten finalists. After this intensive search and after interviewing these finalists, the committee offered the position to David Smith who accepted after talking the offer over with his wife, Sheila.

When David was offered the position of headmaster in August 1974, Brewster had 74 students. When he retired in 2003, Brewster had 74 faculty members. As David Smith began his new role as headmaster at the age of 30, the youngest headmaster in the school's 154-year history, there were two special women who helped him understand the responsibilities of the job and kept him focused on priorities. They also protected him. These two women were the headmaster's secretary, Dottie Swaffield, and David's wife, Sheila.

A joyous groups of seniors on graduation day.

Once again David was young when he assumed this responsibility, but Sheila was even younger when she stepped into the role and responsibilities of the headmaster's wife. To be exact, she was 26 with a two-year-old son Timothy and his brother Danny scheduled to arrive shortly; James would follow two years later. Sheila managed her young family and supported her husband. She also opened her home and acted as hostess (and often chief cook and bottle washer) for individual guests or gatherings that David believed would result in some level of support for the school, particularly in the Admissions Department.

Hiring New Faculty Members

One of the most critical issues facing the new headmaster was hiring new staff. When several faculty members, concerned about the future viability of the Academy, decided to leave, the headmaster was faced with the challenge of hiring new staff who supported the vision of the school. There were, of course, those on whom Headmaster Smith depended who remained and held key positions. The obvious were the administrators beginning with Bob Richardson, Trevor Peard, Fred Djang, and Dave Pollini. Walter Hertz, Bill Morrison, and Harry Widman were key faculty members, but the list included everyone from Rink DeWitt, trustee chairperson, to Andy Halepis, dining room manager, and Sam Oliva, business manager.

Pete Tyler, a trustee, was assigned to be Smith's guardian both in the hiring of new staff as well as approving any expenditure and co-signing every check.

Peter Friend, New English Department Chairman

It was decided that the first to be hired should be an outstanding English Department head. That choice was Peter Friend, who brought with him a commitment to high expectations while at the same time validating the academic contributions of each of his students. Peter would remain a model of excellence in teaching within the school for years to come.

Peter Friend would serve as the spokesperson for Brewster's publicity, the advisor to the yearbook, hockey coach in the winter, and outdoor skills leader in the spring.

Headmaster Smith and the faculty of 1974.

Teaching primarily seniors, Peter had a following of students and then alumni who kept in touch with him for years. While understanding and friendly, Peter was a demanding teacher and brought the best out in all his students. He inspired them to step up and accept the responsibility of meeting the challenges of his courses. They invariably did so and went on to college with high levels of competence and confidence.

Peter retired from Brewster in 1997 after 23 years of service, and at Christmas time in 2008, Peter suffered a sudden heart attack. By his memorial service, well over a hundred students from all over the country from the 70s to the 90s had emailed, telephoned, and wrote letters describing what Peter and his classes meant to them.

Moving the School Forward

The blending of the returning faculty with the newly hired group produced a teaching staff of only thirteen members. This small but remarkable group of individuals quickly united with the young headmaster in a shared mission of building a new school. Although there were dire challenges to the school's very existence, the headmaster assured everyone that the school would build a reputation from which all future growth would take root. Through a core curriculum designed to challenge the individual student in the acquisition of content while, at the same time, supplying the reading, writing and mathematical skills to best prepare students for success in college, Brewster would distinguish itself.

Faculty meetings were held weekly at Lord House. With such a small group, it was easy for all to gather in the living room. During his first faculty meeting as headmaster, David had to announce to the faculty that there would be no raises in the year ahead. The school had an operating deficit of $140,000 against a budget of $300,000. The school also had a line of credit of $100,000 of which $90,000 had already been expended.

The new headmaster moved the school forward while constantly delivering the message, both internally and externally, that Brewster was a student-centered school. Together with the faculty, he pledged to constantly adapt the school's program in response to the needs and the potentials of young people entrusted to the school.

As the truth of that promise became increasingly evident, enrollment grew in number, character and capability. Adjustments took place every week at faculty meeting where the progress and challenges of students were reviewed and refinements were introduced accordingly. In later years, during the formative stages of the Brewster Model program, these meetings were the inspiration for structuring the larger school into teams which would be best positioned to take responsibility for advancing each individual student's development, both academically and socially.

The greatest challenges during those early years from 1970-80, continued to be developing and supporting a strong faculty and administration, enhancing the validity of the academic, athletic, and residential programs, increasing the enrollment, and achieving financial stability. In all of this, David took a "hands on" approach that was directive, supportive, as well as entrepreneurial where opportunities presented themselves (Smith, pp 20-23).

Headmaster and the Board

President of the Board Rink DeWitt states, "We went into survival mode for a year or two and all members of the Board and the Brewster community worked hard and well together. But those years were tough. We had to stop the financial bleeding, and we did. We had enough income from the endowment so that we could mow the grass and keep the buildings painted, but beyond that, major changes had to happen, and they did with the new direction and the new leadership."

Rink and David "partnered" for 15 years. Initially as the school was in crises, most major decisions were centered in the relationship between the headmaster's recommendations and the input and endorsement of the president of the Board. As the school became more secure, policy decisions became more inclusive, first through the Board's committee chairs, then moving on to engagement of the full Board of Trustees.

Building an Administrative and Faculty Team

Director of Admissions

One of the best additions to the administrative team during those early years was David's decision to approach Trevor Peard and ask him to return to Brewster as director of admissions. Coming from a prep school (Cate School) and an Ivy League university (Princeton) background, Trevor's bright spirit, enthusiasm, prized education, and his faith in the intentions and commitment of this new iteration of Brewster came through to all who inquired in the admissions process.

He spent a good deal of his initial efforts visiting educational consultants in order to put Brewster on their radar screen. As he built a Brewster identity, inquiries began to come through, interviews were scheduled, and applications followed.

Trevor and David developed their roles in speaking with perspective parents and students. Trevor would talk to them first and then they would meet with the headmaster. Parents were impressed with the headmaster's energy and sincerity. They came away feeling that Brewster was a different place where the needs of their child would be met.

"As the admissions picture brightened, the school had another reason to feel good about itself. It was at this time that the headmaster asked me to also serve as dean of students in addition to my role in admissions. We had a good cop/ bad cop system in place, and it worked. I took my lead from the headmaster, and students would listen, be remorseful and want to do better. Mr. Smith had a way with young people. He could get them to respect themselves and, in doing so, decide to be the best they could be."

In 1978, Trevor left to go to Choate, and Andrew Wooden would follow as director of admissions and Chuck Esty as dean of students" (Peard, *Transcribed Interview*, August 2008).

Director of Athletics

In 1974, another man who would bring a bundle of enthusiasm and ideas as well as heading up the athletic department and reestablishing its credibility throughout the league came when Steve McCloy was hired as director of athletics.

He also taught English, coached lacrosse, and worked with the Wilderness Program. As Brewster attempted to establish legitimacy, the quest extended to an athletic program that could use some victories. Other than the campus site with its backdrop of the lake and mountains, there wasn't anything that made Brewster stand out amongst New Hampton, Tilton, Proctor and the Holderness School. It is fair to say that Brewster was considered by them to be on the lowest rung of the ladder both academically and athletically.

In athletics, the headmaster was searching for a means to establish a sense of pride within the school community. The thought was, "We have a gym, it takes only five good players to make a team, and we have empty beds." A few good players could make a big difference. And wouldn't it be great for the students to have a team to cheer for during the cold gray days of winter? And that is just what happened. Basketball became the social event of the weekend, and everyone went to the games and rooted for their team.

The first visit was with Coach Ed Burley at Boston English High School. His team had just experienced 37 straight victories led by a high school phenomenon, Michael Bennet,'76, who was assisted by his backcourt mate, Walker Haynes, '77. Together, they enrolled at Brewster in the fall of '75, Mike as a senior and Walker as a junior. When the word flashed

Rogers Gymnasium crowded with fans for Saturday night's game.

out to the tight basketball world that Mike Bennett was going to attend Brewster Academy, all of a sudden another eight players from the greater Boston area sought admission.

In looking back and remembering Mike Bennett, '76, and Walker Haynes, '77, Mike was shy and very quiet and Walker was an extrovert, a showman and anything but quiet. The day of Mike's graduation Adelaide Hughes's 50th class reunion chartered the Mount Washington for a cruise around the Lake. They invited any seniors who wished to join them to do so. Most all were anxious to get home and passed on the invitation, but some seniors joined in. Near the end of the cruise, Headmaster Smith found Mike sitting on the upper deck all by himself. When he told him he was surprised to see him there, Mike said, "Mr. Smith, during my whole life I have never been on a boat of any kind and I loved it here and am taking advantage of every last minute" (Smith, p. 27).

In the first real contest, the team was down by about 8 points at the half. Steve didn't know what was going wrong, so he just attempted to talk tough. He started to rant a little telling them to shape up, but "how" he didn't know. Jimmy Ryan,'76, a tough little point guard from Roxbury's Mission Hill known as James "the Rabbit" Ryan, interrupted and said, "Don't worry coach we know what we are getting paid for. We'll take care of everything," and, of course, they did. The program that was 0 and 16 the prior year went 16 and 0 and averaged 103 points per game. Brewster Academy was no longer the athletic doormat, and the student body had something to cheer for. This was the beginning of outstanding Brewster basketball teams as well as the first big step in the resurrection of Brewster athletics.

Steve McCloy was able to continue the basketball success and developed an athletic program with full varsity and junior varsity schedules which included games with Tilton, Berwick, Proctor, New Hampton, Holderness, and Hebron. A growing girls' enrollment led to the establishment of field hockey team for the fall, basketball in the winter, and lacrosse in the spring. The sailing team was to meet with Proctor and Tilton and Exeter. Recreational tennis and golf, hiking and camping rounded out the program.

Basketball Memory

One special memory of a Brewster basketball game will remain in the hearts and minds of everyone who was in Rogers Gym that night. It was not centered in the glories of the strong varsity program, but like many memorable moments throughout the years, it was a sub-varsity contest.

David Gorfine, '81, was a ninth grader on the junior varsity team. By that time the varsity team was so strong with many postgraduate players headed for Division I basketball scholarships that a number of their games were scheduled with college freshman teams. Some of the younger varsity players would help out on the JV team.

The last game of the season was make-or-break for David, as he had not scored a point during the entire season. Brewster was well ahead when David was sent into the game with just minutes to play. When David ran onto the court, the fans went crazy. Everyone wanted to see David score, to sink just one basket. There was so little hope of that happening in the normal flow of the game that his teammates told David to stay up under their basket and they would get the rebound and pass it to him. He would be all alone and right under the hoop. Moses Camacho, '81, grabbed the rebound, and the crowd screamed in anticipation as he fired it down to David at his end of the floor. The only problem was David couldn't catch the ball. Time was running out fast. So the boys on the floor decided to keep Rick McAleenan back down near the basket where he could catch the pass and basically hand the ball to David.

With less than a minute left in the game, only three players went on defense. David and Rick stayed by the basket. As the final seconds were running out, Moses grabbed another rebound and fired it to Rick who made a soft pass to David who turned and threw it up toward the basket. It bounced on the rim and time ran out and the horn sounded as it bounced to the other side of the rim. The crowd was on its feet yelling and hopping as the ball bounced again and then dropped into the basket. Since David released it before the game ended, the shot counted, and the fans went wild. Streaming onto the floor, they picked David up onto their shoulders and circled the gym cheering for their ninth-grade hero. Even the other team caught the excitement, joining in on the moment.

With all the athletic glories witnessed on campus, this one was one of the very best for all that it said about our community. And to top it all off, David's dad was in the stands that day to share in his son's glorious moment.

Environmental Program

In addition to his responsibilities as athletic director, Steve McCloy was interested in environmental studies. He saw an underutilized asset of the lake, and it led him to an extraordinary idea. When he announced his vision of building a program of water-quality analysis, fish population studies, work with the Fish and Game and conservation commissions to the headmaster, David responded that the school didn't even have a boat. However, led by Steve, the school spent about $400 on ads placed in various national papers. Offers came through and soon the Academy was fully equipped. Suddenly Brewster was a research institution and was seen by the Wolfeboro community as an active contributor to the preservation of the town's most precious asset—the lake itself (Smith, p. 27).

The first of several boats serving the Winnipesaukee Project wintered at the Corinthian Yacht Club: Steve McCloy and John O'Connell.

Director of Learning Skills

Another noteworthy addition to the administrative team was Ed Hooper who was to develop one of the most important individualized learning programs at the Academy. When Ed arrived on campus, he had already served as the principal of a school in Connecticut and planned to set up an antique business in New Hampshire. However, he was soon meeting with David Smith who was looking for just the type of help Ed could give.

"And we certainly needed the help," Bob Richardson remembers. "For the last ten years, the student attrition rate had been too high and pointed to the fact that many of our students were failing because of reading and study skill deficits. We had discussed and debated the issue many times in faculty meetings and had come to the conclusion that 'canned' reading and study skills instruction didn't work. There had to be an on-going program integrated with, or tied to, the student's regular class schedule that included three important components: first, determination of how the individual student learns; second, application of a study plan to develop reading speed and comprehension; and third, follow through on the plan until the student was able to become an independent learner achieving success in the regular academic classroom.

"Ed's meeting with the headmaster marked the beginning of a new chapter for Brewster, and it was destined to bring to the faculty new ideas on how students learn by reinforced study skills in the classroom. Ed un-retired from education a cold day in 1975, and with that decision, another significant member of the leadership team had joined the Brewster program.

"By opening day in September, Ed had designed the first Learning Skills Center in Room 5 at the south end of the Ac's first floor.

"The newly developed Learning Skills Program (LSP) was an individualized program involving the collaboration of instructional support teachers, subject teachers, and the student. A comprehensive program was designed for each student that allowed him/her to learn, practice and receive consistent feedback in skills development within the LSP and

Ed Hooper, founder and director of the Learning Skills Program.

the regular classroom. This was the key to ensuring mastery and growth. The strategies in LSP were applied in each of the student's classes and also practiced in study hall. All faculty and dorm parents were trained in using best practice strategies and methods so they were in the best position to support, guide and reinforce the student's success in becoming all that he/she could be.

"Two significant members who joined Ed's initial team of instructors were Dave Peterson and Shirley Richardson. In order to provide for meeting space, Room 5 had been partitioned into three individualized teaching and learning classrooms."

Expanding the Learning Skills Program

The headmaster had sought out Dave Peterson while visiting Dr. Charles Drake and the Landmark School. He knew that Dave Peterson possessed expertise in enabling the learning of dyslexic students from his Landmark experience.

He also spirited Shirley Richardson away from Kingswood Regional School System to teach study skills and English 9. Shirley understood and valued the school's mission. In addition, Shirley had been working with special needs children in the public school system, and she fully appreciated that all human beings are unique and they learn best in different ways and at different rates.

Dave Peterson felt that there was "a socialization process" that students had to undertake before learning readiness fully set in and, within a boarding school, the dorm was at the center of that process. He would spend endless hours in the evening resolving personal conflict issues, boosting personal skills, and bolstering a student's sense of self and personal responsibility.

Shirley Richardson saw academic success coming from a "ritualized" study schedule that students first had to internalize—completing assigned work was a must. She was totally dedicated to seeing that each student mastered this discipline and kept up with every assignment. As a result of her deep commitment, Shirley's students were able to build up their confidence and develop an "I-can-and-will-do" approach to their studies.

With Ed's expertise, experience and his remarkable ability in making effective use of each teacher's special talent, he blended this hard-working, deeply-committed group into the first learning skills team.

Ed had remarkably fine-tuned gut instincts about kids. He saw them as a picture-puzzle whose parts were a little scattered, and instinctively he knew how he was going to get the student to rearrange his or her academic life to bring the picture together.

To be a teacher and administrator, Ed believed you must be fair and durable, and Ed accepted that it would involve some struggles. He had to be demanding with his teachers about lesson plans, meetings, and discussions with his teachers, but he also knew when to let up. He never took criticism personally and he always finished the job. When presented with a problem, Ed would always come back the next day with a solid suggestion. His drive-in from Ossipee was solution time, and during those twenty minutes he would find the key to unlock the problem and work out a solution.

By 1980, the new Kenison Library was completed, and Ed was able to convince Headmaster Smith to relocate the Learning Skills Department to the upper floor of the "Ac" in the former library space. A new dimension, English as a Second Language, was incorporated under the umbrella of the Learning Skills Department. With the arrival of students from Japan, Thailand, and Korea, their skill development in writing and reading in English was a core focus within their curriculum. This initial ESL program was headed up by Barbara Douglass who made contacts with Asian schools; enrollment continued to rise, not only from Asia, but also from Bermuda, Europe and most all states within the USA.

Introduction of Technology and Expansion of Learning Skills

Today Brewster is renowned in part for its highly effective use of technology. Ed Hooper was the first department chair to recognize the potential of the computer in contributing to individualized instruction. He was the first to put a student face to face with a screen to improve reading, vocabulary, and comprehension. It wasn't long before each teacher within Learning Skills was equipped with a computer and skill development programs. Because of his instinctive understanding of students and his wisdom, Ed Hooper has become a legend in Brewster's history, and his impact is one of the most important keys to Brewster's success.

Upon his retirement, finding a person to assume the leadership and insure the continued advancement of the Learning Skills Program would be a daunting challenge. Fortunately, a young professor from Lehigh University was attracted to this growing school in New Hampshire.

Upon his arrival at the Academy, Dr. Alan Bain assumed leadership of the department. Utilizing research-proven best practices, he quickly provided advancement and refinement to all aspects of the program. As he brought these elements into place, Dr Bain noted that Kim Ross both appreciated the new advancements and rose to the challenges of incorporating them in service to her students. Like Dave Peterson, Kim had come to Brewster from the Landmark School where she had received great training from Dr. Drake in working with dyslexic students. Kim eagerly responded to the methodologies introduced by Dr. Bain. The headmaster was fully aware of Kim's dedication, and before long, he turned over leadership of the department to her, freeing Alan to turn his focus to other components of the school's academic program

Matt Hoopes, a man of many talents who wore many hats.

Through her leadership of the department, Kim has not only brought the advances introduced by Dr. Bain to fruition, she has been responsible for fully integrating Instructional Support within each of the school's seven teaching teams. As a director, Kim works closely with Deans Marilyn Shea and Peter Hess to ensure the accurate application of research-proven best practices throughout all facets of the academic program. Kim has been and continues to be an invaluable leader to the department and to the school.

Matt Hoopes, New Beginnings of Publications

Matt Hoopes, another major addition to the Brewster campus in 1975, thought he would work part time and live in his cottage on Rust Pond. "Hoopes" had never met David Smith, but he wrote to David telling him that he was coming.

Matt remembers, "Not that he had offered me a job, but finally in late August, David, with enrollment secured for the year ahead, offered me a position to teach two sections of the essay class.

"As soon as I got in the door, people started assigning me duties because I was 'part time.' Fred Djang gave me the Student Court, Peter Friend, the yearbook, The *Winnipesaukean*. and I was signed up for weekend duty every weekend. But it was fun with a small young faculty all working together. I think there were 120 students when I arrived, and everyone knew everyone." Thus began the long and special contributions of Matt Hoopes to the very fiber of the Academy.

A History of Publication

While the Brewster students wrote and published various newspapers in various formats and under various banners and names, the Academy did not have a continuously published newspaper or literary magazine until a formal journalism program came into being in 1977. Prior to that time, however, the students, the administrators, and the Alumni Office attempted on several levels with several publications and were successful for periods of years throughout the school's history.

The following is a brief summation of the early record of Brewster's publications.

The first student publication at Brewster appeared in 1892. The hand-written *Academy Ensign* was posted every other week and was promoted as "a medium for development of literary tastes among the students."

The Browser's roots can be traced, vaguely, back to the early1890s when the Academy students felt there was a need for a school paper. The administration, however, felt that the focus should be towards the alumni. Published intermittently over the next few years, this paper was called *The Brewster Review.*

In 1892, the *Review* was replaced by a larger, magazine-style *Winnipesaukean.* At the same period, students also were reporters for the town's *Granite State News* under a column headed "B.F.A." In 1912, *The Brewster* came into being with the students not only writing the news stories, but also setting the type and printing the paper on campus on a small Winter Press. In 1916, the school acquired a hand-cranked Chandler and Price printing press. At that time typesetting was offered as one of the regular subjects of the school curriculum. Over the following years *The Brewster* evolved into an alumni magazine that was then written and published by the Alumni Office, and the student newspaper languished until 1977 when the present *Brewster Browser* was inspired by two junior girls.

The Outcroppings was first published under the same journalism teacher, Matt Hoopes, in 1980. The *Winnipesaukea*n, the Academy's yearbook, originated with the class of 1921, but was then called *The SYB. The BAPA Book*, the photo-address book, also originally published by the students in the journalism classes, made its debut in 1989.

The Years of Journalism: 1977-97 as Remembered by Matt Hoopes

The Browser

"Late in the fall of 1977 I looked up from a stack of essays I was grading to see two girls I vaguely recognized as juniors, but whose names I did not know, enter my English 10 room in the basement of the Academic Building.

'Can you help us?' questioned the shorter of the two, Kathy Morrisette,'79.

'I can try. What's up?'

The taller girl, Terese Valliere,'79, took charge of the conversation.

'Kathy and I were just talking with Headmaster Smith. We told him we felt Brewster needed a newspaper so the students can have their 'voice' in some of the school policies.'

'What was his reaction?' I asked.

'They both smiled down at me in unison. 'We can start one if we can find someone to be the faculty advisor,' Teresa stated, matter of factly.

Kathy exclaimed 'We've already picked out a name, *The Brewster Bee.*'

Together, begging, 'Would you...?'

'I will, on one condition, that you let me select the name. Deal?'

'Deal,' they shouted together.

And so began the school newspaper, *The Browser.*"

The Outcroppings

In 1978 there were quite a number of student artists, photographers, poets, and writers on campus, and they were respected, almost held in as much esteem as BA's competitive varsity basketball players. There were art shows scheduled for Parents Weekends, and on weekends students played guitars and sang songs that they had written in a coffee house kind of setting in the "new" Student Center on the stage of the Rogers Gym. In the spring, as leaves budded and the temperature warmed, after dinner under "the poet tree," one of the few remaining elm trees on the north side of the Academic Building, Brewster poets would meet to read their poems to each other and an ever-increasing band of poet groupies developed.

Matt recalls, "One of the poets, Chuck Peterson, '78, stopped by one day to ask about a student magazine I'd shown him earlier of my previous school that I helped the students publish. After about an hour's chat, Chuck and I decided that we could combine poetry, short fiction, art and photography in a publication to appear in the early spring, just prior to the yearbook's presentation. I had a poster on my classroom wall of NH's Old Man in the Mountain, and Chuck looked up from the copy of the magazine that I showed him to see the poster in the background. 'That's it!'

Puzzled, I questioned, 'What's *it?*'

He pointed at the poster, '*Outcroppings,* that's the perfect name. We can do a salute to the rocks in our first issue.'

Outcroppings came out that spring, be it in a limited manner. The headmaster's secretary, Dottie Swaffield, typed the original on the mimeograph sheets and ran off fifty copies which were read by students and faculty and passed on to others."

Matt reports, "Within three years of my arrival, I had taken on three publications, and the following year established a journalism class out of which came the idea for the student "face book," later named by Shawn Henderson, '89, the *BAPA Book* (Brewster Academy Photo Address).

"So journalism was off and running. We published *The Browser* six times a year, one *BAPA Book*, one *Outcroppings*, and one *Winnipesaukean*, nine publications per year.

"At the same time I was teaching two English classes and quickly realized it would be near impossible to oversee the writing, layout and photography of nine separate publications and do so under the then present volunteer club status as each group came up with an idea for a new publication."

Later Matt offered a course in Journalism and as an afternoon activity as well.

Hoopes: The Student Court and Judicial Board

Soon Dean of Students Fred Djang called on Matt to serve as advisor to the Student Court.

"Over the next few years we were able to have the Student Court evolve into the Judicial Board. Students on both the Student Court and later on the Judicial Board voted on action to be taken on a specific disciplinary case and the recommendation was made to the dean who would confer with the headmaster. About 85% of the time, they would accept the court's decision.

" The board members took their charge very seriously and while it was difficult for them to discipline their peers, they seemed to know that the 'guilty' would learn from their punishment, which usually resulted in being placed on probation for a period of time and often included weekend work hours. The Judicial Board served the students" (Hoopes, 2008).

Matt Hoopes Moves Onward

Matt sailed off to the Bahamas on a year's sabbatical in 1997 and when he returned, there was a new journalism studio filled with computers and printers that he didn't even know how to turn on or off. It was time for change, and the journalism program has continued

Walter Hertz and the fencing team: Burt Johnson, Alex vonKleydorff, Steve Hallberg, Chandler Burpee, Jacqueline Therrien.

to grow with the students doing more of the format work though they were missing out on fun with scissors and glue.

Matt continues to be part of the school as the 'young alum' liaison contact for the Development Office and writing for *Brewster Connections.*

On reunion weekend, June 2006, Head of School Michael Cooper dedicated the Hoopes Journalism Room: *In honor of Matt Hoopes' thirty years of service to the Academy and the founding of the journalism program at Brewster.* "It's really nice to be a bronze plaque and still be alive," Matt noted.

Walter Hertz, Chairman of Foreign Language and Economics

In the fall of 1972, Walter Hertz, who was affectionately called "Toots" by his students, joined the Brewster faculty as chairperson of the Foreign Language Department and instructor of economics. He quickly brought to campus his worldly experience as an international diplomat, economist, and even as a translator when he worked with the Military Intelligence Department during World War II due to his fluency in German. Being German born and educated in Berlin, he also served as a simultaneous interpreter of French, German, and English for NATO in Europe.

His students not only benefited from his outstanding mastery in the field of economics, but his charm, wit, and humor were always part of class as well as school morning meeting time when he shared the latest news and his view of current events with his pipe clenched in his teeth.

"Toots' " classic education included his skill and adeptness in the field of fencing which was an afternoon activity he offered each term to willing students, students who became not only his victims and opponents, but masters at the art of fencing.

Walter Hertz was part of that stalwart group of faculty members who supported the young headmaster and played a significant role as Brewster found its way through the turbulent, difficult, and very challenging years of the 1970s and early 1980s. A classroom was dedicated in his honor in 1995 to commemorate his contributions to the Academy.

Harry Widman and the Study Trips

In 1971, Brewster hired Harry Widman as a history teacher, and within two years, he and his wife Anne would initiate an innovative international study trip program.

While teaching US History and World History, Harry also offered an elective in British History, which eventually became the foundation for the school sponsored Study Trip Program. The first venture in 1973 was to England with seven students, two girls and five boys: Jackie Rankin, '76, Martha Trenholm, '77, David Bergeron, 76, Perry Long, Alan Horowitz,'75, David Kerr, and Todd Matheson, '75. As the young people got off the plane in Heathrow, Harry remembers Todd Matheson's utter amazement as he saw London, Parliament, and Westminster Abbey in the distance.

Lauren Richadson,'77, tells of those special times when the study group would be invited to the Widmans' home. "During the evening, the Widmans would serve British tea and crumpets with marmalade as we studied British currency and prepared for our overseas venture. In appreciation of our memorable journey, our group purchased a traditional British teapot from the famous Harrods Department Store and then proceeded to fill it with sugar packets from every hotel where we had stayed. Upon returning home, we presented the memento to the Widmans with our thanks."

These trips became so popular that Harry decided to approach the Academic Affairs Committee to ask if it would be possible to offer academic credit for the planned trips. Required classes would be held before departure in which students would learn about the history and currency of each country as well as attend informative lectures to prepare for

Harry Widman, a man of faith and counsel, who, with his wife Anne, were founders and leaders of the Study Abroad Program.

the tour. Each student was to keep a daily journal and, upon return, offer a research paper or project to the History Department. The study trips presented an option for experiential learning (Widman, transcribed interview, 2008).

When Harry retired from Brewster, the torch was passed to Robert and Shirley Richardson who had often accompanied the Widmans on the study trips. The tradition of the March Study Trip to foreign lands was to continue for many more years with subsequent trips to Scotland, Ireland, Wales, Holland, France, Switzerland, Germany, Greece, Spain, Italy, Belgium, Russia, Egypt, and South Africa.

Upon Harry's retirement in 1981, the school dedicated Harry's classroom 4 in his honor. It is now the tenth grade faculty team area. (*Note, Harry continues to remain active to this day as the school's main substitute teacher and offering his yearly unique graduation invocation.)

Bill Morrison, Flying Juniors and Science Program

Completing the group of dedicated faculty members who continued on after David Smith became headmaster was Bill Morrison. Bill was not only the mainstay of the Science Department, but also pitched in as Director of Athletics for a short time. In addition, as mentioned previously, he was the point man for the sailing program and the fantastic acquisition of the fleet, six Flying Juniors sailboats. Bill was also a creative and popular science teacher who always had his students involved in hands-on projects. Sometimes it was an egg-dropping contest with the Art Department chaired by Evan Matheson,'72, wherein eggs were dropped from the windows of Chapel Hall to the parking lot below to see if they would survive intact within their protective contraption creations. Later it was joining with the Art Department and Ed Rothfus in constructing cardboard boats that could survive the Winni-Olympic racing challenge. Ed was a major cheerleader and engineer of this unique event. The starting gate was at the Two Pine Point, and the finish line was at Faculty Beach. Most boats, soaking wet, soggy, and many times not with all their cardboard, superstructures or crew, limped across the finish line with pride and glory!

Six Flying Junior sailboats (above) were given to the Academy by the Father's Club.

15. The Wish List Comes to Life

Start by doing what's necessary, then what's possible, and suddenly you are doing the impossible.—St. Francis of Assisi

Looking over the campus in the mid 1970s, there was not a single aspect of the facilities, other than its incredible natural setting, that was in good condition; and yet it made little sense to establish a facilities wish list, because the school did not have the means to even consider such an undertaking.

The Acorn Fund

Once the school was able to operate in the black, David Smith wanted to secure its financial position going forward. He knew the best way to be prepared was to have some "acorns" stored away for a rainy day. A plan was devised to budget 5% over "expenses" and to squirrel it away in the Acorn Fund then move on to 10% over expenses etc. With wise investments by the Board of Trustees, the fund grew to be a substantial amount and eventually became the bedrock for the Master Plan in the 1980s. The key was that the school's growing reputation would produce a growing enrollment and tuition revenue made up about 90% of the budget. The headmaster established the tactic of setting the budget with a conservative increase in enrollment, and when that was surpassed, each year about half of the additional revenue was placed in "The Acorn Fund."

That was the tactic through the latter half of the 70s and early 80s. Enrollment growth supported program, faculty and facility growth, as well as the establishment of an annual contribution to the Acorn Fund. By the early 80s the Academy dared to believe they had set themselves on solid ground and a cautious confidence began to grow. Eventually, the consistent strengthening enrollment and the accompanying growth of the Acorn Fund provided the foundation and the courage to believe that it made sense to establish a Master Plan for the school's facility needs. But that was still some years away. For the time being, glaring immediate needs had to be addressed.

New Student Center

In the 1970s, there were many facility needs. The question became what to address first. True to form, the answer was student centered; in fact, it became a "Student Center" as the Board of Trustees questioned," What do the students want more than anything else?" The answer? Student leadership was asking for some sort of accommodation for a place for students to gather.

The administration began looking for existing space that was underutilized. The best option seemed to be the creative use of the stage area in the school gymnasium. Frank Johnson, a trustee and chairperson of Buildings and Grounds Committee, became architect, engineer, and clerk of the works. He was the major contributor to the design, and he secured a contractor by petitioning the construction class at Kingswood High School to take on the project. When the venture was completed, it was all the students

New Student Center designed and created on the Rogers Building stage, 1976-1977.

had hoped for and more.

Challenge "78"

In 1974, a needs list had been drawn up and a consensus was reached. A Self-Study, a Long-Range Planning Committee of the Board of Trustees, and ultimately, the Visiting Committee of an accreditation association all came to the same conclusion. Brewster needed a new expanded library and greatly expanded modern science facilities. To secure the means to finance these new facilities, Campaign '78 was launched, the first capital campaign since the gymnasium had been built in the early 1950s.

Something had to be done to improve the library situation where the space was so restricted that moving more books into the current library meant moving students out. The Academy needed a quality space that would encourage and support an academic atmosphere in which students would read, do research and establish study groups. And if the library conditions were insufficient, science facilities were virtually non-existent. A room with a sink did not constitute a science lab.

New Library/Science Facility

A groundbreaking ceremony for the new facility took place on August 25, 1978, and construction began immediately. Frank Johnson, the clerk of the works and a member of the Long-Range Planning Committee, stayed right on top of the job, and things went along quickly and smoothly. In August, just prior to the 1979-1980 school year, the new library/ science facility was ready for dedication. As people arrived for the ceremony, they entered the foyer that was filled with beautiful hand crafted display cases exhibiting the famous Nelson bird collection set within scenes of natural environment. On the upper level of the building was the library and the lower level housed the new science department with a wonderful solar heated greenhouse.

The New Science/Library Building (above) built and dedicated to the Kension family in 1979. Below, the interior of the New Kenison Library.

The Kenison family had had a long and special relationship with Brewster Academy, and on that day of celebration, the new library was dedicated to the Kenison family in appreciation of their accomplishments and their contributions in both service to and financial support of their school (*Minutes of the Brewster Academy Board of Trustees,* January 12, 1979).

Arthur E. Kenison had been a member of the Brewster class of 1899. He had three sons—Frank R., Samuel M., and Arthur E., Jr.—all of whom had been boarding students and were graduates of the Academy. A bronze dedication plaque was placed in the library depicting the father standing behind his three sons in their naval uniforms, all three having been naval officers who had served overseas during World War II. The first son, Frank R. Kenison, joined the Board of Trustees and served from 1945 until 1970. The third son, Arthur E. Kenison, Jr., class of 1930, served as a trustee from 1972 to1980 and was recognized as an esteemed trustee *emeritus*. Arthur received the Brewster Alumnus of the Year Award in 1982, and at that time, Headmaster Smith said, "In our 162-year history, Arthur is the most generous of all our alumni." Second son, Samuel M. Kenison, class of 1927, did not serve on the Board himself, but his son, Arthur M. Kenison, accepted the baton when his uncle, Arthur E., retired from the Board.

Moving the Library Collection to Its New Home

In 1978, with nearly 20,000 volumes, 3,300 paperbacks, and a large collection of periodicals, records and tapes, the Kenison Memorial Library was the center of academic life at the Academy. Libby Sanders, the librarian, continued for many years to offer her considerable knowledge and expertise to Brewster students and faculty. Never were her leadership, creativity and expertise more in evidence than when she orchestrated the move of the entire library collection from the second floor of the Academic Building to its new home in the Kenision Library. Under her supervision and the direction of Dean Chuck Esty, Director of Studies Bob Richardson, Harry Widman, and Headmaster Smith, a bucket brigade of students was organized. The brigade began in the old library and wound down two flights of stairs through the lower hallway out onto the driveway between the buildings, through the open door of the new structure, up the stairs and into the new facility where faculty and librarians were waiting to put each volume into proper order and sequence on awaiting shelves in the new library. It was truly an amazing feat. The old library had functioned during that academic day, and through a true community effort, the new library was ready for study hall that evening.

Reusing Valuable Space

During the period that followed the completion of the library/science building, still not quite ready to commit to a grand plan, the school attempted to accommodate the most pressing and yet realistic needs by taking advantage of manageable opportunities that presented themselves. Facility adaptation was a constant. The new library/science facility opened up the previous library space in the Academic Building for use by the Learning Skills Department, the Art Department, and a new classroom.

Also, whenever there was an opportunity to purchase surrounding properties, the headmaster was able to receive the Board's endorsement for the purchase because providing for this need came with the additional tuition dollars to cover the cost.

Admission House and Other House Purchases

The Admissions House (1982) is a prime example of this philosophy. This historic home was located directly across the street from the main campus. With its purchase, the school was able to move the admissions operation out of the hustle and bustle of the main hallway of

This bronze plaque, honoring the Kenison men, hangs in the Kenison Library.

the Academic Building into a charming, historical, attractive, calm, and homelike setting.

In addition to the Admission House, today's athletic director's residence, Berry House (1982), Fox (1984) and Piper Houses (1984) were purchased during that period. And as the school grew in this measured manner, the financial position and the confidence in the school's longevity grew from those incremental steps. Later in 1991, Chamberlain House, which had been the manse for the Congregational Church, would be moved onto campus and redesigned and renovated to provide housing for 12 students and two faculty living quarters. Also during that time period, Kimball House was entirely renovated and rebuilt to provide for updated dorm rooms and two faculty apartments

Additions to The Estabrook and Sargent Hall

The increase in enrollment had grown to the point that the Estabrook dining area and lounges were not large enough to accommodate the faculty and students. The headmaster convinced the trustees of the importance of maintaining the tradition of family dining with the whole community joined together at evening meals. To continue to do so, the dining area had to be expanded and the lounge areas, intended to serve as comfortable gathering areas for pre- and post-meal conversations, enlarged. The dining room sidewall toward the Academic Building was moved out 15 feet, and a faculty entrance was built on that side. The student and faculty lounges were enlarged and renovated, and the inside main stairway was turned to face the front entrance.

Four new faculty apartments were added to the lakeside of Sargent Hall, while former faculty apartments were converted to student rooms to accommodate 12 additional students. The project would be paid for over a three-year period from the tuition and fees of the additional students.

Master Plan

By the mid 80s as confidence had continued to grow, the school increasingly recognized the inefficiencies of converting and reconverting spaces to adapt to the pressures of growth. Courage was mustered to consider establishing and committing to a master facility plan that would best serve the students and faculty alike and would carry forward the mission/business of the school. As the Academy approached the mid 80s, its bond of partnership with the parents had grown to a firm conviction that it "had the right to dream and that dream had a right to be."

By this point, Board President DeWitt had become convinced that it was poor economics to continue following the pattern of "conversions and acquisitions" to make things work. He saw that the Acorn Fund had reached a point where it was a legitimate source of funding for capital projects. He also believed that once you put a plan together, people see the plan, and they think it's doable. All of a sudden they think, "Wow, wouldn't it be great to have that!"

He encouraged a process that led to contracting for the establishment of a facility master plan. Before long the plan was tacked to the wall of the headmaster's office. The plan showed six new dorms, three on each side of campus, a greatly expanded Estabrook Hall that would contain a new dining facility and student center as well as completely renovated student and faculty apartments. It also showed a new athletic complex and renovated arts building. And Rink was right in his prediction, for once the plan was on the wall ,it stimulated the "Wow, wouldn't that be great!" exclamations, and somehow it all seemed more doable.

But again while the trustees recognized that it was time to move beyond the old way of doing things, they were not willing to take out a loan for ten million dollars to put the components of the plan into place. What they were saying was, "Go for it, and raise the necessary funds." Thus the goal was set. The vision and the challenge were established, and

Moving the library from the second floor of the Academic to the new library.

The admissions office was moved from the Academic Building to its new home across Main Street.

the headmaster set out to find the means to make it happen. Fortunately for the Academy, a group of interested, committed, and capable parents came forward to assist him in that quest. At the core of that partnership initially and throughout the remaining years of his headmastership were parents Grant and Helene Wilson (Grant '87 and Kirstin '88), Nick and Penny Harris (Lamont '84 and Henry '88), Jim and Betty Pinckney (Jon '84), and Hank and Ann Spaulding (Tom '85).

The Wilson Family

Grant and Helene Wilson first stopped by to see the headmaster during a Parents Weekend when their son, Grant, and daughter, Kirstin, were students. When they departed, it was with a promise to provide a good deal of stock in a friend's growing company to the school. The second time they came by, the Master Plan hung on the wall.

In that later conversation with Grant, David had indicated that, "the most we had ever raised in a capital campaign was $300,000 for the library/science building and the fulfillment of this Master Plan would cost at least $10 million." He asked, "What should we do? Should we just begin with a million-dollar campaign for the first three of the six proposed dorms?" Grant replied, "David if you know what you're going to do and you are committed to doing it, let people know. Who knows? There might be someone out there who will do 10% of whatever your plan is? Do you want $100,000 towards your million-dollar campaign or would you like 10% of your ten-million-dollar campaign?" David, with an OK from the Board, followed Grant's advice and took on the entire project.

A couple of months later Grant and Helene had seen to it that his prediction came true.

Grant Wilson, President of the Board of Trustees, introduces the master plan.

They understood that there is nothing more challenging than bringing up and educating young people. They devoted their philanthropy toward supporting those who were engaged and effective in helping young people. Their generosity and the extraordinary partnership and friendship that developed between David and Grant would result in a relationship of accomplishment in all the advances the school would make during David's tenure as headmaster—and beyond.

The Pinckney *Family*

With the birth of the Master Plan, came the initial major addition to the campus. The Pinckney Boat House was the first project to be undertaken. That priority position was driven by the Pinckney family's support rather than actual priority of need, but as it turned out, the Pinckney Boathouse made a great opening statement. It not only announced, "We have made it," but also that the rebirth of the Academy would continue in all respects. In addition, it placed that spectacular exclamation point on the Academy's unique and extraordinary physical asset, its half-mile of frontage on the lake.

Jon Pinckney, class of 1984, had arrived at Brewster from California as a sophomore. Jim, his dad, had the California roots while his mother, Betty, was a native of New England. When she became concerned that her second son was being corrupted by what she referred to as "the southern California mentality," she wanted to find a school with rock hard New England values which also had a sailing program because Jon had been a competitive sailor for most all of his young life.

At Parents Weekend, shortly before Jon's graduation from Brewster, Betty and Jim

The Pinckney Boathouse honoring Betty and Jim Pinckney (John, '84).

attended a reception at the headmaster's home. David Smith used that occasion to share with the gathering the newly designed Master Plan. After listening to David's presentation, Betty caught his ear and while expressing her enthusiasm for the vision for the school's future, she offered, "The school should really get the sailboats out from under the snow and ice" where they were 'stored' during the winter months. She suggested that if the trustees agreed to match his contribution, she thought Jon's grandfather would contribute toward the construction of a lean-to for that purpose.

That conversation led to others, and Jon's grandfather advanced his vision in collaboration with the headmaster by devoting himself to the design and the support of a magnificent building that would mean a great deal to both the school and his family. The Pinckney Boat House not only serves the sailing and crew programs, but it provides a spectacular setting for school events as well as a variety of functions in service to various organizations of the greater Wolfeboro community. The Pinckney Boat House was dedicated in 1987.

As the family's legacy of the boathouse was being constructed, Betty joined the Board of Trustees. Her legacy of board service would center on her desire to insure that, as the school's increasing strength provided for additions to the physical plant, its primary attention would remain rooted in the student-centered approach, the true foundation and strength of the school. She encouraged the school to pause in its enrollment growth to insure that the focus of its attention remained centered in fulfilling the promise of its mission to the individual student. Just as has been the case with other parents who joined in the quest to fulfill the vision, through their son's experience, the Pinckneys came to appreciate the crucial difference in Brewster's approach. Partially out of gratitude but more so out of a desire to contribute to sustaining and advancing that special quality, they joined in support.

The Harris Family

Lamont Harris, '84, had just graduated, and his brother Henry, '88, was to follow, when the headmaster received a letter from their father, a soft-spoken and caring man. In his brief note, Nick simply stated, "David, Penny and I want to thank you for all that you and your school have done for our son." A check for $25,000 was enclosed. At that time, that check was the largest single gift in David's tenure.

Staying in touch, David wrote a letter to Nick at this juncture which began, "Nick I am not asking you for anything, but I just wanted to share with you what is happening," and he went on to spell out the vision of the Master Plan. Shortly thereafter, the headmaster received a call from Nick. "If I gave you a check for $100,000, what would you do with it?" David's immediate response was, "I'd stick it in my back pocket." A surprised Nick asked, "What do you mean?"

"I am about to go before the Board of Trustees and try to sell them on a Master Plan that is probably going to cost between ten and twelve million dollars. The most money that has ever been raised for any capital campaign is about $300,000. The Board is going to look at me and say, 'Are you crazy?' and I'll reach into my back pocket pull out your check, put it down on the table and say, 'Here's someone who doesn't think so.' " And that is essentially what happened. From that point on, any time there was a major move forward, Nick and Penny would be there to help.

Another such time that is special in David's memories was the occasion when he was in his office rather late one evening over a Christmas break, and his phone rang. It was Nick with another gift of support. David left his office and walked through the snowy paths home to Lord House. Sheila was in the kitchen, and David asked her, "Who is the patron-saint of Christmas?" She answered, "St. Nicholas?" and he responded, "That's right, and I just talked to him."

Harris House honoring Penny and Nick Harris, parents of Lamont, '84, and Henry, '88.

The Harris' emotional support, as well as their generous contributions, helped to bring the components of the Master Plan into place. Student/faculty housing was the first priority, and when they came into place, one carried the name Harris House. When the pilot program of the Brewster Model program was to be introduced with the freshman class in 1993, it needed a home for a new suite of classrooms, etc. With a lead gift from Nick and Penny, Harris Hall was created in what had been the attic of the Academic Building.

The Harris family, both through the experience of the "boys" and the partnership of their parents, will always be enshrined as special members of the Brewster Family. Both families have suffered the loss of a wonderful husband and father and our great friend, Nick, who left behind yet another magnificent gift of support. He is truly our school's St. Nick.

The Spaulding Family

Tommy Spaulding, the youngest of seven children in his family, enrolled as a freshman in 1980. At that fall's Parents Weekend, Hank and Ann Spaulding arrived on campus to visit with Tommy's teachers, dorm parents, and coach in order to gain a sense of how their son was doing in his first weeks at his new school. Tom's former school experiences had not been positive for him, and they had been searching for a school that would prove to Tom and to everyone else that he could be successful academically. When the headmaster went over to speak to the Spauldings that evening, Ann took his hand and, with a tear in her eye, told him that she had never lost faith that such a school existed, and now they had found it.

Prior to Tommy's sophomore year, the athletic director, in his budget request, had a line item for championship jackets. The headmaster removed that item telling the AD that we had real pressing needs and there was little likelihood we would win any championships.

Tommy was not big of stature, but he was a talented soccer player with a big heart and great, inexhaustible determination. The regular fall season ended with Brewster and Proctor Academy undefeated in league play. They had played each other twice and in both cases the game had ended in a one to one tie after double overtime. The two schools agreed to have a playoff game for the championship on a neutral field, and they decided to play at Tilton School. Since the athletic season was over, all students could attend the game. The Brewster band was there. In reality, the school didn't have a band, but it did that day. One student brought his slide trombone, another a clarinet, a third a trumpet, and a couple of others brought drums. Faculty member Phil Goldstein arrived dragging a little cannon that he intended to fire after each of Brewster's goals. At the end of regulation play, he had fired it only once, for again the score was tied one to one. As time was running out in the second overtime, this little sophomore, Tommy Spaulding, in a cloud of dust, shot the ball up into the upper right hand corner of the net, and the little cannon fired the announcement. Brewster had won the championship!

The headmaster called back to campus with the joyous news. The school's chef/manager immediately went to work creating a huge celebratory cake decorated for the Lakes Region Champions. Bob Richardson grabbed a few students and went to his barn where they retrieved an old sheet and with red paint wrote "Champions" in large letters. They hung it from the second floor windows of the Academic Building. Tommy's goal was one of the most glorious moments in the school's sports history.

Hank Spaulding called David Smith the next day. Before he could say anything, David told Hank, "Your son got me in trouble." "What do you mean? What did he do?" With smile on his face and undoubtedly in his voice, David responded, "I have an athletic director, Bill Pottle, who tries to plan for every possible contingency. Bill was putting the budget together and told me he needed some money in the budget for championship

The Estabrook with the Spaulding-Emerson Student Center honoring the Emerson and Spaulding families (Tom, '85).

jackets. I told him "Are you crazy—we haven't won a championship in years. If we win a championship, I'll find the money for jackets."

"So you see your son got me in trouble yesterday due to his gutsy play and his incredible goal. We have now won a championship, and I have no funds for jackets for the team." And with a swell of pride in his voice, Hank responded, "I will take care of the jackets for those boys. Don't you worry about that!" In addition to taking care of the jackets, Hank had a felt banner made up proclaiming the Lakes Region Championship. That banner started a tradition. If one looks up in the Smith Center today, he or she will see innumerable League and New England Championship banners. With the exception of one, they are all in the school's maroon; that one is bright red and reads Lakes Region Men's Soccer Champions 1982.

That was just the first of the Spaulding family's many annual and capital gifts to the school. They were always quietly behind the scenes, yet when additional scholarship aid was needed, the Spauldings were there. When the students initiated an effort to create a student center on the stage of the old gym in the mid 80s, the Spauldings were there. When the Master Plan called for a new student center within the Estabrook complex, once again the Spauldings were there to help. When David wanted to recognize Hank and Ann by naming that facility the Spaulding Student Center, he knew they would not allow it and so, as the expression goes, "he made them an offer they couldn't refuse." He informed Hank and Ann that, with their permission, it would be named the Spaulding /Emerson Center in memory of their parents.

Years later, when David and Sheila were approaching the end of their careers at the Academy, the school took on the largest single capital project in the school's history.

Gaining the support necessary to construct a second-to-none athletic and wellness center was going to be a monumental challenge. Once again, in their quiet way, Hank and Anne Spaulding supported David in advancing the school's capacity to best serve.

The most extraordinary feature of that facility is a retractable artificial field enabling all of our field sports teams to practice inside. Twenty years after the goal was set, not far from where the '82 banner now hangs, there is a plaque dedicating that "field."

Perhaps the initial support of these families came out of gratitude, but then a sense of partnership developed as they wished to join with the school in the continuing efforts to impact the lives of its young people. As with other great challenges over the last twenty years, the future Smith Center would mean a great deal to the school's capacity to best serve its students; without extraordinary support it would not, it could not happen. Once again it was the partnership with the parents, more than any other factor, that made it happen.

And unlike what occurs at most schools, the partnership with the Wilsons, Harrises, Pinckneys, and Spauldings would continue long after their children graduated as they shared in both the effort and the rewards of their support to the Academy. Other families to follow were the Clarks, the Slyes, the Brooks, the Colkets, the Stabiles, the Turners, the Stones, the Murrays, the Jobes, the Mudges and a continuing line of others, "We could not have done what we have done without you, and we will continue to do all we can do with you."

Six New Faculty/ Student Homes

While the Pinckney Boathouse was the first project undertaken, the immediate question was what need and opportunity holds the priority position for the school's attention within the Master Plan? The answer was a "no-brainer"—quality housing for both faculty and students. Faculty deserved it, students would love it, and parents would appreciate it.

North Campus Faculty/Student Housing Begins and Continues to South Campus

The first three faculty/student homes were constructed behind Sargent Hall. In 1986, they were up and running. Initially referred to as Houses I, II and III, they became Spencer House, Mason House, and Hughes House honoring three long-serving trustees: Carlton Spencer who headed up the Brewster Trust trustees; Arthur Mason who was treasurer of the board during the transition years; and Adelaide Hughes who, in addition to serving as secretary, also contributed her remarkable faith and spirit to the Board and her school for 39 years as a trustee.

Harris House, Vaughan House, and Lamb House were completed in 1988: Harris House in recognition of all the Harris family meant to the school, Vaughan House in recognition of Burtis Vaughan, one of the greatest teachers in the history of the school and the man who served as headmaster in transitioning the school in 1964-1965 when Kingswood Regional High School was constructed; and Lamb House in recognition of the great support of Trustee Herb Lamb and in memory of his love for his wife Sarah "Sally" Lord Lamb.

Last of the Expansion of the 1980s

During the summer of 1988, the old alumni/writing center, which had a most unusual history, was picked up again and moved to a new foundation on the south side of Academy Drive opposite the parking lot for the Estabrook Dining Hall. Faculty members, Evan Matheson, Jason Thatcher, and Ron Nentwig, assisted Tim Radley as he renovated and added an addition to the building that would serve as the school's art center. The new facility accommodated areas for pottery, drawing, painting, and photography. But it had not always been an art building. As mentioned in previous chapters, in the late 1890s, this building had begun its life as an icehouse for the Pavilion Hotel. In 1903, after the fire that destroyed the original academic building, it was brought up from the lakefront on a horse-drawn sled to serve as a temporary classroom. Over its continuing history, it served as a chemistry lab, a chapel, the home economics building followed by a brief stint as a senior student center, as the Alumni/ Development Center on the ground floor with the student publication center upstairs and, finally, as the senior writing class taught by Mary Fallon. Now, after its latest move and incarnation, it had a new purpose and would serve as a student art center.

In the fall of 1989, when students returned to campus, there were several more changes that had been completed over the summer months. The Estabrook had a new bookstore, post office with student mailboxes, and an expanded lounge for faculty. There were renovations to the upstairs dormitory rooms and faculty apartments as well. The dining room and kitchen facilities were enlarged substantially and a folding oak-paneled partition was installed between the dining room and the Student Center, which added flexibility to the functional use of either space. The Student Center had its own entrance and was equipped with a snack bar and tables and chairs. A circular stairway led to the second floor mezzanine and TV lounge with fireplace and meeting room. On the lower level were washers and dryers, game tables, and booths for snacking and socializing. All new oak tables and chairs and paneled walls brought a dramatic new look and feel to the Estabrook dining room.

Revisions in the Academic Building provided for more classrooms, a study hall space, and a new journalism room. The Lake Room in Bearce Hall became a dance studio, and a new plan for roadways and walkways was developed. As the facilities Master Plan process paused to catch its breath, the school community settled in with heightened enthusiasm to take advantage of all that had been brought into place to enrich their experience.

The Business Office
Financial Master Plan

By the time of Bob Simoneau's arrival at Brewster as the new business manager in July 1986, the Academy's trustees had recently approved the development of the facilities master plan. Formulating a facility master plan had been exhilarating, and the resulting vision of what such a reality would mean to the school was exciting. But there was a huge price tag attached to the vision, as discussed above. As a small school with a young private-school alumni base, the opportunity for capital fund raising was very limited.

Municipal Bonds

With the decision to utilize the Acorn fund approved and looking for other funding means, Bob suggested the possibility of floating municipal bonds rather than paying commercial interest rates on monies borrowed as he had been able to do in the past in overseeing the finances of a 35,000 student school district in California. The Academy needed to find a way to replenish its Acorn Fund and work towards raising more annual fund dollars to take care of the newly acquired and built facilities.

In the fall of 1995, on the strength of the Academy's finances and its strong management team, the Academy was successful in securing an investment grade rating and with the help of State Street Bank floated a $6.5 million municipal bond.

At this juncture, led by the Board of Trustees, the leadership of the school met and formulated a Strategic Plan designed to ensure the school's viability while maintaining and enhancing its financial equilibrium. This plan committed to the priorities set out in its facility and programmatic master plans, and the leadership also outlined a comprehensive, aggressive, long-range financial plan. The school that two decades earlier had been on the verge of extinction, focusing on finding the means to pay off its loans, now had confidence that by securing favorable financing, it could establish the facilities and the programs that would thrust the school into a leadership position, thus securing its future.

Enthusiasm for launching the facility plan and all it provided for the obvious blossoming of the school became infectious. The plan stimulated generous support, and securing a second bond at a most favorable rate provided the impetus to keep it going. That bond refinancing, enhanced with a letter of credit from the Allied Irish Banks, at a very favorable interest rate, permitted immediate retirement of the first bond with its much higher rate as well as some additional commercial loans that had carried significantly higher non-municipal commercial interest rates. It also supplemented fund-raising, allowing the construction and purchase of equipment to keep rolling for about four years straight.

In summary, this refinancing strategy saved the Academy millions of actual interest dollars when compared to the original fixed interest rate on the first bond floated and the double digit rates on the commercial notes, especially on leased equipment.

This funding would be employed in the completion of the Wilson Center for Teaching and Learning, which was yet to be constructed, renovation of faculty and student housing provided at Chamberlin House, Kimball House, Haines House, and the Estabrook House as well as reconstruction of an expanded dining hall and the Spaulding-Emerson Student Center.

In addition to this construction and renovation, the school followed guidelines of its master plan, purchasing and renovating various late 19th century homes along South Main Street. These acquisitions included Alt House, Avery House, Goodwin House, Kelley House, Cate House, Holmes House, 6 Estabrook Road, and 100 South Main Street.

Addressing Deferred Maintenance and Infrastructure

Even after the heavy construction subsided, the beat continued. Shortly after Bob Simoneau had become business manager, the school leadership made a priority to address all the school's deferred maintenance issues. They had also determined that each year's budget going forward would contain enough funding to meet current maintenance needs, thus insuring that deferred maintenance would never again become an issue for the school. Improvements to the infrastructure included resurfacing and expanding campus roadways and pathways, installing new electrical services across the campus, and laying down 43 miles of fiber optic cable that provided for 3,000 ports and the establishment of the *Brewsternet.*

Funding for Laptop Computer Program and Renovating Anderson Hall

All the while, Bob continued to explore the State of New Hampshire's municipal bonding availability. Through this program, he secured Revenue Anticipation and Capital Anticipation Notes which have helped the Academy offer to parents an economical way to provide affordable laptops to their students as well as the needed software and network connections to provide a truly ubiquitous tool for student-directed learning in the 21st Century.

The Capital Anticipation notes would also help renovate the Academy's first-class music performance hall, now called Anderson Hall, that was purchased from the Catholic Diocese of Manchester, New Hampshire, in 2004, with lead financial support from the Anderson Family (Jared, '06).

Robert Simoneau Retires as Business Manager

During the years that Bob Simoneau served as chief financial officer/business manager for the Academy, the school not only grew in size but also gradually broadened its mission. As it became increasingly complex to conduct school business, the business office staff expanded to include the cfo/business manager, an assistant business manager, a secretary/ administrative assistant, an accounting systems supervisor, an accounts payables clerk, an accounts receivables clerk, and a bookkeeper.

For seventeen years, David Smith and Bob Simoneau worked closely together. After David retired in 2003, Bob remained to provide transitional business office leadership for Dr. Michael Cooper. In 2009 Bob left his position of CFO/Business Manger and returned to his first love, the classroom. He still made himself available to the head of school, the business office, and the development office for initiatives where his experience and commitment would help the school continue to advance (Simoneau, 2010).

Illustration of the Academy's Growth over a 34 Year Period 1975-2009

1975	1985	1995	2005	2009
Total Enrollment				
128	224	320	365	363
Enrollment (Boarding)				
93	180	265	283	288
Enrollment (Day)				
35	45	55	83	75
Tuition (Boarding)				
$4,400	$9,800	$21,300	$34,980	$42,305
Tuition (Day)				
$2,200	$4,900	$11,800	$20,720	$24,940
Square Footage				
110,414	197,090	317,014	423,631	432,281
Value				
$870,323	$2,700,051	$22,499,468	$43,412,823	$50,983,083
Acreage				
59	61	62	71	82
Financial Aid				
$82,844	$132,645	$1,025,317	$2,334,660	$2,944,393
Market Value				
$334,985	$2,352,771	$3,040,484	$11,122,393	$7,672,101

Invested Funds

*In 2009 the physical plant grew to $50,983,083 with the Curvey gift of an 11.3 acres property in Alton, NH. It included 650 ft of lake frontage and 6 buildings with a square foot increase of 8,650 sq. ft. The investment portfolio suffered with the economic market meltdown during 2008-2009. Financial aid grew by 26% to $3 million. (Robert Simoneau, CFO/ Business Manager, Report, January 2009).

We thank Bob Simoneau for his desire to make a difference; he indeed made a difference and was "the right man at the right time" in the history of the Academy and for that we are grateful.

16. Changing Times of 1980s and 1990s

I hear, and I forget. I see and I remember. I do, and I understand.—Confucius

A Nation at Risk

By 1980, the American people had begun to take a good hard look at the education provided by their public school systems. The Vietnam War and the cultural conflicts of the 1970s had readied them to evaluate thoroughly where they were going in the education of their young people. Added to this was the fact that America still continued to be divided spiritually following the 1954 United States Supreme Court decision in the *Brown v. Board of Education of Topeka, Kansas,* calling for the complete integration of public schools. A central focus emerged on this question: Did the United States compare favorably with other countries when their public school curriculum requirements and student achievement were contrasted?

In 1983, the federal government's National Commission on Excellence in Education published its study, *A Nation at Risk,* which sent shock waves throughout American educational circles and the general populace. By 1964, secondary school curricula had become homogenized and diffused to a point at which there was no central purpose. Student migration from the challenge of the "college preparatory" track to the less challenging "general" track had eroded to a point at which, by 1979, numbers indicated a decrease from 42% to 24%. Twenty-three percent of state colleges lowered their selectivity ratings when admitting new students each year, while publishing companies began to "write down" their student textbooks so that those pupils with low vocabulary skills might survive. Less than 31% of the average graduating classes took Algebra 2, 13% took French 1, Geography, less than 16%, and Calculus at 6% (*A Nation at Risk,* 1983; Archived Information—Findings). This raised the question of how America could possibly compete actively in the world markets of the future.

Brewster Responds to *A Nation at Risk*

As the nation was conducting a self-examination of its educational delivery system, a maturing Brewster Academy was turning its attention to maximizing the contributions of its academic, social, and extracurricular curricula. Director of Studies Robert Richardson received a special assist in placing a focus on this endeavor from the school's new dynamic and committed admissions director.

Andrew Wooden's initial introduction to the Academy came as a candidate for an English teaching position. He was assigned one English class, the position of sailing coach, and assistant dorm parent. Andrew went above and beyond with his contributions. He was committed to the school mission, and he shared the headmaster's vision of what could be. Andrew was soon advanced to the position of director of admissions.

In response to *A Nation at Risk's* attention to educational quality, Andrew Wooden set out to study the matter in detail and to write an appraisal of where the school stood in relation to the concerns expressed within the report and where it could expect to be in the future.

In his resulting monograph, *Brewster Academy's Position within Current Enrollment Trends in Independent Schools,* dated December 1982. Wooden surveyed the trends in independent school enrollment figures. Those trends projected significant declines in the years ahead due to several root causes, namely, the rapid increase in tuition costs, the instability of the international market (devalued currency), doubt about the future of Reaganomics, and a general trend to downgrade the stature of the term "preppies" as no longer carrying the prestige of a good education. A survey by the Northern New England Schools Association found that three schools had a good year, eight stayed constant, and nine opened with substantially lower enrollment statistics—a gloomy picture indeed for a small independent school.

In his concluding assessment, Wooden advised that independent schools that didn't establish a marketing research component within their admissions departments would have great difficulty attracting and enrolling students. To demonstrate just where Brewster stood in admission statistics, he also shared the following table depicting Brewster's admission reports by grade, class averages and year from 1979-80 through 1981-82.

Enrollment Numbers and Academic Averages 1979- 1980 to1981—1982

	1981-82	1980-81	1979-80
Grade 9	28 - 77.32	32 – 75.6	25 - 75.8
Grade 10	58 – 77.3	38 - 75.5	27 - 75.1
Grade 11	52 – 75.9	43 – 78.2	57 - 73.7
Grade 12	44 – 80.2	60 – 79.2	43 – 76.5
Post Graduate	23 – 73.8	19 – 78.3	13 – 73.7
	203 – 77.9	192 – 77.5	165 – 75.2

Due to Wooden's program as admissions director, in combination with the school's growing reputation, the dire national predictions did not materialize at Brewster.

A consultant Andrew engaged concluded that Brewster was one of the "best kept secrets" of independent schools. Believing that "compliment" to be true, Andrew sought and received the resources to market the Academy as a school with a deserved reputation a notch or two above its competition.

Academics Had To Come First

Andrew's monograph helped the Academic Affairs Committee to place the *A Nation at Risk* report in its proper perspective relative to the Academy while emphasizing the need to continue to advance the school's programs.

The committee, under the leadership of Director of Studies Robert Richardson, set out to determine how to best advance the development of Brewster's curriculum. The initial discussions centered upon the consideration of academic challenge, and the committee determined that there must be more challenge for the upper grades in terms of both the depth and breadth of course offerings. They decided that each academic department would offer an Advanced Placement program directed at 11th and 12th graders. By introducing these offerings, the school would not only insure each student was truly challenged; it also would permit students to achieve national recognition and, potentially, college credit for achievement in English, history, foreign languages, mathematics and science.

The Academic Affairs Committee moved on to review and to establish a policy relative to the units of credit required by each department for a Brewster Academy diploma. As policy was involved, the following were recommended to the Board of Trustees for their endorsement:

The faculty 1981.

English—four units
History—three units—American History required
Mathematics—three units—Algebra 2 required
Foreign Language—two units in a single language required
Science—three units—Biology required

The Core Writing Program

In advancing our belief in the importance of skill development, Mary Fallon, an amazingly talented and dedicated English teacher, in conjunction with the Academic Affairs Committee, developed a Core Writing Program to be implemented during the new school year. The program consisted of levels of instruction and a unified process to be followed in each grade. In addition, each academic department reviewed its curriculum with a writing coordinator who helped develop writing topics, make suggestions, and review progress. The coordinator would use one period weekly to evaluate progress, make revision recommendations, and coordinate change with the instructor (*Academic Report,* Robert Richardson, Director of Studies, June 21, 1985, pp. 2-3).

The new core-writing program was scheduled to be placed into practice for the first time in 1985, the same year that a NEASC visiting team would return again to campus for the regular ten-year accreditation review. Although there was some skepticism about the need to begin such an effort at that time, the decision was made to start as soon as possible, and the evaluating committee praised the work done on the program and supported its continuation. Later, elective writing classes would be offered: Writing the Essay for underclassmen and then Intensive Writing for upperclassmen. Each included personal weekly conferences with a writing teacher in order that students would get immediate individualized feedback on their writing skill development.

New Science Curriculum Offerings

The next area of concentration was the Science Department. During the 1984-85 school year, Eric Chamberlain, department chairman, developed an optimal educational program combining academics with field experiences. Such a program offered a varied, but balanced, method of learning. In this approach, learning occurred beyond just the classroom and the textbook and was implemented in Freshwater Ecology, Human Survival, Marine Science, and Natural History.

Environmental Club and Activities

Heightened interest in environmental preservation began within the student body during 1970 and 1971 when Science Department Head Albert Powers first turned the heads of students and teachers toward the spillage of gasoline in the lake. An environmental science class was organized, and a formal club was established in 1992. The club was named Brewster Academy Students for the Environment or BASE, and the group had designed a motto and symbol for a large *Environmental Quilt* about New Hampshire. The plan was then transformed into a beautiful quilt by seamstress Marcella Stewart of Effingham. The quilt was placed inside a specially-made case, constructed by Hab Masse, the school carpenter, and was hung in the Estabrook hallway.

Under Science Department Chairman Bruce Gorrill's direction, the club worked with the kitchen and the bookstore to reduce the cost of garbage and trash disposal, and their first impact calculations and recycling remunerations were encouraging. Throughout the campus, the club had separated paper, glass, plastic, tin and cardboard. Helpers with vehicles of conveyance had been enlisted, and specialized recycle dumpsters had been provided to organize the removal of the refuse in an environmentally sound fashion *(Brewster Connections,* February 1993, p. 5).

Over the years, the Environmental Club has continued its crusade periodically to

Teacher John Bishop conducts a class freshwater ecology field experiment at the lakeshore.

An Environmental Quilt, depicting the tasks undertaken by the club, hangs in the Estabrook entryway: Melissa Bernardin, Noah Magnifico, Erik Jones, and Akari Miki,club leaders 1993.

involve the entire campus and has attempted to build "green" awareness at school, but in the last few years, another strong focus was re-established culminating with the celebration of National Earth Week. The dedicated Environmental Club was active with bringing concerns to the forefront not only with the school use of water and electricity, but also with its commitment to recycling. With the faculty support of Ben Larson, Lauren Hammond,' 79, Gratia Trahn and the student leadership of Kelsey Hammond,'10, Jared Boudreau,'10, and Taylor Roy, 10, an intense campus drive was begun.

The Senior Seminar

Another addition to the curriculum that provided a unique and valuable experience for students was the Senior Seminar. Designed and directed by the Academic Affairs Committee, it offered students a chance to examine a pressing issue of their times. It also presented an opportunity to develop important communication, research, and thinking skills that would serve them well in their college careers. Replacing the students' usual academic schedule, the seminar ran for four weeks at the end of the spring term and included regular seminar meetings and scheduled lectures and films. Participating seniors were required to do extensive reading, make individual seminar presentations, attend lectures and films, participate in discussion, do research, and write a long research paper on a topic related to the central theme of the course.

The goal of the course was not only to encourage students to consider an important issue that would impact their lives, but also to stimulate student initiative and independence in the learning process. The seminar was aimed at self-directed education and open inquiry (*Brewster Review,* Centennial Issue, p.33).

ESL: English as a Second Language

As Brewster admissions increasingly accepted more international students, it became apparent that additional support was required for these young people. In 1985, Barbara Douglas came to Brewster to be part of the Learning Skills Program, but Mrs. Douglas soon found herself organizing and developing an English as a Second Language (ESL) program for the larger number of foreign students. Two different course levels served these students—one centering on basic skills and another more accelerated track. With Mrs. Douglas as a strong advocate for these young people not only as teacher, advisor and friend, but sometimes mother, the ESL program became a remarkable success and has remained an integral part of the curriculum for international students in Brewster's academic offerings. When Mrs. Douglas moved to Maine, Raylene Davis became director.

In 1991, at an All-School Meeting, the international students held a flag dedication program to introduce the entire school to the different cultures and countries that were represented at Brewster. President of the International Club, Matt Wong,'91, was the master of ceremonies, supported by Mrs. Anita Fahy, director of the Student Center, who initiated the program. This tradition has continued as the school honors each new country that is represented on campus. Today there are 19 flags hanging from the rafters in the Student Center.

Nineteen international flags hang from the rafters of the Spaulding-Emerson Student Center.

Music Returns

As the Academy continued to review its curriculum and provide for further varied and expanded offerings, the Board of Trustees endorsed the recommendation of Headmaster Smith to restore the music program to the Academy. Mr. Smith hired Dr. William Gaver, former chair of the Music Department at Mississippi State University to create a music program at the school.

With some support from "alums" that carried fond memories of the Burt Vaughan era with his glee club, band, and choral society, the program gradually grew. Glen Depine, a talented musician and trumpet player, was to follow Bill Gaver, and a new teacher, Colleen Foley, in 1985, joined Glen with an instrument music program, glee club and voice lessons. Finally, a music program was reestablished in the Brewster curriculum, but it wasn't until 1993, when the multitalented "pied piper," Andy Campbell, was hired to head up the music department that the program truly took off.

Drama and Art

Drama was always a part of the school's offerings and tradition, and it continued to be part of Brewster's extracurricular program in the 70s and 80s with a wide variety of activity from school-wide talent shows to drama performances. As with other programs, it too began to grow and build as a viable department with productions such as *The Rain Maker, Antigone, Guys and Dolls, The Phantom Strikes Again, Mouse Trap, Anything Goes, Midsummer Night's Dream, Carnival, The Fantastics, Damn Yankees, GodSpell, Grease and Rashomon.*

The Art Department also became re-energized, and a broader curriculum was added to its offerings. Evan Matheson, a 1972 graduate of Brewster, joined the Art Department in 1980. It didn't take Evan long to revitalize the art and photography program. When the Art Department was moved from the gym to its new home in the Academic Building, Evan lugged equipment, tore out walls, and built up the new Art Studio by himself. In 1981, the students dedicated their yearbook to him for his fairness, understanding, humor, energy, artistic talent, sensitivity, and adventurous spirit, and for coaching them in soccer and skiing.

By 1983, Ed Rothfus had joined Evan in the Art Department. His amazing creativity and unusual art projects caught the interest of the entire student body. From his zany "egg drops" to his weird "boat floats" projects on the waterfront, Ed was a man the students looked to, not only for his remarkable talent and encouragement, but also for his faith which he shared with them. In 1986, the yearbook was dedicated to him too with comments on his shin-splinting X-C teams, pain-gaining wrestling holds, heart-stopping haunted houses, and two-wheeled crazed racers. The Art Department was in good hands

The Arrival of Computers

Another major area of curriculum development was the arrival of the computer on campus. Information technology and the use of the computers in the classroom had its beginning in 1982, when Room 4, one of the most prominent and accessible classrooms in the Academic Building, was given over to computer instruction. Fundraising, design and planning were driven by Headmaster David Smith, Business Manager Samuel Oliva, Mathematics Department Chair David Atwood and the Brewster Academy Parents' Association President Joseph Taft, who together raised thousands of dollars to develop a state-of-the-art, for its time, computer facility. The Tandy Corporation TRS-80 Model III computers were deployed in an open classroom style that presaged the future modular classroom designs that were to be brought to the Academic Building and the Wilson Center in the 90s.

This combination of community involvement and outreach led to one of the true pioneers of computer science lending her name and her support to Brewster's computing

Rear Admiral Grace Murray Hopper, a true pioneer in the computer field.

efforts. Grace Murray Hopper, who summered in Wolfeboro as a child with her family, was one of the true pioneers in the computer field. She also was to hold the distinction as the country's first female rear admiral in the United States Navy.

Grace Murray Hopper had been one of the developers of the Mark I and Mark II calculators that predated the earliest computers. She was on the team that designed UNIVAC I, developed the first ever computer compiler (which allowed for programmers to code in relatively clear source code instead of arcane object code), helped to develop the seminal COBOL computer language, and popularized the terms "computer bug" and "debugging" computers after she corrected a malfunction by extracting a moth caught inside of one of the relay cabinets, an insect that remains in the Smithsonian Institution today.

The Grace Murray Hopper Center for Computer Learning was dedicated on November 7, 1983. Shortly prior to the ceremony, Grace's good friend, Kenneth H. Olsen, the president and founder of Digital Equipment Corporation, saw to it that the center would be infused with their new equipment. Mr. Olsen arrived on campus by helicopter to be the keynote speaker at the dedication.

The governor declared the day Grace Murray Hopper Day in the State of New Hampshire. The ceremony honoring then Captain Hopper with the dedication of the Grace Murray Hopper Center for Computer Learning was attended by officials from Wang Laboratories, Prime Computer, Sanders Associates, Planning Research Corporation, NEC Laboratories, Hewlett-Packard and many other notables, including two other Mark I programming alumni, Richard Bloch and Robert Campbell.

Within ten years, the Grace Murray Hopper Center for Computer Learning had expanded into one of the key components of education at Brewster. Soon Art Department Co-Chair Dale Peterson brought graphics and desktop publishing to the art curriculum, writing his own manual for using the Macintosh in art when he discovered there were no computer art textbooks available for secondary schools at the time.

Change in Leadership of Academic Office

In 1987, a major change in leadership of the academic program occurred when Robert Richardson moved his compass point from academic supervision toward a new tack and returned to being a full-time teacher.

Since coming to Brewster Academy in 1965, Bob had worn many important hats—teacher, coach, assistant to the headmaster, director of studies, dean of college placement, and head of the History Department. Undaunted by the many obstacles along the way, through his determination, fortitude, and resolve, he helped to establish a new path for the Academy.

In 1994, the school was set to launch its systemic model of teaching and learning through a pilot program for incoming freshmen, Bob wanted to be part of this new beginning. He volunteered and was selected as a member of the first teaching team in the Brewster Model; once again he would play an important role in a huge step in the school's historic evolution.

A decade later, in 2004, after almost 40 years of dedicated service, Bob Richardson retired from teaching, but not before Sanborn House, where the Richardson family-Bob, Shirley, Lauren,'77, Susan,'81, and Andrea,'84-had lived for so many years, was named Richardson House in honor of their contributions to the school. The girls would be remembered for their athletic and extra-curricular leadership. Even then Brewster's head resident historian took up yet another endeavor for the Academy when he agreed to research and write the school's history from its earliest beginnings to the present.

Dr. Joyce Ferris the New Academic Dean

Dr. Joyce Ferris was hired as the new academic dean whose goal in education had been to help create "independent learners, creators, thinkers, and risk-takers who will carry away from the classrooms a life-long zest for learning." She arranged numerous faculty workshops, including workshops in creative thinking, learning styles, and ethical and intellectual development. She instituted a new program of senior electives and shared her own creative energy each year by teaching a course in mythology and providing the flexibility of scheduling that allowed for such innovations. Joyce Ferris touched everyone, helping students to bring goals into focus, to care about each other and to reach their best.

Community Life Under Dean Esty

Dean Charles Esty, who came to Brewster in 1975 with his wife, Nancy, and family, was an energetic leader and role model for the group. Under Dean Esty's leadership, several programs were instituted that had a significant influence on campus life with community service at the top of this list.

One of the most important contributions to the school community was the implementation of the Proctor Program. In 1980-81, after a great deal of planning and discussion by the faculty, dorm parents, and administration, a proctor system was instituted at Brewster under the direction of Dean Esty and David Peterson. David was in close contact with students and had a unique sense of knowing immediately when a young man, for whatever reason, needed guidance and direction. He was up front and honest with both parents and students, and his counsel and support often headed off issues before they became problems. He was also the first to give praise and recognition when earned.

Chuck Esty Leaves and Dick Weeks Becomes Dean in 1986

After Chuck Esty retired from the dean's position in 1986, Dick Weeks, who had been director of college placement and coordinator of advising since 1982, became the new dean and turned over his college counseling responsibilities to Shirley Richardson. Under Dick's leadership, the role of the office was expanded and redesigned.

It was important to Dean Weeks that a comprehensive guidance program, tempered with counseling and education, be instituted. He believed that young people needed not only adult support, but also education to deal with the social issues of the times. Throughout his years as dean, Dick Weeks continued to spearhead this philosophy.

Leadership Change in the Dean's Office Again

In 1989, when Dick Weeks left to become a headmaster at a school out West, Ron Nentwig assumed the position of dean of students. Having served as assistant dean, Ron was already well liked and respected by the student body and could always be counted on to be "in the know" of happenings on campus. Ron with his wife, Sue served admirably until the day came when they moved on to take on positions at Avon Old Farms, Connecticut.

With the continued expansion of both the student population and student residential life support services, there was a change in the organization of the dean's office. The responsibilities were divided between a dean of community and residential life and a dean of students. Bill Lyons would be the first to serve as the dean of residential life as Ron continued as dean of students. It was through Bill's energy and commitment that the position was expanded and defined, and through his efforts the importance of the residential life curriculum received its proper emphasis.

Community service was designed on a continuum through a student's years at Brewster

Community Service Project taking little ones fishing.

with the twelfth-graders required to complete more hours of service. When a student fulfills service requirements, some form of public recognition is given through certificates and announcements" (*Brewster Review,* Spring 1996).

New Programs and Expansion of Old

The *Quality of Life Program,* under new direction from Bill Lyons' office, began to highlight the attributes of "goodness and fairness" through quality of life awards and thank you notes. These remembrances were delivered to students and faculty who had been particularly helpful and supportive to an individual.

A proactive role to counseling and health services was established with professional consultants discussing eating disorders, breast cancer, and AIDS, and offering peer counselor training. And, just for fun, community based teams were established for the newly formed Brewster Intramural Flag Football and Softball Leagues.

And finally, Dean Lyons, with the help of Teri Moyer, began a new tradition that has become very important to all senior and pgs, the senior slide show. Throughout the year, Mr. Lyons and Miss Moyer took pictures of members of the class in a wide variety of activities and put them together into a slide show to be presented at the headmaster's senior breakfast held at the boathouse after the prom.

A side note to the prom: Since 1966 there had been no proms on campus for a variety of reasons. Finally, in 1984, the prom was reinstituted. Several senior girls and boys had talked to Mrs. Richardson about holding a formal dinner dance at the end of the year. The class of 1984, a unique, spirited group, had a tendency to bond together in almost any project they attempted. They were a group of jokesters and fun-loving individuals who enjoyed each other immensely. The group was headed by classmates Greg Branzetti, Glen Gordon, Debbie Kelloway, and Andrea Richardson, and they became the planners and organizers of a final dinner dance and in reality the rebirth of the senior prom tradition.

Ice sculpture designs for Winter Carnival.

Today's Winter Carnival

Winter Carnival began in 1922 as a relief from the long winter of short days, cold, and snow. Today's version of the Winter Carnival originated under the enthusiastic direction of Dean Lyons and then passed on to the director of student activities, the indefatigable Tim Radley, who continued the tradition that re-ignites school spirit with a weeklong celebration of fun and friendly competition in late January or early February.

Teams consisting of both faculty and students compete for the year's coveted prize and carnival title. Contests included: team spirit day, team uniform day, a poster competition depicting the team's theme, Pictionary game night, and the wildly popular lip-sync final competition. The week-long event also embraces the Winter Olympic Games of human sled races, ski racing, snowball-archery, snow scooter racing, bicycling in the snow, creating the biggest snowball, then pushing it across the field, and, weather permitting, the traditional ice-sculpture contest. The highlight of the week was the Friday night lip-sync contest presented on the Rogers building's stage for the entertainment of the entire school.

Athletic Director, Bill Pottle

When Athletic Director Steve McCloy left the Academy in 1980, the immediate and overwhelming choice to fill the position was Bill Pottle who had arrived as a science teacher, coach and dorm parent in 1976.

It wasn't long before students realized Mr. Pottle's keen interest in the athletic program, a devotion to physical fitness, and an enthusiasm to support each of his students in the classroom. In 1980, the class chose to dedicate their yearbook to Mr. Pottle.

Bill Pottle, Director of Athletics for almost twenty years.

New Offerings in Athletics During the 80s and Early 90s

During this time, several new programs were added to the athletic offerings. First came wrestling and horseback riding in 1981; then men's and women's lacrosse and biking in 1985; women's field hockey, club ice hockey, aerobic dance and indoor tennis followed in 1986; and then on to club rugby in 1988; and club crew and snowboarding in 1989. Many of these teams began as club or JV teams but quickly moved onto varsity designation as interest and skills levels developed.

With the addition of a sports equipment manager and Kate Turner, as assistant athletic director, by 1987, Rogers Gymnasium and Brewster athletics were well organized and well prepared for the challenge of running a top-notch program as far as our facilities would allow.

Sailing

If accomplishment is measured by championships won, then Brewster's sailing team has had its share of triumphs. In 1981, Andrew Wooden's team had 40 straight victories over determined sailors from such schools as Brookline, Dublin, Northfield-Mt. Hermon, Cardigan Mountain, and Phillips Exeter Academy. At the New England Preparatory Regatta at the Harvard Yacht Club, Bill Esty,'81, and Scott Poole,'81, beat skippers from such powerful sailing schools as St. George's and Tabor.

Marilyn Shea coached the Varsity Sailing Program from 1988 to 1996, and it was under her leadership that Brewster was a state champion from 1989 through 1996.

Brewster's greatest sailor was Jon Pinckney,'84.' A competitive sailor from early childhood, Jon not only led the Brewster team to innumerable league victories as skipper

Andrew Wooden was a major supporter of the sailing program and its sailors.

The Sailing Team on Wolfeboro Bay.

with Bermudian Ray Lambert,'83 as crew, they captured the New England Championship, the banner of which hangs in the Pinckney Boat House.

At his 25th reunion in the summer of 2009, Jon was selected as the Academy's fifth inductee into its Sports Hall of Fame.

Crew

Lynn Herrick Snyder came to Brewster in 1987 while the Pinckney Boathouse was under construction to teach and serve as crew coach. She played a significant role in revitalizing a crew program that had not been part of the athletic line up for several years. With valuable assists from Will Barnett and Terri Moyer, Lynn transformed crew from a recreational offering to a very challenging and well-respected varsity program.

Later as Seth and Carrie Ahlborn joined the Brewster community in the 1990s with Carrie as director of development and Seth as dean of students and crew coach, the crew program moved to the next level becoming a major force in the athletics department and a sport in which its rowers, their families, and the school community rightfully took great deal of pride.

Seth recalls, "Crew is natural on Lake Winnipesauke and with the Pinckney Boathouse as a home base there is no better setting or set up.

In 1987 the Pinckney Boathouse was completed, and the importance of this new addition to waterfront varsity and recreational activities could not be overstated. The building itself met the objective Mr. Smith originally set out for the architects—the standard one would find on the Charles in Boston and the Schuylkill outside Philadelphia. In support of the crew and sailing programs not only was the entire docking facility unbelievable, but also the lower level of the boathouse offered a wonderful space for the winter boat repair program. The area provided for valuable hands-on experience as students worked with fiberglass, wood, canvas and made needed boat repairs so that the sailing and crew fleets would ready for launching as soon as ice out.

Above, getting ready to launch. Below, preparing for the upcoming race.

The Pinckney Boathouse, a major addition and focus for all campus waterfront activities.

As with other sports, championships would be won; but the spirit and dedication of the rowers and sailors as they grasped and developed their skills as individuals and came to understand and appreciate what it means to be a team pulling together to reach a common goal—these are the valued lessons that live on in their lives beyond Brewster.

New Playing Fields

Mr. and Mrs. Howard Brown, parents of Mike, '90, realized that with increased enrollment and more varied sports offerings, there was a need for expanded playing fields; and they offered to have a new field built for Brewster, which would be used for both soccer and lacrosse. During the October 1989 Parents Weekend, the Brewster sports teams dressed in their assorted uniforms and assembled on the new field as Mr. Smith dedicated Brown Field and thanked Mr. and Mrs. Brown for their generosity and faith in the Academy. The new field is positioned in the area behind the Rogers Gymnasium where three old tennis courts had been located. *(Brewster Browser*, October 1989, p.4). Then in 1998, the field area bordering along Clark Road, was cleared, excavated, and prepared for two new playing fields that would accommodate the athletic needs of an expanding student body. The lower of the two was prepared in such a way as to be the location of a suite of tennis courts when the necessary funds became available. Those nine courts, the first on campus since the late 70s, were completed in 2008.

The Fall Pep Rally

One of the traditions that Bill Pottle established to promote spirit and fun was the fall pep rally. Shortly after the opening of the fall term, there would be a night when the Athletic Department scheduled a bon fire. It was usually on the first Friday night in October when the fire would be lit. The major varsity teams sponsored the event. During the afternoon, coaches would lead the players to search for sources of old broken tree limbs, boxes, wood of all kinds, and any old rotted items that needed to be disposed of. They dragged them to the baseball diamond where they were stacked in a mountain high pile. After evening study hall, teams would begin a long war-dance going from dorm to dorm in the pitch dark calling out the students and leading them down to the baseball diamond to form a large circle around the bonfire where all would wait for the moment when the fire would roar and the flames would light the sky and lick the clouds.

Suddenly, a tall muscular figure, posing as a Native American, would emerge, seemingly from the woods behind, dressed completely in Abenaki clothing from head to toe, Native American toe-heel stepping and swirling and circling the fire. In hand, he carried a menacing eight-foot spear decorated with feathers. His mind was strictly absorbed with the accuracy of dance and motion. If asked a question, he would simply ignore it and without a break, continue his dance. He circled and circled the fire without losing step, and soon sweat broke to cover his body and his dance intensified.

At some point, when the fire began to decline in intensity, and after many students tried to determine who the Indian was, the dancer disappeared from the center and faded into the night's darkness well beyond the crowd and into the woods. The team coaches would then introduce each team member to the crowd, and several cheerleaders, shouting and yelling, would conduct the inspired crowd in school cheers. The din and blast of voices could be heard over the quiet, dark lake like an explosion as the enthusiasm and spirit of the students erupted. But the mystery of the Abenaki dancer continues to haunt many. Could it have been the spirit of old "Indian Joe" from the Brewster Beach woods who used to cheer the football and baseball teams of the 1890s? Or was it some imposter? But since 1999, the Indian has not returned!

Bill Pottle continued to head the Athletic Department until 1999 when a teaching opportunity in chemistry and coaching was offered to him. Upon Bill's departure in 1999, Doug Algate was appointed the new athletic director. Unfortunately, Bill was not on campus when his dream of a field house and athletic center with an indoor turf field was fulfilled in 2002 by the completion of the Smith Center.

Summer Programs

Doug Fallon was hired as director of summer programming in 1988 and has spent many years developing just how best the campus could be used during the summer months while still protecting the school's identity and facilities. In the summer, Brewster has become an active, vibrant community serving many needs and populations with a continuous stream of programs, events and activities.

Summer programs actually began in earnest in the early 1970s when the school hosted six and seven weeks of the Gordon Research Institute. Top scientists from the world over gathered for weekly exchanges of the latest research centered in their specialties. Now there are three major programs that utilize the campus from late June until mid August: The Royal Thai Scholars Program, an intense college preparatory program, the Brewster Academy Summer School and the Heifetz International Music Institute under the leadership of founder-director Daniel Heifetz for young advanced musician from around the world. In addition, there are several sports camps and other special programs that are hosted on campus.

A major asset to the program's organization is Chris Brown,'87, faculty daughter and graduate of Brewster. She began in 1987 as an office helper for the Gordon Research Group and now is co-director of the Thai Program and office manager of the Summer Programs office. For years, Chris has been a wonderful friend to the Thai scholars, as well as an incredible benefit to summer programming.

Over the years the Summer Programs has become vital to the Academy not only with gross earnings of well over a million dollars, but from the admissions perspective as well for each year about a dozen students choose to attend Brewster after their summer experience. In addition, summer programs contribute to the greater Wolfeboro community by offering diverse and varied opportunities and providing its campus for a host summer activities (*Brewster Review,* Fall '04: Annual Report). Upon Doug Fallon's retirement in 2010, Raylene Davis would follow as director of summer programming.

Tragedy and Legacy of Friendship and Tradition

One of Brewster's darkest hours came in May 1989 when the campus experienced the death of a popular and promising student. From that darkest hour, however, and out of that pain, has grown a legacy of friendship and opportunity that continues to be a defining feature of Brewster's identity.

None of us who were a part of Brewster at the time will ever forget when Trey Whitfield, a Brewster senior, drowned in a boating accident on a nearby lake. The time was one week before graduation. Trey was poised for a brilliant career, headed to the University of Richmond where, in addition to his studies, he would play Division I basketball.

Trey was the most beloved and respected student in the entire community. On Saturday evening, May 27, 1989, Trey and several friends were returning by rowboat from visiting a classmate at her lakeside camp. The crowded boat flipped over and when Trey grabbed its side, it flipped again and caught him with a knockout blow to his head. His friends dove repeatedly into the dark water in a desperate effort to find him until, exhausted and desperate, they had to swim for shore.

Trey Whitfield, #34, Class of 1989.

Looking back, no incident in recent history was more painful and yet more demonstrative of the strength of the community of the school. The universal love for this young man was a product of that strength and what he meant to the community. It brought both the pain and the surge of shared supportive emotion to bind the wound and celebrate Trey's life. As one letter of condolence to Headmaster David Smith, stated, "In times of crisis and tragedy, the weak and ill prepared crumble; the strong rally together to learn and grow from the experience" (William Cooper, Head Wolfeboro Camp School, *Letter of Condolence).*

A major source of our strength came from Trey's parents, Janie Whitney and Argyle Whitfield. Argyle "AB" came to Wolfeboro immediately with Trey's brother, Alvin. After seeing Trey and speaking with the doctor at the hospital, Mr. Whitfield walked into Lord House's back door; and after tearful hugs with the Smiths, his first words were "Who needs me most?" and Mr. Smith pointed to Trey's friends in the living room and specifically the girl whose camp they had visited. Mr. Whitfield immediately went in sat down on the couch next to her and threw his big arms around her.

At the memorial assembly, led by the headmaster, the entire community came together to celebrate a young man who lived his life with faith and optimism in the "dream."

The Whitfield Foundation 1989

Trey's legacy has far-reaching benefits beyond Brewster Academy. The Trey Whitfield Foundation, established by Trey's parents in 1989, was founded to commemorate his life with the mission to pursue his dream that every child, regardless of ethnic background, have equal access to educational opportunity and be enabled to reach their potential in life. The foundation provides recognition, encouragement and financial scholarship assistance to deserving young people. Many of these students have been provided the opportunity of a Brewster Academy education through the support and encouragement of the foundation in partnership with the Academy. The foundation has also provided recipients scholarships to other independent schools in New England and New York City. Furthermore, at the Annual Trey Whitfield Foundation Dinner they honor that year's selected young people "who are positive and productive young citizens" and adults "whose love and support inspire others and who give unselfishly to the greater good of mankind" are also recognized. A number of Brewster administrators and faculty, including Dr. Joyce Ferris, Mr. Stewart Dunlap, Mr. David Smith, Mrs. Shirley Richardson, Mr. and Mrs. Tim Radley, Ms. Beth Hayes, Mrs. Lynn Palmer, T.J. Palmer, and Mrs. Maureen Simoneau have been so honored.

Brewster treasures its relationship with Argyle Whitfield, Janie Whitney and the Whitfield Foundation and its special relationship with the faculty and staff and the gospel choir of the Trey Whitfield School—all of which return each year and re-infuse Trey's spirit through the Trey MLK Memorial Day celebration.

The legacy that emerged out of Brewster's darkest hour has become one of hope, optimism and joy. That legacy challenges us to ask, as one of our recent speakers, Orlando Vondross, Class of 1988, so aptly questioned, "What will each of us do in our lives that will be remembered and have a positive impact for future generations as Trey is remembered so fondly and with such continuing influence after such a brief life?" (Ferris, *2008).*

Argyle Whitfield was selected as the speaker at David Smith's last commencement in 2003 and currently serves as a trustee of the Academy.

Facilities Master Plan for the 80s and 90s

The focus developed and implemented during this period of the Academy's history had found success because it directed all of its resources in the best service to its students. As a result, a decade after David Smith assumed the leadership of the school, the Academy had acquired an excellent ever-expanding reputation. Enrollment was on the rise, the physical

Above, the Trey Whitfield School Gospel Choir performing, Anderson Hall. Below, Argyle and Janie Whitfield with their students in front of the Academic building as they prepared to leave campus.

plant had been transformed, the administration, faculty, and staff were strong and devoted to the school, and an invigorated Board of Trustees was committed to ensuring the school's future prosperity. Just as it had carried out the initial stages of its Facilities Master Plan in the 80s and early 90s with the construction of six brand new dormitories, the addition of two completely rebuilt and refurbished dormitories, a new library science facility, a redesigned Estabrook with a new kitchen facility, and the Spaulding/Emerson Student Center addition, not to mention the magnificent Pinckney Boathouse at the water's edge of Winnipesauke, it was now time for the Academy to move forward in developing and executing an extensive educational master plan soon to be referred to as The School Design Model in furthering efforts to best serve its students.

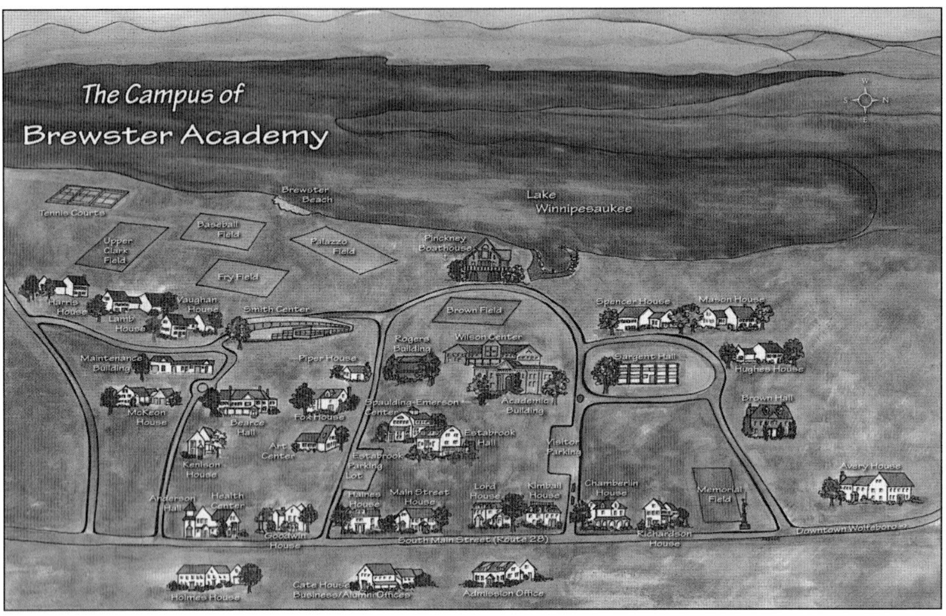

Brewster Campus 2010.

17. Formulating and Delivering a New Educational Paradigm

If we teach today as we taught yesterday, we rob our children of tomorrow.
—John Dewey

If a child can't learn the way we teach, maybe we should teach the way they learn.
—Ignacio Estrada

Introduction

For Brewster Academy the years between 1985 and 2002 would prove to be as critical to the evolution of the school as 1887, the date of its founding under terms of John Brewster's Will, and 1965, the year when the Board of Trustees rejected the State of New Hampshire's invitation to become a regional high school but instead reaffirmed Brewster's status as an independent school in the tradition of the old New England Academy.

In 1985, almost a hundred years after the school's founding, another dramatic, ambitious transformation began to take place. During that year the school's leadership embarked on a mission to transform Brewster Academy from its traditional New England Academy image into a modern secondary educational institution. David Smith would be the point man for this new journey. He recognized that the school had reached a point where further improvement must come, not from continuous renovation of the physical plant and adjustments to curriculum and programs already in place, but rather from reformation and re-creation of the school. He began to speak about developing a master plan to revise the total curriculum of the school, recognizing that any such well-considered plan could result only from extensive collaboration among all members of the school community—trustees, administrators, faculty, students, parents, alumni and friends. That collaboration would prove far more involved and extensive than he or anyone else had envisioned. The final product would require commitment to a new educational paradigm and would position the school to provide the best educational experience available anywhere. That transformation became known simply as "The Model."

Strategic Planning Committee Develops Plan

A formal Strategic Planning Committee composed of representatives of the faculty, administration, and trustees met for a planning retreat at Waterville Valley. Their charge was to develop a "Policy Plan for the 90s." At the end of the retreat, the committee summarized its findings as follows:

- Educational Master Plan and Implementation Considerations
  The creation of an educational master plan will bring a central focus to the academic, athletic, and student life programs of the school to assure that all are directed toward fulfilling the priorities established within the school's stated mission. Similarly, all considerations of trustee policy setting and allocation of faculty, administrative staff, facilities, and financial resources

will be based on the degree to which they contribute toward carrying out the goals of the master education plan, the intent of which is to best achieve the school's mission.

- Communications and Accountability
  The school will work to improve communication between and among the Academy's constituencies, students, trustees, administrators, faculty, and staff, to improve participation in the decision-making processes; and to strengthen accountability for communicated expectations. Growth of the school has also brought a challenge to communication and the spirit of togetherness that originally fired the engine. The leadership must provide an environment that encourages sharing in the decision-making process, communication of decisions and responsibilities, and mechanisms for feedback, evaluation, and accountability.
- Final Areas
  Brewster Academy must place high priority on attracting and retaining the best people, facilities, finances, policies and leadership to execute and support this mission.

Strategic Plan Presented at Special Board of Trustees Meeting

Within the framework of their discussion outlined above, the Strategic Planning Committee presented a plan to the full Board of Trustees, which suggested minor alterations and additions before giving the report their wholehearted endorsement. The Policy Plan in its final form stated:

- Brewster Academy's mission for the 1990s will not be changed.
- The Academy will remain a coeducational college preparatory school serving students of varying abilities and talents and from diverse socioeconomic, racial, ethnic, religious, geographic, and international backgrounds who are in harmony in the school's mission.
- A subcommittee would study and recommend what would be the optimum size of the school; until that recommendation is made, enrollment will not increase further.
- A master educational plan that links all current and projected new programs toward best fulfilling the promise of the mission statement will be constructed.
- A special faculty task force, appointed by the headmaster, will lead the effort to develop this master plan in consultation with all faculty members.
- The implementation of this educational master plan will ensure that all considerations of the staff, administration, policy setting, building, maintenance, and finance are consistent with fulfilling the school's mission.
- In developing the master plan, the following implementation suggestions will be considered in greater depth:
    - computer-assisted instruction
    - a core humanities curriculum
    - grouping by skills and learning styles
    - an ongoing program of educational research and development
    - required community service
    - strengthening "writing across the curriculum"
    - thinking across the curriculum
    - special needs of day student

- involvement in the greater Wolfeboro community
- financial aid services
- summer programs

The Policy Plan concluded with the following directives:

- Establish programs that improve involvement and communication about decisions and assure accountability for fulfilling those decisions.
- Make professional working conditions of the administration, faculty, and staff a top priority to ensure that the school continues to attract and retain outstanding professionals.
- Provide a comprehensive, ongoing, and environmentally progressive program for restoring, maintaining, and enhancing the school's buildings and grounds.
- Ensure that the structure, policies, procedures, and membership of the Board of Trustees enable the school to meet its future needs.

Additional Driver for Curriculum Master Plan Identified

Brewster Academy's development of the Master Plan for Facilities brought to the forefront a need to first determine targeted outcomes for each and every aspect of Brewster's curricula. The headmaster's desire was to establish a consensus on outcomes and then to move forward in establishing the scope and sequence of the various academic, athletic, and social curricula that would best enable students to attain those outcomes. The emphasis was to be intentional in all that the school did. Firing away with a shotgun of good intentions was no longer sufficient; the school needed to apply its resources more wisely, aiming and expending all its "ammunition" toward the agreed-upon targets, and those desired outcomes.

The Brewster Model

It is one thing to envision what a school should be, but it is a vastly different and greater challenge to determine how best to reach that goal. In almost all prior instances, the headmaster did not set out an objective without having in mind a process which would accomplish that objective. Not so in this case. The various drivers called for a change in *modus operandi*; the headmaster recognized that the school could no longer get where it needed to be by playing it safe. The school must have the courage and the conviction to step into the world of the unknown.

The School Leadership Team Expands

To meet this challenge as well as to provide a replacement for the retiring Ed Hooper, the founding father of Brewster's oh-so-important Learning Skills Department, another major transition in leadership was underway. In response to an ad placed in the *Chronicle of Higher Education,* which gave a brief description of the school's overall quest, Dr. Alan Bain, then teaching Ph.D. candidates at Lehigh University, became interested in learning more about Brewster.

Alan Bain, Ph.D., Becomes Director of Instructional Support

As an assistant professor of special education in the School of Education at Lehigh, Dr. Alan Bain lectured about those practices that research had proved to be the most successful practices of effective schools. He worked with graduate students in programs to assess and teach elementary and secondary school students with a variety of learning styles.

Alan met in interview with the headmaster at Lord House, and as David spoke about

Dr. Alan Bain, Director of Learning Skills and Assistant Headmaster.

the Brewster drivers and the passion that drove Brewster's mission to offer the best service to its students, Alan recognized that the school's objective was congruent with his hopes to develop and implement a systemic model of education centered in and disciplined by research-proven best practices. In addition, he saw represented in the headmaster's enthusiasm a commitment by the school community to getting just such a program in place at Brewster Academy.

In 1991, Alan Bain came to Brewster first to replace retiring Edward Hooper as director of instructional support. He brought with him a new vision for integrating our traditional Learning Skills and classroom programs. He worked quickly with all faculty members within his department to develop those strategies and to define those methods which would enhance students' abilities to manage their own studies.

What had been a rather isolated Learning Skills Program became an integrated Instructional Support Program, and within a few short weeks, Kim Ross had been selected to lead the transformed program. Alan Bain was ready and anxious to shift his attention to aiding in the transformation of the school as a whole.

The Faculty Prepare for a Different Year

After two years of self-study and strategic thinking had established consensus around goals and objectives for the school's future, the Board of Trustees had a dynamic new leader in Grant Wilson, and the school had acquired new leadership and expanded vision in Alan Bain and Pete Caesar who had succeeded Joyce Ferris as academic dean.

Prior to and in preparation for the opening faculty meeting of the 1992-93 school year, David Smith, Alan Bain, and Pete Caesar met and structured the agenda for that meeting—steps which would set them on the path to transform the school. The faculty meeting was opened with the premise that this was going to be a different year, but just how different it would be no one could yet fully appreciate.

After being introduced by the headmaster, Pete Caesar led an exercise in which faculty and administrators brainstormed the various aspects of the school, identifying strengths and comparative weaknesses.

At this point Dr. Bain was introduced. Within his initial presentation, he identified the tenets of those practices found in the most effective schools. They are as follows.

- The school can demonstrate the way in which its mission, policy, curriculum, professional development, and evaluation are directly linked in service to teaching and learning.
- Evidence of those things that are valued by the school can be found in clear and unambiguous ways in the everyday life of the school—the way teachers teach, and administrators administer, and in the way students learn. "Good practice is intentional, not coincidental."
- Valid and reliable procedures exist to monitor and evaluate all-important outcomes of the school's mission and policy. The school knows how it is doing.
- Curriculum is coordinated across grade levels and subjects. It focuses on what students know and are able to do.
- Collaboration and teamwork are valued and are built into the way in which the school is organized at all levels.
- The school has a planned approach to professional development that is directly linked to its policy and curriculum.

When the group considered the listing of identified weaknesses, they noted that, while the list of strengths was a positive affirmation of the tenets, the weaknesses were present in areas where the tenets were absent from the school's current *modus operandi*. They concluded, therefore, that the first step toward transformation of the school should be conducting a thorough needs assessment and taking an honest look with a critically-focused eye at just where the school was in relation to research-proven best practices. Under Alan Bain's leadership, the school set out to do just that.

A core team considering how to proceed included David Smith, Alan Bain, Pete Caesar, and Dean of Students Bill Lyons. They quickly realized that each aspect of the school must be connected to all the other aspects. Pete Caesar put the essential components up on a white Board, in the form of a jigsaw puzzle showing pieces fitting together. Looking at the configuration, Pete said, "This is our model." From that defining moment on, the program was called the 'Brewster Model," "The School Design Model," or just "The Model."

The core team had just reached the conclusion that they were committed to building a systemic model of education that incorporated the tenets of best practice in each and every aspect of the school. By working to develop all the components, Brewster Academy would indeed fulfill the core promise of her mission statement to "maximize student growth."

"The Model" Presented to the Board of Trustees

The Board of Trustees' Education Committee reviewed "The Model" components, and then members Helen Hamilton, Fred Stephens, and Carl Simon presented the drafted policies to the full Board for their consideration, for discussion and input, and, ultimately, for adoption.

"The Model" concepts were approved by the Board and included the following additions in policy:

- The Model supports only those practices which have been shown to be effective in improving student achievement, self-esteem, and social growth.
- The student experience is multifaceted, and the Model is composed of residential, athletic, and academic components which serve the student body in an integrated fashion.
- Before adopting any new or additional curriculum components, the following should be determined:
- The applicability of the curriculum to student advancement and an enumeration of the groups affected by it.
- The intended learning outcome defined in terms of how the learning is to be applied.
- The justification of the curriculum in terms of the school's learned outcomes and mission.
- The resources that its implementation would require.
- A plan for ongoing assessment (David Smith, 2008).

Communicating the New Beginning for Brewster Academy

To introduce "The Model" to the various Academy constituencies, an article outlining concisely the dimensions of this new direction was prepared for *The Brewster Review*:

"The year 1993-1994 was a busy year as the school sought to transform itself into the best school in the world.

"We are making ourselves into a school for the 21st century, a school that is changing the way teachers teach because they recognize how students learn; that is changing how students do homework, take notes and quizzes, and even how people communicate with each other; that is changing the way classrooms look. We are helping our students become active and involved as they work together and take charge of their education. In short, the Brewster Model, as we call it, is defining what a high school should be.

"The key to Brewster's evolution in the last year is not new—indeed, it is one of the oldest concepts that we have, that of 'mastery.' The concept of mastery is crucial to the way our students progress. Just as one would not jump into the deep end of a swimming pool without having mastered basic swimming strokes, students cannot be expected to move on to tasks of increasing difficulty if they have not mastered the basic and progressive skills of a discipline."

Implementing "The Brewster Model" in Four Stages

The project was to be broken into four stages.

Stage One

Starting with a pilot program for the incoming freshman class, Brewster took the dusty, dingy attic of the Academic Building and transformed it into a very modern and "cool" learning area. Remodeling the space was an essential consideration in creating this systemic model. By assigning to each team its own space, the Academy could recapture the advantages of the small school; each team would have the ultimate flexibility to best deliver and achieve the outcomes of its curriculum objectives. In addition to accommodating 45-50 students and the six teachers who made up the freshman team, the space had to be wired for the network. Construction began in June 1993, immediately after graduation.

Elissa Paquette instructs a 9th English class in the new third floor academic area.

Workmen effected a near miraculous transformation of the space, providing three classrooms and a science lab, individual areas as well as a conference area for teachers, an auditorium for 60 students, and a student lounge. High ceilings and dramatic rooflines were added. Brickwork for the chimneys and the massive roof beam remained exposed while corridors and classrooms were finished with oak wainscoting and trim.

This new third floor teaching and learning space was dedicated in honor of Nick and Penny Harris (Lamont, '84, and Henry, '88) with its lecture hall named in honor of Tristram and Ruth Colkets (Bryan, '94). This new area, soon to be named "the Bubble" by upperclassmen because it separated the freshmen from the rest of the students, was introduced to freshmen and their parents during a special orientation that took place at the beginning of the school year. Parents immediately asked how the school would carry on this program into the sophomore year, and they were assured that the school would continue its physical and programmatic transformation as their youngsters progressed toward their graduation.

Brewster Net: Preparing Students for the 21st Century

A sophisticated fiber optic computer network was established which connected the freshman area, the library, the administrative offices, and the freshmen dormitories. Consistent with the ways other academic components interfaced, best practice applications of technology needed to serve each aspect of the program and play a major role in their intercommunication. Over the next two years, this network would expand like a venous system throughout the entire campus. The Trellis Corporation of Nashua, New Hampshire, worked with Dr. Bain in creating the network architecture and installed the cabling. The Siemon Company of Watertown, Connecticut, provided the 3,000 connecting ports through which students and faculty accessed the network. Carl Siemon, a member of the Brewster Board of Trustees, was a past president of the company, and his son, Hank, a 1976 graduate of the Academy, was now a principal manager of the company.

The Model's first computer, an Apple 850 model, is used by freshmen Chris Callahan and Josh Ladieu.

The impact and applications of technology became ubiquitous. In a class, the teacher could make his or presentation using a LCD projector connected to a Macintosh Power Book. Instead of attempting to scribble down notes while still remaining focused on the presentation, students were now able to download the presentation from the network to their own computers for later review and study.

From their dormitories, students could reach their teachers by email to ask questions or to seek clarification. They could do research on several CD-ROM databases in the library, some of which included video and sound as well as traditional text and graphic material. The aim was to make the laptop computer a tool as easy for students to use as were paper and pencil. Within months students found that it was easier and a lot more fun.

Ultimately, students would be able to carry on research over the network, connect with college or university courses available through satellite downlinks, or share their own work through satellite uplinks. At all times, however, it was recognized that technology is only a tool, and in order to best harness the power of technology, its role was carefully defined within the overall curriculum structure that was developing.

The Brewster faculty would continue to teach a challenging, college-preparatory curriculum designed to meet students at their current level of performance and accelerate them in their mastery of content and skill to a defined level of graduation outcomes. Curriculum design and delivery were based in the school's commitment to provide each student with the appropriate curriculum, instruction, and materials, and to give them appropriate time to master both the advancing levels of skills and content within each progressive unit of study.

To progress in the curriculum a student must demonstrate evidence of skill and content mastery through assessment on a set of rubrics.

Everyone in the Brewster Model Program carried a laptop computer in order to take best advantage of the teaching and learning opportunities. The technology-rich environment and the team approach enabled teachers to deliver a traditional independent education with a new sophistication. The result was more personal attention to each student in every class.

Stage Two

Each new school year would bring advancement of the pilot class to the next stage and would require new instructional spaces. In September 1994, the initial freshman class was joined by new sophomores who were developed into two sophomore teams.

To accommodate this stage of the process, perhaps the biggest stage of all, required tearing down the "old" library and science building and starting over. The new building would be twice as big as the historic Academic Building and would be named The Wilson Center for Teaching and Learning, honoring Grant and Helene Wilson and their children, Grant '87, Kristen '88, and Sara.

The date for the ground-breaking was the spring of 1994, and the construction crews started digging the foundation for the new center as soon as the ground had thawed. As spring wore on, construction continued with a sense of urgency. After the whole building was framed and enclosed, focus shifted to that half that would house the oncoming two teams of the pilot class.

With the paint still drying on opening day of '94 the sophomore teams moved into brand new team spaces, located on the upper and lower levels in one wing of the Wilson Center.

Each of the new team areas included a teaching team office and conference area, a science lab and classroom, and three classrooms for English, math, social science and foreign languages as well as two instructional support rooms. Each team had access to a

The new Kenison Library with view of lake, mountains, and Wolfeboro Bay.

The completed Wilson Center for Teaching and Learning.

lecture room known as the "Link" built into the lower level between the buildings. At the heart of the new construction was a multi-media technology area which served as the hub for developing and supporting the technological capability of the school.

The Wilson Center was linked to the main academic building by a corridor that included space for the college office, academic and instructional support offices, and an additional classroom.

The New Kenison Library

John Sandeen was hired as a consultant in establishing the design and operating plan for the new Kenison Library. John offered a proposal to enhance the service of the library through electronic media, taking full advantage of access to the Internet. The architectural design for the library space was spectacular with huge floor to ceiling windows looking out to the vista of playing fields, the lake and its islands, and the distant Belknap mountain range. The library opened in rough form in October and was fully completed by January 1995. John was hired as the library director in July 1995 and solidified and fully empowered its operation during his next four years of its leadership.

Stage Three

The third stage was one of the easiest to complete, simply finishing the northwest side of Wilson Center as an exact mirror image of the teaching and learning suites built during the second stage. In honor of their contributions to the Academy over the years, the upper floor was dedicated to Robert and Rosie Clark and the lower level to the Roy Foundation.

Stage Four

After graduation in 1997, the only areas that remained to be remodeled were the first and second floors of the Academic Building. During the summer, the second floor was converted to new classrooms. The Learning Skills Center was changed into a science

An early classroom in the Wilson Center.

lab and classroom, and old classrooms were updated and improved. A faculty team area and instructional support classrooms were added, and all were infused with Brewsternet. Although the Academic Building still carried its traditional look outside, its interior had been refined and upgraded to the standards set for the Brewster Model program.

Over the course of four years as the pilot class progressed toward their graduation, Brewster had set into place all the various components of its new programs. The New Brewster had been born (*Brewster Browser*, Fall 1997).

Preparing our Teachers—The Brewster Summer Institute

Brewster Academy was committed to excellence in education and believed that a quality education for students was definable, attainable and begins with an investment in the expertise of faculty. The Brewster Summer Institute (BSI) of 1993 marked the introduction of a unique school-based program of high quality professional development. The BSI trained the first pilot team and has been carried on each successive year as the Academy trains its teachers. It is a six-week, highly intensive experience for all new faculty, regardless of prior teaching experience. BSI provides comprehensive training in adolescent development, teaching methodologies, and learning styles, all based on the best available research in the field of education. The Institute also provides instruction in the school's technology platform and the software used to enhance educational experiences. Each participant learns the theories and practices associated with the Brewster Model, and then he or she spends concentrated time with his or her department chair, applying the methods to actual curriculum that they will be teaching.

Left, the entrance to the Kenison Library. Right, the Kenison Library, the focal point of the Wilson Center.

Curriculum Development

Curriculum development, under the direction of department chairs, began by identifying desired learner outcomes and the types of assessment recommended to measure those outcomes. Originally, in order to actually get a written curriculum in place, all faculty were required to devote a portion of the summer to curriculum writing, and they were paid to do so. After the curriculum was completed, the school was able to step back from such intense demands and leave curriculum writing to those department members who want to undertake revisions. Revisions are planned under the leadership of the department chair and are approved by the Teaching and Learning Team, a group made up of administrators and department heads. This group is the gatekeeper for curriculum changes and takes responsibility to ensure that changes are in keeping with our commitment to best practices, mastery learning, and value-added education (Shea, 2008).

The construction of multi-sophisticated instruction with multi-leveled curriculum proved to be a monumental task; but because each lesson constituted a mastery-based game plan to best advance individual student growth, it was the key ingredient in the success of all that went into the Model reformation.

The Collaborative Process

The Brewster program was grounded in a belief that schools need to be collaborative communities in which all the stakeholders have a vested interest. All meetings—whether the teaching teams, various committees, dorm groups, or others—used the collaborative process which helped ensure that each member of the group had an opportunity to voice thoughts as the groups worked towards decisions that all members could support. Interestingly, our graduates repeatedly cited this commitment to collaboration and to

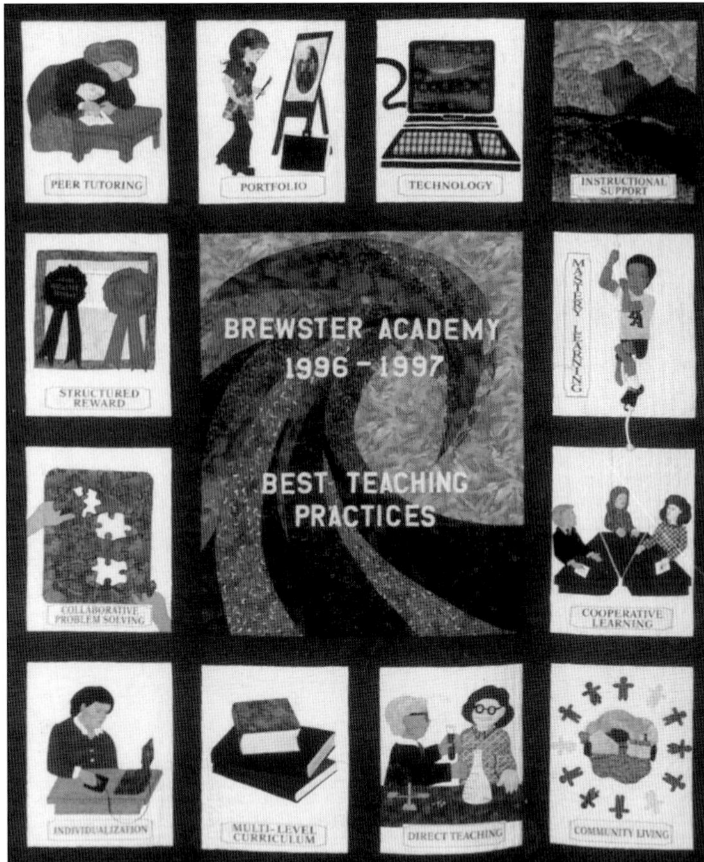

The Best Practices Quilt now hangs in the Wilson Center.

teamwork as the experience they most retained as they made the transition to college and life. Brewster graduates find that the life skills they develop from working in groups have proven to be invaluable.

Effect on Faculty Relations

The commitment to teamwork and collaboration has fostered a strong sense of professionalism among faculty. Because faculty can participate in developing collaborated solutions to problems, they bring a high level of energy to the implementation of those solutions that is often missing when decisions come from the top down.

In a monograph written in September 2008, Marilyn Shea, a member of the first freshman team, sums up faculty response to the changing way of doing things at Brewster Academy: "Institutions are always slow to change, and often resistant to change. The "Model" was no different. Early on, it had its champions, and it had a strong dose of resistance as well. The community divided into camps—those who embraced the coming change and were energized by its prospects, and those who saw change as a threat. It would actually take several years for the tensions to resolve, and for turnover to deliver the Academy to a stability and sense of harmony. As people elected to leave, newcomers joined us because they believed in the program" (Shea, 2008).

Mr. TJ Palmer instructing Lindsay Turner and others in history class.

Technology and Impact on Learning

Brewster was a leader in a very new era, and familiarity with technology was a must, plain and simple. The faculty was able to integrate technology into the curriculum and remain committed to evolving technologies that allow for greater facility in teaching and learning. Technology empowered and integrated all aspects of the Academy's program. Brewster's School Design Model is systemic with each piece serving all the other components and technology facilitating all those interconnections.

Change in Peer Culture

Marilyn Shea observes, "The Model changed peer culture as well. It moved us from a place where adults tried to push/pull students over the finish line to a place where students and adults facilitated students in learning how to reach the finish line on their own and really relish the challenge and engagement along the way. It did this by offering curriculum and instruction that gave kids the success they needed to sustain their motivation. It did this by praising students for making good choices and creating an environment in which, the headmaster so often observed, 'it's cool to be good.' The success rests really with the fact that the model was comprehensive in its vision: it understood the need to serve the whole student—not just academics. It understood that reform needs to put all the pieces together, and that change based on patchwork and piecemeal efforts tends to just shift problems from one area to another without really moving the needle for most kids. 'To do it right, we had to do it all,' and we did" (Shea, 2008).

Faculty team areas, teachers collaborate on solving and implementing education issues.

Peer Managed Living

Dormitory life is a key component of the experience at a boarding school, and like any other aspect of the school experience, it too needed to have identified objectives and an intentional program designed to enable students to obtain the potential benefits from the experience.

During the '80s, Brewster had built new dormitories—faculty/students homes—and renovated existing buildings to provide comfortable and inviting living space for both students and faculty. With the introduction of the freshman model, the ninth grade students were moved from the larger dorms into the more family like Chamberlin, Kimball, and Estabrook dorm/homes. A new community living program was instituted which supported students in taking responsibility for the creation of a positive supportive culture as well as the management of their lives in their dormitories.

Under the program, dormitory students met twice weekly in forty-five minute meetings. At the beginning of the meeting, students identify the issues they wish to discuss. Using the same collaborative decision-making process incorporated at all levels of decision-making within the school, they reach consensus as to how they would best resolve those issues of concern. At the end of the meeting, the dorm parent gives the students a critique, reinforcing the positive aspects of their approach and making suggestions where they might continue to improve their technique in future gatherings.

The Recognition System

The Recognition System that first developed in 1994 strengthened an environment where students would be supported and encouraged to develop their unique abilities and potentials both as individuals and as contributing members of a vital caring community.

The Brewster Browser published an article defining the Recognition System.

"Brewster Academy defines itself not as a school structured by rules and punishments, but rather as a school governed by a set of positive values which promote excellence. The goal of the Recognition System is to encourage, support, and reward each student as they progress in the achievement of their potential academically, athletically, and socially. Our Recognition System is based on the following values:

- We believe in the value of each human being.
- We are responsible for caring for ourselves and for one another.
- We respect and support each other's goals, needs, and differences.
- We respect our physical environment.
- We strive to be helpful and contribute to the well being of all.
- We strive to bring our best to all that we do.

We have tremendous faith in our young people. We believe that they want to contribute, that they want to grow, that they want to serve, that they want to become the best that they can be.

"In order to encourage and support them in the attainment of these goals, the Academy believes in the concept of teamwork. It is teamwork first, meaning that each and every member of the community shares in a common responsibility to assist one another in the achievement of their individual potentials.

"The Recognition System fosters this growth process by:

- Building and defining commonly held standards, values, and goals in all aspects of Brewster life: academic, athletic, and residential.
- Recognizing and rewarding students for sustained effort and tangible growth toward their attainment.

"Formal recognition of that attainment comes in two levels that will be measured at four points during the academic year through the Student Recognition Surveys.

"Students who are considered by their teachers, coaches, and dorm parents to be exhibiting these values and standards most of the time receive our recognition of Citizenship. Those who do so virtually without exception and provide leadership by example and support receive the distinction and privileges of being a John Brewster Scholar. It is our expectation that, with the support and encouragement within this community, every student can ultimately reach these levels of performance, recognition, and privilege/independence.

The Brewster Motto

The Latin phrase, *Meus Dux Sit Veritas*, appears on the Brewster Crest. It translates "Let Truth Be My Leader" This motto calls members of the Brewster community to live by the highest standards, to reach above the commonplace, and to accept the challenge of excellence. During this important period of change the community developed an expanded version of this motto to serve as a guidepost for all everyone does here at Brewster Academy—"*Respect, be helpful, and contribute. Serve yourself and others with your best in all you do.*"

Faculty Recognition: Teaching Awards Program
When The Model had been fully instituted throughout the school by 1996-97, in addition to recognition for students, an awards program to honor faculty was established. Two important awards make up this program:

The Faculty Teaching Award is granted for excellence in teaching and performance, and *The Career Growth Award* is given in recognition of the faculty member who has demonstrated the most accelerated professional growth within the Brewster program.

These award programs are open to all returning faculty who have taught at Brewster for a minimum of one year and have completed one evaluation cycle. Nominations may be made by any member of the school community and are reviewed by the academic directors who serve as the selection committee. Each award is scholarly, involves a significant monetary component, and is valued highly by the faculty. Most importantly, it provides for public recognition.

Editor's Note:
Mary Fallon, long-time faculty member and a superior, highly dedicated and much appreciated teacher, wrote this essay about her feelings that came with the changes that The Model transformation brought to the Brewster she knew so well.

"Good Is Not Enough"
"'It was the best of times; it was the worst of times.' Or, putting a different twist on Dickens' famous words, it would be more accurate to say, 'It was the worst of times that became the best of times.' You see, I am a survivor of whole school change. I have borne witness to eight

Mary Fallon, gifted, longtime writing and English literature teacher, expresses her views on the Model Program.

years of the hard work, the long hours, the frustrations, the excitement, the stimulation, sorrows, pain, and the joys that are all part of the process of change

"In 1992, Brewster Academy set out to completely recreate itself. In the years that followed, I have cried and cheered, applauded and 'booed,' as my school has transformed itself from a well-intended and caring school into an excellent school for preparing our students for the twenty-first century. Whether I was in the midst of the fray brainstorming across yards and yards of white Board or a fly on the wall observing quietly from a distance, I have watched and waited and wondered and worried.

"I remember the feelings of rejection I experienced as we all worked our way from a new approach to curriculum design through new techniques of classroom management through new strategies for teacher training and evaluation.

"They're telling me I'm not good enough, a teacher the headmaster once called the best writing teacher in the country, Brewster's secret weapon in the fight to make our students among the most literate. Why fix what isn't broken? I can stand-alone and catch any student that comes through Brewster and single handedly teach him/her to write for college. After all, I was the senior college prep writing teacher. All seniors took my class; all seniors learned to write so what was the problem?

"The problem was that it was wearing me out. The problem was student preparation before they got to me was a hit or miss proposition. The problem was our curriculum wasn't fully coordinated. We didn't move our students through a sequential skill-building program that met each student where he/she was and supplied the appropriate challenges to maximize student growth. The problem was we weren't preparing our young people for the technologies of the new century. The problem was that there was no on-going, clarified, and articulated means of measuring mastery. "Did the students really master that skill? Can they apply it independently? Are we really empowering our students or just passing them through?"

"Yes, there were problems, but I was a hero, and I would fix things. I and the other writing teachers would teach sequential skill building, would measure mastery through portfolio products, would employ collaborative learning techniques, guided-practice, appropriate models, a fully developed and intentional curriculum. We had it all. I knew these approaches would benefit the rest of the school. But why did we have to change too?

"First, let me make this clear. I was indeed an 'old dog' learning 'new tricks,' a seasoned veteran of the classroom. When I came to Brewster Academy in 1984, I had already completed a teaching career teaching Spanish and ESL. I had taught in both public secondary schools and in universities. At Brewster I would be embarking on my "second life" in education, the teaching of English and writing. I had two master's degrees and an all-but-dissertation Ph.D. and had logged in thirteen years of teaching already. My coming to Brewster was a quick decision to try boarding school life and give a stable environment to my own kids. I never dreamed how deeply involved, how totally loyal, how much a part of this school I would become.

"After my first seven years at Brewster, I had become an institution myself, the 'writing guru' as my academic dean now says. But it was during my eighth year that things began to rumble, and we were launched into whole scale change, the type of educational change that soon educators and politicians and philosophers and administrators will be calling for across the nation.

"I participated in the early meetings, the early planning, and maintained my position at the senior exit level as the new program was progressively built into the school. It was first integrated into the freshman year. I watched as the first teaching team was chosen. I watched as those first teachers in the new program received their PowerBooks and plugged into the fiber optic system, which now united the campus. I watched as they attended the first Brewster Summer Institute to prepare them in the practices and skills they would need to implement the new school-wide curriculum. I watched throughout that first year as they worked tirelessly to create intentional curriculum, to integrate collaborative teaching strategies into their classroom, to employ the new technologies we had adopted as tools of learning. I remember their sometimes drawn and exhausted expressions as they tried once again to energize themselves for yet another meeting, another planning session, another 'stab' at curriculum writing.

"As I watched, I felt conflicting emotions. I was jealous. After all, all attention was focused on the new program. But I was also relieved. I didn't have to build new pedagogical strategies into my curriculum. I didn't have to surrender my autonomy to be part of a teaching team. I didn't have to handle the stress of being continuously monitored and observed and evaluated and 'taught' how to do things. Maybe, in fact, it would all die out on the way and never reach me. At times, that was a tempting and consoling thought.

"But it was coming. And the metaphors blossomed. The new program was a recipe we had developed together, a cookie we would bake. The new program was a truck that had been totally unloaded and repacked with a whole new program including new technologies, new evaluation tools, new curriculum designs, new professional development demands, new practices and guidelines, new support systems. Then it all picked up momentum. The new program was a train rushing full steam down the track. What was familiar was embedded within a new, technologized, steam-lined, professionalized, and strategized design. I waited and that fast moving streamlined engine pounded down the rail toward me. Should I climb on or run for the bushes at the side of the track? Could I climb on? Did I want to? Maybe I could just hide in the shadows of my classroom and they wouldn't know I was there. Just keep up the work, deliver the goods, stay out of their way, and hang on, unnoticed, at the back of the caboose. Do my thing!

"There was grief and fear and pain in those first years. I felt it. We all did. After all, it was incredibly hard work, designing curriculum, mastering and implementing best practices in both direct and collaborative learning, being constantly visited and measured in your classroom, being held to standards of pedagogy and professionalism, engaging in on-going professional development programs, rising up an incredibly steep learning curve. Many of my colleagues decided it wasn't for them. Their careers had already been set. In their eyes, their approaches had proven successful. Many moved on, and we all experienced the sense of loss that always accompanies change.

"I was engaging similar thoughts. Was this for me? After all, I was an intuitive teacher, and a very good one at that. I could assess the needs of each of my students and adjust my expectations. If I taught a class of twelve students, I literally had twelve IEP's in my head. I was gifted, inspiring, motivational. I knew all that. Why did I now have to learn the technology? Why did I have to preplan and write out my entire curriculum down to the goals and outcomes, the practices and materials I would use each day? Why did I have to sacrifice my own autonomy to work with a team under the principle of team primacy? I knew what to do with kids and how to treat them. What I had always done was good stuff. Maybe I just needed to leave and find a school where I would be 'appreciated' as I was.

"Yes, what I did in the classroom every day was good enough, had always been good enough, would continue to be good enough. What I didn't realize at first was that good was not enough. Something bigger than good was happening here. You were either part of it or you weren't. And good wasn't the goal. Maximum growth of our students in terms of skills and knowledge was the goal. Maximum preparation of each child we taught for the new technology and information age we were entering, were, in fact, living in, was the goal. Excellence in achieving the outcomes we had articulated for our kids was the goal. Not my ego. Not my indignation. Not my personal comfort.

"It took me two and a quarter years teaching in the new program on a senior team to finally make this breakthrough for myself. And it came to me one day in the classroom when I was delivering that planned and intentional and fully articulated curriculum I had designed, that direct teaching/peer tutoring plan I had developed in the summer and was now implementing in my classroom. I realized in that moment as I moved through my PowerPoint presentation that I was teaching a group of kids that I knew had the foundation to accept and practice and internalize what I was adding to their repertoire because I knew what had come before me from previous English teachers. We were building something solid here for our kids, no more hit or miss, no more broadcast education. I didn't have to go back and reinvent the wheel each time I wanted to introduce a new skill or concept. I knew what each of them had already mastered and where I could meet them and go forward with each group. Yea!

"And yea again! We had done something remarkable...something I know now in my very intuitive heart. What I had to do to be part of the change that would so benefit our kids was lose my ego, adopt the humility of a true learner open to new things, embrace a program bigger than my classroom because that was best for my kids. Whole school change demands that we all become part of something bigger than ourselves, simply because it is best for our students. And it is.

"I now teach in an excellent school. I now teach as a completely integrated part of a working, organic team of teachers, supporting one another, supporting their team of students in a combined and structured system. It provides clear goals for our young people, action plans to pull them back when they stray, consistency to provide them with a sense of security and clarity, fully embedded technology systems to prepare them for the information workplace and the benefit of a team of professional adults working together for their benefit and for their well-being, adults who ask the best from them and supply the best in return.

"Old dogs do learn new tricks, and in the process old dogs are re-energized and renewed. I know. I did and I am."

At the end of the 2010 school year, Mary Fallon retired after 26 years of dedicated teaching and service to the community. Mary and Doug will be living in their new home in Arizona for the winter months and will return to their Wolfeboro residence to teach in the summer Thai Scholar Institute.

18. Doing it All and Doing it Right Across the Campus

If every day you do a little more than is expected of you, everyday a little more will be expected of you.—Mother Teresa

The School Model in Place, Now the Rest of the School

In 1997, the Wilson Center for Teaching and Learning was completed, and all grade levels were now actively involved in the program. The Brewster School Design Model had taken form and was now the fabric of school life. As The Model was implemented in the academic program, other components of the Brewster program and community were developed and expanded, applying the same intentionality toward desired outcomes which undergirded the academic program.

Interconnecting all these departments was a comprehensive communication network that utilized technological information infrastructure to serve the evolving communication needs. Developing this all-important asset was the challenge of the newly established "Tech Office."

Computer Technology: A Bold Step

In 1993, Brewster Academy had taken a bold step, an all-out commitment, to create a systemic model of best practices in the evolution of teaching and learning. This model would be new not just at the Academy but in education in general. As presented in past chapters, the Brewster Model was the result of an exhaustive program of self study, needs identification, and integration of proven, researched best practices into a classroom designed to individualize and improve how teachers teach and how students learn.

Early on Headmaster Smith and Dr. Bain, now serving as assistant headmaster, had determined that communication and information processing would be absolutely essential for the model to function effectively. To that end, they created a pioneering laptop computer program that, for the first time in primary or secondary school education, made computers an integral part of the student experience. All Brewster students had their own computers which they carried to each class. Likewise, all teachers had a computer they used to demonstrate problems, develop and distribute curriculum and communicate with their students.

To use the technology to its fullest extent in supporting The Model, the computers needed to communicate with one another. Therefore, Brewster Academy developed the "Brewster Net," a comprehensive, school-wide network, supported by dedicated information technology professionals.

Expansion of the Technology Department

When it became clear that the Academy needed to be able to quickly repair and return computers to students, new personnel were hired to assume this responsibility. As the "Tech Office" evolved, a full-time programmer and a networking and software specialist were added. A "Help Desk" was placed at the entrance of the "Tech Office" where an accommodating individual offered initial support and direction for more complex problems. In addition, an internship program was established that brought some of the best and brightest students into the Information Technology Department.

Creating Brewster Database; Curriculum, Homework, Grading Systems

In 2001, a new core Brewster database system was created that eliminated redundancy and inconsistency and was accessible from anywhere on Earth via the World Wide Web. With this database system came the development of related curriculum, homework, and grading systems.

One of Alan Bain's pioneering principles was, and remains, to identify classroom needs and create new technology or methodology to meet them, rather than finding a technology and trying to adapt classroom practices to meet it. As a result, new technologies are used rather than simply appearing in class. Faculty members were given the opportunity to test, develop their skills, and utilize computers in ways that make teaching easier and more effective. During the summer, using their computer toolboxes, experienced teachers in each department were employed by the school to develop and evaluate new curriculum that was mastery based and employed the concepts of "best practice" methods of delivery within the classroom. The new curriculum enabled students to approach their assigned work in ways best suited to their learning styles.

Admissions: Impact of School Design Model on Admissions

Just after Stuart Dunlop became director in December 1986, Admission House was remodeled to provide four additional offices for interviewing, and Peg Radley joined the department as coordinator and secretary. For the next 22 years, Peg would be the right hand lady and organization guru for the admissions office.

In his annual report to the Board in February 1991, Dunlop reported, "There was a three-year down trend in Northern New England Prep School admission with the exception of Brewster; however, financial aid needs were escalating and now schools in Southern New England were competing for our market while still others were offering learning skills and slicing into our pool." Stu attributed Brewster's growth to a clear and unique mission, a faculty who understood it, continuity of leadership, and a strong, highly personalized admissions program. He advised that Brewster should continue to refine its mission and focus marketing on that mission, improve teaching expertise, provide program and facilities in support of the mission, and become a national leader in across-the-curriculum mainstream learning support. By 1992, when Stuart Dunlop moved on in his career, the Academy was in the formative stages of implementing the model which reflected the vision he had presented to the Board.

In the July 1994 issue of the *Parents Newsletter*, Admissions Director Paul Amadio reported: "With the onset of the School Design Model, our program is so comprehensive it sells itself. We validate how our community offers students the optimum environment for them to reach their potential. We demonstrate how our program is supportive, interactive, nurturing, and show the results with quantitative information. Brewster does exactly as it says it does in the view book, and overall numbers show Brewster continues to attract inquiries from an ever-expanding demographic nationally and internationally.

"The validity of our program is reinforced by our student tour guides now being called our 'Gold Key members.' Day in and day out, this dynamic group of young people represents the best of everything that is good about Brewster. Every family that tours walks away impressed with our students. Ninety-four percent of the prospective candidates that tour our school make application."

New Admissions Benchmark and Expansion of Leadership

When Paul Amadio became assistant headmaster for advancement in 1997, Lynne Palmer was asked to serve as director of admissions. In Lynne, the headmaster saw a person who shared his intense focus on the school's mission and whose belief in the impact of the Brewster Model on the lives of individuals would lead to a consistent promotion of its strengths internally and externally. As director of admissions, Lynne saw her work not as much as salesmanship but as a drive to get the word out and attract students who, by their presence within the Brewster community, would make a significant contribution to campus life. She saw how a clear understanding of the school, advanced through the work of the admissions department, would help the Academy capitalize on its assets. She was confident in her message and brought energy, enthusiasm, direction and leadership to the office.

As the number of applications grew and the sophistication of the department increased, Lynne, Associate Director Sheila Smith, and Office Manager Peg Radley were joined by associates Margaret Martin, Jason Smith, and upon Sheila's retirement, Fred Garnesy and later Allie Cooper.

As the pieces of The Model were put into place, the admissions operation underwent a thorough analysis; the school affirmed its obligation to accept only those students who could be projected to succeed as well as to contribute to the success of others. Through a study, which compared entry profiles of recent students with their subsequent success at Brewster, the school developed a "benchmark" system to identify and quantify those qualities and standards that students needed to bring if they were to be successful as well as make positive contributions to the community. Student-centered admission decisions could then be made as each application was evaluated in terms of character, attitude, I.Q., past performance, and skills in writing, reading, and math.

As the admission staff carefully scrutinized applicants in relation to the benchmark and as the strengths of incoming students increased, involuntary and voluntary attrition

The Admissions Team: Margaret Martin, Denise Morrill, Fred Garnsey, Peg Radley, Lynne Palmer, and Jason Smith.

decreased significantly.

With the central objective of demonstrating how Brewster Academy delivered on the promise of its mission statement, the school's first website had been launched in 1995. Under Lynne's leadership, the site is constantly evaluated and enhanced to reflect a student's immersion within the various components of the school's distinctive program as well as to illustrate the excitement of daily life on campus.

It had long been recognized by the school that students and their families who visited Brewster Academy very often sought admission. Now, through the website, an effective pre-visit opportunity was available to prospective families, resulting in a dramatic increase of students who actually made enrollment visits to the campus each year.

Sports Impact on Admission

Upon assuming leadership for the admissions department, Lynne also faced the challenge of the historic imbalance between boys and girls with boys significantly outnumbering girls within the student body. Contributing factors in bringing greater gender balance to the school population was not only the growing reputation of the "intentional academic and social curriculum," but the results from a major decision to identify which sports played by both girls and boys had the greatest potential for success in New England. Soccer, ice hockey, basketball and lacrosse were selected for emphasis, and that emphasis carried over into the admissions process. While the benchmark insured both character and capability, the school's focus in attracting student-athletes in these selected areas resulted in increasingly flourishing programs. And as the expression goes, "Success breeds success."

Thus the admissions decision became self-fulfilling and its influence was felt throughout the school.

The Alumni and Development Office

In the spirit of intentionality and expansion, The Alumni and Development Office continues to improve and provide an important liaison between the school and our parents, grandparents, alumni, and friends. Major responsibilities include coordinating reunions and special events, developing alumni/parent programming, promoting the annual fund, organizing phonathons, and preparing mailings. News about upcoming events, schedules, and campus weekend activities is now made available to all through a state-of-the-art messaging system. Tenacity, attention to detail, and a friendly and warm spirit characterize each alumni and development staff member as they make such an important contribution toward fulfilling the mission of the Academy.

During a critical time of fundraising, the Alumni and Development Office was fortunate to have the Mudge family become part of the Brewster community. Daughter Tapley Ann enrolled as a freshman in 1994. Parents Dan and Kathy volunteered to serve in any way they could to support the school. Development staff wasted no time in getting them involved, and they became active leaders of the Parents' Association. When their youngest daughter Ashley arrived in 1999 as a sophomore, Dan and Kathy both moved up to join the Board of Trustees. Dan's expertise and strong commitment led to his appointment as the Board's treasurer, chairperson of the finance committee, and a member of the strategic planning and development committees.

Meanwhile Kathy advanced quickly to the equally crucial position of chair of the development committee and became an animated member of the education committee. Kathy was the leader in the fund-raising efforts for the Smith Athletic and Wellness Center that at the time, was the largest fund-raising campaign in the history of the school. It was through the effort of the Mudges that, over time, Brewster's current parents have become a significant constituency to the fundraising efforts of the Development Office.

Birth of the Spring Fling Thing/Parents' Benefit

In 1989, two very talented and enthusiastic "moms," Rosie Clark (Hadley, '91) president of the Parents Association and Barbara Daly (Cristine, '91), asked Lynne Palmer to join them in developing their fabulous idea for a major fund-raising event that would bring family members together for an evening of fun and entertainment. It would be held on campus in the spring and would become the first significant Parents' Benefit.

Thus, the traditional Spring Benefit, which was eventually moved to the fall when more families were able to attend, was born.

The committee chose to have all proceeds from the event go directly to the "Faculty Support Endowment Fund" and to scholarship financial aid programs so that other children might have the same opportunity (*Brewster Connections Annual* Report *1994/95*, p.16).

Today the goal of the Alumni and Development Office remains constant—to raise funds to best serve our students and to stay in touch with Brewster's wider community.

New Centralized Communication Office

By the 1998-1999 school year with the Brewster Model firmly in place, it became increasingly clear that Brewster required a central office to be responsible for broadcasting the Brewster story by presenting the Brewster difference to as many diverse markets as possible and showing that here was a unique school offering students a highly effective, individualized education. This office would essentially become responsible for all external communication.

Marcia Eldredge was selected to head the newly-created communication office. Under her direction, the office took on a larger role incorporating media relations, publicity, marketing, advertising, and the evolving Internet Web Site that had first been developed under Alan Bain in the mid 1990s. The school's expanding website (www.brewsteracademy.org) provided a new way to communicate with Brewster's constituency for quick and current information.

First Full-Time Dean of College Office

In 1986 the services of the College Office were expanded as part of the mission, "Doing It All and Doing it Right," was implemented. After teaching freshman English and being a valued member of the Learning Skills Department since 1977, Shirley Richardson became the first full-time dean of college placement in 1986. The headmaster had determined that the whole college placement process needed a higher level of priority and a greater allocation of resources, beginning with a full time dean. He saw in Shirley Richardson all the qualities needed to make the office operational; he knew if she accepted the position, she would become knowledgeable and connected with colleges so that she would be positioned to best advocate for her students. Her tenacity, her problem solving and organizational skills, her ability to communicate with people, her energy and enthusiasm, her ability to analyze a situation and take quick action—all were a great benefit to the College Office. She also possessed a special ability to work with young people as she gained their confidence and encouraged them to stretch themselves to be the best they could be.

Expanded Services of College Office

At the time, computer resources were rare, but the College Office had its own computer for students to investigate research options and gain information. In time, the computer became an integral part of every student's college application process.

Shirley printed the first *Brewster College Handbook*, which served as a basic guide offering concise and substantive information for parents and students. Mike Gefers, our in-house math wizard, offered a SAT prep course for seniors and a quick review for the Junior PSATs.

Shirley Richardson, the first full time Dean of College Placement.

A college fair was organized for fall Parents Weekend and a special "college dinner" was planned at the Boathouse for all juniors as they entered the admissions process.

Under the leadership of the Alumni Office and later the College Office, a "Young Alum Program" was begun. On a Saturday morning in February, young alums were invited back to campus to be part of a panel to share their college experiences and be helpful to the seniors as they prepared for their transition to college.

The advancements of the College Office did not go unnoticed by the colleges' admission offices and their representatives who visited with students on campus or called to encourage a student's application to their school. They either had the direct evidence of the success of Brewster graduates at their college or university or they had overheard comments in their professional circles about something special going on at Brewster Academy as evidenced by the performance of their graduates.

The direct evidence was based on the fact that, while national statistics revealed that 15% of all entering freshman left their college or university after 6 weeks and 30% did not return for the sophomore year, on average, 98% of Brewster's "model" graduates returned for their sophomore year. Brewster graduates were arriving on their campuses with refined academic skills, as well as the social skills that enabled them to be successful and contributing members of their college community.

Establishing Traditions

The College Office also worked closely with the senior class on the tradition of a class gift to the Academy. The selection of the senior gift and the raising of funds for it emanated from the College Office. Over the years, the seniors have presented the Academy with gifts such as the restoration of the front doors of the Academic Building, the marble seal in the senior patio, the water garden behind the senior team area in the Wilson Center, the clock above the front door of the Academic Building, and many other additions to the Brewster campus.

Senior Class gifts to the School. From left to right, from the top: School Seal and Bricks, Gazebo with Academic Building in the background, Seniors carving bricks to be placed in the senior patio, Senior Swing and Patio, Water Fountain, Score Board, Main Building Clock, The Victory Bell, and Water Garden.

While those gifts remain as monuments to each class, other traditions were also established or resurrected. Despite the fact that the school's roots extended back to 1820, its rebirth in 1965 as a college preparatory boarding school left it with few established traditions.

The senior prom disappeared in 1965 when, after the transition, the school was initially all boys. In 1984, Brewster again restored the prom tradition with an added feature, the senior breakfast cooked and served by the headmaster at the Student Center then located in the Rogers' Gym. Later the senior slide show would be added to the breakfast, and the event would be held at the Pinckney Boathouse. Other traditions established were the senior walk, senior bricks, senior auction, senior cookie bake, and the passing of the gavel. The winter formal, the lighting and celebration of the traditional campus Christmas tree, holiday vespers, and the planting of daffodils were also among the new contributions to life on campus.

One of the most meaningful traditions can be heard throughout the school day. The "Westminster Chimes" sing over the campus and surrounding neighborhood each hour as they announce the call to class, the call to lunch, dinner, and evening study. They have become part of the very fabric of the school and the surrounding community

The 2003-04 school year marked the retirement of Shirley Richardson as dean of college placement and her service to the Brewster community for almost 40 years; students come first was her motto.

At the time of her official retirement, her associate, Laura Duffy, was to become the next dean with the support of Bill Lee.

The Fine and Performing Arts and Computer Graphics Department

Music Department Has a New Leader

The arrival of Andrew Campbell at the Academy had a dramatic impact on music and the arts at Brewster and, indeed, on the broader Wolfeboro community.

After completing two masters degrees at the Yale School of Music and teaching at the Cate School in Santa Barbara, California, Andy accepted a position at Brewster in 1993. In his first year, teaching music was not even a full-time position. Andy recalls, "It did not take long to fill my schedule with piano students, but I knew that we had to have other music classes as well."

Jazz Band and Chorus

The first addition was the expansion of the Jazz Band. Andy also began a Brewster Chorus with a small group of girls; not one boy showed up for the first meeting. In order to fill the ranks, Andy started to cajole boys in the halls, in the dorms, and in the dining room. Eventually a few brave souls did wander over to see what was happening, and the Chorus became co-ed. Classes in music history, jazz, and choir began to slowly emerge. Soon some recording equipment was pieced together, and a recording studio became part of the Music Department.

Chamber Orchestra

Andy recounts the continuing expansion of the program. "We hired Chris Nourse to teach the chamber orchestra in 1995; I added other classes such as Music Production and Technology and Music Theory to my own schedule when I handed over the jazz group to Candice Graham. Later Candice introduced Wind Ensemble as well as jazz. In 1996, a Foundation Arts and Chorus Program became required for all 9th and 10th grade students who could fit it into their schedule.

Andy Campbell, Pied Piper of the Music Department.

Chorale and Howl!

About this time, John Sandeen, school librarian and a member of the Clearlakes Chorale in Wolfeboro, approached Andy and asked if he would consider accepting the Chorale directorship. For the next two and a half years, the Brewster Choir operated as part of the Chorale.

As student interest increased, the headmaster suggested that Andy begin a similar chorale on campus. In response, Andy's idea was to take the student group in a different direction. "I wanted to make it fun and funky, but we needed a name," he explained. "When I talked with the students about it, the idea of the Stomp group on TV got the boys interested. Their music was cool. So I thought, 'Stomp is to dance as singing is to what?' *Howl* came to mind. So *Howl* it was!'"

Howl Takes To the Road

Howl quickly became and has remained part of the fabric of the school community. They have spread the school's image and reputation through concerts ranging from an invitational concert on the UNH campus to Carnegie Hall where they preformed for audiences of over 2,800. In addition to the standard choral repertoire, *Howl* regularly performs in operas such as *HMS Pinafore, Pirates of Penance, Dido and Aeneas,* and *Amahl and the Night Visitors.* And the pride in and enjoyment of their contribution is a special part of numerous other events on campus throughout the year including an always emotional send off to each year's graduates and their families at commencement.

Andy Campbell has been the school's pied piper, and his music has enriched the spirit of the community. The Rogers building is as busy now as it ever was in its earlier incarnation as the school gymnasium. Nowadays this brick building truly functions as the "hub" of the Arts at Brewster.

Chamber Orchestra musicians.

Drama Department

As Andy Campbell's contributions have resurrected what music meant to the Academy under the direction of Burtis Vaughan, during the Smith era a number of dedicated, talented and inspirational teachers restored the "role" that drama had played in school life. By 1995, exemplified by Susan Dean Olsen's direction of a major production of *Fiddler on the Roof*, the program had spread its wings. In 1996, Donita Coburn was hired to be Brewster's first official drama director and give the students a truly professional experience. A core company of players played significant roles from their sophomore through their senior years. That core group included the President of the Student Body Lindsey Turner and Vice President Topher Grace. Lindsey went on to write and direct an Off Broadway production of *Beowulf* while Topher has gone on to star in television and movies, including *That 70s Show, Traffic, In Good Company, Spider-Man 3, PS, Valentine's Day, Win a Date with Tad Hamilton, Predators, and Kids in America.* He and classmate Gordon Kaywin established their own production company, Sargent Hall Productions, named after their sophomore dorm where they first met. When Donita moved on in 2001, Dan Clay accepted the position of director of drama.

Music and Drama Partnership

Clay shared the vision Campbell had for developing an expanded arts community on the Brewster campus. For the next six years, the synergy of their partnership resulted in an incredible vitality in the arts department. From the sole theater production previously staged each year, Clay was able to expand Brewster's offerings to one main stage production per trimester as well as a major musical performance. Clay had a unique ability to recruit other faculty members, departments, and off-campus organizations to collaborate with Brewster's drama department. As an example, he staged *Pirates of Penzance* by teaming Brewster students with the Clearlakes Chorale and Wolfeboro's community theater group, The Village Players.

A new chorus on campus, Howl!

Under Clay's direction, Brewster students were able to experience a wide variety of drama from Shakespearean classics to modern plays, including tragedies, comedies, musicals, operas, skits and scenes. When Clay was determined to produce *Alice in Wonderland,* he approached Andy Campbell about composing the score for the many stories and poems in the book. The final production showcased Campbell's original compositions alongside the considerable acting and vocal talent of the students. Other memorable productions during Clay's tenure were *Arsenic and Old Lace, Big River, Little Shop of Horrors,* and *The Fairy Queen.*

The Drama Department had grown from a small troupe of faithful followers to a fully developed department that provided its casts and its community with multiple varied productions of high quality performances.

Art/Computer Graphics Department

Our Model pledge of "Doing It All, Doing It Right," by definition, extended to each and every aspect of the school, and the evolution of the art and computer graphics area provided an active visual illustration of how the school led the way in secondary education.

Dale Peterson came to Brewster in 1987 and was quick to recognize that a goodly number of the students were best able to discover and reveal the power and diversity of their intellect through the arts. With that in mind, a noteworthy curriculum for art was established with beginning and advanced offerings in pottery, studio art, and photography. In addition, college placement art and art history became part of the program.

Over the years, the department has also made a concerted effort to have students participating in a variety of art shows and have often submitted pieces to the Scholastic Art Show of Massachusetts and the Scholastic Art Show of New Hampshire and have won "vision" awards, which have allowed them to move on to the national competition in Washington, DC. Other art shows in which students have entered pieces and won prizes for their entries include the Currier Art Show, The New Hampshire Art Association, and Friends of the Arts at Plymouth State University.

Advanced art students who intend to pursue the study in college attend Portfolio Day in Boston. This occasion offers Brewster students a firsthand opportunity to discover what it takes to prepare and present a portfolio for college admission.

Dale also launched and established the school's vibrant and cutting edge computer

Drama production, Little Shop of Horrors.

graphics department and set the standard of constantly introducing new applications as they became developed and available.

After a decade of building the foundation of the department, Dale entrusted his department to a local man of the arts and Brewster alum, BG Hodges.

Computer Graphics Goes Big Time

BG Hodges came to Brewster as a computer graphics teacher in 1997 directly from a successful graphic design career. While Dale Peterson had set the foundations, the rapidly changing landscape of communication, desktop publishing, and personal computing dictated that the computer graphic arts program needed to expand. Again staying true to the promise of Brewster's mission, it was determined that developing skills in these areas was a necessary and important part of preparing students for their futures.

Spearheading these changes, BG brought the design skills he had used as a sign maker and commercial graphic artist and coupled them with the goal of equipping students with ever-expanding computer graphic skills. The program he developed grew out of the components of the Apple iLife suite, Adobe Photoshop, 3D skills and video production. BG wanted students to produce tangible work they could use in the "real world," and so he began to equip his classroom with tools to enable the students to finish their assignments with "real world" products. High quality printers and laminators expanded the applications of the students' design work, and button makers and a tee-shirt press enabled the students to reach out and create interesting products for clubs and activities on campus.

The New Century Communication Tools

With BG's vision, each successive year brought an expansion of the program. BG's approach is from a layout and design standpoint; students learn a skill set and produce a product. With BG in charge, the Computer Graphics Department has created a first rate studio. He developed a comprehensive, multi-layered program, developing skills in a sequential manner. At the end of the year, students produce a DVD of all their work, leaving with a final record of their class projects.

The computer world has a constantly changing and expanding horizon, which has meant that the Brewster Computer Graphic Arts Program also needs to be constantly "upgrading."

BG Hodges, computer graphics director, explaining ideas in the new computer graphic department developed in the Rogers Building.

English as a Second Language
In 1997, Raylene Davis joined the faculty as the director of international student programs and in short order brought Model best practices to all aspects of the English as a Second Language (ESL) program. Previously, Ms. Davis had taught ESL for five years at Bunyko University High School in Shinagawa, Japan, and at Kanagawa Prefectural Foreign Language High School in Yokohama, Japan. Prior to teaching in Japan, she taught at high schools in her native South Australia. Ray was attracted to Brewster by the opportunity to work with computer-assisted language learning and the student-centered approach to education that emphasized skills in learning as much as content.

ESL Curriculum
As in other sectors of the academic program, under Ms. Davis's leadership the ESL core curriculum underwent significant changes, resulting in an intentionally designed curriculum on two levels in order to best serve the needs of Brewster's international population.

Given the nature of the international students' cultures, which all value education highly, most come to Brewster with a strong emphasis on academic performance and do not consider community or athletic commitments of similar importance. The constant theme within the ESL program is "developing a well-rounded student." Raylene also observes, "The quality of the international students has changed over the years. For the most part, their English is far better than it was ten years ago. This is due to a greater focus on English both at home and in schools throughout the world."

Raylene tells us, "ESL students represent 14 percent of the school's population and have a significant representation on honor roll, citizenship, and John Brewster scholar lists. Once students have been in mainstream classes for 6-8 weeks, they often become the best workers in the class."

Raylene Davis and ESL class.

Raylene Davis troubleshoots not only for the educational needs of her students, but also for the behavioral and social issues that they may be confronting. In addition, she keeps in close contact with all international parents and collaborates with the Admissions and Alumni and Development Offices as they work to build a more consistent presence in the Asian market and develop a partnership with parents and past students.

Director of Student Activities

Another area that received a good deal of attention during this time of establishing what it means to be "Doing It All and Doing It Right" was the development of the position of director of student activities.

After several years away from Brewster, in 1988, Tim Radley was re-hired to teach chemistry, coach and be a dorm-master. It was ten years later, after a decision was made to have a full-time director of student activities, that Tim was drafted as the obvious choice for the position.

Early on, Mr. Radley placed an emphasis on providing students with the opportunity to be of service to others. He challenged students to look beyond themselves to serve others. The idea of a formal community service program was first discussed when the Brewster Principle, "Respect, integrity, and service: serve yourself and others with your best in all you do," was adopted in 1993. Under Mr. Radley's leadership, the program became a major force on campus and has also generated numerous service-oriented clubs.

Students Dedicated to Community Service

A wide range of new service opportunities from which students could choose was generated. Students have donated blood to the Red Cross, raked leaves for the elderly, picked up roadside trash with the Adopt-a-Highway Program, and volunteered at Huggins Hospital, Sunbridge Retirement Home and the Humane Animal Shelter. Student volunteers have worked with preschoolers in the area children's center and tutored students in after school programs. They have also served meals at soup kitchens, volunteered in homeless shelters in the Boston area, helped build homes with Habitat for Humanity, provided fleece blankets for Project Linus to comfort children in distress, and raised money to help the child soldiers of Uganda through the Invisible Children Foundation.

Martin Luther King Day

One of the most notable community service projects began in 1997, when Harris House dorm, with the leadership of Mr. Radley, initiated a project to encourage the State of New Hampshire's government to join with the other states of the nation by officially recognizing Martin Luther King, Jr. Day as a state holiday. Over the next three years, Brewster enlisted other public and private schools across New Hampshire to join in a march and rally at the State House Capitol steps in Concord on Martin Luther King, Jr. Day. In the spring of 1999, culminating a 10-year effort by various organizations, including Brewster, the New Hampshire legislature and governor established Martin Luther King, Jr./Civil Rights Day as an official state holiday.

Relay For Life

Also initiated from the director's office was the annual Relay for Life event that now takes place each spring at the Smith Center. Students sign up on teams for this compelling all-night walk-run relay that begins at 11:00 PM with a commemorative ceremony. All during the night until 6:00 AM the next morning, students, faculty, and local residents walk the oval, earning pledged funding for cancer research. Each team also provides fun activities to occupy participants during their overnight stay. That first year, 2006, the students raised $17,000 (*Brewster Connections*, Spring 2005, pp.6-9).

Other Extra-curricular Traditions Established

Recognizing that much of campus life is geared toward academic and sports commitments, as activities director, Mr. Radley concentrated on providing opportunities just for pure entertainment and fun. Such initiatives have included dances, coffee house nights, ping pong tournaments, mall/movie and paintball trips, rides to concerts in Boston and Concord, ski trips, and intramural night football and softball leagues. He stocked his second floor office in the Student Center with all kinds of resources for creating fun: board games, DVDs, posters, handcrafts, prizes, sports equipment, and party decorations. And his door was always open to students to hear new ideas or just as a retreat from the pressures of school. Considering those pressures that grow in mid winter or in exam periods, Mr. Radley developed or enhanced Winter Carnival Week and the wacky weekend activities of Spring Fest.

Most importantly, Tim took a space called the Student Center and made it the Students' Center. It is a welcoming hub of campus life where students can come and interact in a variety of ways.

When the Smith Center was dedicated in the fall of 2002, Tim's impact on campus life was recognized with the dedication of Radley Basketball Court.

After many years of dedicated service, Tim Radley retired in 2009.

Annual Relay For Life event: Peggy McBride, Tim Radley, Lauren Hammond, Nate Billings.

Athletics

As in all the other areas of the school, the Athletic Department was also in a position to anticipate many changes over the next several years. As enrollment of boys and girls increased, many had the opportunity to be involved in interscholastic sports and experience the joy, the pride and the lessons of sportsmanship as members of a team. As enrollment continued to grow, so too did the need to expand the number of offerings, fields and facilities, coaches and support services.

As with academics, the following question was asked: "What does the school intend for its students to gain from their athletic experience?" Through a thorough self-study analysis, the desired outcomes were identified in terms of sportsmanship, teamwork, skill development and fitness. A program was established wherein the importance of acquiring these benefits was underscored by the coaches at all levels of athletic commitment.

Athletic success on the courts, fields, and rink spilled over into the classroom engendering spirit and enthusiasm in the halls. At home games, the sidelines and stands are often filled with cheering students and faculty, and along with them are many parents, Wolfeboro town folks, and old alums on the sidelines rooting and applauding the players.

Due to the increasing degree of athletic talent and with the combination of excellent coaching, many teams, both men and women, have won Northern New England Championships in both Class C and Class A as well as NEPAC and have earned Division I status: basketball, lacrosse, baseball, hockey, soccer, cross country, alpine skiing, nordic skiing, snowboarding field hockey, tennis, crew, sailing.

In 1996, the Brewster athletic program was supplemented by an unusual request by two students, Jamie Butler, '98, and Kevin Ginest,'96, who wanted to improve student life and activities on campus. They approached the headmaster with a novel idea of creating a climbing gym for the students. They saw it as a facility that could be used by sports programs, dorms, and clubs for team building.

BREWSTER
LACROSSE
24
8

SOUTH

20

8

104

25

Fans in the stands supporting the Academy teams.

With the support of faculty members Mike Hanewald, David Harris and Byron Martin, who were leading the Outing Club at the time, a proposal for an Outing Club shack and climbing wall was submitted to the Board of Trustees. The Board approved the project and the raising of $3500 to fund the venture. They also gave permission for the use of Haines Barn as the home of the new facility.

To raise funds, Eladio Moriera, Spanish teacher, designed a T-shirt to sell. Parents and faculty made donations, and Business Manager Bob Simoneau found some money in the school budget. In the fall of 1996, the students held an open house during Parents Weekend to gain attention and support. With funds becoming available, work on the barn was begun and a major overhaul took place as the barn was gutted to create the necessary high ceilings for a climbing wall. Mike Hanewald, David Harris, and Byron Martin spent weeks ripping the loft down and tearing up the floor boards; students were not permitted to join in at this stage because of unsafe conditions.

With professional advice and direction, the main climbing wall design was ready, and students were finally able to participate in the construction work. Inner walls were built to make the barn structurally sound for the climbing wall; a boulder cave was also constructed. Recycled shredded tires and mattresses were put into service for the floor, and the Academy purchased a Flash propane heater and lights with the students and their fund raising campaign paying for the rest of the expenses. Through a true grassroots effort, by fall of 1997, the Climbing Barn was fully equipped and operational.

Over the years, with the faculty supervision and the coaching of Jonathan Fouser (who himself is a mountaineer, having climbed in the Alps and the Himalayas), the Outdoor Skills Program is in capable hands and has contributed greatly to the expansion and improvement of the Climbing Barn. Not only is it a top-notch facility and the base of operation for the Outing Club, it also offers storage lockers for sleeping bags, tents, and other equipment as well as a lounge area for all to come and enjoy a unique opportunity.

Another outdoor event is the traditional Polar Bear Plunge that coincides with the

Climbing Wall located in Haines Barn.

Polar Bear plunge April 18, 2011 recognizing "ice out" and open waters for sailing and crew activities.

official "ice out" in Wolfeboro Bay. Daring students and faculty charge to the boathouse docks at sunrise to take the frigid plunge celebrating the arrival of spring and open waters. This event dates back to over one hundred years.

Moving into the 21st Century

As Brewster embarked on its innovative educational journey, its goal was to march into the 21st century with the highest quality of educational reform imaginable supported by a sophisticated technology system, and an exceedingly well-trained faculty. It had taken time, incredible financial resources, the personal commitment of faculty, and the dedication of an administration led by the support of the Board of Trustees. The transformation had been achieved. Brewster Academy emerged as a school absolutely committed to "Doing It All and Doing It Right." As was the case in the school's origins, the new foundation had been established, driven by, and centered in addressing the learning style and education needs of its students.

19. September 11, 2001: A Day To Be Remembered

There is not grief that does not speak.—Henry Wadsworth Longfellow

It was a warm Tuesday morning, the first day of the 2001-2002 school year. The bright sun spreading through the Brewster classroom windows greeted students as they made their way from their first period class to the next one. Two seniors, hurrying out of their dorm, heard a startling announcement on CNN and watched in amazement as they saw the top floors of one of the "Twin Towers" of the World Trade Center in New York ablaze. One student lingered to learn more and moments later saw an explosion as a second large passenger jet swung around the southeast side of the towers and ripped into the upper floors of the north tower.

As fear and chaos terrified the early crowds in the streets of lower Manhattan, that first senior burst into to Mr. Bob Carter's physics class in the Wilson Center, reporting what he had just seen.

Impact on Campus That Morning

Carter was shaken by what he heard and instructed his students to check the latest news on their laptops. As classes changed, other students learned the news of the tragedy. Students who lived in the New York area were gripped by fear as they listened to the incredible news bulletins, and some rushed to a phone to call home for more details. The news that a terrible incident had happened in New York and that the federal authorities had grounded all air traffic in the country spread rapidly from hallway to hallway throughout the school. By 9:37 AM, a third hijacked airliner, American Air Flight 77 from Washington Dulles to Los Angeles, had crashed into the Pentagon building in Washington, D.C., killing over 200. At 10:05 AM, the South Tower of the World Trade Center collapsed, and at 10:28 AM, the North Tower collapsed. United Air Flight 93 from Newark to San Francisco had taken off and headed west, but soon turned around and crashed near Shanksville, Pennsylvania, but not before some passengers had made an heroic attempt to seize control of the plane which sadly failed.

As morning approached noon, almost everyone at Brewster knew about the terrible disaster that had taken place in New York and Washington.

Plan of Action

After getting the latest facts about the tragedy, Headmaster David Smith called an immediate meeting of faculty and staff where he relayed all he knew about the loss and shared with them the spectrum of anticipated student reactions and their resulting needs. He noted particular concern for those students whose parents were returning home to the New York area after opening day registration and for students who might have relatives and friends who lived and worked in or around the World Trade Center. Mr. Smith then gathered the entire community at the Estabrook where students were seated at tables with their advisors who offered emotional support and assisted advisees in making phone calls to parents,

Tommy Palazzo riding his bike on campus 1973.

relatives or friends in that stricken area. The Health Center personnel as well as additional counselors were made available to support any who seemed to be experiencing difficulty.

Central to the headmaster's message was the faith we all shared in the strength of our community, especially in the most difficult of times. He rallied that community strength, saying we would face its challenge by supporting each other as we carried on in our classes and afternoon athletics activities. He also announced there would be a candlelight vigil that night for all who wished to attend.

Headmaster Receives a Call the Night of 9/11

In early evening, Mr. Smith's phone rang with a call from Kevin Mulvey, '75, who began by saying, "We lost a good one today, Mr. Smith. Tommy's gone." Mr. Smith knew Kevin was referring to his classmate and long-time friend Tommy Palazzo, '75, but hoping by some miracle Kevin was wrong. There was no miracle. The school would lose another family member before it was over. Word soon came that Peter Fry, '83, was among those lost in the attack on the World Trade Center. Devastating news for all. During the candlelight vigil held that evening Headmaster Smith spoke of Tommy and Peter. He shared that he often told students upon graduation that part of them would remain here to live on in our memories as 18 year-olds forever. He said those words would now be especially true for Tommy and Peter, both of whom had possessed the qualities that created a sense of brotherhood with their friends, bonds which had remained strong throughout their lives. Through the joyous memories of their friends, their teachers, and their families, Tommy and Peter would live on.

As he recalled Kevin's call that night, Headmaster Smith remembered, "There was Tommy in my mind's eye with his brother Robbie,'74, beside him, Brewster letters across their chests. And when the games began, Robbie was smiling, as Tommy tore around nonstop giving his all to secure a game victory. And during the years since his graduation as a member of the school's advisory council, there was Tommy calling time and time again with one of the million and one ideas that would pop into his head. "Hey, Mr. Smith, did you ever think of …?"

And there was Peter, the poster boy, the stabilizing influence, the leader by example, a young man who would know just what was needed, what was the right thing to do under any circumstance. Peter was able to do what many people, especially adolescents, find difficult to do. He was both cool and cool headed and he always represented what was right. That combination led to his being highly respected by the entire community.

Tommy and Peter

Tommy was a graduate from the State University of New York at Purchase. At the time of his death, he worked as a government bond broker at Cantor Fitzgerald. He was 44 years old and lived in Armonk, New York, with his wife Lisa and their three daughters, Kristine 17, Carrie 14, and Katie 12.

Peter was a graduate of Curry College where he was an All-American lacrosse player. At the time of his death, he was a vice president of Institutional Money Markets at Euro Brokers Incorporated, a global securities firm. Peter was 36 and lived in Wilton, Connecticut, with his wife Meredith Loomis Fry and their two daughters, Taylor, 6 and Caley, 3 (*Brewster Connections,* Spring 2002, p.15).

The Academy would soon honor these fine young men.

Palazzo Field Dedicated

Under sunny skies, Reunion 2002 attendees and other members of the Brewster community gathered on the former Lakeside Field to dedicate it to Tommy Palazzo, '75, and also to his brother Robbie, '74, an outstanding athlete at Brewster who had set the example for Tommy. Headmaster David Smith presented each of Tommy's children with a Brewster Academy sweatshirt embroidered with *Palazzo #4*, Tommy's hockey uniform number. Robbie spoke about how much the school had meant to the two boys and how they had

Classmates and friends Rick Storm, Peter Fry, and David Hope as students on campus.

#17 Robbie Palazzo and #24 Tommy Palazzo, 1974.

matured. "They were the finest years of our lives as we learned how to become adults here" (*Brewster Connections,* Fall 2002, p. 15).

A long time passed before Robbie could examine Tom's personal things. Deep in Tom's closet he found his old equipment bag. From the bottom of the bag, he found an old cardboard sign:

> *If you think you can't, you're probably right.*
> *If you dare not, you don't.*
> *If you think you'll lose, you've lost.*—Arnold Palmer

Along with the sign was a rolled-up old Brewster game jersey, bearing number "17," the same number Robbie had worn at Brewster his senior year. When Rob graduated, Tom had asked the athletic department to assign him number "17" for his senior year (Palazzo, *Transcribed Interview,* 2006).

Fry Field Dedication

On the Saturday of Reunion 2003, at the soccer and lacrosse field in front of the new Smith Center, the dedication of Fry Field took place. In Headmaster Smith's remarks during the dedication, he talked about Brewster Academy being Peter's school. "As headmaster, there were times I thought he was just about to take over my job. He was a one-man welcome wagon for new students or anyone he saw in need. Peter was always on the lookout to help kids who were a little lost. And once you established a relationship, you had a most loyal friend."

Peter's wife, Meredith, and their daughters, were at the dedication as were Peter's father Charles, Michael Towey, Peter's brother-in-law, other family members, and Peter's good friend Rick Storm, '83 who remembered that, "Peter was the kind of friend-to-the-end sort who was full of energy and forever joking. He was sincere, kind and helpful, and the first person to console you if he noticed hurt in your eyes" (*Brewster Connections*, Summer, 2003. p. 17).

The tragic events of September 11 shook the students, faculty, and alumni of the Academy; but the community spirit, so completely inculcated in each member of the Brewster family, absorbed the shock and the pain and saw the community through the tragedy. As Hubert H. Humphrey so aptly observed, "The greatest healing therapy is friendship and love."

Above, the dedication of Palazzo Field - L to R: Todd Matheson, Greg Cefalo, Kevin Mulvey, Jeff Swecker, Clay Goodwin, John MacDonald, John Ford, Scott Swann and Robbie Palazzo. Below, Family and friends at the dedication of Fry Field: left to right standing: Samatha Loomis Patterson, Lucy Fred, Charles Fry, Michael Towey, Andrea Loomis Towey, Meredith Loomis Fry, Arthur Loomis, Consuelo Loomis, David M. Smith. Front row: Jeff Woods, Cary Loomis Woods, Griffin Patterson, John Patterson, Jordon Patterson, Caley Fry, Taylor Fry. Below, left side of sign standing: Samatha Loomis Patterson, Lucy Fred, Charles Fry, Michael Towey, Andrea Loomis Towey. Left side kneeling: Jeff Woods, Cary Loomis Woods. Standing left side of sign: Meredith Loomis Fry, Arthur Loomis, Consuelo Loomis, David M. Smith. Front of sign: Griffin Patterson John Patterson, Jordon Patterson, Caley Fry, Taylor Fry.

20. David Minton Smith: Concluding Years

If your actions inspire others to dream more, learn more, do more and become more, you are a leader.—John Quincy Adams

Daniel Mudge, New President of the Board of Trustees

With David Smith's retirement approaching and having served as Board president for thirteen years, Grant Wilson determined it best to pass the leadership of the Board to a man who he recognized would be a most capable, respected and dedicated successor. Daniel T. Mudge had served on the Board since 1994 and was elected as the succeeding president in May of 2001.

Dan became president of the Brewster Board of Trustees at a time when the school continued to attract attention and interest from educators worldwide and decisions were being considered regarding the scope of our response to their desire to share in the benefits of our advances.

The foundation for the future of the school's program was well advanced, deeply rooted and valued. The headmaster had great faith in and appreciation of the school's leadership beginning with Academic Deans Marilyn Shea and Peter Hess (initial members of the first freshman Model Team); Director of Instructional Support Kim Ross, who had accepted the reins from Dr. Bain eleven years before; Admission Director Lynne Palmer and Business Manager Bob Simoneau who always applied their talents and deep dedication to insuring the vitality of the business of the school; and Doug Algate and Kate Turner, who served student growth through athletic offerings. In addition Headmaster's Secretary Susan Nichols brought quiet order and facilitation to the office, and Director of Personnel Bonnie Medico was always prepared and capable of assisting with virtually any challenge and any opportunities that came daily to the office.

The school was ready to move forward, refining the newly created potential in all that had already been brought into place and completing the unfinished business on the master facilities plan.

The Facility Master Plan, the Final Push

At this time, the final two major needs left on the original Master Plan drawing board were venues for athletics and the arts. The school was justifiably proud of all that had been brought into place but recognized that it could not fulfill the promise of its mission statement with inadequate facilities in support of the athletic and artistic potentials of its students. The administration and the Board of Trustees felt the time had come, and they set out to do something about it.

How It All Began

It all began one night in 1998 when Bonnie and Terry Turner, who were highly experienced in both film and television production, came to Brewster to see the play *Godspell* in which their daughter, Lindsey, was one of the student performers. Inspired by the performance,

School Management Team: Doug Algate, athletic director; Dr Alan Bain, assistant headmaster; Kim Ross, director of instructional support; Peter Hess, dean of studies; Bob Simoneau, business manager; Bonnie Medico, director of personnel; Marilyn Shea, academic dean; Susan LeBlanc, dean of students; Laura Duffy, dean of college counseling; Lynne Palmer, director of admissions.

Bonnie Turner suggested to Grant Wilson that, in order to upgrade the school's current facilities, "We have to get outside the box, literally, and do it right." The Turners then stepped up to underwrite a "study" of facilities for athletics and the arts (Smith, *Transcribed Interview*, 2007).

The Study and the Challenge

Over the next few months, the study committee, coordinated by an architectural planner, Patricia Sherman, selected and visited a number of schools that were noted for their athletic and/or art facilities. Those schools included Middlesex, Groton, Fay, Walnut Hill, Berkshire, and Providence Country Day schools as well as Brown University and Brandeis University.

An initial question that no one was anxious to prioritize was which facility should come first—athletics or the arts. Ultimately, the answer came with the realization that because the arts would be part of the academic day as well as the afternoon extracurricular program, its facility should adjoin or be adjacent to the Academic Building. It followed then that the space occupied by the current gymnasium would be the logical space for the arts.

The next big question and challenge was, where does the school believe it can acquire the level of funds to have the confidence to make it happen? From the beginning of the Master Facility Plan process, major priorities had been identified, but smaller projects had kept gobbling up any accumulated funds. Fortunately, a new generation of parents became interested and involved; and unlike the case in many schools, the former generation of supportive parents continued to remain loyal and committed to seeing the vision of the plan through to reality.

Fund Raising

Trustee Kathy Mudge who chaired the development committee called for a meeting of her committee at the Wolfeboro Inn. It was billed as a meeting to determine whether it was to be "go or no go" for a new facility. The central question before the committee was: "Will the committee endorse taking on this challenge and pledge to do whatever it takes to make it happen?" She called the vote and just as she secured unanimous endorsement, Grant Wilson walked through the door. With enthusiasm he congratulated the group for their decision and commitment and added his major pledge. The dream was launched (David Smith, *Transcribed Interview*, September 2007).

A combination of Board members and friends who were in tune with the needs of the school entering the 21st Century led the way, and foundation dollars and support from many friends of Brewster followed.

Selecting the Builder

As planning for construction got underway, several individuals and companies came together to initiate the process leading to a new athletic facility. The Lee Kennedy Company with Robert J. McCluskey as principal was hired to oversee the whole process. Very early on Mr. McCluskey recommended that the school engage George Oommen to head up the concept design aspect of the program. Dr. Oommen had been engaged in designing athletic facilities for 30 years, and he told them, "If you want a facility that is above anything that you can find, I can do that, but I need to meet with all your coaches and all other people who will be involved. This is very crucial so I can help you design a secondary school facility to meet the needs of all constituents" (Robert Simoneau, Recorded Interview, February 2009).

Assembling the Team

After listening to everyone and appreciating their "wish list," Mr. Oommen produced a design incorporating major concept ideas for Brewster's decision makers and the architects to review. The vision created by those ingredients was enthusiastically accepted. An example of Mr. Oommen's ingenuity was that the building should have no corners, but be oval in design for corners waste both heat and light. At this juncture Lee Kennedy, overseer of the project, identified and brought in four architectural firms for consideration. The Banwell Company was selected. David Smith and Bob Simoneau were familiar with the company because it was the firm that had designed the Pinckney Boathouse. When Oommen's concepts were advanced to architectural plans, Eckman Construction and Builders was selected from a group of four companies to build the Oommen/Banwell design.

With the input of Dr. Oommen, The Banwell Company completed the Smith Center which was dedicated in 2003. This impressive facility is nestled into the campus hillside, overlooking the playing fields, Wolfeboro Bay, and the mountains. It is one of the finest athletic and wellness centers among independent schools. It's where the Brewster Bobcats interscholastic sports teams train and play, where intramurals and recreational sports games are generated and enjoyed, and where the entire campus community stays in shape and cheers on their teams together. And certainly the athletic leadership, support staff and coaches are now both proud and fully enabled to instill the benefits of fitness, team work and sportsmanship.

Four Lane Track and Convertible

While each and every aspect of the 50,000-square-foot facility is second to none, it is truly distinguished by its convertible turf floor and 200 meter tuned track. In the initial stages of the planning process, George Oommen had stated emphatically and unequivocally, "There is no such thing as a multipurpose floor surface. Basketball needs a floating wooden floor and field sports need an Astroturf-like surface." So once again following a policy of not compromising on quality and "thinking outside the box," the school stepped up, and the facility would provide both surfaces.

Two full size collegiate practice courts run perpendicular through a richly designed

The new Smith Center at winter dawn.

tournament court. At center circle of the tournament court in the building that carries his parents' names is a distinctive bobcat logo designed by Tim Smith, '91, son of David and Sheila Smith.

Conversion of the floor for field sports baseball, lacrosse, soccer, field hockey as well as tennis is accomplished in less than 20 minutes as the artificial turf rolls out across the court and floor-to-ceiling netting provides for multi-purpose use.

The turf offers an additional place to practice that is especially valuable in northern New England during early spring and inclement weather. It also encourages and provides for more interscholastic teams as well as an array of intramural and recreational options.

Fitness and Training Center

Those panoramic views of the playing fields, the lake and the mountains, also provide added inspiration for those working out in the Kaywin Fitness Center and Stabile Weight Area. This modern fitness center features fifty stations of cardiovascular equipment from exercise bikes, to Stairmasters, Tectriz steppers, treadmills, Body Masters Selecterized equipment and a Smith machine as well as numerous benches and free weights in the Stabile section. The fitness center is also used for rehabilitation by the school's trainers whose adjacent, fully equipped Trainer's Room and Therapy Center is available for students, faculty and staff.

The Center's latest unique feature came with the addition of an eight seat rowing tank for year-round crew practice located in "The Crescent" adjacent to another special feature of the Smith Center, the Athletic Hall of Fame and classroom which is located on the ground floor to the right as you enter the Smith Center.

The Brewster Hall of Fame

During a visit to Harvard, the committee decided to incorporate their concept of a Hall of Fame that could also serve as a classroom and a VIP meeting space. The Hall of Fame was created to recognize members of the Brewster family who have distinguished themselves by outstanding contributions in athletics at Brewster Academy, and afterwards by a continuing

Above, BasketBall Court Full Wooden Floor Smith Center. Below, full turf convertible field, Smith Center.

Four Lane Track, Smith Center.

commitment to, and promotion of, the values and philosophy of sportsmanship. Included in the Hall of Fame are:

Paul "Pop" Whalen

On December 1, 2001, Paul (Pop) Whalen became the first person inducted into the Brewster Hall of Fame. Pop had touched hundreds of lives as teacher, coach, mentor and friend at Brewster Academy. To his professional colleagues he had provided an example of what it meant to dedicate your life in service to the lives of young people, and through athletics he had instilled a love of the game, the desire to do your best, the rewards for hard work, fairness in play, and the virtues of good sportsmanship. Thus, the standard had been set as to what it meant to be selected as a member of the Hall of Fame.

Anthony "Tony" Giglio, '70

The second inductee had arrived at Brewster as a post-graduate in the fall of '69. Tony Giglio proved to be a great football player, a pretty good basketball player and a very good baseball player. Football was by far his best sport, and he smashed the Academy's scoring records with 17 touchdowns in just seven games.

In terms of academics, Tony became a high-honors student. During his commencement, Tony was the 1970 recipient of the William Lord Award given to the top student/athlete as well as the Bausch Lomb Award for the top science scholar in the graduating class.

Tony was inducted into Brewster's Hall of Fame in 2004 at his 34th reunion. As he had told Mr. Smith, "I probably won't make it to my 35th." Tony was fighting for his life against a virulent form of brain cancer, and despite his incredible spirit and the support of the loves of his life, his wife Kelly and his children Tony,'08, and Annie, sadly he was right in his prediction.

At the close of the induction ceremony for Tony Giglio, Headmaster David Smith said:

"Tony, from this day forward you will live on at your school as an example as to what it means to discover all you can be by giving your best in all your endeavors."

Bobcat Design Center Court by Tim Smith.

David Pollini, '57

Under the Hall's central criteria of accomplishment and leadership through athletics, David Pollini's record stands unparalleled in the annals of the school's history.

At Brewster Academy Dave Pollini:

- Lettered in soccer, basketball and baseball each of his four years.
- In soccer, he was his team's high scorer in his sophomore, junior and senior years and was selected as the team's most valuable player in his junior and senior years.
- In baseball, he advanced steadily becoming both the team's best hitter and pitcher. He batted over 300 as a sophomore, 338 as a junior and an extraordinary 420 in his senior season. As a pitcher over the four years he had the superlative record of 20 wins and only 2 losses.

Upon graduation from Brewster, Dave went on to Boston University where he was co-captain of both the soccer and baseball teams.

In 1961, upon graduating from Boston University, Dave returned to Brewster where he taught biology and coached soccer, basketball, golf and baseball. His soccer teams won four consecutive Lakes Region Championships, and the National Soccer Guide ranked them as one of the top prep school teams in the country. In 1965 his baseball team achieved a similar distinction.

In June 2005, David Pollini, '57, became the third inductee of the Brewster Academy Hall of Fame.

Rebecca Seaman, '97

Rebecca Seaman was also inducted into the Hall of Fame in June of 2005. When Rebecca became a student at Brewster, she found herself at a school without a women's ice hockey team. She played for the New Hampshire Select Girls Elite Team; and as a result of her persistence, the school agreed to allow her to join the boy's junior varsity team. She spent the next four years minding the net for the team and was twice selected as the captain and

Above, Kaywin Fitness Center, Smith Center. Below, the Rowing Tank, Smith Center.

MVP. She was also recognized with the Coach's Award for the example she set and the leadership she provided. While at Brewster, Rebecca also played goalie in both field hockey and lacrosse and held the distinction of being the only 12-season athlete in her graduating class.

Rebecca was recruited by and played for the Division I Boston College women's ice hockey team. She has coached ice hockey for the New England College development league girls' all stars in Boston, for Brewster Academy, and for the Wolfeboro Junior She-Wolves. Rebecca was the fourth inductee into the Hall of Fame.

Jonathan Pinckney, '84

Before Jon Pinckney arrived on Brewster's campus, our sailing team had never won enough races during the season to be invited to compete in the New England Championship Regatta. The big sailing schools, Tabor Academy in Marion, Massachusetts, and St Marks in Newport, Rhode Island, were in southern New England where their "home court" was not "frozen in" during the beginning of the competitive season. When Jon came to Brewster, he had already won many sailing championships in his early years in California.

Then in 1984, the Pinckney led team earned an invitation, and coach Andrew Wooden took the Brewster team to the New England Championships. All hope for any success rested solely on Jon and his crewmate, Ray Lambert of Bermuda. Together they brought home the New England Championship—the one and only one in sailing ever won by the school.

For his great accomplishments in his sport, for all the reflected glory he brought to his school and for the example he set by what he took with him from his experience at the Academy, on June 7, 2009, Jon Pinckney became the fifth inductee into the Brewster Academy Hall of Fame.

Dr. Alan Bain Moves On

As the Smith Center was completed and the Academy was in the midst of addressing the pending retirement of its long-time headmaster, another noteworthy change was about to happen. The community paused to recognize Dr. Alan Bain who was concluding his contribution to Brewster and returning to an expanded role in education leadership at the university level. The connection of one to the other became evident in the publication of his new book, *The Self Organizing School,* in which he described all that was involved in the creation of the systemic model of education, grounded in research-proven, best practices, which he had developed and advanced during his years at the Academy. During those 11 years, Dr. Bain had contributed his broad and profound knowledge and understanding of the body of research on effective educational practices. With his dedication, wisdom, and boundless energy, he led the school through the process of designing and implementing an intentional systemic model of education, thereby advancing the fulfillment of its mission to maximize the learning experience of every Brewster student. He also was a leader in organizing an international workshop and institute in an effort to enable other schools to advance similar reforms.

In recognition of his extraordinary contribution, the Academy placed a dedication plaque at the entrance to his office, which reads:

> Dedicated to Dr. Alan Bain
> *As an expression of appreciation for his great contribution and*
> *as a pledge to continue our efforts in carrying out the mission for which he*
> *set such a firm and enduring foundation.*

Grant Wilson Remembers the Smiths and Their Years at Brewster

As Mr. and Mrs. Smith prepared to leave the Academy, Grant Wilson remarked, "Thirty years ago, no sane person would have bet a plugged nickel on the likelihood that Brewster would have ever survived into the twenty-first century; the school has not only done so—it has prospered through the efforts of David and Sheila Smith."

At the dedication of the Smith Center, Grant offered these remarks in honor and remembrance of the Smith's faithful and dedicated years at the Academy. In his address, he highlighted the Smiths' many contributions to Brewster, including loyalty, dedication and a deep sense of mission.

He noted that when David took over the school had well under 100 students, most of whom came from the local communities or the Northeast. During his tenure the enrollment had quadrupled to 360 students from 37 states and 22 other countries.

Further, Grant stated that David was always striving to answer the question, "What do we want our students to know and be able to do to be best prepared for college and life, and how do we best use all available to us to ensure we achieve these outcomes?" David had the courage and conviction to lead that commitment to achieving these outcomes.

Finally, Grant added, "It is fitting that a facility that represents strength and permanence bears the names David M. and Sheila H. Smith to commemorate their great legacy to Brewster. The trustees and community were unanimous in deciding to honor the Smiths by naming the new facility after them (Grant Wilson, President of the Board of Trustees, *Brewster Connections* Summer 2002).

David and Sheila Smith Retire

After serving Brewster Academy for 34 years, David and Sheila Smith planned for retirement in June 2003. Alumni, friends, past and present parents, faculty, and trustees organized events in Dallas, Chicago, Washington DC, San Francisco, and Los Angeles to honor, reminisce with and express appreciation to the Smiths. A final recognition banquet was held at the Hawthorne Hotel in Salem, Massachusetts, which included many speakers, mementos, toasts of gratitude, and a slide show recalling their years and their impact.

Then came the day when Headmaster Smith presided at his last commencement, May 29, 2003. Trey Whitfield's dad, Argyle, was the guest speaker.

During the awarding of diplomas, it had become a tradition for each senior to hand the headmaster some small memento symbolic of their time together. Mr. Smith invariably recognized the symbolism and took a moment to inform the "audience." But this time he was puzzled as each senior handed him a feather as he handed out diplomas. Then the class awarded the Smiths an honorary diploma, proudly announcing that the Smiths would forever be a member of their graduating class; and the mystery of the feathers was revealed. The music began and Senior Jenny Cooper sang to the headmaster a special version of "You [Were] the Wind Beneath [Our] Wings."

David closed the ceremony with what had become his legendary expression, saying to the class, "Today is the first day of the rest of your lives," adding that "on this special day Mrs. Smith and I are joining you as you move on because for us today is also the first day of the rest of our lives."

Author's Note

As our presentation of the Smith years comes to a conclusion, it is important to note that David Smith's tenure of 29 years as headmaster is the longest in the school's history, surpassing the previous record by a dozen years or so. Like almost any other history, we have found it almost impossible to separate the institution's history from the leader's biography or the impact of national events on the evolution and survival of an independent school.

Headmaster David M. Smith and Mrs. Sheila Smith as they retired in 2003. Grant and Helene Wilson, and Dan and Kathy Mudge honoring the Smiths' 34 year of service.

Our full and detailed presentation of The Brewster Model and its implementation is important, almost as important is the story of how the school arrived at the concept, refined it, undertook a pilot project, and within a decade incorporated its basic principles throughout every facet of the school.

As early as the Bearce administration, it had become apparent that the school must change substantially if it were to survive in the competitive world of independent education. This slow process began and continued under successive heads of school for decades until the Board of Trustees and Headmaster Smith put all the school's resources of funds, staff, and equipment behind its assertion that Brewster Academy exists solely to serve each student by offering the best education possible.

With the model firmly in place and its premises proven, the Smith administration handed off to Dr. Michael Cooper a much stronger institution than had been inherited almost three decades earlier. Because The Model calls for continuing searches for and implementation of best practices, the school will not likely again fall into a crisis like the near-death crisis it faced in the late 60s and the 70s. That is the true legacy of the administration of David M. Smith.

21. Dr. Michael E. Cooper, 2003–present: The First "Head of School"

Things do not happen. Things are made to happen.—John F. Kennedy

Selection of the New Head of School

Transition in the leadership of independent schools is never an easy process, but both Board President Grant Wilson and Headmaster Smith were committed to passing their batons to their successors smoothly and effectively.

Throughout the long tenure of Headmaster David Smith, the close and productive partnership between headmaster and board chairman had paved the way for the monumental changes that had taken place. By 2001, the board president and headmaster knew they had to take up the question of transition in leadership, and thus it had been sometime in 1997 that Grant Wilson asked David when he might want to retire. Looking ahead, and after much thought and sharing with Sheila, David had set a date of 2003 with Grant. Now that date was fast approaching. Their shared objective was not only to allow adequate time for the board to orchestrate and execute a search for the right person to become the next headmaster, but to do so in such a way that the strength in the school's leadership formula could be retained.

Dr. Michael Cooper, eleventh Head of School and Mrs. Andrea Cooper.

Nearing the end of his third decade as headmaster, David had partnered with only two presidents of the Board, Rink DeWitt for fifteen years and Grant Wilson for thirteen. Such lengthy tenures are rare and provide an insight into the difference that they had provided to the Academy.

Grant and David recognized that they should not retire together, and thus, Grant with a smile, told David since he [Grant] was the ultimate boss he would retire first. In doing so, they sought a replacement for a board president who could work with David, establish the *modus operandi*, and thus be positioned to provide the continuation of support and partnership with the incoming headmaster. Fortunately, they knew they had just the right man for the job, and Dan Mudge stepped in and seamlessly brought about and maintained the tradition of partnership.

The Search Begins

Upon assuming the presidency of the board, Dan Mudge immediately approached Rex Jobe to chair a search committee for a new school leader. A search/selection committee composed of Jobe, Janet Rogers, Helen Hamilton, Les MacLeod, and now trustee emeritus Grant Wilson, was established. As the voice of the Brewster community, Academic Dean Marilyn Shea was also named to the committee. The board retained Dr. Margaret Huling Bonz of Educational Directions, Inc. in Portsmouth, Rhode Island, to lead the process and guide the Brewster community through this challenging and crucially important task.

From the outset, the search committee and the Board were clear about the profile of the individual for whom they were searching. In the announcement of the position, they wrote:

> The next Head of Brewster Academy must be an experienced, reform-minded educational leader whose educational philosophy is compatible with the School Design Model and whose leadership style favors collaborative decision-making. Visionary and capable of translating vision to action, the new Head must possess the intellectual strength and confidence necessary to help Brewster Academy realize the fullest potential of its successful, yet ever-evolving, educational paradigm.

From over one hundred applicants, the Brewster search team identified seven semi-finalists. After reviewing their credentials, the committee invited three candidates to come to campus for visits during October and November 2002. Each of the finalists, along with their spouses, toured the campus; met with students, faculty, trustees, and local parents; and observed classes and evening dorm activities.

One of the three candidates selected was Dr. Michael Cooper. His resume was both lengthy and impressive. His formal education included a bachelor's degree in psychology from The State University of New York at Albany, a master's in education from St. Lawrence University and his doctorate in Child and Family Studies from Syracuse University.

During the five years leading up to his appointment, Dr. Cooper served as vice president for institutional advancement at Clarkson University in Potsdam, New York. During this time, he helped raise \$115 million (toward an original goal of \$70 million) for the Campaign for Clarkson which was completed a year ahead of the original schedule. Cooper previously served as vice president of student affairs and dean of students at Clarkson.

Having experienced the significant evolution of the re-unification of East and West Germany while on a Fulbright Scholarship in Germany in 1993, he taught a course in that subject at Clarkson. His prior teaching experience included a course in statistics as well as a research methods course offered to graduate students in education at St. Lawrence

University. Prior to his work at Clarkson, he was associate dean of student life and director of housing at The State University of New York in Canton.

From the 6th through the 9th of November 2002, Michael and Andrea Cooper formally visited the campus. The members of the search committee first recognized the simple but powerful and important fact that they were a genuine and very thoughtful couple. Probing deeper, they saw that Dr. Cooper's personal style separated him from the other candidates in an all-important characteristic. They saw in Dr. Cooper his appreciation of the Brewster philosophy and mission and came to understand that in this man's personal qualities and management style was a leader who would commit to, effectively implement, and further develop the School Design Model in fulfilling the promise of the Academy's mission statement.

It was evident that Dr. Cooper was a good listener who would invest himself in developing a thorough appreciation of these ingredients and then and only then set out to further develop and refine the programs of the school. They also came to understand that he was a team builder who was good at reading people and putting them in a position to be successful. And in their own fiscal responsibility, they were attracted by the fact that Dr. Cooper was knowledgeable about budgets and very effective at fund raising.

An Appointment Is Made

With all these considerations in mind, Board President Dan Mudge offered Dr. Michael E. Cooper the position of head of school, and his name was recommended to the full Board of Trustees and approved during its November 22, 2002, meeting. On July 1, 2003, Dr. Michael E. Cooper became Brewster Academy's 11th head of school.

This appointment formalized a change in the title of the position. As Brewster entered the 21st century, the Board thought the title head of school was more appropriate, giving a mark of respect to the office by being non-gender specific. Such a title change had historical precedent, the school having changed the title from principal to headmaster decades earlier and now this new title reflected the changing times.

Michael and Andrea Cooper

Michael Cooper's comments during an early interview as he arrived on campus in 2003 illustrate why he made such a positive impression and underscore the personal and profession characteristics that made him the front-runner during the search. Mike quickly realized that here was a school with a strong sense of community with close associations amongst its members. At Brewster, all adults had a great opportunity to serve as mentors and educators as they influenced the lives of students at such a critical stage of their development. Looking back on his own experience, he understood the importance of this role.

Growing up in Albany, New York, Mike played baseball, football, skied in the winter and enjoyed fly-fishing and golf. Andrea also grew up in the Albany area where she and Mike went to kindergarten through high school together. After their marriage, the Coopers lived in the northern New York area where daughter, Allie, and son, Adam, were born.

Before coming to Brewster in 2003, Andrea had spent twenty-seven years teaching art in the elementary schools; and as she became comfortable on campus and with Mike's coaxing, she assumed responsibility of advisor to the Academy's yearbook. The yearbook staff was in for a series of challenges under her direction, but the end product over the years has been an outstanding publication with a vibrant new look that has won many awards using the latest in computer and digital technology.

One tradition that the Coopers started soon after their arrival was their welcoming visits to student residences. The Coopers also invited students to Lord House for an evening of fun and conversation as they enjoyed Mrs. Cooper's famous oatmeal chocolate chip cookies and brownies.

The Coopers entertaining student in Lord House with their famous cookies.

Instituting a Strategic Plan: Future Challenges and Opportunities

In July 2003, with the transition of the Academy leadership in place, the Board of Trustees made it a priority to develop a comprehensive Strategic Plan with strategies for the future. The Board recognized its own need to attain an intimate understanding of the current evolutionary stage of the school and then to consider the future challenges and opportunities that would become apparent in a strategic study. The intended goal was the establishment of short and long-range objectives involving the academic, the residential life, and the athletic programs for the decade ahead.

It was also important that this engagement take place with the new head of school as he was beginning to develop his working relationships with the Board, the administration and the faculty.

The Board commented, "Besides reaffirming who we are, another desired outcome is finding our competitive advantage within our environment of independent secondary schools. As much as the plan will assist us in charting our future, another aim is to bring the entire community together working toward s shared vision of the future success of Brewster" (*Strategic Plan Summary*, 2003, p.2).

From Plans to Actions – New Initiatives for a New Century

If schools are not moving forward, they are moving backward.—Alan Bain

Clearly, Brewster had been a leader in recognizing these challenges and had been nationally celebrated for planning, formulating, and implementing a school-wide approach to addressing them. It had undertaken and put in place an enormous number of initiatives that had re-engineered its approaches to teaching and learning, curricular development, management, social growth programming, and athletics during the previous decade. The faculty and staff had been challenged to assimilate the full measure of these changes in a relatively short period of time. Imagine, then, the position Mike Cooper found himself in as he took over the reins of this dynamic, innovative institution.

As mentioned above, the Board had chosen him over other candidates, in part, because they saw him as having recognized the importance of the Academy's recent developments that he was expected to embrace and further nurture. His mandate was evolution, not revolution. Since Brewster's teaching and learning approaches had been so radically transformed and were so markedly different from the way education was being delivered in other, more traditional high school classrooms, it made sense for Mike to take some time to observe and learn Brewster's approaches before making changes or adding more to the faculty's newly acquired curricular responsibilities. Dr. Cooper, the administration, and the faculty were able to use some time to more fully assimilate those academic initiatives that had been recently installed before taking up new academic initiatives later in the year. In the meantime, Mike turned his attention to student life on campus.

Impact of the New Head of School on Student Life

With Dr. Cooper's advanced work in child and family studies, his experience as vice president for student affairs and his role as dean of students at Clarkson, it was obvious that he possessed considerable understanding and responsiveness to adolescent behavior. With confidence in his ability to contribute within this area, and with the theme of the strategic plan in place, revisions began to be established in the student life program. Dr. Cooper placed an increased emphasis on the importance of building positive relationships between the adults in the Brewster community and its students.

A review of all policy statements was undertaken to ascertain how it either did or did not support the growth of adolescents. This resulted in a complete re-writing of the Brewster regulations to include a newly developed code of student conduct. Placing less emphasis on a series of prohibitive rules and regulations, the new code focused on expected modes of behavior. The simple reorientation of emphasis from one of a prescriptive list to one of "modes of behavior," began to change the underlying relationship that existed between the school and the students.

The first manifestation to come out of this revision that was specifically focused on relationship development was the creation of what are called "weeklies," or once a week reviews. These reviews provide an opportunity between the student and advisor to engage in developing a positive relationship. Students with their advisors reflect upon their school week, assess their successes, and focus on areas where they would like to concentrate in order to improve where needed. These reflections are recorded and entered in the school's portal system so that parents can respond to their child's comments. This helps to create a greater connection between the school and parent, and to force students into taking the time to consider their strengths and weaknesses along with how they plan to keep things moving in a positive direction.

The zero tolerance policy relative to the use of drugs or alcohol was also re-vamped. Rather than simply punishing or dismissing a student for a major infraction, the intention became to institute a program wherein students would be supported in making wise choices and carrying out good decisions.

Other changes were reviewed and implemented as well, including a fine-tuning of the recognition system and residential life.

Being More Responsive to Adolescent Behavior—Director of Residential Life

In 2005, Jamie Laurent assumed the position of director of residential life, overseeing all aspects of student campus life. As Jamie explained it, "The role of director of residence life covers a broad spectrum of opportunities and challenges. Being able to see the big picture of student life and how all the parts fit together is extremely important. In all areas of my responsibility—whether it is in community service, health care, student government, campus activities, all-school meetings, or educational and social programming—all areas work in concert to serve students as we carry out the mission of the school with intentionality."

Jamie recognized that dorm life is the heart of community satisfaction and happiness. The relationships built between dorm parents and their students are essential in making the campus "home" to the students and for establishing a safe and supportive place for practicing student leadership skills and responsibility. To build these relationships dorm parents might celebrate birthdays, go on movie or laser-tag trips, "kidnap" their dorm residents and take them to the climbing barn, arrange a surprise walk in the first snowfall, go to Smith Center to play a game on the turf floor, organize intra-dorm challenges, and/or develop community service activities together. In short, it is these adults who set the tone of dorm life, teaching by example and building and maintaining a responsible and supportive culture within the dorm.

Recognizing that dorm life is the heart of community, Jamie in turn meets weekly with the eighteen dorm parents to talk over and share successful ideas as well as collaborate on common concerns. One primary focus for the director is supporting and equipping this essential group. Another is the supervision of those students who are functioning in

Charlie Hossack, director of student development and activities, Tim Radley, director of student activities, Joe Fernald, dean of students, and Jamie Laurent, director of residential life.

leadership positions: proctors in the dorm and prefects in student government. Establishing an open relationship with these campus leaders is vital to her being able to keep a finger on the pulse of the Academy.

Youth Behavior Survey

In 2006, the school was weary of hearing what questionable behaviors students might be involved in. Dr. Cooper encouraged the leadership of the school to "get a read on our own kids." As a result, Director Laurent conducted the Youth Risk Behavior Survey (YRBS) on campus.

The survey feedback helped Director Laurent meet the challenge of planning effective, meaningful content for all-school gatherings and the weekly morning meetings. "The research data from the YRBS could tease out the health and development priorities for different age, sex, and ethnicity groups with a final result that became the driver for school programming. The school now had a valuable tool that targeted the specific needs of the community and determines what kids were doing and what their needs were. We now had the drivers to set priorities and deliver appropriate grade level programming, and this we have done in all areas that come under my supervision" (Jaime Laurent, *Interview*, February 2008).

All School Meetings Change

The old "All School Meeting" also evolved. The administration still believes that it is very important that the entire school gathers together for assembly programs that focus on cultural, international, and entertainment events, as well as for recognition of student achievements. To better serve the school community, however, two meetings are scheduled every week, each with a different focus.

According to the new plan, "Morning Meeting" is held from 10:00 to 10:30AM on Tuesdays offering an opportunity for the community to gather for a particular message. The Head of School or some unique circumstances occurring in the school, community or world may drive the program content. Faculty members, clubs or organizations sometimes make presentations celebrating or recognizing students or events. "Brewster News," an innovative student electronic news program became a universally popular addition.

"All School Meetings" are scheduled every other week on Friday morning. The agenda for this meeting is more programmatically driven and appearances are planned well in advance and may include: technology ethics, The Trey Whitfield/MLK program, sports and academic awards, showcases of student talent, or motivational speakers whose topics might cover such areas as the health and human development issues, bullying /harassment, drug and alcohol, or overcoming great odds. Also Alumni Career Day, Black History, Diversity Day and other topics of social value are showcased.

In addition to these community gatherings, weekly formal dinner has been replaced with "Community Dinner." These dinners have been designed to do just that—build community. For example, a variety of theme dinners are arranged by international students that might include Korean and Chinese/Taiwanese meals. Other examples include a special program to promote tolerance and celebrate our differences, a foreign language fair with Latin/Caribbean music, and the Jazz Club Dinner celebrating Black history month. In addition, holiday meals are served that share and celebrate different cultures and traditions around the world. The routine of "Community Dinner" is now clearly established and has worked out so well that faculty and students often stepped forward to suggest and design a distinctive occasion.

The School Community sharing an All School Meeting in the Smith Center.

Change in Discipline System/Dean of Students

Joe Fernald, dean of students, remarked, "I arrived on campus in 2004, and after a year of working with students and their individual circumstances in regards to discipline, I realized that it was necessary to orchestrate a different approach to changing behaviors. Head of School Michael Cooper's training and education in the field of counseling led to the decision to revisit and revamp the disciplinary system during the 2004-2005 academic year.

The resulting shift has created a more positive environment for everyone on campus. Many problems are now approached through counseling and guidance and handled directly by the dean and judicial board.

This new approach is referred to as the Engaged Discipline System (EDS) and includes six steps for those placed on discipline probation (DP). The goal of each of the following steps is to have students learn from their mistakes. This innovative approach to developing personal life skills in students reflects the focus of the "21st Century Skills" presented later in this chapter.

- Keep a journal with entries dealing with their own morality, decision-making and values.
- Interview a person who has been hurt or impacted by their poor decisions.
- Respond to, in writing, a moral dilemma question assigned to them by the school's counselor.
- Find some way to give back to the community that has been affected by the action that led to the disciplinary action.
- Work with their advisor to create a way to share what they have learned as a way of educating a segment of the student body.
- Write a reflection piece to be shared with the Judicial Board as part of petitioning to come off disciplinary status.

Since the implementation of EDS, results have shown that adult supervision and support has a major influence.

The dean of students and the director of residential life also meet with the student to address any issue at the initial level, but disciplinary decisions are still determined jointly with the Judicial Board, the head of school, and the dean.

Counseling

When the new Engaged Discipline System was in place and with valuable information available from the Youth Behavior Survey conducted in 2006, Brewster Academy hired its first fulltime counselor to support the new program. Anne Marie Allwine, who first came to Brewster in 1996, set up an office in the new Health Services facility which is attached to Anderson Hall. This allowed for the consolidation of all the health services under one roof.

A major function of the office is to work closely with the director of residential life in organizing and providing programming for the students and develop strategies for building social skills, good decision-making skills, and tools to confront problems. Understanding the unique stresses faced by incoming freshman, a Freshman Retreat is organized consisting of three days of workshops focusing on health and wellness, and social and emotional issues including: adolescent development, abstinence, harassment, self-esteem, alcohol and drug abuse, and stress management. In addition, student development programs are introduced for the rest of the school community as well.

Students entertaining in Anderson Hall.

Evening seminars are offered several times a year focusing on many of these same topics as well as AIDS education and sexually transmitted diseases. The four Senior Seminars concentrate on transitioning into college, understanding legal issues that could impact them, managing money, and decision-making on different levels. Seniors have guest speakers and movies and a mature delivery of information. Feedback and evaluation of these programs are very positive.

Counselor Allwine also provides advice and guidance to faculty in developing Action Plans for individual students who are struggling academically and/or socially. Easily accessible to students and faculty, she is also available for training on many other topics such as depression, anxiety, eating disorders, conflict resolution, and over-the-counter and prescription drug abuse (Allwine, 2008).

With all of these social programs in place, Brewster students have experienced a broad understanding of what is required to succeed in the 21st century.

Athletics in the 21st Century

The athletics department was also experiencing adjustments as the new Athletics and Wellness Center came on line and Doug Algate, a native of Australia who came to Brewster in 1997, was athletic director.

With the new Smith Center on line, the strategic goal established for athletics was to "deliver an intentional athletic experience that fosters fitness and health, sportsmanship and teamwork, spirit and pride, self confidence, and the opportunity to perform at a competitive level"(*Strategic Plan 2003*, p.5).

Sitting in his new office in the Smith Center, Doug related that, "the vision of developing additional school educational facilities was not just restricted to new classrooms and new programs. It went further into addressing all the daily needs and developmental opportunities for our students. The associated sense of obligation dictated the design of

A committed group of young people enjoying a tricky game of croquet.

Above, dance, as an afternoon activity. Below, afternoon Athletic Activities.

a completely new athletic facility that would be shaped around these requirements. The new facility provides basketball courts that convert to a field house with a practice baseball diamond, soccer/lacrosse field or tennis court upon demand. It provides for locker rooms and also includes a study room where coaches and players can evaluate game films, theory and strategy. It is a place where students, under the guidance of a trainer, can profit from the best advice about physical fitness and therapy. It allows the crew team to jog four miles on an indoor track as well as provide a center for students to learn how to live healthy lives and develop lifetime skills."

When Doug became athletic director, there were many afternoon programs offered in art and computer graphics as an option to athletics, and they all were fully enrolled. But when the attraction of the Smith Center came on line, many students elected to enroll in athletic opportunities instead of art, music or dramatics. The new sports-oriented electives were very popular. Ultimate frisbee, intramural tennis and soccer, whiffle ball, yoga, volleyball, cross country skiing, snowboarding, softball, girls JV hockey, and dance were choices now available.

Doug remarked that "fitness was one of the core objectives of the athletic program, and as result, fitness testing is conducted four times a year for all students. Evaluations are done to determine flexibility with the sit and reach; with pinch test for percent body fat; and through a two-mile run for endurance. Results show that during the year, students lower their percentage of body fat and become a fitter population, but also that more fit students are coming in the door. Students are anxious to learn the changes in body fat or muscle and the program also educates young people on healthy choices.

"With the Smith Center and all it offers, it is interesting to note that seventy-five boys signed up to play basketball with twenty-five never having played on a team before. In addition to the Center itself, another factor in the growth of this program is the enthusiasm that is generated by the boys' varsity basketball program. Coach Jason Smith and his incredibly successful basketball teams have built a pride and spirit that flows throughout the school.

"Other schools in our league used to be the ones that was good at everything. They were the teams to beat. They were the best. Now Brewster shares that role. Two-thirds of our young people choose to participate in two athletic competitive seasons when only one is required.

"The mental attitude and expectation that we are winners and that we must never give up has a snowball effect. It was a slow but steady process changing the mind-set, but it has changed. The entire school culture reflects that optimistic way of thinking and sports and winning seasons have created this momentum. This year six field hockey games went into overtime and we won five of them. This was a great example of our mental attitude and toughness. The same feeling exists throughout our interscholastic offerings resulting in several League Championships on an annual basis."

Clearly, Brewster Academy's athletic program with its five person staff:(the director of athletics, associate director of athletics, a full time trainer, a part time trainer, and a full time equipment room manager, who also doubles as court Zamboni operator) fulfills the target laid out in the 2003 strategic plan. The program is well rounded and supports the development of the whole person as it builds self-esteem, confidence and a sense of pride. The spirit that happens in athletics transfers to a student's academic life. Young people are happier and more positive in the Academic Building because of our formal athletic program and our expanded intramural program. Students are doing what they enjoy doing and gain positive feedback as they participate.

At the end of the school year in 2010, Doug Algate retired from Brewster and returned to his home in Australia. Matt Lawlor, who was hired as the new Director of Athletics, comes

Atheltic staff as the Smith Center was dedicated in 2003: Angelo Varrone, Kerry O'Donoghue, Kate Turner, and Doug Algate.

with a strong resume, accreditation in the field of athletics, and private school experience including service at Loomis Chaffee School and Chase Collegiate School in Connecticut.

Championships Record 1999-2010

The Brewster athletic championships record from 1999-2010 is impressive in girls' and boys' sports, with teams winning 26 Lakes Region Championships and/or being champions or finalists in NEPAC. The girls' ice hockey, soccer, field hockey, and tennis teams have been outstanding.

In 2007, the girls' soccer team, coached by Matt Butcher and Laura Cooper, was honored by the Board of Trustees for their undefeated season with a 16-0 record and for winning the NEPSAC Class C division and Lake Region Championship. Again in 2009 the girls performed brilliantly with an 18-0 record and winning the NEPAC Class C and Lakes Region League championships.

The boys' lacrosse team warrants a special note for they had another outstanding record in 2009 under Coach Bill Lee. Brewster was ranked 24th in the country and the team averaged 14 goals a game and gave up only 5 goals a game. As true lacrosse junkies, eight players of that team will play in college ranked programs. Several Bobcats received accolades for their outstanding play that season, and not only did we have a player named as an "All-American," but for the first time one of Brewster's players was named Northern New England Lacrosse League Academic Player of the Year,-a wonderful recognition for the player and the school.

Brewster's varsity field hockey team championed the spirit of teamwork and character throughout the 2010 season. Well known and respected for these qualities, the players made

Girls 2007 championship soccer team with coaches Matt Butcher and Laura Cooper.

Academy history by capturing, for the first time, both the New England Preparatory School Athletic Council (NEPSAC) Class C Championship and the Lakes Region Championship. It was a season in which the team openly embraced change and saw challenges as real opportunities. Continuing in the winning tradition of Brewster field hockey, it became the eighth team to earn a spot in the New England Tournament in the past nine seasons. Field Hockey is a highly successful sport on campus.

Demonstrating the Bobcat drive and fortitude, the team finished its season with exciting wins over New Hampton and Proctor before a cheering crowd led by Head of School Dr. Michael Cooper and Mrs. Cooper to capture the Lakes Region Championship and a bid for the NEPSAC tournament

The 2010 Varsity Field Hockey Team with Head of School Dr. Michael Cooper and coaches Kim Yau and Janis Cornwall.

The 2010 Basketball New England and national champions with coaches Jason Smith, Josh Lee, and Al Simoes.

Craig Brackins, outstanding basketball player.

In the tournament finals, the Bobcats faced off against the undefeated #1 seed, Newton Country Day School. With the strength of willpower and commitment, evident throughout the regular season, a 3-1 victory translated the dream of winning New England Championship into a reality. The team and coaches, Kim Yau and Janis Cornwell, deserve high accolades for their outstanding teamwork and leadership.

"Adversity causes some men to break, and others to break records."—Unknown

Since the 2001-02 season, Brewster boys' basketball has participated in the NEPSAC, Class A division, which is the most competitive division not only in New England but also in the nation. During Jason Smith's ten year tenure to date, the team has over 200 victories; the program has sent 54 student-athletes to NCAA Division I programs and many others to NCAA DII and DIII programs. Jason comments, "In 2007-08, Brewster basketball had its most successful season in the school history to date, with 31 wins and 4 losses. The 31 victories established a new school record and earned the team a final ranking of fourth nationally." Quite an impressive accomplishment!

Yet in 2010, Brewster's Bobcats exceeded all expectations by winning not only the NEPSAC Class A title, but then went on to win for the very first time the National Prep School Championship, defeating its opponent in overtime. Accolades for the 2010 Basketball Team!

In honor of their outstanding winning seasons, the Board of Trustees recognized the team's accomplishments and offered its heartfelt congratulations and thanks to the members of the team for their outstanding accomplishment as the first team to win a national championship.

Another distinguished honor came home to Brewster in 2010 as a direct result of its superior basketball program. After his graduation from Brewster, Craig Brackins,'07, was selected by Iowa State University to be part of its basketball program. While there, Craig earned recognition as the "Big Twelve Player of the Week" three times in one season, and he appeared on the pre-season Naismith and Wooden awards watch list. In 2009 Brackins was selected to open the Iowa Special Olympics, declaring the beginning of the 2009 games. A young man of high character and skill, when the opportunity came for a NBA draft pick, Craig was chosen by the Oklahoma City Thunders and later traded to the New Orleans Hornets. This was the first time any Brewster player had reached the NBA level of play. In a note to Coach Smith, Craig wrote, "I couldn't be more grateful to Brewster Academy for the experience I had there. In the classroom, it provided me with the necessary tools to succeed in college. On the basketball court, I was pushed every day to develop my game and given the opportunity to compete against the best competition in the country. Brewster provides an environment where you know people care about you as a person. That level of support aided me greatly in becoming the 21st overall pick in the NBA 2010 draft."

"One man can be a crucial ingredient on a team, but one man cannot make a team."
—Kareem Abdul Jabbar

22. Preparing for the 21st Century

What's past is prologue, what's to come is yours and my discharge.—William Shakespeare

New Academic Initiatives, and 21st Century Skills

After a brief period of latency in the evolution of the academic program, Dr. Cooper set in motion a new set of initiatives compatible with the Brewster Model and based on current educational research. At the heart of these new approaches was the principle of "habits of mind." It is interesting to note that the concluding remarks of the 2010 graduating class commencement speaker Pierce B. Dunn, whose son was a member of the class, reflected the essence of the principles that underpin those approaches.

> I leave you with one of my favorite quotations, author unknown:
> *Watch your thoughts for they become words*
> *Watch your words for they become actions*
> *Watch your actions for they become habits*
> *Watch your habits for they become character*
> *Watch your character for it becomes your destiny.*
> "To the great class of 2010.... I congratulate you and may most of your habits be good and your destinies worthy of who you want to be."

Scottish bagpiper, performing at commencement.

21st Academic Skills and Habits of the Mind

As the world moved into the 21st century, there was a great deal of research and study taking place in the field of education. The phrase "21st century skills" was fast becoming a well-known term characterizing an important trend in education, and the world was changing in ways and at rates that were unprecedented in human history. Studies told us, "Today's education system faces irrelevance unless it bridges the gap between how students live and how they learn. The next generation of students will spend their adult lives in a multitasking, multifaceted, technology-driven, diverse, vibrant world, and they must be equipped to do so" (*Gateway to 21st Century Skills, n. d., 2009).* Brewster, under Dr. Cooper's leadership, needed to be alert to the fact that these unique literacy skills were as significant as reading literacy had been to the 19th century.

Through Brewster's professional development program, Peter Hess, veteran teacher and administrator who came to Brewster in 1988 was selected as the first team leader of the ninth grade model program in 1993, named director of the lower school in 1995, and appointed dean of studies in 2006, had read and heard what several experts were saying about 21st century academic skills and habits of the mind.

He noted that in reality nobody has a clue about what the world will look like in even five years. Despite all the expertise that has been published how can we prepare our graduates for the world in which they will be living? What skills will they need? What knowledge will they need? What skills will be needed for college and the 21st century?

But he was struck by the following commonality of several themes that emerged as the world shifts from an Information Age to a Conceptual Age.

- **Globalization:** Students will face greater competition for jobs in a global marketplace and will need to work collaboratively with people from other countries, and must be able to solve complex, multidisciplinary, open-ended problems with creative and entrepreneurial thinking.
- **Technology:** The growth of technology will be exponential, not linear, which translates into 20,000 years of progress rather than 100 years during the 21st century.
- **A New Definition of Literacy:** In the 21st century, the 3 Rs—reading, writing and arithmetic—will have a different look. Reading will be more than decoding. It will be about finding information, critically evaluating it, and then organizing it. Writing will be about communicating ideas in compelling ways that involve images and sounds in addition to the written word. Math will be about employing information to solve problems, and skills of accessing and discerning information will become increasingly vital.
- **Creativity:** Success will depend far more on application of knowledge, critical-thinking skills, and problem-solving abilities rather than on memorization of information.

How Is Brewster Responding?

Hess explained, "By design, with Brewster's forward-looking, innovative mindset, it remains at the forefront of educational programming. It provides a solid foundation from which to respond to these challenges of a rapidly changing world. Among the steps being taken to help prepare Brewster students for the new century are the following:

- ***Curriculum Evolution*****:** The "habits of mind" required for college success have been identified and more activities that call on students to apply their knowledge have been infused into the curriculum. Ensuring that creative problem solving is sufficiently represented in the curriculum, especially in interdisciplinary projects, is a curriculum goal.

- ***Technology Integration:*** Brewster has long been a leader in the meaningful integration of technology in the classroom. The next challenge will be engaging the Web 2.0 technology for collaborative knowledge creation: weblogs (blogs), podcast and wikis are finding valuable uses in the delivery of curriculum.
- ***Multimedia in the Arts:*** As technology is increasingly being viewed as an invaluable tool in the creation and communication of ideas, rich arrays of art and computer course are being offered—filmmaking, digital photography, web design, and 3D animation.
- ***Study Abroad:*** To provide more opportunities for our students to experience global connections, Brewster has partnered with the Experiment in International Living, a partnership that allows interested students to travel abroad and to experience the culture of a foreign country by living with a host family. In addition, international opportunities are always planned for the March break and during the summer.
- ***Character Education***: To advance the ethical dimension of a student's experience, several programs have been initiated: the Engaged Discipline System which was discussed earlier takes advantage of teaching opportunities in a disciplinary event; presentations and workshops by outside resource people are presented; and senior seminars to help prepare students for the transition to college are offered (*Brewster Connections* 2008, p. 5-6).

Bruce Gorrill innovative teacher and academic leader.

Project Based Learning
Looking toward the skills required for the 21st century and in response to the current research, a significant initiative was instituted into the curriculum by Brewster's Teaching and Learning Team.

Project Based Learning (PBL) was added to its arsenal of teaching techniques. It was clear that PBL would give students an opportunity to engage in critical thinking, creative problem solving, higher learning/thinking skills, making judgments, and applying what they had learned in novel settings all skills required for 21st century. The result was that students learned more, took on greater amounts of personal responsibility for their own learning, and experienced a satisfaction that came with real learning, not just attaining good grades. Since research has also noted that the benefits of PBL are enhanced when technology is used, this approach made maximal use of Brewster's well-established technology program.

Bruce Gorrill was one of the first teachers at Brewster to make use of PBL in the science curriculum. As science department chair, Bruce has been teaching at Brewster since 1988. He has been immersed in the Brewster Model and best practices since its inception in 1993, and he continues to identify the most innovative ideas in hands-on, collaborative learning through technology. PBL was an ideal practice for him to explore, and he began to search for a venue for this new application of skills.

Just steps from the largest lake in New Hampshire with its 7,800 acres of water to study and sample, students are never far from their subject. With access to the latest Web 2.0 technologies and a veteran teacher dedicated to the idea that education is more meaningful to students when they learn within the context of solving real world applications, the students have an empowering and invigorating learning environment. Students learn right away that their work cannot be done in a vacuum. They know that their studies are real and how they report and share their findings are likely to have implications beyond the classroom. They also learn how to share what they are learning through such Web 2.0 technologies as podcasts, blogs, wikis, and a Ning network.

Through their class projects students gain lifelong learning skills—critical thinking, information literacy, creativity, and collaboration—all increasingly vital to their success in the 21st century. Fifteen years after Brewster began its Model program, much continues to be developed and grown through technology, and each year Brewster is doing just that (Bruce Gorrill, *Brewster Academy Annual Report 2007-08, p. 9-12*).

In other areas of the academic program, Maria Found and Bret Barnett, math; Matt Butcher, English; Doug Kiley, history; Michelle Rafalowski-Houseman, science, all leaders in their respective departments, are at the forefront as they incorporate PBL within their disciplines. Students work in groups to solve challenging problems that are authentic curriculum-based activities designed to help students to see connections across disciplines. Learners make choices, decide how to approach a problem, and figure out what activities to pursue. They gather information from a variety of sources, synthesize, analyze, and then communicate their work creatively using a variety of media that can include tests, sound, images, and videos. At the end of the project, students are judged by how they have learned and how well they communicate their project.

By engaging in this process, students have a unique opportunity to develop the academic skills, the thinking skills, the problem-solving skills, the technology skills, and the interpersonal skills that reflect those needed for the 21st century (Brewster Academy, *Annual Report 2008-2009*).

Media Arts and Technology: 21st Century Communication Tools
Along with academic innovation and in response to the 21st century skills needed in the fast moving pace within the media arts field, Brewster continues each year to expand its

Above, Maria Found using best practices in math class. Below, Byron Martin instructing Connor Dunn.

Doug Kiley demonstrating PBL in history class.

program. BG Hodges, chairperson of computer graphics, affirms, "Whatever you have to say, you can say it better and communicate it further in digital media, web pages, blogs, video, Facebook, Ning, or Pod-casts. These are today's communication tools. Because of increasing computer horsepower and software improvements, what used to take hours and hours and special equipment to produce can now be accomplished in your own home on your desktop computer in minutes." With BG in charge, the computer graphics and photography department has created a first rate studio. Two years ago the department moved to offering digital photography and creating a muti-leveled digital photo classroom.

The graphics arts faculty also collaborates with students in producing a short weekly newscast which is aired each week at All School Meeting and is available on the Academy's website.

Acknowledging the continuing changes in the communications world and realizing that all of these skills are necessary as our culture communicates in the 21st century, Brewster has made the decision to move in the direction of digital media and tools for use in all classrooms. Associated continuing professional development, including several workshops, empowers faculty with cutting edge computing literacy including digital photo, sound, web pages, basic video, and DVD production.

Peter Hess remarked as all these innovative approaches were being initiated at Brewster, "I have seen lots of changes in my twenty years at Brewster. Change, innovation, and evolution seem to be part of the very fabric of the Academy. The challenge of preparing our students for the 21st century is an exciting proposition and one that we take very seriously. It is our mission to continue to prepare our young people for the 21st century and provide them with best education as they move forward" (*Brewster Connections* 2008, p. 5-6).

A Student's Pilgrimage Through the Brewster Curriculum: The Connor Dunn Story

When Connor joined our community, he had already had his share of educational frustration. Despite his superior intellect, Connor had to face the many challenges of being a dyslexic student. Nevertheless, he was determined to find success in his new school. As Connor prepared for graduation, his mom and dad wrote this letter in appreciation of all that their son had accomplished during his years at Brewster.

"It seems like yesterday that we left our son Connor at the Estabrook parking lot to embark on what has proven to be a life changing journey. As we exchanged embraces and tears three years ago, the dark foreboding skies that had been hovering over Lake Winnipesaukee let loose torrential rain and a wind to match the raw emotions of the moment. All three of us wondered whether the decision to attend Brewster (the first child in either family to attend a boarding school) was fortuitous or calamitous. What type of journey had we embarked upon?

"Little did we know that it was the beginning of a remarkable journey of discovery for Connor (and us). All our misgivings about relinquishing our son to "strangers" were quickly replaced with genuine awe and respect for a remarkable and supportive community that has nurtured and stimulated Connor. Like every student at Brewster, Connor was embraced by teachers, staff and their families. Adults, peers and young families all became part of Connor's life. Close ties of friendship were forged with families on and off campus. Teachers, advisors and coaches provided guidance, encouragement and frequently inspiration. Our concerns about Connor's dyslexia were replaced by admiration for the flexible curriculum and educational support system that empowered Connor to develop a clear vision of himself as a lifelong learner. His teachers and advisors provided him with practical tools and solid habits that have convinced Connor that he is capable of mastering any material.

"Connor's teachers, advisors and coaches have challenged him to do his best and to plumb his potential. The Brewster community reassured Connor that it was a safe place to take risks. Opportunities to lead in the classroom, on the water (Connor is a rower) or in the community were offered and taken. During his years at Brewster, we have witnessed Connor grow as a confident student, athlete and leader.

"So what is the value of this wonderful community to us and to our child? How do we thank Brewster Academy and each member of its community for the journey they have encouraged Connor to take? These are difficult and very personal questions. Brewster Academy is a very special place."

Pierce B. Dunn and Lee Hoyt
Parents of Connor Dunn, Class of 2010

Planning Admissions and Marketing for the New Century

With the goals of the 2003-2004 strategic plan in place and with the social athletic and academic needs for the 21st century firmly in process with a course of action, the school determined that developing a comprehensive admissions marketing initiative was it next objective that would help the administration understand how Brewster Academy was being perceived in the marketplace and among its own constituencies. It would also determine if Brewster had a distinctive market advantage due to its School Design Model.

With the comprehensive research data in place, critical marketing tools were developed to move the school forward with a compelling, integrated and dynamic message that would reflect Brewster's growing reputation.

All publications including the school's viewbook, search piece, mailing envelope, application guide and other supporting materials were redesigned as well as the web site. The new website provided the opportunity for a better connection with parents and the outside world, but more than that, the site (www.brewsteracademy.com) also evolved into a workplace where faculty, staff and students could interact and where parents could access student grades and progress reports

All external messages focused on colors that embodied strong tradition and prominence, and reflected a new tag line: "*Live. Learn. Lead. Great Expectations: Expect More. Expect Great Things...of Us...of Yourself.*"

An appealing new magazine with a fresh look, *Brewster Connections,* debuted in the fall of 2004. The new bi-yearly format was well received as readers valued having a printed communication from their school to help them feel connected

Along with the forward-looking direction for academics, athletics, admissions and communication, the Academy was also advancing into the 21st century with new facilities.

Anderson Hall, the new all-school meeting hall and performance center.

New Facilities On Campus

This administration's first addition to campus was the 3.1-acre property that formerly contained St. Cecilia's Catholic Church and rectory and abuts the campus along South Main Street. It was purchased for $950,000 on July 2, 2005, from the Catholic Diocese of Manchester.

A year later, on Saturday, October 24, 2006, the school held a dedication and naming ceremony for its newest campus facility. During the official dedication, the building was named in honor of the Anderson family of Morristown, New Jersey, whose son Jared is a 2006 graduate.

By 2007, to fulfill the dream of Mr. Anderson, the Academy had completed significant renovations to Anderson Hall including the construction of a proscenium theater complete with sound and projection systems, and internet-accessibility with PC tower and DVD, CD, and VHS players. Eight microphones placed throughout the Hall with control access from the balcony offer the opportunity for recording performances or live broadcasts.

Not only does Anderson Hall provide for an extraordinary space for the entire school community to gather for All School Meeting, but it also provides a grand opportunity to better serve the performing arts needs of Brewster. The Hall also hosts other community programs including the Heifetz International Music Institute, Clearlakes Chorale, and Friends of Music.

The Health Center

With the purchase of the Catholic Church and Rectory, the school was able to take advantage of the spacious rectory as an ideal setting for the Academy Health Center. The new facility increased the need for additional health staff as well tripled the area available for meeting the healthcare issues of students, and, as mentioned earlier, includes the office of the school counselor.

The new and expanded Health Center adjacent to Anderson Hall.

Tennis Courts

The next significant addition to the campus was a beautiful outdoor tennis facility located on the former Lower Clark Field that boasts a picturesque view of the Lake Winnipesaukee shoreline. A gravel walkway from Mudge Lane in front of the Smith Center leads players and spectators to the site. Courtside umbrella tables offer seating and shade for spectators. In July 2008, the nine courts were named for the following leadership donors:

The Zarkin Family Foundation (Ally Reiner '10)
The John P. Stabile Family Foundation (Ryan '92, Jake '00)
The Silverstein Family (Charlie '10)
The Rehnert Family (Taylour Holden '07)
The Reichenbach Family (Emily '09)
A collective reunion gift from the Class of 1954.

Additional support was received by a collection of alumni, parents and friends to make this on campus facility a reality

Curvey Property, "Beaver Brook Campus"

The most significant addition to Brewster Academy which would have a far-reaching impact on campus programming and service to its students was the Curvey property gift. In 2008, former Fidelity Investments President James C. Curvey and his family donated more than 11 acres of Winnipesaukee lakefront property on Roberts Cove which is valued at $6.3 million and includes seven cottages and 615 feet of lakefront. It is the largest single donation in the school's history. Each year, this gift will fund three full four-year scholarships to Brewster Academy for students from the greater Alton and Wolfeboro area.

The school now has 9 new tennis courts located along Clark Road (above.) On opening, the Bobcat (below) played his first match.

Head of School Dr. Michael E. Cooper commented that "we are honored that the Curvey family has recognized Brewster Academy with this extraordinary donation that we never anticipated coming our way. The generosity of the Curvey family, whose donation will expand the academy's lakefront resources and provide the setting for more hands-on educational opportunities, will enhance current offerings such as Fresh Water Ecology, Environmental Science, Character Leadership, and other experiential learning programs. Students will have a chance to learn from one of the Northeast's most important and largest resources, Lake Winnipesaukee."

Henceforth the Curvey property will be called the Beaver Brook campus on Roberts Cove *(Brewster Connections*, Spring 2009, p. 7).

The Lamb Green Renovations

The last of the changes or additions to the campus was the renovation of Lamb Green. During the summer of 2009, a major redesign of the area, located directly between the Academic Building and Main Street, was undertaken to render the space both more aesthetically appealing and more conducive to social gathering. The changes included the removal of a large blue spruce in order to afford a view of the Ac and the addition of a cobblestone terrace, surrounded by a stone wall and a seating area that would welcome students and faculty as they left The Estabrook. On Main Street, a stone wall containing a large granite stone upon which the name of the school is embossed was created to define and identify the campus. In front of the stone wall is a lovely perennial garden dedicated to Mary Fallon when she retired in June 2010. What better tribute to honor Mary and her years of commitment to her students and her love of flowers.

Perhaps the most fascinating aspect of the entire project was the resurrection of the stone pillars that had marked the entrance to the original academic building built in 1890. When the fire of 1903 destroyed the building, the rubble was buried in the general area of the burned-out structure. Amazingly, in 1953, while the construction company was

At left, one of seven cottages. At right, the beach and water view of the Curvey Property, Roberts Cove.

preparing the site for the new Memorial Gymnasium, lo and behold, the granite pillars that had marked the old south entrance staircase were found. Fortunately, an alert construction crew recognized that amid the vast rubble was something of importance. As they dug deeper, they uncovered the original pillars in excellent condition. Protecting their find, they removed and settled the columns in a place behind the new Rogers Gymnasium for safekeeping. Years later they were dragged away to a wooded area near the Maintenance Building on Green Street, there to remain out of sight and out of mind for over thirty-five years until the author, remembering they were there, suggested to the architect that he may want to incorporate them once again on the campus grounds bringing them full circle from 1890 to 2010.

What a better place than the entrance to The Estabrook, one of the oldest buildings on campus and the past summer home of Arthur Estabrook.

A New Tradition: The Brewster Medal

Along with new facilities and expanded additions to the campus, new traditions were also being established at Brewster, the first of which was the Brewster Medal.

On January 24, 2009, trustees, faculty, friends and guests of the Academy came together to celebrate its first Brewster Medal ceremony held at the Boston Museum of Fine Arts. It was a night to honor two individuals for their excellent and distinguished service and extraordinary commitment to the growth and betterment of the Academy. It was a moment to express appreciation and thanks to Nick Harris and retired Headmaster David Smith who had dedicated themselves to the advancement of the Brewster mission and to the vision of John Brewster. The criteria for recognition included:

- Loyalty of service and/or support to the Academy
- Personal characteristics that reflect the Brewster Principle
- Commitment of excellence in personal and professional pursuits

(*Brewster Connections,* Spring, 2009, p.4).

Other Traditions Introduced

Building on the Head of School's philosophy of recognition and appreciation, additional traditions were finding their way into the Brewster community infusing spirit and goodwill.

Class Colors: The Academy's old tradition of class-colors was re-instituted.

Faculty Recognition: A tradition of honoring faculty members who have served the community for a period of 10, 15, 20, or 25 years was initiated in 2010.

Alumni Golden Bobcat: In 2004, a tribute to Golden Bobcats, celebrating their very special 50th reunion, was established with an exclusive ceremonial banquet and the awarding of a gold lapel pin embossed with the Brewster crest. This proves to be an exceptional way to reconnect with old friends, relive past memories, and continue a connection to Brewster.

Head of School Michael E. Cooper Assesses the Past and Future

As the year 2010 was coming to an end, Michael Cooper offered his comments on the future of the Academy.

"As I write this brief personal reflection of where the school is at this point, there is much to contemplate about our future. Most would agree that the United States, along with much of the rest of the world, including the Academy, has been through one of the

The newly designed Lamb Green. Note the Estabrook entranceway pillars from the original 1890 Academy Building.

more challenging economic times since the Great Depression. The result for the Academy has been the need to react to, and learn from, a sea-changing experience while maintaining our resolve and purpose. What was most reassuring throughout these past months was remembering the great history that this wonderful school has and how we have weathered many storms in our almost 200 years of existence; and we would once again. As we worked our way through the challenges that we were facing, that fact stood as our beacon. Once again, as in our past, it was the dedication and strength of the people associated with the school that helped to carry the day. I firmly believe that we will emerge from these challenging times a stronger school, with an even greater sense of purpose and direction. It is my fervent wish that future generations will favorably judge us for how we managed the school during these turbulent times so that they, too, may be inspired, as we were inspired by our predecessors, when those ever-present cyclical challenges that seem to confront each generation present themselves to the future leaders of the school."

Afterword

What have we learned from the history of Brewster Academy? Although the cast of characters, the challenges faced, and the major directions have varied through the years, some common denominators become apparent:

- Each generation of students and teachers has fallen in love with and been inspired by the beautiful Lake Winnipesaukee campus.
- From Edwin Lord to Michael Cooper, the Academy has attracted leaders who believed in John Brewster's vision and worked tirelessly to fulfill it.
- Faculty members across the years have focused unselfishly on the growth and development of their students, accepting each student as a unique individual.
- "People helping people" has been a central attribute of the school's program from the first students enrolled to the most recent graduating class.

The Brewster Story is a remarkable one, and we have been privileged to relate it beginning with when this land was home to the Abenaki Tribes and ending with the year 2010.

We look forward to the future and reading the next chapters in the history of this extraordinary school.

"The work goes on, the cause endures, the hope still lives, and the dreams shall never die." —Edward M. Kennedy.

Board of Trustees, 1887–2010

1887-1892 Joseph L. Avery
1887-1923 Charles U. Bell
1887-1910 John L. Brewster
1887-1919 William Brewster
1887-1919 Arthur F. Estabrook
1887-1922 John K. Lord
1887-1901 Benjamin F. Parker
1887-1894 Charles H. Parker
1887-1891 Jeremiah Smith
1887-1894 Albert W. Wiggin

1891-1893 James W. Patterson

1893-1894 Charles H. Hersey
1893-1910 Charles S. Murkland
1893-1934 Nathaniel H. Scott

1894-1935 Sewall W. Abbott
1894-1898 Fred Gowing
1894-1894 Isaac Pearl
1894-1904 Charles F. Piper

1901-1906 James C. Melvin

1905-1910 George E. Mackintire

1907-1910 Carroll D. Wright

1908-1945 Oscar L. Young '95

1910-1915 W. Lucius Tuttle

1911-1926 Stedman Buttrick
1911-1920 Joseph B. Russell

1917-1940 George H. Evans '95

1920-1945 Frederick R. Galloupe
1920-1939 Lydia A. Osborne '94

1922-1934 Charles R. Lingley
1923-1933 Ernest H. Trickey

1926-1938 John Abbott

1928-1965 Justin M. Tibbetts '92

1934-1944 William J. Britton '92
1934-1958 Arthur P. Gale '00

1935-1939 Edwin T. Brewster

1936-1941 Fred E. Clow '00

1938-1972 John P. Carr

1940-1944 Fred Engelhardt
1940-1947 Lawrence S. Mayo

1941-1964 Edwin B. Edgerly '03
1941-1949 Fred E. Hanson '03

1944-1979 Fred A. Stackpole '09

1945-1956 John H. Joy
1945-1970 Frank R. Kenison '25
1945-1974 Chester E. Merrow '25

1948-1980 Hugh Wilkin

1951-1968 Howard Avery '22
1951-1957 Frank J. Berry '11
1951-1955 Charles H. Watts

1953-1958 Hadley Case
1953-1964 Ernest Gile
1953-1992 Adelaide R. Hughes '26

1956-1965 Herman Pike
1956-1963 Charles H. Watts, Jr.
1957-1963 Clinton T. Piper '38
1958-1985 Charles D. Cilley '27
1958-1968 Harold E. Gregory '30

1964-1968 Francis E. Moore
1964-1972 Charlesworth K. Neilson

1965-1979 Dana M. Cotton
1965-1968 Charles C. Noble

1966-1968 Henry F. Hurlburt
1966-1997 Carlton W. Spencer

1967-1973 Fred C. Brokaw
1967-1992 Arthur J. Mason

1968-1977 Elvira Z. Avery
1968-1972 John J. Ballentine '46
1968-1976 Dorothy Bovaird

1968-1975	Warren P. Tyler
1969-1970	Walter N. DeWitt '54
1970-1973	L. Thurston Pendleton
1970-1973	Herbert P. VanBlarcom
1972-1993	Walter N. DeWitt '54
1972-1974	David E. Gregory
1972-1998	P. Fred Gridley '53
1972-1980	Arthur E. Kenison, Jr. '30
1972-1974	Patrick A. Requa
1973-1976	T. William Bigelow
1973-1977	Robert F. W. Meader '25
1973-1996	Lloyd B. Waring
1974-	Helen S. Hamilton
1974-1975	James E. O'Neil, Sr.
1975-1976	Frank Denieotolis
1975-1976	Shirley Dunham
1975-1976	Charles E. Hugel
1976-1990	Russell C. Chase
1976-1987	Franklyn L. Johnson
1976-1978	Walter S. Marson '50
1976-1978	Clinton T. Piper '38
1976-1977	Glen Potter
1977-1977	Leon Botstein
1977-1988	John W. McDermott
1977-1982	Wendy Scharin
1978-1979	Bradley J. Hayes
1978-2004	Herbert W. Lamb
1978-1980	Leslie H. York '31
1979-1980	Robert R. Engisch
1979-1999	Arthur M. Kenison
1979-1985	Frederick A. Piehl
1980-1982	Davena R. DeWolf '52
1981-2000	George W. Sullivan, Jr.
1981-1982	Joseph W. Taft
1982-1987	Elvira Z. Avery
1982-1984	Leslie H. York '31
1983-1989	John M. Grant, Jr.
1984-1985	Hope W. MacDonald '45
1985-1987	Penny S. Duncan '63
1985-2000	Bradley J. Hayes
1986-2001	Bryce Blynn
1986-1988	Bruce Keller
1986-	Leslie N. H. MacLeod
1986-1988	Barrant V. Merrill
1986-1991	Betty Pinckney
1986-1997	Burtis F. Vaughan, Jr.

1986-1988	Patricia Weatherly
1986-2001	Grant M. Wilson
1987-1991	Sylvio Dupuis
1988-2000	Rosalie C. Clark
1989-1990	Harrison D. Moore '46
1989-2001	Alan Stone
1990-1991	Dianne Rogers '56
1990-1993	George E. Slye
1991-1992	Gregory P. Branzetti '84
1991-	David L. Carlson '54
1991-1994	Judi Kaufman
1991-1993	Anthony J. Leitner '61
1992-1993	Donald O. Brookes '65
1992-1995	Carl Siemon
1992-	Nancy Spencer Smith
1993-1994	Edward Heald
1993-1994	Harrison D. Moore '46
1993-2007	Derek J. Murphy '77
1994-1995	Allan E. Bailey, Jr. '60
1994-1998	Anne Marie Diemert
1994-1996	John Gribi
1994-1998	David Wright
1995-1997	Bruce H. Crowther '64
1996-	C. Richard Carlson
1996-2010	James E. Nicholson
1997-	Arthur O. Ricci
1997-2000	Frederick H. Stephens
1997-2000	Cory N. Strupp
1997-1999	Janie Whitney
1997-1999	Kristianne Widman-Johnson '80
1998-2000	George Eaton
1998-	Daniel Mudge
1998-2006	Kathleen Mudge
1998-2003	Janet Rogers
1999-2000	Jennifer Huntley
1999-2003	David W. Merrill '86
1999-2004	Bonnie Turner
2000-2001	Patrick Donahue
2000-2003	Mei-Ling Henrichson
2000-2001	Bonnie Hofmann
2000-2010	Rex V. Jobe
2000-2001	Judi Kollmorgen
2000-2001	Matt Kollmorgen
2000-2003	Francis McCarthy
2001-2007	Todd P. Parola '89
2001-2010	Nancy M. Black
2002-	Michael Keys

2002-2008	Anthony J. Leitner '61	2006-	Roy Ballentine
		2006-	Candace Crawshaw '64
2003-2004	Jennye Greene	2006-	Peter Ford '80
2003-2006	John C. Naramore	2006-2008	Mitch Sanders '82
2003-2006	James O'Brien	2006-	Steven R. Webster
2003-2004	Zack Pringle '92		
		2007-	Michael Appe
2004-2006	William B. Bradford '69	2007-	Claudine Curran
2004-	George J. Dohrmann III		
2004-2005	Peggy G. Herrington	2008-2009	Christopher J. Britt '02
		2008-	Barbara Naramore
2005-2007	Susan M. Harger	2008-	A.B. Whitfield
2005-2007	Lynn F. Kravis		
2005-2010	Shawn K. Smith	2009-	Arthur W. Coviello, Jr.
		2009-	Stephen C. Farrell
		2009-	Douglas Greeff

PRINCIPALS AND HEADMASTERS, 1887–2010

Head of School, Michael E. Cooper: 2003 to Present

Headmaster David M. Smith: 1974 – 2003

Headmaster C. Richard Vaughan: 1969 – 1974

Headmaster Wilfred E. Paro: 1965 – 1969

Principal Burtis F. Vaughan, Jr: 1959 – 1965

Principal Vincent D. Rogers: 1942 – 1959

Principal Walter F. Greenall, Jr: 1935 – 1942

Principal Ralph K. Bearce: 1924 – 1935

Acting Principal Carroll D. Piper:(two terms) 1923 – 1924

Acting Principal Herbert E. Sargent:(one term) 1923-1924

Principal Charles W. Haley: 1911 - 1923

Acting Principal Herbert E. Sargent: 1910 – 1911

Principal Charles S. Murkland; 1907 – 1910

Principal Edwin H. Lord: 1887 - 1907

Bibliography

Algate, Doug. *Interview with Robert and Shirley Richardson.* Transcribed from Tape Recording. December 2008.

Allwine, Anne Marie. *Interview with Robert and Shirley Richardson.* Transcribed from Tape Recording. February 2008.

A Nation at Risk: The Imperative for Educational Reform. Washington, DC: The National Commission on Excellence in Education. 1983. (An archived version of this book is available at: www2.ed.gov/pubs/NatAtRisk/index.html)

Avery, Howard C. *Letter to J. P. Carr.* February 3, 1962.

Bailey, Allan. *Interview with Robert and Shirley Richardson.* Transcribed from Tape Recording. April 2008.

Ball, Jr., Travis. *Looking Back: 1969-1972 at Brewster Academy.* Unpublished Monograph. 2008.

Barak, Jr., Oscar T. and Hugh T. Lefler. *Colonial America.* New York: Macmillan, 1968.

Barak, Jr., Oscar T. and Nelson Manfred Blake. *Since 1900: A History of the United States in our Times.* New York: The Macmillan Company, 1949.

Bean, Howard. *Interview with Bob and Shirley Richardson.* Transcription from Tape Recording. February 2007.

Blum, John M. *et. al. The National Experience: A History of the United States.* Third Edition. Fort Worth: Harcourt College Publishers, 1973.

Bowers, Quentin David. *History of Wolfeboro, NH, 1770-1994.* Vols. 1-3. Wolfeboro: Wolfeboro Historical Society, 1996.

Bradford, William. *Personal Narrative.* Unpublished Monograph. June 2007.

Brewster Academy Board of Trustees and Executive Committee Minutes (sometimes referred to as the Executive Board). Unpublished minutes from 1878 to the present are housed in the Brewster Academy Head of School's Office.

Brewster Academy Principal's Report. Unpublished reports from 1878 to the present are contained in the Brewster Academy Archives. [Note: As the title of the office changed, the title of the reports became *Headmaster's Report* and *Head of School's Report.* Various other administrative reports across the years are also in the Academy Archives.]

Brewster Banner. Wolfeboro, NH: Brewster Academy Students, 1910.

Brewster, Blair. Unpublished letter, *Family Tree of Wolfeboro Letter,* May 2, 2005, from the Brewster Academy Archives.

Brewster Bulletin. Wolfeboro, NH: Brewster Academy. [This publication the school's admission catalog for a number of years, and copies of many issues are in the Brewster Academy Archives.]

Brewster, E. W. *Letter.* Unpublished and unpaginated letter from the Brewster Academy Archives.

Brewster Free Academy Catalog. Wolfeborough, NH: The Press of *Granite State News,* 1890-1911.

Brewster Academy Catalog. Wolfeboro, NH: Brewster Academy. [The *Catalog* replaced the *Bulletin* as a student recruitment tool.]

Brewster Review. Wolfeborough, NH: Brewster Academy. [Note: this title has been used for both student and Academy publications. An incomplete file of issues is available in the Academy archives.]

Brewster, William. *October Farm: Diaries and Journal.* Introduction by D. C. French. Cambridge, MA: Harvard University Press, 1932.

Brookes, Donald "Chip." *Interview with Robert and Shirley Richardson.* Transcription from Tape Recording. April 2008.

Bullock, Ned. *Interviews with Bob and Shirley Richardson.* Transcription from Tape Recordings. 2004, 2007.

Bylaws of the Wolfeboro and Tuftonboro Academy. Dover, NH: J. T. Gibbs, Gazette Office, 1836.

Carr, John P. *Letter to Howard C. Avery.* April 2, 1962.

Cleary, Jacqueline Rogers. *Waiting for William: Letters from Wolfeborough New Hampshire.* West

Conshohocken, PA: Infinity Publishing Company, 2004.
Columbia Electronic Encyclopedia. New York: Columbia University Press, 2005.
Concord Journal, May 4, 1989: Malcolm Ferguson, special, p. 13).
Cooper, William. *Letter of Condolence*. Unpublished. 1989.
Davis, William Thomas. *Professional and Industrial History of Suffolk County, Massachusetts.* Vols. 1-2. Boston: Boston History Company, 1894.
DeWitt, Walter N. Unpublished Monograph. 2006.
Dow, Jr., Albert H. *Interview with Robert and Shirley Richardson.* Transcription from Tape Recording. January 2005.
Fallon, Mary. *Good is Not Good Enough.* Unpublished Essay. 2010.
Ferguson, Malcolm, Special to the *Concord Journal*, May 4, 1989.
Ferris, Joyce. *Monograph.* Unpublished. 2008.
Ford, Dan. *When Brewster Lost the Free.* Unpublished Monograph. 2005.
Granite Monthly. October 1920. Wolfeborough, NH: Granite State News. [Note: As the local newspaper, *Granite Monthly* and the later *Granite State News* are "newspapers of record" for Brewster Academy. Archives of issues are available at the newspaper and local historical societies.]
Granite State News. See note above for *Granite Monthly.*
Greer, Peter. *Monograph.* Unpublished. 1968.
Hale, Anita Thompson. *Interview with Robert and Shirley Richardson.* Transcribed from Tape Recording. March 2007.
Hanson, Robert. *Interview with Robert and Shirley Richardson.* Transcribed from Tape Recording. March 2004.
Hanson, F. Ernest. *Brewster Free Academy: Income and Funds.* Letters to Jason M. Tibbetts, 1940, 1943. These letters are in the Brewster Academy Archives.
Hatch, Steve. *Interview with Robert and Shirley Richardson*. Transcription from Telephone Interview. February 2007.
Hatfield, Mark O. *Senate Historical Office.* Washington, DC: U.S. Government Printing Office, 1997.
Hawley, John W. *Wolfeboro and Tuftonboro Academy—1821-1887.* Wolfeboro: M.G.F. Roberts, Printer, 1915.
Heywood, Janet. *Person of the Week*. Cambridge, MA: Mount Auburn Cemetery, 2001.
Heywood, Janet. *Three Ornithologists at Mount Auburn.* Cambridge, MA: Mount Auburn Cemetery, 2005.
History of the YMCA. This history is online at www.ymca.net.
Hoopes, Matt. *Monograph*. Unpublished. 2008.
Jones Company. *Report to the Brewster Academy Board of Trustees*, New York, NY: John Price Jones Company, 1950.
Knight, Clementine. *Interview with Robert and Shirley Richardson*. Taped in 2006.
Laurent, Jamie. *Interview with Robert and Shirley Richardson.* Transcription from Tape Recording. 2008.
Lehan, Edward. *The Brewster*. Wolfeboro, NH: Brewster Academy Students, 1920.
MacDonald, Hope Whittum. *Interview with Robert and Shirley Richardson.* Transcription from Tape Recording. January 2006.
McDermott, John W. "Study Committee Laid Groundwork for KRHS." *Granite State News*, Friday, November 13, 1964, p. 1.
Maher, P. F. *Report on Examination of Books and Trust Accounts.* May 1945, pp. 1-3.
Masters, Hilary. *Unpublished Letter to Marcia Eldredge*. Sept., 13, 2007.
Meader, Robert F. W. "Wolfeboro Past and Present." *The Wolfeboro Bicentennial Banner 1759-1959.* Wolfeboro: The Bicentennial Committee, 1959.
Merrill, Georgia Drew. *History of Carroll County, New Hampshire.* Boston: W. A. Fergusson and Company, 1889.
Mitchell, John Hanson. *Looking for Mr. Gilbert: The Reimagined Life of an African American.* Berkeley, CA: Shoemaker-Hoard, 2005.
Moore, Cara R. *Interview with Robert and Shirley Richardson.* Transcription form Tape Recording . February 2005.
Murkland, Charles Sumner. *Presidential Papers.* Durham, NH: University Archives of the University of New Hampshire.
Nason, Elias and Thomas Russell. *The Life of Henry Wilson.* Boston: B. B. Russell, 1876.
Old Cambridge. Cambridge, MA: Cambridge Historical Commission, 1973.
Financial Report to the Board of Trustees. (As business manager Samuel A. Oliva periodically prepared these reports, many of which are still available in the Academy Achives; later his successor Robert

Simoneau issued similar reports.)
Palazzo, Robert. *Interview with Robert and Shirley Richardson.* Transcription from Tape Recording. June 2006.
Parker, Benjamin F. *History of the Town of Wolfeboro, New Hampshire.* Wolfeboro: Town of Wolfeboro, 1901.
Peard, Trevor. Interview with Robert and Shirley Richardson. Transcription from Tape Recording. July 2008.
Peters, H.W. *Letter to C. S. Merrow.* January 22, 1951, pp. 1-2.
Pike, Curtis. *Interview with Robert and Shirley Richardson.* Transcription from Tape Recording. February 2006.
Pond, Bremer Whidden. *Letter to Vincent D. Rogers,* May 21, 1949, pp. 1-7.
Price, Chester B. *Historic Indian Trails of New Hampshire.* Concord: New Hampshire Archeologist Society, 1958.
Quayle, Dianne Rogers. *A Daughter's Reminiscence.* Unpublished Monograph, May 2008.
Secretary's Records of Wolfeborough-Tuftonborough Academy. Unpublished minutes from 1820 to 1871 are housed in the Brewster Academy Head of School's Office.
Shea, Marilyn. *Monograph.* Unpublished. 2008.
Simoneau, Robert. *Interview with Robert and Shirley Richardson.* Transcription from Tape Recording. 2010.
Simoneau, Robert. *Monograph.* Unpublished. 2010.
Smart. Mary Haley. *Interview with Robert and Shirley Richardson.* Transcription from Tape Recording, March 5, 2005.
Smith, David M. *Interview with Robert and Shirley Richardson.* Transcription from Tape Recording, 2007.
Smith, David M. *Monograph.* Unpublished. 2008.
SYB (The Senior Yearbook). Wolfeboro, NH: Brewster Academy Students. [Copies of many issues are in the Brewster Academy Archives.]
Minutes of the Transition Committee. Wolfeboro: Brewster Academy. 1965-66.
Wallace, James. *The Scott Twins at Brewster Free Academy, 1911-1915.* Unpublished Manuscript.
Widman, Harry. *Interview with Robert and Shirley Richardson.* Transcription from Tape Recording. 2008.
Winnepesaukean. Wolfeboro: Brewster Academy [Note: This title has been used for both student and Academy publications—for a newspaper, yearbook, and alumni newsletter. Incomplete files of these publications are available in the Academy archives.]
Wolfeborough Christian Institute Exposition. Vol. 1. Wolfeborough: Wolfeborough Christian Institute, 1874.
Wolfeboro-Tuftonborough Academy Alumni Association Secretary's Records. Unpublished minutes and notes from 1909 to 1911 which are housed in the Brewster Academy Head of School's Office.
Wolfeborough-Tuftonborough Academy School Catalogue. Wolfeborough, NH: Wolfeborough-Tuftonborough Academy, 1823.
Wooden, Andrew. *Brewster Academy's Position within Current Enrollment Trends in Independent Schools.* Unpublished monograph. 1982.
Young, Nancy A. Email Smith College Archivist to Robert and Shirley Richardson.
Young, Nancy A. *Smith College Archives.* www.smith.edu/libraries/libs/archives.
Zulauf, Barbara Lewando. *Brewster Academy and Family,* (Unpublished Monograph). 2004.

Index

A Nation at Risk, 234ff.
A Sound Mind in a Sound Body, 139
Abenaki, xi, 17, 103
Academic Affairs Committee, 217, 235-236, 238
Academic Building, 12, 46, 55, 60, 63, 77, 85, 102, 115, 120, 127, 136, 177-178, 195, 213, 221-224, 231, 240, 253, 260, 263-265, 280-281, 290, 337
Academic Changes, 1911-1914, 67
Acorn Fund, 218, 223, 231
Act of Incorporation, 20
Admission House, 221, 276
Admissions, 28, 44, 67, 89, 96, 156, 158, 161, 170, 176, 180, 191, 194-195, 204, 206, 276-278, 288, 333
Advanced Placement, 185, 235
Ahlborn, Carrie, 247
Ahlborn, Seth, 247
Air Raid Drills, 110-111
All School Meetings, 17, 88, 170, 316-317, 332
Allwine, Anne Marie, 319
Alumni and Development Office, 278-279, 288
Amadio, Paul, 276
Amanita, Miss, 126
Ambrose, Thomas L., 24
Anderson Hall, 232, 253, 319, 334
Anti-slavery Movement, 36
Armistice, 65, 74, 76
Athletics, 58, 64, 113, 115, 146, 179, 206, 217, 245-247, 290, 300, 303-308, 315, 320-322, 333
Atwood, David, 240
Avery, Howard C.
BFA Alumni Association, x, 29, 94, 108, 139, 171, 194
Bailey, Allan, 152
Bain, Dr. Alan, 211, 257-259, 276, 279, 308, 314
Ball, Travis, ix, 184-186
Ballad of the Front Door, 57
Ballentine, John J., 138, 197, 342
Barnett, Will, 247
Baseball, 50, 54, 58-59, 63-64, 73-74, 90, 94, 105, 126, 152, 155, 188, 250, 290, 303, 322
Basketball, 52-53, 58, 63, 78, 105, 113-114, 128, 146, 155-158, 171, 188, 206-208, 289, 290, 302, 304, 322, 325
Bassett, Charles, 76
Bean, Howard, 106, 111
Bearce Hall, 29, 85, 97, 175, 191, 231
Bearce, Ellen Bradford, 85, 97
Bearce, Ralph King, 83ff., 343
Beaver Brook Campus, 337
Benchmarks, 59, 191, 277-278
Bennett, Mike, 207
Bernardin, Melissa, 238
Bigelow, T. William, 342
Blake, Jonathan, 20
Board of Trustees, x, 20, 32, 36, 59, 63, 66, 77, 83, 88, 95, 96-97, 98, 102, 107, 109, 112, 131, 133-140, 144, 149, 151, 161, 165, 167, 175, 182-184, 193, 196-198, 202, 218, 231, 254, 255-258-259, 293, 294, 300, 313, 314, 341
Boston and Maine Railroad, 100
Boston Brewster Club, 109, 116, 143, 194
Boston Society of Natural History, 38
Bowles, Doug, 106
Boys' Sports, 323
Brackins, Craig, 326
Branzetti, Greg, 244, 342
Brattle Street, 32, 34-36
Brewster Beach, 52, 120, 250
Brewster Bulletin, 89, 99, 345
Brewster College Handbook, 279
Brewster Connections, viii, 215, 333
Brewster Data, 276
Brewster Free Academy, x, 19, 32, 37, 38, 39, 43, 44, 48, 49, 58, 64, 67, 78, 83, 88, 102, 131, 149, 345
Brewster Hall of Fame, 303, 305-308
Brewster Memorial Hall, 56, 90
Brewster Motto, 270
Brewster Net, 261, 275
Brewster Recreation Hall and Museum Committee, 134
Brewster Summer School, 38, 139, 194, 213
Brewster Transition 1962-64, 161
Brewster Winnipesaukee Project, 208-209
Brewster, Arabella, 33
Brewster, Basset & Company, 31
Brewster, Cobb & Estabrook, 31
Brewster, Cushman & Bancroft, 31
Brewster, Daniel, 30
Brewster, Elder William, 84
Brewster, George, 30
Brewster, John L., 28, 44, 57, 341
Brewster, John, ix, x, 11, 28, 30ff., 43, 59, 108, 113, 149, 177, 270, 338,
Brewster, Sweet & Company, 31
Brewster, William, 28, 34ff., 57, 78, 132, 341

Bridge Village, 18-31
Bridges, Senator H. Styles, 103, 107, 149
Britton, Esther, 131,
Britton, Judge William, 102, 113, 114
Bronze Plaque, 29, 77, 215, 222
Brookes, Donald "Chip," 52, 342
Brookes, Lillian Osgood, 121, 139, 142
Brower, Dorothy, "A Sweater Soliloquy," 72
Brown Field, 189, 249
Brown Hall, 79, 81, 85, 101, 110, 120, 124, 154
Brown Trust, 110, 124
Brown, Rupert, 138, 147, 161, 169
Browser, 213-214
Building Committee, 57, 131
Bullock, Ned, 103, 106, 110, 138
Butcher, Matt, 323-324, 330
Camacho, Moses, 208
Campbell, Andy, 240, 283-285
Carpenter II, Ralph, 172, 173
Carpenter School, 29, 79, 94, 105, 113, 116, 147-148, 158-159, 188
Carpenter, George. A., 29
Carr Report, 160
Carter, Bob, 295
Cate Fund, 116
Cefalo, Greg, 299
Center Street, 19
Chadwick, Lydia Remick, 45, 48
Challenge "78," 219
Chamber Orchestra, 282, 284
Chamberlain House, 222
Chamberlain, Eric, 237
Chapel Hall, 29, 76, 87, 88, 90, 95, 105, 110, 115, 122, 157, 202, 217
Character Education, 329
Civil Air Patrol, 110, 116, 119
Civilian Conservation Corps, 100
Clark Field, 335
Clark, Greenleaf B., 29
Clark, Rosie, 264, 279
Clay, Dan, 284
Cleveland, John Paine, 22
Climbing Barn, 113, 293, 316
Clow, Dr. Fred, 89, 103, 107
Clow, John H., 131
Cobham Hall, 29, 97, 172-173
Coburn, Donita, 284
Code of Behavior, 89, 111
Cole, Frank, 202
Cole, Peter, 191, 194
Colket Family, 230, 261
College Office, 264, 279, 280
Comeau, Peggy, viii
Communication Office, 279
Community Dinner, 317
Community Life Program, 242
Community Service, 241, 243, 256, 288-289, 316
Computer Graphics, 282, 285-287, 322, 332
Computer Technology, 275
Concord River, 36-37
Cooper, Andrea, 311, 313
Cooper, Dr. Michael E., 313ff., 343
Cooper, Laura, 323, 329
Cornwall, Janis, 324
Counseling, 243, 318, 319
Cowan Estate, 133
Crew, 178, 188, 247, 290, 303, 322
Cross Country Running, 178, 290
Cunningham, Leaman, 76
Curriculum, 24, 47, 63, 67, 105, 117, 172, 185, 235-238, 240, 255ff.,259, 260 ff, 266, 276, 332
Currier, Roland , 75
Curvey Property, 335
Curvey, James C., 335
Daly, Barbara, 279
Dana, Richard Henry, 34
Dartmouth College, 24
Davis, Raylene, 239, 251, 287, 288
Dea, Eugene, 168, 172
Dean of Students, 155, 167, 169, 179, 186, 197, 201, 206, 214, 243, 247, 259, 301, 315, 316, 318
Dean-Olsen, Susan, 284
Depression, 11, 92, 95, 98, 99-101, 103, 106-107, 109, 111, 112, 339
Development Office, 142, 215, 233, 278
DeWitt, Walter N. "Rink," xi, 146, 147, 197, 202, 205, 223, 312, 342
Director of Admissions, 156, 162, 206, 234, 277, 301
Director of Development, 138, 181, 186, 247, 278
Director of Student Activities, 245, 288, 316
District #19, 27-28
Djang, Fred, 204, 212, 214
Doing It All, Doing It Right, 285
Douglas, Barbara, 211, 239
Dow, Albert, 57, 79
Dow, Jr., Albert H., 58, 131
Dow, Sandy, 106
Drama Department, 284
Dunlop, Stuart, 276
Durkee, Forest, 106
Eckman Construction and Builders, 302
Edgerly, Edwin, 131
Eldredge, Marcia, 279
Engaged Discipline System (EDS), 318, 329
Englehardt, Dr. Fred, 103
English as a Second Language (ESL), 211, 239, 287
Enrollment, 23, 24, 27, 47, 50, 71, 88, 95, 101, 110, 113, 119, 125-126, 135, 140, 147, 148, 156-158, 165, 175, 176, 193, 195, 205, 233, 235, 256
Environmental Club, 237
Environmental Program, 208
Estabrook & Co., 31
Estabrook and Main Street Houses, History of, 39
Estabrook as a Bed and Breakfast, 40
Estabrook, Arthur, 28, 31, 37, 38-41
Esty, Charles, 242
Evolution Debate, 93
Excellence in Teaching Award, 166, 271
Executive Board, 114, 119
Executive Committee, xii, 102, 126, 128, 132,

134, 136, 159, 180
Expect More–Exceed Your Greatest Expectation, 333
Fahy, Anita, 239
Fahy, Richard, 196
Fall Pep Rally, 249
Fallon, Doug, ix, 250, 251
Fallon, Mary, ix, 231, 236, 271
Fernald, Joe, 316, 318
Ferris, Joyce, 242, 252, 258
Field Hockey, 80, 81, 196, 208, 246, 290, 303, 322, 323, 324
Finance Committee, 131, 278
Fine and Performing Arts, 282ff.
Fire in the Estabrook, 40
First Congregational Church, 45, 85, 96, 166, 222
First Time Tuition Charged, 102
Fitness Program, 188, 245, 290, 302-303, 307, 320, 322
Fletcher, Ida, 42
Flexible Modular Scheduling, 185
Flying Juniors, 217
Foley, Colleen, 240
For a Better Brewster, 139
Ford, Daniel, 152
Ford. John, 299
Fouser, Jonathan, 293
Francis Harriman, 45
French and Indian War, 18
French, Daniel Chester, 11, 27, 34, 35, 37
Fresh Water Ecology, 337
Friend, Peter, 204, 212
Fry Field, 298-299
Fry, Peter, 296, 297
Fund Raising, 95, 108, 131, 132, 133, 136, 140, 164, 176, 231, 278-279, 293, 301
Gale, Arthur, 101, 131
Garnsey, Fred, 277
Gaver, Dr. William, 240
Gefers, Mike, 279
GI Bill, Service's Readjustment Act, 124ff.
Giglio, Anthony 'Tony," 305
GIs, 124ff.
Glee Clubs, 116, 117, 120, 143, 146, 152, 153, 154, 170, 240
Goldstein, Phil, 288
Goodwin, George, 161
Goose Corners, 20
Gordon Research, 250
Gordon, Glen, 244
Gorfine, David, 208
Gorrill, Bruce, 237, 329, 330
Grace, Topher, 284
Graham, Candice, 282
Grant, General Ulysses S., 25
Greenall, Walter G., 98ff., 343
Gregory, Dr. Harold, 154, 159, 161, 164, 175
Gridley, Lee, 184, 193
Gridley, P. Fred, 342
Ground Breaking in 1953, 143-144
Guppy, William, 27
Haines Barn, 113, 115, 293, 294
Haircut Issue, 189
Hale, Anita Thompson, 111
Hale, Clayton E., 111
Haley, Charles Webster, 66ff., 343
Hamilton, Helen, x, 259, 312
Hanson, F. E., 95, 108, 341
Hanson, Robert, 111
Harlow, Chris, 184, 185, 200
Harris Family, 227-228
Harris, Henry, 227-228
Harris, Lamont, 227-228
Harris, Nick, 227-228
Hatch, Charles, 93
Hatch, Marjorie, 120, 131
Hatfield, Mark O., 25
Hawley, Rev. John W., xi
Haynes, Walker, 206-207
Health Center, 123, 296, 334, 335
Heifetz Institute, 250, 334
Hersey, Charles A., 29
Hertz, Walter, 204, 215, 217
Hess, Peter, 212, 300, 301, 328, 332
Hockey, 78, 80, 103, 104, 111, 121, 129, 130, 155, 157, 176, 179, 180, 181, 188, 196, 246, 278, 290, 303, 306, 322, 323
Hodges, BG, viii, 286, 287, 332
Hoit, William H., 23
Hooper, Ed, 209, 210, 211
Hoopes, Matt, 212-215
Hopper, Grace Murray, 241-242
Hossack, Charlie, 316
Howl, 283, 285
Huggins Hospital, 102, 131, 289
Hughes, Adelaide (Mrs. Roland), 97, 142, 151, 159, 161, 164, 173, 175, 177, 197, 230, 341
Human Survival, 237
Hurlburt III, Henry F., 341
Idea of Mindset, 328,
Impact of 1954 New Building, 146
Indian Joe, 52, 250
Influenza Pandemic of 1918-1919
Instructional Support Program, 258
Intramural Flag Football, 244
Jazz Band, 282
Jobe, Rex, 312, 342
John Brewster Trust, 95
John Price Jones Company, 133
Johnson, Frank, 218-219
Joined at the Heart, 29
Jones Report, 133
Jones, Erik, 238
Josiah Brown Trust, 110
Journalism, 213-215
Judicial Board, 214, 318-319
Kaywin, Gordon, 284
Kelloway, Debbie, 244
Kelsea, Carrie Frances, 66, 82
Kenison Library, 37, 211, 220, 222, 263, 264, 266
Kenison, Arthur E., 221
Kenison, Frank R., 221
Kenison, Jr., Arthur E., 221, 342

Kenison, Samuel M., 221
Keys, Michael, 342
Kimball House, 39, 45, 85, 125, 136, 137, 222
Kimball, George C., 52
Kimball, John, 131
Korean Conflict, 135
Kramer, Beryl M., 131
Lacrosse, 206, 246, 249, 278, 290, 298, 303, 322, 323
Lake Room, 231
Lake Wentworth, 89
Lakes Region Championship, 229, 324
Lamb, Herbert, x, 230, 337, 339, 342
Lamb, Sarah Lord, 230
Landman, Bernie, 131
Laurent, Jamie, 316
Learning Skills Department, 211, 221, 257
Lee Kennedy Company, 302
Leitner, Tony, 342, 343
Libby Museum, 29, 70, 123
Libby, Dr. Henry Forrest, 29
Libby, Ichabod, 20
Liberty Bonds, 72
Library, 12, 19, 29, 36, 37, 87, 105, 133, 152, 164, 168, 175, 177-178, 211, 219-223, 263, 264, 266
Long Range Planning Committee, 175-176
Longfellow, Henry Wadsworth, 32, 69
Lord House, 38, 39, 45, 46, 58, 85, 112, 115, 143, 147, 151, 156, 169, 191, 205, 313-314
Lord, Edwin H., 43ff., 61, 343
Lord's Boathouse, 56, 162
Lovering, Earl N., 72
Lyceum, 24-26
Lyons, Bill, 243-244, 259
MacDonald, Hope Whittum, 121, 342
MacLeod, Les, viii, 312
Marine Science, 237
Martin, Byron, 293, 331
Martin, Margaret, 277
Mason, Arthur, 183, 230
Masonic Hall, 142
Massachusetts Audubon Society, 38
Master Facility Plan, 223, 301
Masters, Hilary, 126
Matheson, Evan, 217, 230, 240
Matheson, Todd, 299
McCloy, Steve, 206-208, 209, 245
McDermott, Dr. John, 342
McDonough, Hubert V., 149
Meader, Robert, 126
Melanson, Joseph, 121, 135
Memorial Building, 48, 136, 141, 143-145
Merrow, Chester E., 97, 131, 135, 138, 139, 140, 149, 164, 314
Mikulus, George, 185
Mirror Lake, 70
Monroe, Mr., 126
Moore, Cara R., 40
Moore, Harrison, 40
Moore, Linley, 76
Morning Meeting, 122, 215, 317
Morning Star Lodge, 85
Morrisette, Kathy, 213
Morrison, Bill, 184, 204, 217
Morse Code, 116, 119
Mount Auburn Cemetery, xi, 33, 42
Mount Washington, 115, 207
Moving of Old Academy, 28
Moyer, Terri, 247
Mudge, Ashley, 278
Mudge, Daniel, xi, 278, 300, 310, 312-313, 342
Mudge, Kathy, 278, 301. 310, 342
Mudge, Tapley Ann, 278
Multimedia in the Arts, 329
Mulvey, Kevin, 296
Murkland, Dr. Charles Sumner, 47, 59, 61ff., 67, 341, 343
Murray, Mal, 184, 185, 193
Music and Drama Partnership, 284
Music Department, 282, 283
Music Program, 57, 63, 116, 143, 146, 154, 232, 240, 283
Natick, MA, 26
Natural History, 38, 237
Neilson, Charlesworth, 175, 183, 197, 341
Nentwig, Ron, 230, 243
NEPSAC, 323, 324, 326
New England Association of Colleges and Secondary Schools, 134, 236
New England College Entrance Board, 67
New England Prep School Tournament, 157
Newall-Goodspeed Architects and Engineers, 140
Nicholson, Jim, 342
Noble, Carlos, 184
Noble, Dr. Charles C., 142, 341
Noble, Jr. Carlos, 179
Nourse, Chris, 282
Noyes, Rebecca, 32
Nuttall Ornithological Club, 38
October Farm, 34, 36
O'Donoghue, Kerry, 323
Olfene, Rick, 202
Oliva, Samuel A., 204, 240
Olsen, Ella S., 99
Oommen, George, 302
Orne, Martha, 25
Outing Club, 178, 188, 293
Palazzo Field, 297, 299
Palazzo, Robbie, 298, 299
Palazzo, Tommy, 296, 297, 298
Palmer, Lynne, 277, 279, 300, 301
Palmer, T.J., 252
Paro, Betty, 167, 171, 182
Paro, Wilfred, 167ff., 183, 184, 189, 343
Paul Revere Bell, 22
Pavilion Inn, 36, 42, 45, 55, 56, 230-231
Peard, Trevor, 188, 189, 204, 206
Pearl Harbor, 109, 112
Pendleton, L. T., 181, 183, 342
Perkins, Clarence L., 73, 78
Perkins, Perley, 76, 103

Peters, H.W., 136, 138
Peterson, Chuck, 214
Peterson, Dale, 242, 285, 286
Peterson, David, 242,
Pickering, Daniel, 19-21, 28, 39
Pike, Curtis, 106, 116, 119
Pill, 174
Pinckney Family, 225
Pinckney, Jonathan (Jon), 225, 246, 308
Piper, Audra, 154
Piper, Carroll, 50, 66, 82, 83, 87, 89, 131
Pitman, Anna Leila, 69
Pollini, David, 169, 184, 186, 306
Portsmouth, 18, 22, 30, 64, 69
Pottle, Bill, 228, 245, 249, 250
Powder Point School, 84, 85, 99
Powers, Albert, 184, 193, 237
Proctor Academy, 27, 125, 180, 228
Proctor Program, 242
Project Based Learning, 11, 330
Publications, History of, 212-214
Quality of Life Committee, 214
Quayle, Dianne Rogers, 112, 113, 115, 149, 342
Radio, 90, 92, 101, 154
Radley, Peg, 276, 277, 252
Radley, Tim, 230, 245, 252, 288-289
Ramsey, James, 178, 179
Recycling, 227, 238
Red Cross, 71, 72, 75, 110, 116, 118, 120, 289
Rehnert Family, 335
Reichenbach Family, 335
Relay for Life, 289, 290
Remick, Lydia, 45, 48
Richardson House, 39, 45, 152
Richardson, Andrea, 244
Richardson, Fred, 76
Richardson, Lauren, 70, 195, 196
Richardson, Lucy, 40
Richardson, Robert "Bob," 17, 168, 179, 180, 184, 185, 192, 194, 200, 201, 203, 209, 217, 221, 228, 234, 235, 236, 242
Richardson, Shirley, 210-211, 217, 243, 252, 279, 280, 282
Risky Behavior Survey, 317, 319
Roaring Twenties, 89, 91, 185
Rogers Gymnasium, 40, 143, 146, 207, 208, 214, 246, 249, 282, 338
Rogers, Janet, 312, 342
Rogers, Jr., V. David, 112, 114, 154, 155, 169, 184, 185
Rogers, Lillian Sanborn, 112, 113, 143, 149, 150
Rogers, Vincent David, 112ff., 124ff., 132ff. , 343
Rogers, William, 25
Roosevelt, President Franklin, 99, 110, 121
Ross, Kim, 211, 258, 300, 301
Rothfus, Ed, 217, 240
Royal Thai Scholar Program, 250
Rust Rond, 178, 212,
Ryan, Jimmy, 207
Sailing, 188-189, 208, 217, 225, 226, 234, 246, 290, 308
Sanbornville, 93, 100, 113, 133, 158
Sanders, Elizabeth "Libby," 168, 177, 184, 221
Sardella, Joseph, 136
Sargent Hall, 163-164, 165, 184, 222, 230
Sargent, Herbert, 46, 50, 66, 67, 80, 82, 83, 108, 110, 123,
Sargent, Ned, 123
Scala, Beth Hayes, 252
Scanlon, Bob, 202
School Design Model, 254, 255, 259, 260, 268, 271, 275, 276, 277, 310, 312, 313, 333
School Dress Code, 91, 169, 170, 172, 185
School Management Team, 186, 301
Science Facility, 219, 221, 254
Scott, Dr. Nathaniel Harvey, 38, 68, 89, 341
Scott, Ethel and Edith, The Scott Twins, 68, 69-71
Scott's Palace, 68
Seaman, Rebecca, 306
Senior Carnival, 140, 141
Senior Gift, 280
Senior Project (SAVE), 188
Senior Seminar, 188
September 11, 2001, 295ff.
Severance, Charles, 131
Sherman, Patricia, 301
Siemon Family, 261, 342
Silverstein Family, 335
Singing School, 24-25
Skiing, 80, 103, 120, 179, 188, 240, 290, 322
Slack, Bill, 184, 185
Slide Show, 244, 282, 309
Smart, Mary Haley, 80
Smith Athletic and Wellness Center, 229, 230, 250, 278, 289, 302, 303-305, 309, 316, 318, 320-323
Smith River, 19
Smith, David Minton, 199ff., 218ff., 234ff., 255ff., 275ff., 299ff., 300ff., 343
Smith, Jason, 277, 322, 325, 326
Smith, Shelia, 199, 203-204, 227, 277, 303, 309, 310
Snyder, Lynn, 247
Soccer, 152, 155, 157, 188, 189, 196, 228, 229, 240, 249, 278, 290, 298, 322, 323, 324
Softball, 196, 244, 289, 322
Solar Green House, 219
South Main Street, 19, 21, 23, 44, 45, 69, 90, 96, 123, 232, 334
South Wolfeboro, 111
Spaudling, Hank, 228
Spaulding Family, 228-229
Spaulding, Tom, 228
Spencer, Carlton, 197, 230, 341
Spring Fling Thing, 279
Stabile Family, 335
Stabile Weight Area, 303
Stackpole, Fred, 131, 135, 341
Staples, John, 180, 186
Stone, Alan, 342
Storm, Rick, 297, 298
Strategic Plan, 231, 256, 314, 315, 322, 333

Stubblebine, Hazel, 172
Student Center, 40, 214, 218, 219, 223, 229, 231, 239, 254, 282, 289
Student Court, 212, 214
Student Handbook, 172, 189
Studio Art, 56, 133, 136, 147, 214, 217, 221, 240, 242, 285, 329
Study Abroad, 329
Study Trips, 317
Subterranean, 181, 187
Swaffield, Dorothy, 203, 214
Symonds, J.W., 27
Taft, Joseph, 240
Tech Office, 275
Tennis Courts, 51, 87, 103, 176, 188, 190, 191, 249, 335, 336
Thatcher, Jason, 230
Thayer, Dr. Gordon O., 163
The BAPA (Brewster Academy Photo Address), 213-214
The Brewster Banner, 64
The Brewster Medal, 338
The Lake Bank, 19
The Minds of Our Children, 142
The Outcroppings, 213, 214
The SYB, 78, 91, 93, 105, 213,
Thousand Miles of Pennies, 140
Tibbetts, Justin, 101, 108, 164, 341
Tinker, Herbert D., 38, 71, 153, 154
Tinklam, Peter, 202
Toonerville Kids, 93,
Town Garden, 99
Town Hall, 20, 23, 28, 29, 36, 45, 49, 87, 101, 177
Traditions, 58, 128, 169, 249, 280, 282, 289, 317, 338
Train Kids, 88
Turner, Bonnie, 301, 342
Turner, Kate, 246, 300, 323
Turner, Lindsey, 268,
Tuttle, Fred, 116
Twenty-first Century, 199, 272, 309
Twin Towers, 295
Tyler, Warren P. "Pete," 183, 197, 204, 342
Valarioti, Dominic, 202
VanBlarcum, Herbert P., 197, 342
Vandross, Orlando, 252
Vaughan, Burtis F., 143, 149, 151ff., 342, 343
Vaughan, C. Richard "Dick," 183ff., 201, 202, 343
Vaughan, Margaret "Peg," 184, 198
Victory Garden, 111, 115
Vietnam War, 11, 173, 176, 187, 234
Vocational Education, 140
Wallace, Clayton, 70, 71, 78
Wallace, Dr. James M., 68
Web Site, 279, 333
Weeks, Dick, 242, 243
Whalen, Paul, 146, 156, 181, 191, 193, 195, 200, 201, 305
Whitfield Foundation, 252
Whitfield Gospel Choir, 252, 253
Whitfield, Argyle, 252, 343
Whitfield, Trey, 251-252, 253, 317
Whiting, Virginia Paige, 152
Whitney, Janie, 252, 342
Widman, Harry 204, 217
Wilkin, Col. Hugh, 159, 197, 341
William Brewster Fund, 132
Williams & Brewster, 31
Wilson Center for Teaching and Learning, 232, 263, 264, 275
Wilson Family, 224
Wilson, Grant, xi, 225, 258, 300, 301, 302, 309, 311-312
Wilson, Henry, 25, 26, 27
Wilson, Jr., Grant, 224
Wilson, Kirsten, 224
Winnipesaukean, 213
Winter Carnival, 80, 129, 162, 171, 244, 289
Wolfeboro Bay, 85, 189, 216, 247, 263, 302
Wolfeborough Christian Institute, 27
Wolfeboro Historical Society, 29
Wolfeboro's Tax Bill, 184
Wolfeborough and Tuftonborough Academy, x, xi, 20-21, 24, 26, 28, 29
Wolfeborough and Tuftonborough Academy Corporation, 20, 28
Wong, Matt, 239
Wooden, Andrew, 206, 234, 246, 308
World Trade Center, 295-299
World War I, xi, 65, 77, 99, 124
World War II, x-xi, 115, 116, 122, 171, 193, 215, 221, 314
Wright, David, 342
Wright, James, 168, 179
Writing Program, 236
WTA Alumni Association, 29
Yau, Kim, 324, 326
Young, Oscar, 71, 101
Zulauf, Barbara Lewando, viii, 106, 116, 164, 177